EVIDENTIALITY:

*The
Linguistic Coding
of
Epistemology*

edited by
Wallace Chafe
University of California, Santa Barbara

Johanna Nichols
University of California, Berkeley

**Volume XX in the Series
ADVANCES IN DISCOURSE PROCESSES
Roy O. Freedle, Editor**

ABLEX PUBLISHING CORPORATION
Norwood, New Jersey

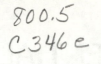

Copyright © 1986 by Ablex Publishing Corporation

Printed in the United States of America

Library of Congress Cataloging-in-Publication Data

Evidentiality : the linguistic coding of epistemology.

  (Advances in discourse processes ; v. 20)
  Bibliography: p.
  Includes indexes.
  1. Grammar, Comparative and General. 2. Semantics. 3. Languages—Philosophy. I. Chafe, Wallace L. II. Nichols, Johanna. III. Series.
P201.E95   1986   415   86-10873
ISBN 0-89391-203-4

Ablex Publishing Corporation
355 Chestnut Street
Norwood, New Jersey 07648

Contents

Preface to the Series

Roy O. Freedle
Series Editor

This series of volumes provides a forum for the cross-fertilization of ideas from a diverse number of disciplines, all of which share a common interest in discourse—be it prose comprehension and recall, dialogue analysis, text grammar construction, computer simulation of natural language, cross-cultural comparisons of communicative competence, or other related topics. The problems posed by multisentence contexts and the methods required to investigate them, while not always unique to discourse, are still sufficiently distinct as to benefit from the organized mode of scientific interaction made possible by this series.

Scholars working in the discourse area from the perspective of sociolinguistics, psycholinguistics, ethnomethodology and the sociology of language, educational psychology (e.g., teacher–student interaction), the philosophy of language, computational linguistics, and related subareas are invited to submit manuscripts of monograph or book length to the series editor. Edited collections of original papers resulting from conferences will also be considered.

Volumes in the Series

Introduction

This book is about human awareness that truth is relative, and particularly about the ways in which such awareness is expressed in language. There are some things people are sure of, either because they have reliable evidence for them, or—probably more often—because they have unquestioning faith that they are true. There are other things people are less sure of, and some things they think are only within the realm of possibility. Languages typically provide a repertoire of devices for conveying these various attitudes toward knowledge. Often enough, speakers present things as unquestionably true; for example, 'It's raining.' On other occasions English speakers, for example, may use an adverb to show something about the reliability of what they say, the probability of its truth: 'It's probably raining' or 'Maybe it's raining.' Inference from some kind of evidence may be expressed with a modal auxiliary: 'It must be raining.' Or the specific kind of evidence on which an inference is based may be indicated with a separate verb: 'It sounds like it's raining.' The view that a piece of knowledge does not match the prototypical meaning of a verbal category may be shown formulaically: 'It's sort of raining.' Or an adverb may suggest that some knowledge is different from what might have been expected: 'Actually, it's raining.'

Other languages express these and other attitudes toward knowledge in sometimes similar, sometimes quite different ways. The contributors to this volume have been concerned with the nature of such devices in one or in several languages. The data and analyses which they present can, for one thing, show us much about what we might regard as 'natural epistemology', the ways in which ordinary people, unhampered by philosophical traditions, naturally regard the source and reliability of their knowledge. Simultaneously we can learn a great deal about an important ingredient of language itself, the ways in which languages agree and differ in their emphases, and in the kinds of devices they make available to their speakers.

The term EVIDENTIAL has come to be used for such a device. As will be seen, it now covers much more than the marking of evidence per se. We do not wish, for the moment at least, to suggest what the boundaries of evidentiality in the broad sense are. Although evidentiality has been studied in individual languages, no one has at yet undertaken a comprehensive treatment of it. As a first step, in the spring of 1981 the editors of this volume organized a symposium in Berkeley at which the authors represented here, along with several other participants, met and discussed the state of the art. So far as we know, it was the first conference ever assembled to compare evidentiality in a variety of languages and to explore such general questions as the areas of epistemology for which different languages provide evidential markings, the nature of such markings, and the ways in which they arise and spread.

This book contains revised versions of many of the papers that were presented at the symposium. It does not attempt to offer a single, unified approach to evidentiality, because we believe that the time is not yet ripe for such a treatment. We are necessarily in a stage of exploration, a stage where we should welcome relevant data of all kinds, and where we should also remain receptive to a variety of viewpoints and interpretations. The heterogeneous perspectives of the authors in this volume offer a store of ideas from which, sooner or later, a more unified interpretation will, we can hope, be constructed. For now, the interested reader can find enjoyment in the discovery of a large range of evidential phenomena which are marked by a number of different languages in different places in the world, and in the range of linguistic devices which these languages use for such marking.

Much of the original interest in evidentiality was aroused by American Indian languages, and especially those of Northern California, where the marking of evidentiality through verb suffixes is widespread. One can easily believe, in fact, that the entire Western Hemisphere shows an unusual concern for the linguistic marking of epistemology. We begin the volume, therefore, with eight papers focused on languages in various parts of North and South America.

The first paper, by William Jacobsen, begins with a useful summary of references that have been made to evidentiality in the earlier published literature on American Indian languages, and demonstrates the poor recognition which has been given to this category in standard surveys and textbooks of linguistics. The bulk of his paper describes in detail the variety of evidential markers to be found in Makah, a Nootkan language spoken at the tip of the Olympic Peninsula in Washington. He shows that the evidentials in this language are rich and varied, and that they do not constitute a homogeneous morphological class.

In contrast, the paper by Robert Oswalt on Kashaya, a Pomo language spoken north of San Francisco, shows a language in which evidentials do form a morphologically coherent category. As he remarks, the systems in Kashaya, Southern Pomo, and Central Pomo 'rank among the most elaborated and discriminating of any in the world'. Both the Jacobsen and the Oswalt papers, then, describe a richness of evidential discriminations, but with structural heterogeneity in the first case and homogeneity in the second.

Alice Schlichter's paper deals with Wintu, another Northern California language, whose evidential properties were first pointed out by Dorothy Demetracopoulou Lee and later systematically described by Harvey Pitkin. Wintu shows an evidential system whose complexity parallels that of Kashaya, but whose origins seem to have been quite recent. The origins of the Wintu evidential suffixes are fairly transparent, and suggest that the idea of marking evidentiality in this way was borrowed from neighboring languages. Schlichter also draws a parallel between tense deixis in European languages and evidential deixis in a language like Wintu.

Kenneth Whistler describes evidentiality in Patwin, another Northern California language. Patwin is closely related to Wintu, and thus provides an opportunity for historical comparison of evidentiality within a single language family. The Patwin system is less homogeneous than that of Wintu: 'There is little reason to posit the category "evidential" as constituting a formal/functional subsystem.' Since 'only a few of the Patwin evidentials . . . can be projected back to a Proto-Wintun stage', Patwin gives further evidence that the better known Wintu system is of recent origin, just as it seems that 'most of the Patwin evidentials . . . are recent functional developments in Patwin'.

Lynn Gordon takes us to the Maricopa language of Arizona, a member of the Yuman language family. Maricopa has evidential markers which are not present in other Yuman languages, and Gordon explains how they were derived from independent verbs meaning 'see', 'hear', and 'say'. The explanation leads us through various related complexities of Maricopa verb morphology and clause structure.

Marianne Mithun shifts the scene to the Northern Iroquoian languages, spoken principally in New York, Quebec, and Ontario. She extends the range of evidential phenomena to include not only 'evidence,' but also precision, probability, and expectations, noting that the same markers may be used for several of these functions, and furthermore that there are shifts among these functions over time. Evidentiality is expressed in the Northern Iroquoian languages partly through verb affixes, partly through lexical predicates meaning 'think', 'say', 'be certain', and the like, and partly through a rich collection of particles. Mithun shows how the affixes have been the most resistant to change and the particles the most volatile, with the lexical predicates occupying an intermediate degree of stability.

With Martha Hardman we shift our focus to South America and the Jaqi language family, consisting of three languages spoken in Peru, Bolivia, and Chile. In these languages evidentiality is 'pervasive and uncompromising; an integral part of the world view.' Speakers of Jaqi languages find it obligatory to indicate whether they are talking from personal knowledge, from knowledge acquired through language, or from nonpersonal knowledge, with various intermediate distinctions also possible. Hardman uses the term 'data source marking' as a substitute for 'evidential' in order to avoid the narrow implications of the latter term. She discusses a wide range of phenomena associated with such marking in these languages, including its effect on the Spanish which is spoken in the area.

David Weber describes three evidential suffixes in the Quechua language of Peru, and raises the question of whether their function is primarily evidential (expressing the source of a speaker's knowledge) or validational (expressing a speaker's attitude toward his knowledge), opting for the evidential function. He then discusses the interaction between these evidential markers and a topic marker to produce what he calls the 'information profile' of a sentence, its progression from theme to rheme.

With Aksu and Slobin's paper we leave the New World and its evidential exuberance to examine a single Turkish suffix whose basic function is to convey inference and hearsay. The authors examine its pragmatic extensions, historical origins, and development in child language, aiming at a psychological explanation of its use and development. On the most general level, they find that it 'represents intrusions into consciousness from psychologically more distant, less directly apprehended worlds of thought and experience'.

Victor Friedman takes us to the Balkans, where Bulgarian and Macedonian have often been said to possess a distinct set of verb forms which express reported, as opposed to directly experienced knowledge. He presents evidence that the forms in question do not consistently have an evidential function, but that, rather, their evidentiality is a product of their interaction with particular contexts in which they occur. Friedman also discusses the so-called admirative form of the Albanian verb, which expresses surprise, disbelief, and reportedness.

Anthony Woodbury explores the interaction of an evidential category with tense in Sherpa, drawing conclusions about the relation of grammatical organization to speakers' awareness of it. Tense skews both the meaning and the distribution of evidential categories. The pattern of intersection is based entirely on semantics, although native speakers' reflections on it—and hence their comments regarding it—are based rather on form. This observation is supported by a comparison of English and Sherpa evidentiality, and an analysis of speakers' English glosses and their comments on Sherpa forms.

Scott DeLancey brings us to Tibetan, where a distinction is made on the basis of whether the speaker is talking about something novel, or about something already well integrated within his knowledge system. He describes the interaction of this distinction with the category of volitionality, as well as with the more typical Tibetan marking of inference, and discusses the conceptual overlap which leads to the marking of all three with the same grammatical material.

Graham Thurgood describes evidentiality in Akha, a language of the Lolo-Burmese family, where it is coded by several sets of sentence-final particles. Tracing their etymologies, he finds that, although functionally homogeneous and formally paradigmatic in the modern language, they stem from a variety of older sources, some of them as ancient as Proto-Tibeto-Burman.

Haruo Aoki presents various evidentials in Japanese, having a variety of grammatical manifestations. They cover three major areas of evidentiality: reporting sensations experienced by someone other than the speaker, reporting as a fact something which is ordinarily not directly knowable, and showing that some piece of knowledge was arrived at by hearsay or inference. He mentions the use of evidentials to signal politeness, and discusses questions regarding the origin of Japanese evidentials, whether from native sources or as borrowings from Chinese.

Johanna Nichols explores evidentiality in one dialect of Chinese pidgin Russian, a jargon which arose in Russian-Chinese trade beginning in the 18th century. This dialect shows an evidential opposition of inferential vs. immediate as its only verbal inflection. That a pidgin should choose to grammaticalize evidentiality in its sole inflectional opposition is of interest. The particular meanings involved, and their interaction with tense and person, support generalizations offered by other authors in this volume.

The last three papers introduce some general considerations which may help to clarify the overall nature of evidentiality. We have placed these papers at the end because they are best understood against the background of the earlier papers. On the other hand, readers interested in a general orientation may find it useful to begin with these discussions.

Wallace Chafe provides a taxonomy of evidential phenomena, subcategorizing them into those which involve the reliability of knowledge, the mode of knowing, the source of knowledge, and the matching of knowledge, either against the verbal resources which are available to express it, or against prior expectations. He goes on to show how these various subtypes of evidentiality are marked in conversational English and in academic written English. As might be expected, epistemology is handled somewhat differently in the two styles.

Lloyd Anderson provides a broad ranging discussion of evidentiality in general, and an overall perspective on much of the material presented in the other papers. He constructs a 'map' of evidential space which shows the degree of distance between evidential types. The map is useful for the comparison of evidentiality in different languages, and also in showing paths of historical change. A change in the function of a particular evidential marker can be usefully conceptualized in terms of movement through evidential space.

John DuBois carries us into the realm of ritual language, where he sees a variety of devices converging to produce the impression that ritual knowledge is self-evident. He discusses the nature of ritual speech, identifying fourteen properties which distinguish it from ordinary speech. He then introduces the notion of 'authority' as a larger category under which evidence is subsumed. Finally, he provides an explanation of the relation between the form of ritual speech and the social constitution of the speech event.

We are grateful to the participants in the symposium, both those whose contributions are represented here and the others who contributed to its success. We are also grateful to the authors of the volume *Discourse and Syntax* (Academic Press, 1978), and especially to the editor of that volume, Talmy Givón, for providing the royalty funds without which this symposium would never have occurred. The royalties from the present volume will be reserved for a similar purpose.

PART ONE

EVIDENTIALITY IN NORTH AND SOUTH AMERICA

ONE

The Heterogeneity of Evidentials in Makah

William H. Jacobsen, Jr.
University of Nevada, Reno

I take evidentials to constitute a linguistic category which applies to predications that the speaker assumes have a reasonable likelihood of being true, but which he cannot vouch for out of direct observation or experience. This is distinct from mood, in which the speaker disavows the factual truth of a predication.[1] Since the category is semantically defined, it will often fail to be structurally homogeneous in a language, either because its exponents are contained in paradigms which also express other concepts, or because they are dispersed among several paradigms. This structural heterogeneity will be illustrated for Makah and, more cursorily, a few other languages.

A BRIEF HISTORICAL REVIEW

The concept of evidentials as a category seems to have existed in Americanist circles for several generations; it is but scantily attested in print, however, and the label EVIDENTIAL itself is relatively recent. The concept probably derives from the work of Franz Boas on Kwakiutl. In his influential introduction to the *Handbook of American Indian Languages,* Boas (1911a:43) employs it in commenting on the example *The man is sick:* '. . . in case the speaker had not seen the sick person himself, he would have to express whether he knows by hearsay or by evidence that the person is sick, or whether he has dreamed it'; this is supposed to illustrate 'modalities of the verb'. In his grammatical sketch of Kwakiutl in the *Handbook,* a similar statement is found: 'To the suffixes expressing subjective relation belong those expressing the source of subjective

---

[1] In making this distinction between mood and evidential(s) I follow Jakobson (1957:4; 1971:135), who cites Vinogradov's formulation that mood 'reflects the speaker's view of the character of the connection between the action and the actor or the goal'; evidential, I would correspondingly say, reflects the speaker's evidence for asserting the combination of action and actor or goal.

knowledge—as by hearsay, or by a dream' (Boas 1911b:443), and four suffixes are treated together under the heading 'Suffixes denoting the source of information' (p. 496). This represents a change from Boas's 1900 *Sketch* of Kwakiutl, which does not invoke the category at all (although the quotative -ʔ*la* occurs several times in the sample text [pp. 720–1]). The concept is retained in Boas's posthumously published *Kwakiutl Grammar* (1947), with the statement that 'a small group of suffixes expresses source and certainty of knowledge . . .' (p. 206) and a listing of three of the suffixes in one section (pp. 237, 245). Here the term EVIDENTIAL occurs, but is applied to just one of the suffixes (-*x̣ənt*), expressing a category that would probably now be called INFERENTIAL.

Boas does not mention evidentials in his several treatments of grammatical categories and their possible diffusion among Indian languages, but he touches on them again in some general essays in his last years. In his chapter *Language,* he briefly mentions 'source of information—whether seen, heard, or inferred' as an obligatory category in an unspecified language (Boas 1938:133), and in his essay *Language and Culture* (1942:182), he humorously commends the Kwakiutl evidential categories to our newspaper reporters.

In his book *Language* (1921), Edward Sapir, a student of Boas's, shows his awareness of evidentiality when he mentions, in a lengthy list of grammatical categories, 'how frequently the form expresses the source or nature of the speaker's knowledge (known by actual experience, by hearsay, by inference)' (pp. 114–5). In his own work on individual languages however, Sapir seems not to have had occasion to deal with evidentials as a separate category. Thus, in his compact early report on Nootka (1911)—a language related distantly to Kwakiutl and closely to Makah—he only mentions, in discussing pronominal categories, 'a series of forms . . . implying that the statement is not made on the authority of the speaker' (p. 19), and in his exemplary treatment of Takelma (1922) the inferential is treated as just one of six tense-mode categories of the verb,—although with careful delineation of its meaning, especially as contrasted with that of the aorist (pp. 157–9).

Morris Swadesh was a student of Sapir's who collaborated closely with him in the analysis and description of Nootka. In his 1939 *Nootka Internal Syntax,* a revision of a 1933 dissertation, Swadesh groups the quotative and the inferential together as 'modes of evidence', contrasted with 'modes of predication' and 'relational modes'; in a chart of examples of inflection of modes, he places the label 'evidential' over forms of the inferential (alongside the indicative, absolute, and interrogative, all of which are 'modes of predication') (1939:82).

In several articles, starting in the late 1930s, Dorothy D. Lee was concerned with the interpretation of Wintu grammatical categories as evidence for the speaker's cognitive orientation. In some of them she recognizes and discusses evidentiality (1938:89–92, 94, 102; 1944:183; 1959:124–5; 1950:542; 1959:137–8), referring to it by labels such as 'suffixes giving the source of information' (1938:102). These suffixes are differentiated from others with modal force. Lee found a paradigm of five evidential suffixes in Wintu (see the display of five ways to say 'Harry is chopping wood' [1938:92]). Lee reported the occurrence of similar suffixes in unrelated neighboring languages, and the consequent possibility of borrowing (1938:102). Her articles doubtless helped to increase anthropological linguists' awareness of evidentials.

A more recent recognition of this concept in the Americanist tradition is found in a paper by Harry Hoijer, another student of Sapir's. In *Some Problems of American Indian Linguistic Research* (1954), Hoijer lists ten phenomena found in some Indian languages and recognized by scholars as distinguishing them from more familiar languages. One of these, although not labelled as such, is the category of evidentials: 'the technique, in a number of languages, whereby statements are classed as known from the speaker's experience, from hearsay, or from cultural tradition' (Hoijer 1954:10).

Roman Jakobson was a friend of Boas's and wrote two papers characterizing his linguistic work, *Franz Boas' Approach to Language* (1944/1971) and *Boas' View of Grammatical Meaning* (1959/1971). In them he cites the passages alluding to evidentials in Boas' late work that have already been mentioned. Of most interest, however, is his important (1957/1971) treatise *Shifters, Verbal Categories, and the Russian Verb*. This introduces the term EVIDENTIAL as a 'tentative label' for the generic verbal category. Four possible sources of evidential information are suggested: someone else's report (quotative, i.e. hearsay evidence), a dream (revelative evidence), a guess (presumptive evidence), and one's own previous experience (memory evidence). Evidential is distinguished from mood, and is fitted into Jakobson's typology of grammatical categories with reference to speech, narrated matter, events, and participants.[2] Reference is made to the occurrence of quotatives, not only in American Indian Kwakiutl (as described by Boas), Hopi (as described by Whorf), and Tunica (as described by Haas), but also in Slavic Bulgarian and Macedonian (Jakobson 1957:1,4; 1971:130–1, 135).

A somewhat more independent reference to evidentiality occurs in Heinz-Jürgen Pinnow's textbook-like *Die nordamerikanischen Indianersprachen* (1964:82–3), with strong emphasis on the quotative. Examples of suffixes and free forms are given for Athabaskan Mattole and Navaho, Iroquoian Seneca, and Siouan Dakota, but only for Navaho are nonquotative categories exemplified.

---

[2] Jakobson's formula for an evidential, E^nE^{ns}/E^s, is perhaps too closely linked to the quotative, bringing in as it does two speech events, immediate (E^s) and narrated (E^{ns}). I find it significant that in quoting Boas (1938:133), Jakobson inserted the explanation '[i.e. known by hearsay]' after 'heard'. This would be appropriate if the language were assumed to be Kwakiutl, but otherwise excludes the possibility of evidence coming directly from the sound of an event, the auditory rather than the quotative category. Perhaps by analogy with the formula P^nE^n/P^s for mood, where P^s, participant of the speech event, actually represents the speaker's attitude, an evidential should be merely E^n/P^s (E^n = the narrated *event*)—which is to say that evidentiality does not concern the relationship between the narrated event and its participants in the way that mood does.

The term 'evidential' seems to have become established by the mid 1960s, due largely, it seems, to the teaching of Mary R. Haas at Berkeley. Haas, another student of Sapir's, collaborated with Swadesh in work on Nitinat, which is closely related to Nootka and Makah. Sherzer (1968, 1976) also includes a category 'Evidential or source of information markers' for verbals (of which more below).

One additional passage recognizing essentially the same concept in a general survey has come to my attention. Uriel Weinreich's (1963:120–1) outline of the semiotic stratification of language, under the heading 'pragmatic operators', discusses devices for the neutralization or suspension of assertiveness of sentences, which correspond to the traditional concept of mood. Within these he singles out 'motivated' cases that indicate the speaker's uncertainty or disclaim his responsibility. Examples include the Hopi quotative (after Whorf), the Bulgarian nonevidential (after Jakobson 1957), Turkish -miş, and the German change from indicative to subjunctive. The influence of Jakobson seems likely here.

Even recent Americanists have used the concept of evidentials rather infrequently, although instances do occur, as in Laurence C. Thompson's (1979:744) report on Salishan languages, under the topic 'modal categories', that 'one category includes a number of evidentials—e.g. "hearsay information", "observed situation", "presumably" ", and Wallace L. Chafe's (1979:228) brief mention that verb prefixes in the Caddoan languages express evidentiality and modality, among other things.

Just as we saw with Sapir, other workers on individual languages have also not employed the generic concept of evidentials because of its lack of structural appropriateness. Thus, Haas treats the Tunica quotative -áni as one of some thirty enclitic particles (1946:363–4) or one of a subset of ten tense and modal postfixes (1941:117–8). Similarly, Hoijer (1946:309–10) groups the Tonkawa quotative -noʔo and narrative -laknoʔo as members of a set of ten enclitics.

Benjamin Lee Whorf, who also studied under Sapir, circulated an outline of language structure in 1938 which included grammatical categories. The outline lacks the generic concept of evidentials, and certain categories that might be so construed are put into two different classes: the inferential is treated as a mode (mood) along with other categories conventionally so labeled, but the quotative is treated as a status along with interrogative, negative, and emphatic (1956b:131). This doubtless reflects, in part, Whorf's description of Uto-Aztecan Hopi, which treats the quotative and the concessive (seemingly close to an inferential) as simply two out of nine modalities (1938:280–6; 1956:118–23; 1946:177). Modality in this case roughly corresponds to mood (mode) (while the label 'mode' is used idiosyncratically for types of hypotactic constructions) and the description of Hopi thus diverges from the outline in treating the quotative as a modality rather than a status, although the latter category is still present. In certain passages (1956a:85; 1938:283, fn. 5; 1956:120, fn. 5), however, Whorf comes closer to our topic, as he discusses the differing Hopi grammatical treatments of information from sensory evidence in the presence of a verb for 'see' or 'hear': the verb expressing this information may occur in either the indicative, quotative, or concessive modalities, or the transrelative 'mode'.

In describing Algonquian Menomini, Leonard Bloomfield (1962:51–2) treated the quotative as one of five modes. This is reflected in Hockett's textbook *A Course in Modern Linguistics* (1958:237–8) and secondarily in Lyons's *Introduction to Theoretical Linguistics* (1968:311), which do not otherwise recognize evidentials. Bloomfield's own *Language* (1933) does not even mention the quotative.

Aside from the few cases that have been mentioned, for which I have tried to suggest a primarily Americanist inspiration, the concept of evidentials seems to be lacking in the standard linguistics textbooks and surveys of grammatical categories. This must be due in large part to the absence of distinctive evidential forms in the better-known European and classical languages.[3] One finds merely passing mention of marginal phenomena, such as the use in indirect discourse of the accusative with infinitive construction in Latin or the subjunctive in German and other Germanic languages (Jespersen 1924:295–7; Hall 1964:220–1).[4] One undercover evidential in English is the inferential value of polysemous *must*, distinct from its obligational one, as nicely delineated by Chafe (1970:179–84), but this has not traditionally been segregated as inherently different from the meanings of other modals with which this word is in a paradigmatic relationship; thus Bolinger (1975:189) treats *must* along with *could, may,* and *might* as remnants of higher sentences.

AREAL DISTRIBUTION OF EVIDENTIALS

Clearly, evidentials are fairly widespread in North American Indian languages, and they tend to differ from the European cases in the specificity with which the channel of information is indicated. Speculation has been expressed that the evidentials described for northern California (Pomoan and Wintun) and the Northwest Coast (Makah) in this volume might point to a widespread areal

---

[3] One western European language that does have an evidential marker is Basque, with a particle *omen* (*emen,* Roncalese *emon,* Vizcayan *ei*) that is a sort of impersonal quotative or generalized inferential meaning 'reportedly', 'as they say', 'it seems', as in *etorri omen da* 'he is said to have come, he seems to have come' (cf. *etorri da* 'he has come'). The same slot before an auxiliary verb can be occupied by other markers of mood or aspect, such as *bide* 'probably', *ote* (*othe,* Vizcayan *ete*) 'perhaps, maybe', *ohi* (*oi, ei*) usitative, and *al* yes-no question marker (cf. Azkue 1923–5:467–71; De Rijk 1969:328, 340; 1972:131–2; Lafitte 1962:47–9, 412; Trask 1981:298–9; Wilbur 1981:171–4). *Omen* also occurs as a noun meaning 'rumor; fame, reputation; honor, virtue'.

[4] An analog to this use of the subjunctive occurs in the Sierra Miwok narrative mode, used in myths or anecdotes of old days, which has arisen as an extension of the use of the subordinate mode (Freeland 1951:86–8).

phenomenon. I would urge caution in this matter, which has yet to be adequately studied.

The only study we have of areal distributions is Sherzer's (1968, 1976). In surveying languages for the presence of any members of the generic category, he finds evidentials to be a 'central areal trait' of the Northwest Coast (1976:78, 230), Great Basin (pp. 163, 165, 245–6), and Plains (pp. 183, 185, 248), and a 'regional areal trait' of northern-central California (pp. 125, 128, 238) and the Papago-Apachean-Tanoan region of the Southwest (p. 147). Evidentiality is felt to be a 'family trait' of several families or stocks: Wakashan, Salishan, and Siouan, and perhaps also Nadene, Athabaskan, Chimakuan, Uto-Aztecan, Algonquian, Hokan, and Penutian (pp. 78, 125, 163, 183, 198). Its geographical spread is thought to be at least partly the result of diffusion in California, the Great Basin, the Plains, and perhaps the Southwest (pp. 131, 167, 186–7, 246). Specific languages are singled out as possibly having developed the category under the influence of their neighbors: Yana in California (pp. 125, 130), Washo in the Great Basin (pp. 163, 166), Kiowa and Tonkawa in the Plains (p. 183).

Lamentably, Sherzer's study is largely vitiated, in my opinion, by its failure to treat separately the individual evidential categories, such as quotative, visual, auditory, and inferential. It seems clear that the individual categories are what might have diffused, rather than a more generalized concept of evidentiality. Making these distinctions would certainly have revealed greater geographical discontinuity. Moreover, some of the instances of evidentials accepted by Sherzer would not be evidentials as defined here: 'narrative' may be a category of tense or aspect, 'quotative' may be a kind of spoken quotation mark (like Sanskrit *iti*).[5]

A good example of the blurred picture that arises from this approach can be found in Washo, a language of the western Great Basin conventionally assigned to the disparate Hokan stock. Washo has three evidential suffixes: visual *-iyeʔ*, auditory *-delem*, and *-áʔyiʔ* expressing an ex post facto inference with some connotation of surprise.[6] They are structurally part of a set of 16 prefinal verb suffixes, whose meanings include categories of tense, aspect, and mode. Sherzer suggests (1976:163, 166) that Washo may have developed its evidentials as a result of contact with contiguous Penutian (Maiduan and Miwokan) and Uto-Aztecan (Numic) languages. Information available on these language families, however, shows no clear case of congruence with categories in Washo.[7]

---

[5] This kind looms large in Munro's (1978) useful survey of northern Uto-Aztecan quotative patterns. Cf. also Weinreich 1963:130, 158, fn. 26.

[6] Cf. Jacobsen (1964:626–30), where these are labeled respectively visual, auditive, and mirative. Washo belies the hypothesized dependency relationship that if a language has any evidentials, it will have a quotative.

[7] Although the Maidu 'evidential' *-wéw* (Shipley 1964:45) might correspond somewhat to the Washo visual, and the (unexemplified) Sierra Miwok 'circumstantial evidence' marker *taʔ, tat, ʔiš-* (Freeland 1951:169) may correspond to the Washo inferential (mirative).

THE EVIDENTIALS OF MAKAH

I now turn to an examination of the evidentials of Makah, identified in accordance with the relatively narrow definition given earlier.[8] I will be especially interested in their morphological localization and their connections to the rest of Makah linguistic structure, as well as in their etymology, when evidence is available.

Makah is a language of the Nootkan branch of the Wakashan family. It is the southernmost language of the family, spoken around Cape Flattery at the northwestern tip of Washington State on the Olympic Peninsula. The other closely related Nootkan languages, Nitinat and Nootka, are spoken on the west coast of Vancouver Island. The other branch of the Wakashan family is located farther north, and its best described language is (Southern) Kwakiutl, sometimes known, nowadays, as Kwakwala.[9] The Makah were in close contact with the Quileute, their neighbors to the south, whose language belongs to the Chimakuan family.[10] Some comparisons to evidential categories of Quileute will be made, which are suggestive of an areal relationship.[11]

The Wakashan languages are highly polysynthetic, and in them the evidentials are rather sharply distinguished from indicators of person and tense. In Nootkan pronominal indications are given for subject and object by suffixes showing three persons and two numbers. Unmarked present opposed to marked past is the main tense distinction, but inner-layer indications of future tense also occur.

Let us look first at some contrastive sets in Makah which will illustrate common evidential suffixes applied to the same stems.[12] Our first group shows *wiki·čaxak* 'bad weather'. These two examples are indicative, with contrasting present and past tense forms, and the usual zero marking of direct experience:

---

[8] My field work on Makah has been supported by the National Science Foundation, the Desert Research Institute of the University of Nevada, and the Research Advisory Board of the University of Nevada, Reno.

[9] For fuller information on Wakashan see Jacobsen (1979b).

[10] Cf. Jacobsen 1979c on Chimakuan, including lexical borrowing between Quileute and Makah.

[11] The following are the sources of information used for discussion of the languages mentioned. All complete Nitinat forms shown are taken from the Nitinat Lexical File prepared by Mary R. Haas and Morris Swadesh, made available to me by Haas (cf. Haas 1969:109; 1972:84). Other sources for Nitinat are Haas (1969, 1972); Klokeid (1968, 1976, 1978); and Carlson and Thomas (1979). Information on Nootka comes from Sapir (1924); Sapir and Swadesh (1939); Swadesh (1939, 1948); and Haas (1969, 1972). Kwakiutl is from Boas (1911b and 1947). Quileute forms come from Powell and Woodruff (1976), or, when so indicated, from Andrade (1933).

[12] I use the orthographic symbols of Sapir and Swadesh (1939), except that *u* is substituted for *o*. When following the vowel *u*, dorsals (*k*'s, *q*'s, and *x*'s) are always labialized (*k*ʷ, etc.); this is, however, not indicated in my orthography, even when a vowel follows. Morphemes cited in isolation are in their morphophonemically underlying form. The extensive morphophonemics includes loss of short final vowels and shortening of final long vowels. Wakashan words from other sources are retranscribed into these symbols. (Cf. Sapir and Swadesh 1939:12–3; Jacobsen 1969:127, sec. 0.3, for listings of Nootka phonemes.)

(1)   *wiki·čaxaw*
      'It's bad weather.'   (seen or experienced directly)

(2)   *wiki·čaxak?u*
      'It was bad weather.'

The following are forms with evidential suffixes:

(3)   *wiki·čaxakpi·d*
      'It looks like bad weather.'   (with an inference from physical evidence)

(4)   *wiki·čaxakq̇ad?i*
      'It sounds like bad weather.'   (on the evidence of hearing)

(5)   *wiki·čaxakwa·d*
      'I'm told there's bad weather.'   (the quotative)

(6)   *wiki·čaxakitwa·d*
      ' I'm told it was bad weather.'   (the corresponding past tense form)

The next two forms are indicative and quotative, based on the graduative form *wi·kičax* of this stem:

(7)   *wi·kičaxšil*
      'A storm is coming.'

(8)   *wi·kičaxšiƛwa·d*
      'I'm told a storm is coming.'

Another group of contrastive examples is based on *ča·?u·qił* '(to be) drunk', with present indicative followed by evidential forms:

(9)   *ča·?u·qił*
      'He's drunk.'   (implying direct observation)

(10) *ča·?u·qiłpi·dił*
      'They must have been drunk.'   (with an ex post facto inference from physical evidence such as the debris they have left)

(11) *ča·?u·qiłq̇ad?ił*
      'They must be drunk.'   (evidence of hearing without visual observation)

(12) *ča·?u·qiłq̇ad?ic*
      'It looks like you're drunk.'   (evidence of visual observation as applied to the second person)

(13) *ča·?u·qiłcaqilił*
      'It looks like they're drunk.'   (based on uncertain visual evidence)

(14) *ča·?u·qiłxa·łš*
      'They might be drunk.'   (with a logical inference from unspecified evidence)

The suffixes of the Nootkan languages have been recognized by Sapir and Swadesh (1939:236) as falling into two broad groups, an inner layer of FORMATIVE suffixes, and an outer layer called INCREMENTAL suffixes.[13] Evidentials occur in both groups, although the suffixes that are clearly specialized as evidentials belong to the latter group, and are in paradigmatic relationship to other suffixes with a modal value. The incremental evidentials fall into two groups according to whether the pronominal suffixes following them are of the indicative or nonindicative type, the former indicating a greater degree of the speaker's personal responsibility for the assertion than the latter.[14] There is evidence that some incremental evidentials have developed from former formative suffixes.

The formative suffixes are of the type often referred to as LEXICAL suffixes. Among them a distinction is made between GOVERNING and RESTRICTIVE suffixes, and the formative evidentials seem to line up with the governing suffixes. The governing suffixes among themselves are quite disparate in terms of semantic and combinatorial possibilities. Some are verbs that take their stems as objects. Others are more nominal in meaning, such as those indicating body parts, in which case their stems may describe them, act upon them, or take them as actors or instruments. Still other governing suffixes act as numeral classifiers.

INDICATIVE INCREMENTAL SUFFIXES

The first evidential suffixes that will be individually examined are incremental suffixes. These are outer-layer suffixes that occur just preceding the pronominal endings, and following suffixes indicating causative, passive, and tense. The suffixes that I am treating are somewhat arbitrarily segregated, from a structural standpoint, from a larger set of modal suffixes, some of which could be construed as evidentials in a broader sense: conditional -*qey,* counterfactual -*qeyča·,* and absolutive -*Ø* (used, inter alia, in the apodosis of conditions). (Even interrogative formations could be mentioned here, indicating as they do the complete absence of information on a given point.)

Among the incremental suffixes I will first treat three that always occur in the indicative mode, and only in main clauses. (Thus a combination with modal categories such as interrogative, quotative, subordinate, or conditional, is necessarily excluded.) They are usually found in the present tense, never in the past tense; they can be preceded by a marker of future tense.

---

[13] Cf. also Swadesh (1948:107). Boas earlier used the labels *stem-suffixes* and *word-suffixes* (1911b:448), continued by Swadesh (1939:79).

[14] There is an analytical problem in Makah and Nitinat, as discussed in Jacobsen (1979a:149–50, fn. 22), as to whether there is a separate morpheme marking the indicative mode. If there is, it follows the evidential suffixes. Information on these pronominal series is found, for Makah, in Jacobsen (1973); for Nitinat, in Haas (1969:111–4); Klokeid (1976, 1978); and Carlson and Thomas (1979); and for Nootka, in Sapir (1923); Sapir and Swadesh (1939:242–3); Swadesh (1939:82); and Haas (1969:108–14).

The first of the indicative incremental suffixes is *-pi:t,* which indicates an inference from physical evidence, usually the result of the inferred action, which has not itself been witnessed (contrasting indicative forms are given in parentheses):[15]

(15)   *haʔukaƛpi·dic*
       'I see you ate.'   (cf. *haʔukalic* 'You're eating.')

(16)   *diqšiƛpi·d*
       'He must have been sewing.'   (cf. *diqšil* 'He's sewing.')

(17)   *weʔičaƛpi·tid*
       'We must've been sleeping.'   (*weʔič* 'to sleep')

(18)   *caxʷi·ʔasaƛpi·d*
       'It must have run over it.'   (seeing results, remains, damage) (cf. *caxʷi·ʔasal* 'It ran over it.')

(19)   *qu·ʔasaƛpi·dic*
       'You must have been strong (to endure such a strenuous experience).'

The evidence may also imply intentions for future actions:

(20)   *diqšiƛe·ʔispi·d*
       'It looks like he's going to sew.'   (cf. *diqšiƛe·ʔis* 'He's going to sew.')

In Wakashan languages nouns may be the stems of predications, and may occur with evidentials;[16] here the stems are *ʔaƛi·tqʷał* 'bear' and *ƛicuxadi·* 'person':

(21)   *ʔaƛi·tqʷałpi·d*
       'It must have been a bear.'   (when seeing the tracks) (cf. *ʔaƛi·tqʷał* 'It's a bear.')

(22)   *ƛicuxadi·pi·d*
       'It must have been a person.'   (when seeing footprints)

Contrast (21) with:

(23)   *ʔaƛi·tqʷałi·č ƛi·yit*
       'It's bear tracks.'   (*ƛi·yit* 'tracks')

The suffix *-pi:t* occurs with a similar value in Nitinat, but cognate suffixes are not known in other Wakashan languages. (See fn. 20 for a suggested etymology

---

[15] The *V:* in this suffix indicates a persistently long vowel, which resists shortening in a third or later syllable. Cf. Jacobsen (1979a:145–6, fn. 3) for discussion.

[16] This overlapping of parts of speech is an areal feature found also in Chimakuan and Salishan; cf. Jacobsen (1979a).

involving the passive of an incorporated stem *pi·- 'to observe'.) A Quileute 'inferential' -ca (Andrade 1933:206) may have a similar meaning.

The second indicative incremental suffix is -q̇adi. Its predominant meaning seems to be evidence obtained from hearing, in the absence of direct experience or visual observation. Thus we have:

(24)   dudu·kq̇ad?i
      'I hear him/it singing.'   (cf. dudu· 'He's/it's singing.')

(25)   pu·pu·q̇ad?i
      'He's blowing a whistle.'

(26)   babaɫdiq̇ad?i
      'He sounds like a white man.'   (cf. babaɫd?i 'He's a white man.')

(27)   ƛiƛiƛq̇ada·l
      'There are sparks.' (when they are heard rather than seen)

(28)   qi·qeyac̆q̇ad?i
      'It sounds like thunder.'   (cf. qi·qeyac̆ 'There's thunder.') (Note that since thunder is a necessarily auditory event, the use of the evidential indicates not only this sense channel but also a certain degree of tentativeness or uncertainty.)

I have noted that evidentials are especially favored in Makah with second person subjects, often with special functions. They seem to be a way to avoid insulting a person's intelligence by appearing to tell him what he already knows about himself.[17] This is true of the following example, where this suffix refers not just to a noise but to the content of an utterance:

(29)   ƛa·ci·wiƛq̇ad?ic
      'It sounds like you're getting fat.'   (if someone says e.g. that their clothes are tight) (cf. ƛa·ci·w?alic 'You're getting fat.')

The next two examples show that the suffix -q̇adi sometimes refers to evidence from feeling rather than hearing. This can occur even in first person reports of an internal state:

(30)   ƛuɫu·q̇ada·ƛs
      'I feel fine.'   (cf. ƛuɫu·?aƛs 'I'm fine.')

as well as for evidence of external happenings:

---

[17] A more explicit encoding of this concern can be found in Kwakiutl -əmskʷ 'as I told you before', which Boas originally (1911b:496) regarded as one of four evidentials, and in the Washo 'redundant' -le, indicating that the information conveyed already is, or should be, known to the hearer (Jacobsen 1964:655–6).

(31)   *taqi·q̓ad ʔi*
       'It seems like an earthquake.'

Some examples in the second person illustrate the use of this suffix to indicate evidence based on direct observation rather than hearing or feeling or, as with *-pi:t,* indirect inference:

(32)   *ʔuxu·q̓ada·lic*
       'It seems to be you.'   (a greeting)

(33)   *haʔukq̓adʔic, haʔukq̓ada·lic*
       'You are eating.'   (cf. *haʔuwic, haʔukalic* 'You are eating.')

(34)   *ƛi·ʔiłdakq̓adʔic*
       'I see you've got a lot of company.'

(35)   *diqšiƛe·ʔisq̓adʔic*
       'It looks like you're going to sew.'

The generalized force of the suffix shown in the examples is probably a more recent innovation, that perhaps began with its use, noted above, to refer to the contents of spoken messages.

Nitinat and Nootka exhibit two possibly cognate suffixes. In Nitinat the phonologically corresponding *-ːad* seems to be descriptive of sounds made by certain beings:

(36)   *yaya·d̓ːad*
       'changing voice of boy'

(37)   *hihid̓ːad*
       'noise of dogs growling'

(38)   *hu·x̣ːad*
       'noise of shouting'

(39)   *ya·c̓ːadiʔł*
       'noise of walking in house',

whereas *-e·ʔid* seems to be more oriented towards the act of making a sound:

(40)   *mu·smu·se·ʔid*
       'A cow makes a noise.'

(41)   *mu·smu·se·ʔids*
       'I am making the sound of a cow.'

(42)   *bucubuxaqe·ʔid*
       'A bear is making a noise.'

Nootka shows two corresponding forms, -ʔin and -ʼin, which may embody a similar slight difference of meaning concerning sounds.[18] These thus suggest an origin of the Makah evidential from a verb-like formative suffix descriptive of noises. There are also compatible occurrences in Makah, such as

(43)   ƛiƛi·čǧad
       'a creaking sound',

and perhaps also

(44)   ƛuƛubuǧad
       'a boat with a motor'[19]

Kwakiutl, however, seems to have two different potentially cognate suffixes for these forms, one (-ʼala) concerning noise or continued action with the voice, the other (-ǧa) meaning 'to feel'. Quileute has a comparable lexical suffix -layo 'sound of something'.

A somewhat different source for an auditory evidential, relating to the reception rather than the production or description of sounds, can be seen in Washo -delem, which is clearly derived from the transitive verb dámal 'to hear'.

Our third clearly evidential indicative incremental suffix is -caqiƛ, indicating uncertain visual evidence, as when trying to make out something at a distance:

(45)   čapaccaqil
       'It looks like a canoe.'   (cf. čapač 'It's a canoe.')

(46)   ʔaƛi·tqʷałbadaxcaqil
       'It looks like bears.'   (cf. ʔaƛi·tqʷałbadax 'They're bears.')

(47)   łapsčiƛcaqil
       'It looks like something dived.'   (cf. łapsčil 'He dived in.')

I would compare this to Nootka -caq-, -ca·q- 'paying attention to' plus momentaneous aspect marker -iƛ, thus again suggesting an origin from a verb-like formative suffix.

---

[18] Nootka and Nitinat ʔ comes from Proto-Nootkan *q̓ (or *q̓ʷ), retained in Makah. The alternate shape -ʔin might have arisen from the glottalizing effect of -ʼin on a preceding -q, which commonly occurs on combining forms of stems, to give *-q̓in (Jacobsen 1969:142, sec. 5.2). A change in function from formative to evidential incremental suffix would have encouraged a resegmentation to make this consonant part of the suffix.

[19] Cf. Jacobsen (1969:131, sec. 2.3).

NONINDICATIVE INCREMENTAL SUFFIXES

Our next group of incremental evidential suffixes are those that occur with nonindicative pronominal series. They have a somewhat more modal and tentative force than the preceding group, and they are less constrained as to tense and person.

The first of these suffixes to be considered is the quotative marker -wa:t. It indicates hearsay evidence, and occurs constantly in the narration of tales and myths, although its excessive repetition can be avoided by the use of absolutive forms. This ending is incompatible with other modes such as interrogative and imperative, but does occur with usitative and responsive postclitics; there is, however, another way of marking the quotative in combination with interrogative and subordinate endings. Our first example is in the past tense (marked by the preceding -bit-):

(48) xu·biɫadibitwa·d
      'He was snoring (I was told).'   (cf. xu·biɫadibʔu 'He was snoring.')

Here as elsewhere, of course, tense indications always apply to the action described by the verb stem, and not to the time of the speech act that is the source of information. The next example is in the present tense, but, as always with the quotative, interpretation must refer to the past, to allow for time between the utterance quoted and its subsequent report:

(49) hi·dawʔaƛwa·d
      'I hear he found it.'   (cf. hi·dawʔal 'He found it.')

This example includes the usitative postclitic:

(50) dudu·kwa·di·k
      'He sings (I hear).'   (cf. dudu·wi·k 'He sings.')

The next two examples show second and first person subjects:

(51) ʔakyadakwa·tsu
      'You've got a lot (I hear).'   (cf. ʔakyadawic 'You've got a lot.')

(52) ƛaʔu·ʔe·ʔiswa·tdu ba·dapaƛ
      'We're going to practice again (I'm told).' (ƛaʔu·- 'again')

A final example:

(53) bu·scačiƛwa·d
      'He went somewhere (don't know where).'   (cf. bu·scačil 'He went somewhere
      (don't know where but saw him go).')

shows uncertainty about a destination in the indicative version, and uncertainty about even the fact of someone going when the quotative is used.

The forms of the indicative quotative markers differ somewhat among the Nootkan languages, but all are based on an incorporation of the verb *wa·* 'to say', as has been pointed out by Sapir (1924:89, no. 57) and Swadesh (1948:109). In Nootka this occurs also as a formative suffix, *-wa·ł-, -wa·* 'to say'. The Makah *-t* in *-wa:t* is doubtless to be equated with the passive suffix -'*it*, so that this would have meant 'I am told'. Note Sapir's comment (1924:96, no. 122) that in Nootka 'passives of *wa·*- refer to the person addressed, not the thing spoken of', with his example *wa·-ʔat-aḥ* 'I am told'. The vowel contraction in *-wa·-ʔit > -wa:t* is otherwise attested for the passive suffix in Makah.[20]

The Nootka quotative marker is *-we·ʔin* (secondarily *-weʔin*). Sapir (1924:89, no. 57) refers to this as a 'petrified nominal derivative', from *-wa-ʔin* (the *a >* e is regular before *ʔi*). Swadesh derives this from *-wa·ỹin*, from *-wa·ł-* plus an *-ʔin* which he equates with a formative suffix meaning 'so treated'. I would opt for *-wa·-ʔin*, but would suggest taking the Nootka auditory suffix -'*in* (p. 15) as the second part, so that this would have meant something like 'he said and I heard him'.

Finally, as the last Nootkan example, the Nitinat quotative marker is *-uw* (*-u:w, -u:*).[21] This would have arisen from *-wa·* through regular sound changes applying to Nitinat, which include shortening of long vowels in the third or later syllable, loss of final short vowels, insertion of short vowels (here *-u-*) under certain conditions, and change of preconsonantal *uw* to *u:* in certain positions.

For Kwakiutl the quotative marker is *-ʔla*, which Swadesh (1948:116) compares to the word *ĺagʷala* 'wail, shout, call' and to the Nootka formative suffix *-č-ła·* 'called, named'. Boas (1947:224, 375), showing the stem as *ĺaqʷəla* 'to shout', compares it to a suffix *-laqʷəla* 'to talk about', which might be an intermediate stage between stem and evidential.

Andrade (1933:205, 206) reports a Quileute suffix for hearsay evidence, *-ku* in *-ku-l-ač*, which he equates with the feminine invisible unknown pronominal suffix *-kʷ*. This *-ku* is doubtless the same as the *-kʷo-* in Powell and Woodruff's

---

[20] The fact that the vowel in *-wa:t* is persistently long is additional evidence for its origin by contraction (cf. Jacobsen 1979b:780–1). The Makah-Nitinat evidential *-pi:t* (p. 12) may also etymologically contain passive -'*it*, but no suffixal first part *-pi·* presents itself. One does think of comparing, though, the Makah and Nitinat stems *pi·x̣-*, with specialization of the meaning seen in cognate Nootka *piḥ-* 'to observe, study, judge; look in mirror' (Jacobsen 1969:135). There is evidence indicating that *-x̣* or *-ḥ* may have been added to some stems as a 'stem extender' (Haas 1972:82–5, sec. 2.1; 1969:118–9, sec. 6.21; Jacobsen 1969:149–52, sec. 6.11–5). (Note the similar formal relationship in Kwakiutl between stem *p̓aq-* and suffix *-p̓a*, both meaning 'to taste' [p. 24, below]; *-q* is another 'stem-extender'.) Thus we can think of a stem *-pi·-* which became incorporated as a formative suffix, and went on to become frozen in the passive as an evidential incremental suffix, *-pi·-ʔit*, which would have literally meant 'it is observed'.

[21] See Carlson and Thomas (1979:325) for a sample paradigm.

(1976) -*kʷolas* 'assumed, presumed, supposed' and -*kʷokʷ* 'supposed, presumed' (the latter indeed ending with the -*kʷ* pronominal suffix, glossed by Powell and Woodruff as 'she [unknown reference]').

A parallel to the Nootkan case of a quotative marker arising from a suffixed verb 'to say' is seen in Hokan Yana of northern California, where the Central and Northern dialects' quotative mode (i.e. evidential) suffix -*ti(ʔa)* and the Yahi quotative particle -*tii* must originally have been identical with the stem *tii-* 'to say' (Sapir and Swadesh 1960:157; cf. Sapir 1923:289, no. 182). Similarly, in northern Uto-Aztecan, rather impersonal and stative evidential quotatives have arisen from verbs for 'to say', in some cases becoming suffixes and in others remaining stems (Munro 1978:159–60).

Makah has forms that seem to be nonindicative quotatives, formed with a suffix -*ča:* that also occurs elsewhere. The quotative interrogative, used in asking about hearsay or inferential information, has the ending -*i:-ča:* instead of -*a:ł* in the third person:

(54)   *ba·qi·daxa·ƛi·ča teʔiłiq*
       'How did he say the sick person is?'   (cf. *ba·qi·daxa·ƛa·ł teʔiłiq* 'How is the sick person?')

This -*ča:* also occurs, preceded by -*x*- and followed by personal endings, in a quotative subordinate form:

(55)   *łaxa·s kabatsa·p kupa·ʔe·ʔisxča·s*
       'I just found out that I'm supposed to point.'   (-*ʔe:ʔis*- 'distant future', -*s* 'first person singular')

-*ča:* also follows conditional -*qey* to form counterfactual forms:

(56)   *waha·kitqeyča·si·k*
       'I wish I had gone.'   (-*it*- 'past tense', -*i:k* 'usitative')

Nootka also has quotative forms corresponding to nonindicative modes: interrogative, relative, conditional, relative inferential, and subject relative; these are formed with -*č* (Sapir 1924:89, nos. 57, 58; 102, no. 184; Swadesh 1939:82; 1948:110).[22] Swadesh (1948:110) compares this -*č* to Bella Bella (northern Kwakiutlan) -*k* 'to say'. There is also a quotative or inferential particle -*ča* (Sapir 1924:90, no. 66; 101, no. 78; Swadesh 1948:110, 112).

Nitinat is described as having a quotative interrogative with a segment -*ʾi:t*, which precedes the usual interrogative endings (Carlson and Thomas 1979:325–6). This is probably a derived function of the suffix marking the passive voice,

---

22 These are the evidential forms alluded to in the quotation from Sapir (1911) on p. 4.

although one thinks of comparing the Nootka auditory suffix -'in (a Nootkan morpheme-final *n ~ *t alternation being well attested). It can be preceded by a past tense marker -ʔ-.

Inferred probability is marked in Makah by -x̣aː-..-š, where the -š comes after the pronominal suffix. This indicates a probability inferred from unspecified evidence. Examples are:

(57)   dudu·kax̣λx̣a·š
       'He's probably singing.'   (cf. dudu·kal 'He's singing.')

(58)   dudu·kix̣λx̣a·š
       'He'll probably sing.'

(59)   ʔukye·ʔitx̣a·su·ƚš
       'They probably gave it to you.'
       (This last is passive with pronominal indication of second person singular patient
           and plural agent.)

Nitinat has comparable forms marked with -x̣i-..-iš. Carlson and Thomas (1979:321–5) feel that these have evidential value only in the past tense; they gloss the present tense forms with *I guess, I think,* and *might;* Klokeid (1976, 1978) calls this category UNKNOWN; Haas (1969:113) labels the forms MAYBE.[23]

Corresponding past inferential forms in Makah are marked by -x̣učaʔaː-..-š:

(60)   dudu·kax̣λx̣učaʔa·š
       'He probably sang.'   (cf. dudu·kax̣λʔu 'He sang.')

(61)   λi·x̣ʷawe·ʔitx̣učaʔa·si·š
       'He probably made fun of me.'
       (This second example is again passive, with an indication of first person singular
           patient.)

These forms probably contain a past tense marker -'u-, which occurs elsewhere, and the -ča- of the nonindicative quotative forms. In Nitinat the past inferential is marked by -ʔ- (giving -x̣ʔi-..-iš); this may relate to the -ʔ- in Makah. This ending also recalls the Nootka inferential in -ča·ʔaš, meaning 'apparently' (categorized, it will be remembered, along with the quotative, as an evidential by Swadesh [1939:82]).

The related ending -ºaː-..-škub indicates that the speaker has only belatedly become aware of a fact or event:

(62)   čapaca·škub
       'It's a canoe.'   (after you finally make out what it is)   (cf. čapac 'It's a canoe.')

---

[23] The -x̣- here is perhaps to be equated with a marker of the RELATIVE paradigm (Jacobsen 1973), called by Carlson and Thomas (1979:323) SUBJECT FOCUS.

(63)   *pe·dišatχa·škub*
       '(We found out that) it was the Spanish.'
       (This refers to the Makahs' belated learning that it was the Spanish who had left
            certain remains in their territory.)

A final example has a second person singular pronominal suffix:

(64)   *hitaqeyala·su·škub*
       '(I see) you have arrived.'

This is, of course, like the present tense form of the previous section without
the preceding *-χ-*, but with an added segment *-kub*. This *-kub* might be compared
to Kwakiutl *-kəm* 'sign (of . . .), omen'.
     There is also a past tense form with added *-ʔu-* to yield *-ʔuʔa:-...-škub*:

(65)   *ʔo· čapačuʔa·škub*
       'Oh, so it was a canoe.'

which could be a response to:

(66)   *čapacpi·d*
       'It must have been a canoe.'

GOVERNING FORMATIVE SUFFIXES

The last group of evidentials that we will examine are governing formative
suffixes. They all occur preponderantly with substantival or descriptive, rather
than evidential, value, but seem to play the latter role in certain circumstances.
There is also usually a distributional correlation, in that when they have evidential value they do not occur with bound stems or with combining-forms of free
stems, as they do in their other meanings. They may thus provide a further
indication of how evidentials may arise from morphemes with these kinds of
concrete meanings, in connection with a move to a less central layer of the word.
     The suffix *-ckʷi·* (combining-form *-ckʷiq-*) usually forms nouns referring to
remains or debris resulting from a particular action. However, when added to the
free noun stem *bukwač* 'deer' it underlies a predication indicating tracks as the
source of evidence:

(67)   *bukwačckʔi*
       'It was a deer.'   (when seeing the tracks)   (cf. *bukwač* 'It's a deer.', *bukwačʔu*
       'It was a deer.')[24]

---

[24] A regular rule of dissimilation of labialization accounts for the *-k-* rather than
-kʷ- in the suffix.

Contrast

(68) *bukwači·č̓ x̌i·yit*
      'It's deer tracks.'   (*x̌i·yit* 'tracks')

when explicitly identifying the tracks as such, and also the previously cited

(21) *ʔax̌i·tqʷałpi·d*
      'It must have been a bear.'

which is less specific about the nature of the evidence. The following example, with stem *q̓idi·x̌* 'dog', would apply to tentative identification of a tooth found lying alone:

(69) *q̓idi·x̌icckʷi·ʔ čiči ʔi*
      'It must've been a dog's tooth.'   (*čiči ʔi:* 'tooth')

Examples follow of the more numerous cases where formations with this suffix either label the remains or debris itself,

(70) *x̌aščkʷi*
      'skeleton, bony remains'   (*x̌aš-* 'bone')

(71) *łux̌cki*
      'skull'   (*łux̌-* 'head')

(72) *čitckʷi*
      'sawdust'   (*čit-* 'to saw')

or assert its existence or identification, when predicative:

(73) *hisckʷi·ʔ*
      'It's chips from chopping.'   (*his-* 'to chop')

(74) *kʷi·x̌kʷi·yackʔi*
      'It's powder from sharpening mussel shells.'   (repetitive form of *kʷi-* 'to sharpen, grind')

(75) *qułcki·ʔ*
      'He's from a slave family.'   (*quł-* 'slave')

(76) *łux̌cki·bʔu*
      'It was a skull.'   (past tense)

Cognate suffixes occur in Nitinat and Nootka. A similar meaning is seen in Kwakiutl *-sʔo* 'piece of, remains of', and apparently also in Quileute *-stake·tił* 'remainder, waste' (Andrade 1933:195). These are not known to have evidential functions. There is also a Nootka suffix *-yit* 'showing evidence, traces, marks of . . .', and a Nitinat cognate *-yit* (*-yt*) 'evidence, signs, tracks of . . .':

(77) *ʔałevt*
       'tracks of two'   (*ʔał* 'two')

(78) *bu·yit*
       'tracks of four'   (*bu·* 'four')

(79) *buwčeyt*
       'deer tracks, signs'   (*buwač* 'deer')

The Makah cognate -*yit* is not well attested, but occurs in

(80) *łi·yit*
       'tracks'   (*łi·-* 'to walk')

The formative suffix -*kuk* has been noted as an evidential only in the second person, where it indicates evidence based on appearances, as in:

(81) *ła·ci·wiłkuwic*
       'You look like you're getting fat.'   (cf. *ła·ci·wʔalic* 'You're getting fat.')

This suffix occurs much more commonly, with initial CV- reduplication, on combining-forms of stems, to express idiomatic nominal derivation involving physical resemblance, as in:

(82) *babačaskuk*
       'wheat, grain', lit. 'looks like fleas'   (*bačas-* 'flea')

(83) *čičiyupkuk*
       'spaghetti, macaroni', lit. 'looks like intestines'   (*čiyup-* 'intestines')

(84) *čičisaqkuk*
       'sugar', lit. 'looks like sand'   (*čisaq-* 'sand')

(85) *xaxaškuk*
       'hardtack, pilot bread, crackers', lit. 'looks like bones'   (*xaš-* 'bone')

(86) *hihisckʷiqkuk*
       'soda crackers', lit. 'looks like chips from chopping'   (*hisckʷiq-* 'chips from chopping')[25]

The evidential force of -*kuk* is not necessarily recent, however, as both values are also described for the cognate Nootka suffix -*kuk*. Nitinat also has a cognate suffix -*kuk* (more common allomorph -*kkʷ*), attested in available materials only in a nonevidential value. One thinks of comparing here also the Kwakiutl suffix -*kəm* 'sign (of . . .), omen' (cf. p. 20). Quileute has a comparable lexical suffix

---

[25] Numerous additional examples of this Makah suffix occurring in neologisms are given in Jacobsen (1980, pp. 170, 174–7), and some also of the Nitinat suffix, from Klokeid (1968, on p. 178).

-čaqal 'similar, like in appearance' (Andrade [1933:197] shows -čaq 'to be like, look like').

With our final formative suffix, -pał, we are scraping the bottom of the barrel in the search for evidentials. It clearly has a primarily descriptive value in describing smells or tastes, but verges on being an evidential which indicates evidence from these sense modalities in certain examples. Thus

(87)   daʔa·pałs
        'I smell it.'   (cf. daʔa·s 'I hear it.')

can be taken literally as 'I hear (i.e. sense) it by the evidence of its smell.', and the stem bis- 'to smell' rather redundantly takes this suffix in

(88)   bisi·pałs
        'I smell something.'   (cf. bisšiƛ 'Smell it.')

Examples like the following hover on the borderline between description and evidentiality:

(89)   čabaspał
        'It smells good, tastes sweet.'   (cf. čabas 'It tastes good, sweet.')
(90)   cixi·pał
        'It's sour.'   (cix- 'sour')
(91)   čupał
        'It stinks.'   (ču- 'to stink'),

while those below seem more evidential in nature:

(92)   ba·dawi·pał
        'It smells like smelt.'   (cf. ba·dawi·ʔ 'It's a smelt.')
(93)   ƛušaktpał
        'It smells like dried fish.'   (cf. ƛušakd 'It's dried fish.')

Cognate suffixes with about the same range of meanings are found in Nitinat -pał (-pł) and Nootka (-pał). Nitinat examples are:

(94)   ƛułipł
        'good smell, smell something good'
(95)   su·pupł
        'soap smell'
(96)   bucubuxqapł
        'smell of bear'

(97)   *łu·łičχqapł*
       'smell of flowers'

Kwakiutl has -*pa* 'to taste', from which is probably derived -*pala* 'to smell' (cf. also -*pałto* 'to see'). Boas (1911b:446; 1947:224), followed by Swadesh (1948:117), also compares the Kwakiutl stem *paq-* 'to taste'. Quileute also has a suffix with corresponding meanings, -*łada* 'odor, smell, taste'.

As mentioned earlier (pp. 3–4), Kwakiutl has an evidential suffix referring to the experience of a dream; this has the form -*ʔənga*.[26] Makah has no comparable evidential, but there is a formative suffix meaning 'to dream (of) . . . , to have a . . . dream', -*ʔapuł* (with CV- reduplication). Available Makah examples describe the quality of the dream:

(98)   *λuλu·lapułaλits*
       'I had a good dream.' (*λuł-* 'good')

(99)   *łałakʷapułaλits*
       'I had a sad dream, bad dream.' (*łakʷ-* 'sad, poor')

Nitinat examples with cognate -*ʔapł* (also with reduplication) express a more material content:

(100) *bubuwačapł*
       'to dream about a deer' (*buwač* 'deer')

(101) *ququʔačapł*
       'to dream about a person' (*quʔac-* 'person')

There is a semantically comparable Nootka suffix -*ʔituł* (also with reduplication), but the cognate suffix may be -*(q)apuł* 'to imitate, impersonate, represent . . . '. Quileute also has a comparable suffix, -*kʷsil*. Since Kwakiutl seems, on the other hand, to lack a parallel formative suffix for predications explicitly about dreaming, it appears very possible that such a suffix may have been the source of this evidential.

SUMMARY

The evidentials among the formative suffixes give rather specific indications of physical evidence or evidence from sensory modalities, and most of them are etymologically or descriptively related to suffixes with nominal, verbal, or descriptive values. Their evidential function can be seen to arise from a kind of semantic subordination, where the focus of the predication shifts from the suffix

---

[26]There is another Kwakiutl suffix, -*xsłaakʷ* 'apparently, seemingly, it seems like', which is said to also mean 'in a dream' in the Koskimo dialect (Boas 1947:245, 371).

to the stem, the suffix coming to provide merely a kind of epistemological orientation.

The evidentials among the incremental suffixes that occur with indicative pronominal endings also have relatively concrete and specific meanings, applying to evidence obtained approximately at the time of speaking. Incremental evidential suffixes taking nonindicative pronominal endings, on the other hand, express more diffuse evidence that may be more distant in time.

For both formative and incremental suffixes we have discussed semantically defined subsets of paradigmatically opposed suffixes. Evidentials, in other words, are not a morphologically unitary or distinct category in Makah.

REFERENCES

Andrade, Manuel J. 1933. Quileute. Handbook of American Indian languages, Part 3, ed. by Franz Boas, 149–292. Glückstadt and New York: J. J. Augustin.

Azkue, Resurrección María de. 1923–5. Morfología vasca. Euskera 4.i–viii, 1–404, 5.405–804, 6.805–930. (Also published separately, 1925. Bilbao: Editorial Vasca.)

Bloomfield, Leonard. 1933. Language. New York: Henry Holt and Company.

———. 1962. The Menomini language. New Haven and London: Yale University Press.

Boas, Franz. 1900. Sketch of the Kwakiutl language. American Anthropologist 2.708–21. (Reprinted in The shaping of American anthropology 1883–1911: A Franz Boas reader, ed. by George W. Stocking, Jr. New York: Basic Books, Inc. 1974.)

———. 1911a. Introduction. Boas, ed. 1911:1–83.

———. 1911b. Kwakiutl. Boas, ed. 1911:423–557.

———. 1938. Language. General anthropology, ed. by Franz Boas, 124–45. Boston: D. C. Heath and Company.

———. 1942. Language and culture. Studies in the history of culture: The disciplines of the humanities, 178–84. Menasha, WI: The George Banta Publishing Co.

———. 1947. Kwakiutl grammar, with a glossary of the suffixes. Transactions of the American Philosophical Society 37(3).201–377.

———, ed. 1911. Handbook of American Indian languages, Part 1. (Smithsonian Institution, Bureau of American Ethnology, Bulletin 40.) Washington: Government Printing Office.

Bolinger, Dwight. 1975. Aspects of language. 2nd ed. New York: Harcourt Brace Jovanovich Inc.

Campbell, Lyle, and Marianne Mithun, eds. 1979. The languages of native America: Historical and comparative assessment. Austin and London: University of Texas Press.

Carlson, Barry F., and John Thomas. 1979. The Nitinaht inferential. Anthropological Linguistics 21.317–27.

Chafe, Wallace L. 1970. Meaning and the structure of language. Chicago and London: The University of Chicago Press.

———. 1979. Caddoan. Campbell and Mithun, eds. 1979:213–35.

De Rijk, Rudolf P. G. 1969. Is Basque an S. O. V. language? Fontes linguae vasconum 1.319–51.

———. 1972. Partitive assignment in Basque. Anuario del Seminario de Filología Vasca 'Julio de Urquijo' 6.130–73.

Freeland, L. S. 1951. Language of the Sierra Miwok. Indiana University Publications in Anthropology and Linguistics. (International Journal of American Linguistics, Memoir 6.) Baltimore: Waverly Press, Inc.

Haas, Mary R. 1941. Tunica. Handbook of American Indian languages, Vol. 4, 1–143. New York: J. J. Augustin.

_____. 1946. A grammatical sketch of Tunica. Hoijer et al. 1946:337–66.

_____. 1969. Internal reconstruction of the Nootka–Nitinat pronominal suffixes. International Journal of American Linguistics 35.108–24.

_____. 1972. The structure of stems and roots in Nootka–Nitinat. International Journal of American Linguistics 38.83–92.

Hall, Robert A., Jr. 1964. Introductory linguistics. Philadelphia: Chilton Books.

Hockett, Charles F. 1958. A course in modern linguistics. New York: The Macmillan Company.

Hoijer, Harry. 1946. Tonkawa. Hoijer et al. 1946:289–311.

_____. 1954. Some problems of American Indian linguistic research. Papers from the Symposium on American Indian Linguistics held at Berkeley July 7, 1951, 3–12. (University of California Publications in Linguistics, 10.) Berkeley and Los Angeles: University of California Press.

Hoijer, Harry, et al. 1946. Linguistic structures of native America. (Viking Fund Publications in Anthropology, 6.) New York: The Viking Fund.

Jacobsen, William H., Jr. 1964. A grammar of the Washo language. University of California, Berkeley dissertation.

_____. 1969. Origin of the Nootka pharyngeals. International Journal of American Linguistics 35.125–53.

_____. 1973. The pattern of Makah pronouns. Paper presented to the Eighth International Conference on Salish Languages, Eugene.

_____. 1979a. Noun and verb in Nootkan. The Victoria Conference on Northwestern Languages, ed. by Barbara S. Efrat, 83–155. (British Columbia Provincial Museum Heritage Record, 4.) Victoria: British Columbia Provincial Museum.

_____. 1979b. Wakashan comparative studies. Campbell and Mithun, eds. 1979:766–91.

_____. 1979c. Chimakuan comparative studies. Campbell and Mithun, eds. 1979:792–802.

_____. 1980. Metaphors in Makah neologisms. Proceedings of the Sixth Annual Meeting of the Berkeley Linguistics Society, February 16–18, 1980, ed. by Bruce R. Caron et al., 166–79. Berkeley: Berkeley Linguistics Society.

Jakobson, Roman. 1944. Franz Boas' approach to language. International Journal of American Linguistics 10.188–95. (Reprinted in Jakobson 1971:477–88.)

_____. 1957. Shifters, verbal categories, and the Russian verb. Cambridge, Mass.: Department of Slavic Languages and Literatures, Harvard University. (Reprinted in Jakobson 1971:130–47.)

_____. 1959. Boas' view of grammatical meaning. The anthropology of Franz Boas: Essays on the centennial of his birth, ed. by Walter Goldschmidt, 139–45. (American Anthropological Association, Memoir 89.) (Reprinted in Jakobson 1971:489–96.)

_____. 1971. Selected writings 2: Word and language. The Hague and Paris: Mouton.

Jespersen, Otto. 1924. The philosophy of grammar. London: George Allen & Unwin Ltd.

Klokeid, Terry J. 1968. Linguistic acculturation in Nitinat. Paper presented to the Third International Conference on Salish Languages, Victoria.

_____. 1976. Encliticization in Nitinaht. Working papers for the XI International Conference on Salishan Languages, August 12–14, 1976, University of Washington, Seattle, Washington, compiled by Carol M. Eastman and Robert L. Welsch, 211–46. Seattle: Department of Anthropology, University of Washington.

_____. 1978. Surface structure constraints and Nitinaht enclitics. Linguistic structures of native Canada, ed. by Eung–Do Cook and Jonathan Kaye, 157–76. Vancouver: University of British Columbia Press.

Lafitte, Pierre. 1962. Grammaire basque (Navarro–labourdin littéraire). Revised ed. Bayonne: Editions des 'Amis du Musée Basque' et 'Ikas'.

Lee, Dorothy Demetracopoulou. 1938. Conceptual implications of an Indian language. Philosophy of Science 5.89–102.

————. 1944. Linguistic reflection of Wintu·'thought. International Journal of American Linguistics 10.181–7. (Reprinted in Lee 1959:121–30.)

————. 1950. Notes on the conception of the self among the Wintu Indians. The Journal of Abnormal and Social Psychology 45.538–43. (Reprinted in Lee 1959:131–40.)

————. 1959. Freedom and culture. (Spectrum Books S–6.) Englewood Cliffs: Prentice–Hall.

Lyons, John. 1968. Introduction to theoretical linguistics. Cambridge: Cambridge University Press.

Munro, Pamela. 1978. Chemehuevi 'say' and the Uto–Aztecan quotative pattern. Selected papers from the 14th Great Basin Anthropological Conference, ed. by Donald R. Tuohy, 149–71. (Ballena Press Publications in Archaeology, Ethnology and History, 11.) Socorro, New Mexico: Ballena Press.

Pinnow, Heinz–Jürgen. 1964. Die nordamerikanischen Indianersprachen: Ein Überblick über ihren Bau und ihre Besonderheiten. Wiesbaden: Otto Harrassowitz.

Powell, J. V., and Fred Woodruff, Sr. 1976. Quileute dictionary. (Northwest Anthropological Research Notes, Memoir 3.) Moscow, Idaho.

Sapir, Edward. 1911. Some aspects of Nootka language and culture. American Anthropologist 13.15–28.

————. 1921. Language: An introduction to the study of speech. New York: Harcourt, Brace and Co.

————. 1922. Takelma. Handbook of American Indian Languages, Part 2, ed. by Franz Boas, 1–296. (Smithsonian Institution, Bureau of American Ethnology, Bulletin 40.) Washington: Government Printing Office.

————. 1923. Text analyses of three Yana dialects. University of California Publications in American Archaeology and Ethnology 20.263–94.

————. 1924. The rival whalers, a Nitinat story (Nootka text with translation and grammatical analysis). International Journal of American Linguistics 3.76–102.

Sapir, Edward, and Morris Swadesh. 1939. Nootka texts: Tales and ethnological narratives, with grammatical notes and lexical materials. Philadelphia: Linguistic Society of America.

————. 1960. Yana dictionary. Ed. by Mary R. Haas. (University of California Publications in Linguistics, 22.) Berkeley and Los Angeles: University of California Press.

Sherzer, Joel F. 1968. An areal–typological study of the American Indian languages north of Mexico. University of Pennsylvania dissertation.

————. 1976. An areal–typological study of American Indian languages north of Mexico. (North–Holland Linguistic Series, 20.) Amsterdam: North–Holland Publishing Company. [Revised version of Sherzer 1968.]

Shipley, William F. 1964. Maidu grammar. (University of California Publications in Linguistics, 41.) Berkeley and Los Angeles: University of California Press.

Swadesh, Morris. 1933. The internal economy of the Nootka word. Yale University dissertation.

—— ————. 1939. Nootka internal syntax. International Journal of American Linguistics 9.77–102. [Revised version of Swadesh 1933.]

————. 1948. A structural trend in Nootka. Word 4.106–19.

Thompson, Laurence C. 1979. Salishan and the Northwest. Campbell and Mithun, eds. 1979:692–765.

Trask, Robert L. 1981. Basque verbal morphology. Euskalarien nazioarteko jardunaldiak, 285–304. (Iker, 1.) Bilbao: Euskaltzaindia.

Weinreich, Uriel. 1963. On the semantic structure of language. Universals of language, ed. by Joseph H. Greenberg, 114–71. Cambridge, Mass.: MIT Press.

Whorf, Benjamin Lee. 1938. Some verbal categories of Hopi. Language 14.275–86. (Reprinted in Whorf 1956c:112–24.)

————. 1946. The Hopi language, Toreva dialect. Hoijer et al. 1946:158–83.

————. 1956a. A linguistic consideration of thinking in primitive communities. Whorf 1956c:65–86. [Written about late 1936.]

———. 1956b. Language: Plan and conception of arrangement. Whorf 1956c:125–33. [Originally circulated in 1938.]

———. 1956c. Language, thought, and reality: Selected writings of Benjamin Lee Whorf. Edited by John B. Carroll. New York: The Technology Press of MIT and John Wiley and Sons, Inc.

Wilbur, Terence H. 1981. Basque syntax. Euskalarien nazioarteko jardunaldiak, 169–86. (Iker, 1.) Bilbao: Euskaltzaindia.

TWO

The Evidential System
of Kashaya

Robert L. Oswalt
California Indian Language Center

1. INTRODUCTION

Kashaya[1] is one of seven languages of the Pomo family, all native to northern California. The three most closely related—Kashaya, Southern Pomo, and Central Pomo (about as divergent one from another as Spanish, Italian, and French)—share a cognate set of evidential verbal suffixes, elements which express the means by which the speaker has learned whereof he speaks. The systems in these three languages rank among the most elaborated and discriminating of any in the world; descriptions of the Pomo languages other than these three do not reveal as complex a development.[2] The evidential suffixes of Kashaya, Southern Pomo, and Central Pomo are close to a "pure play"; most are solely evidentials and are not detectably related to, or derivative from, anything else within the three languages. This is in contrast to many of the elements

---

[1] Most of the Kashaya material on which this paper is based was collected in the summers 1957–1961, in the course of fieldwork sponsored by the Survey of California Indian Languages, Department of Linguistics, University of California, Berkeley. Later work among the Southern and Central Pomo, in the period 1965–68, was assisted by the National Science Foundation, Grants GS–711 and GS–1463.

Example sentences are identified by a preceding S plus a number which is incremented sequentially through the entire body of the chapter. Some of the example sentences are from a published source, *Kashaya Texts* (Oswalt, 1964); these are cited with the abbreviation KT followed by text, paragraph, and sentence numbers.

[2] Table 1 shows suffixes for Kashaya evidentials. Of the suffixes in the table, the two with reflexes most widely distributed in the Pomo languages are *-do* Quotative and *-ya* Visual (although this latter is apparently not always limited to a visual meaning). The cognate sets are given in Oswalt (1976:25). The data therein on the Western Pomo languages are from my own fieldwork; that on Eastern Pomo from McLendon's dissertation (published in 1975); that on Southeastern Pomo from Moshinsky's dissertation (published in 1974).

described for other languages, for which the evidential function is often peripheral to, or derived from, some other use.

2. LINGUISTIC PRELIMINARIES

2.1 Overview

The system of Kashaya evidentials is presented in Table 1. The suffixes are
divided into three groups by horizontal lines extending the full width of the chart.
The first division, with six suffixes named in the leftmost column, applies in
general to events or states perceived directly by the speaker but also includes
general truths and inferences based on circumstantial, although directly observed, evidence (Sections 3.0–3.6). The second division consists of one suffix,
-do, for information the speaker has learned from someone else (Section 3.7).
These first two divisions constitute the main part of the system, and the suffixes
in them are mutually exclusive—only one can appear on any one verb. The third
division consists of one suffix, -bi- (Section 3.8). It is notionally an evidential,
having an inferential meaning, but is different in that it is necessarily followed by
some other suffix, which may be certain of the core evidentials.

The first five lines of suffixes are concerned with evidence acquired at the
time and place of the event and are not compatible with the future tense or
uncertainty. The suffixes on the bottom three lines, the two Inferentials and the
Quotative, concern evidence acquired apart from the event and can co-occur in a

Table 1. Kashaya Evidentials

	Spontaneous	Responsive (with Suffix −m˘)	Narrative	Remote
Performative (Imperfective)	-ẁela	-ẁǎ		
Performative (Perfective)	-mela	-yǎ		
Factual (Imperfective)	-ẁǎ		-yoẁǎ	-miyǎ
Visual (Perfective)	-yǎ			
Auditory	-V̂nnǎ			
Inferential I	-qǎ			
Quotative	-do			
Inferential II	-bi-			

sentence with a future tense. The significance of the vertical order in the table will be discussed further below.

Before the detailed description and exemplification of the evidential suffixes, it is necessary to give some preliminary information on Kashaya phonemics and morphophonemics and on several elements and features which are important to the operation of the system: the Assertive verb, the Absolutive suffix, Aspect, and the Spontaneous, Responsive, and Narrative modes (which pertain to the different columns in Table 1).

2.2 Phonemics

The Kashaya language has five vowels, *a, e, i, o, u;* vowel length, ·; and pitch accent, ´. The consonants include three complete series of stops in six positions—labial, dental, alveolar, palatal, velar, uvular—symbolized in the plain series by *p, t, ṭ, c, k, q;* in the aspirated series by the same symbols plus a superscript *h* (*p^h*, etc.); and in the glottalized series by the same series plus a superscript comma (*ṗ*, etc.). Voiced stops and nasals occur only in the labial and alveolar positions *b, d, m, n;* other resonants are *w, y, l;* sibilants *s, š;* glottalized affricate *ŝ;* and laryngeals *h, ʔ*.

The forms at the head end of arrows and most full word and sentence examples are in a surface phonemic representation. The constituent boundaries of some of the surface forms are marked by hyphenation, although the fusion between neighboring elements may be so great as to preclude strict delimitation, except in a morphophonemic representation.

2.3 Morphophonemics

The segmented forms at the tail end of arrows, and the suffixes in Table 1 and in isolation in the text, are in an underlying morphophonemic representation (marked by a preceding □). The special symbols used in representing the suffixes are as follows:

ŵ   symbolizes an alternation between Ø after a stem ending in a consonant and *w* after a vowel: *cad-ŵela* → *cadela* 'I see,' versus *miṭi-ŵela* → *miṭiwéla* 'I am lying (down)'.

V̂   symbolizes Ø after a vowel, and various vowels determined by a preceding consonant: *u* after *d, o* after a uvular preceded by *o, a* after labials and uvulars elsewhere, and *i* after other consonants.

ă   symbolizes Ø before a word-boundary and most vowels, and /a/ before certain suffixes. Even when it is realized phonemically as Ø, ă can be detected as being morphophonemically present when a preceding syllable has a long vowel: *biře°l-ŵă* → *biře·l* 'is sewing'; without the ă, the word would end in a consonant in its underlying form and the preceding vowel would become short. Underlying plain stops become aspirated stops before an ă that becomes Ø before word boundary (see S8) and this too is different from the development of the same

underlying plain stops directly before word boundary—in this latter
situation they all become a phonemic glottal stop ?.

A complete statement of the alternations in the verb stems is not possible in a
short paper, but occasional formulaic explanations are given along with some of
the early examples.

2.4 Assertive

The Assertive can be the main verb 'be' in simple assertions but also has several
specialized auxiliary uses, one of which is of great importance in the operation of
the evidential system. The Assertive verb is enclitic (marked by a preceding = in
the examples) and thus cannot appear initially in a sentence, although it can
appear almost anywhere else. When followed by additional suffixes, it has the
form =? after words ending in a vowel and =i after consonants, with glottalization of preceding plain stops.

In Kashaya, there are a very large number of mutually exclusive suffixes,
some of which (including the evidentials) form finite verbs, while others form
subordinated verbs. However, a clause whose principal verb has some suffix
other than an evidential may have an evidential introduced into it with the
Assertive as a "dummy" carrier of the additional suffix. This allows the evidentials which are not specifically present-past to be introduced into a clause with a
future tense, and it allows certain evidentials to be introduced into subordinate
clauses (which would otherwise normally be assumed to have the same evidentiality as the superordinate clause). In the narrative construction (Section 2.9), it
serves as the carrier of the evidential, while the main verb is placed in the
Absolutive.

2.5 Absolutive

The Absolutive has multiple functions: citation form of verbs, gerund, participle
(active and passive), and the main verb of sentences in the narrative construction.
It also provides an escape from the evidential system. Sentences elicited from
English with third person agents are often given in the Absolutive since the
translator may have no clue to the type of evidence involved. However, if the
translator pictures a situation in which he would use the sentence, he will often
supply an evidential suffix.

The Absolutive has the allomorphs -w after a vowel stem, -u after d, -? after a
resonant, and $\emptyset$ after any other consonant. Stem-final stops become ? when this
suffix is $\emptyset$.

2.6 Aspect

Some Kashaya verb roots and stems are innately imperfective and refer to a state
or a continuing or repeated act. Others are innately perfective and refer to a
single short act or to one moment of a longer act. Still others are aspectless and

indifferent to the distinction. There are suffixes that form derived stems, converting from one aspect to the other.

Aspect is important to two pairs of suffixes, the Performative pair and the Factual-Visual pair. Perfective stems can be suffixed only by the perfective members of these pairs; imperfective stems only by the imperfective members. Aspectless stems can be suffixed by either member of the pairs and then the aspectual distinction is carried by the suffix. The other evidential suffixes have no such contrast and any aspectual information would have to be shown by the preceding stem. With negative verbs (formed by a suffix that precedes the evidential suffix) there is a collapse of the aspectual distinction; negative verbs accept only the imperfective suffixes of the pairs, whether the stem without the negative suffix is imperfective, perfective, or aspectless.

2.7   Spontaneous remarks

When a remark is spontaneous or prompted by the event or state being described (and not as part of a continuing discussion or conversation), then the suffixes show the maximum discrimination in types of evidence, and are those in the leftmost column of Table 1. No other suffix is added if the verb is final in its clause; if it is not, a suffix called NONFINAL VERB is necessary: -a· after -qǎ, -e· after other instances of -ǎ, · (vowel length) after other vowels.

Since it is usually the event or state itself that induces the act of speech, a present or immediate past tense is implied. The aspect of the verb stem or of the suffix has a great deal to do with the tense of translation. A perfective act would most frequently be one completed just before the act of speaking; English 'just' plus the past or present perfect tense would then be a good translation (S2, S9, S11), but the tense could be at an earlier time in a properly supporting context, even as English, 'A car just ran off that cliff,' would normally imply a moment earlier, but the time of 'just' is stretchable with an adverb like 'last week'. An imperfective act is often one going on at the moment of speaking (S1, S8, S13), but, in the proper context, it too could be one that continued at an earlier time.

2.8   Responsive

When a remark is prompted not by the state or event being talked about, but by the words of someone else—that is, by a question or in the give and take of conversation—the Responsive construction is required: -m suffixed to the verb with the evidential and a rising intonation at the end of the sentence (marked ˇ), and often with the particle ṭa somewhere in the sentence (Examples S7, S28). This construction occurs with all the evidentials except the Performative pair (Section 3.1). The tense tends to be intermediate past, since the matters discussed in conversations tend not to be immediate and present.

2.9   Narrative

If the topic of discussion shifts to happenings more remote in time and one speaker comes to dominate a stretch of discourse with some account, the radically different narrative construction comes into use, with a simplification of the evidential distinctions to two: Personal Experience (Section 3.5) and the Quotative (Section 3.7). What is semantically the main verb is put in the Absolutive (2.5) and the evidential is suffixed to a 'dummy' verb, the Assertive (2.4). The combination is postpositive, appearing almost anywhere in the sentence except initially, but it is preponderantly placed after the first word of the sentence. That first word is usually a sentence connector like *mul* 'that, then' (S25, S27, S33), *ma?u* 'this, now', *men* 'thus', *menšiba* 'having done so (with a continuation of the agent of the preceding sentence)', *menši·li* 'having done so (with a switch in agent)', etc.

3. THE SUFFIXES

3.0 Direct Evidence

Since almost all the suffixes in the first division (above the Quotative line in Table 1) end in the morphophoneme -*ă*, one could segment these into two parts and label the final -*ă* as a morpheme which designates events or states perceived, by some means, directly by the speaker. In fact, this -*ă* could be identified as the Factual suffix -*ŵă;* since in collocations such as -*y-ŵă*, -*V̂nn-ŵă*, and -*q-ŵă*, the -*ŵ*- follows a consonant and can never surface and be realized phonemically as anything but $\emptyset$. In the narrative construction, the -*yowă* of personal experience is more clearly identifiable as containing -*ŵă* Factual added to an element -*yo*-, which terminates in a vowel. However, since none of the prior components of these indicators of direct evidence occur apart from the -*ă*, these possibly compound suffixes are treated as units in the following discussion. It should be kept in mind that in most occurrences of these suffixes the -*ă* is realized phonemically as $\emptyset$ (Section 2.3).

3.1 Performative Pair, -ŵela, -mela

The Performative[3] suffixes signify that the speaker knows of what he speaks because he is performing the act himself or has just performed it. The subject, of course, is always the first person, singular or plural, but I prefer not to classify this pair simply as first person endings because the category of person is not developed in the Kashaya verb, occurring only incidentally, as when the Imperative suffixes are second person. The evidentials, on the other hand, are a well-developed category. As a conversational interchange develops from the opening remarks, the Performative pair drops out of use, replaced by the all-person Factual-Visual pair, and thus this incidental first person distinction is lost in the verb and carried solely by independent pronouns.

---

[3] The term Performative for this pair was chosen about 1959 and used in *A Kashaya Grammar* (Oswalt 1961) before its use in speech act studies, in a different sense, was widespread. There is a contrast in application: the Performative here is a verbal suffix, the speech act term applies to a type of verb or larger unit.

It would seem that the shared element -*ela* is the morpheme for the Performative. One might then postulate that the initial elements, -*ŵ*- and -*m*-, are imperfective and perfective markers. These initials cannot convincingly be identified morphemically with anything else in the language. A claim that the -*ŵ*- of -*ŵela* is the Factual suffix would be difficult to support—a number of diverse suffixes begin with -*ŵ*- and a fair case could be made that it developed phonologically as a glide to separate the vowel of the preceding stem from the vowel of the suffix (there are no vowel clusters in the language). As for -*m*-, it is a common verbal suffix, most frequently forming derivative verbs of state, all imperfective, quite different from the perfective use of -*mela*.

The final -*a* of the Performative pair differs from the final -*ă* of the other suffixes of direct experience in that it always surfaces as a phonemic -*a* and is never Ø before word boundary.

The first three examples below are with a verb root indifferent to the aspectual distinction:

(S1) Performative-Imperfective: □*qowa°q-ŵela* → *qowá·qala*.
      'I am packing (a suitcase).'   *e* → *a*/*q*(*ŵ*)__.

(S2) Performative-Perfective: □*qowa°q–mela* → *qowáhmela*.
      'I just packed.'   *q* → *h*/__*m*, *tʰ*, *y*.

(S3) Performative-Negative: □*qowa°q-tʰ-ŵela* → *qowáhtʰela*.
      'I am not packing, I haven't packed.'

There is no negative form with -*mela*.

That a perfective statement can be made during the moment of an act is illustrated by the word in (S4), commonly used in the situation in which an English speaker says 'Good-bye'.

(S4) *cohtoc-mela* → *cohtócʰmela*.
      'I am leaving.'

There is no *cohtocéla* because *cohtoc*- is innately perfective; an imperfective stem can be derived from it, however, with the Durative suffix:

(S5) *cohtoc-V̂°d-ŵela* → *cohtocí·dela*.
      'I am continuing to leave.'

That the act itself need not have just happened is illustrated by the following textual example in which the sight of the children of a man killed years earlier has brought forth the spontaneous statement:

(S6) (KT7:7.4) *mi·-li*   *ʔa   me-ʔe-l*   *pʰakúm-mela*.
                    there-VISIBLE   I your-father-OBJ.   kill-PERFORM.
                    'Right there I killed your father.'

As an example of a response to a remark by someone else there is

(S7) *hú·ʔ·* *men* *ší - ya*   *- m*   *ṭa* *ʔa·*
      Yes.   thus   do - VISUAL - RESP.   I.
      'Yes, I have done that.'

Here, the Visual suffix takes over in the Responsive mode for the Performative. Although *men šímela* (without the Responsive suffix) 'I have done that' is normal as an isolated remark, **men šímelam* (with the Responsive) does not occur.

3.2   Factual-Visual Pair, -ŵă, -yă

The suffix labeled Factual is imperfective and that labeled Visual is perfective; the two form a complementary pair, as did the Performative pair, and signify that the speaker knows of what he speaks because he sees, or saw, it. However, in addition to this application to specific events, the Factual (not the Visual) also applies to classes of actions or states which have been observed enough by the speaker for him to generalize them as true and to classes which may simply be common knowledge.

(S8) Factual (Imperfective):   □*qowa°q-ŵă* → *qowá·qʰ.*
      '(I see) he is packing.'

There is no segment in the surface form of (S8) that can be said to be the Factual, but its presence is shown by the vowel length in the final surface syllable and by the realization of the stem-final consonant as an aspirate (Cf. Section 2.3).

(S9) Visual (Perfective):   □*qowa°q-yă* → *qowahy.*
      '(I just saw) he packed, I just saw him pack.'

(S10) Negative: □*qowa°q-tʰ-(ŵă ?)* → *qowahtʰ.*
      '(I see/saw) he isn't packing/he hasn't packed.'

Whether the underlying form in (S10) actually contains the -*ŵă* suffix cannot be told from the surface result as -*ŵă* would end up Ø and there would be no effect on the preceding stem. There is no negative with the -*yă* suffix.

The following is an example of a verb stem made perfective by the suffix -*ma°c-* 'in hence' added to the root □*mo-* 'run'.

(S11) □*mo-ma°c-yă* → *momá·y.*
      '(I just saw) he ran in.'
      c → · / __ *tʰ, y.*

The above verb stem can be suffixed only by -*yă*, not by -*ŵă*. However, in the negative, the stem cannot be suffixed by -*yă*, (only by -*ŵă ?*).

(S12)   □*mo-ma°c-tʰ-(-w̌ǎ ?)* → *momá·tʰ*.
        '(I saw) he didn't run in.'

The following can be interpreted as the general truth use of the Factual or as a specific action that was seen.

(S13)   *šihta=yacʰma   cahno-w*.
        bird=PL.SUBJ.   sound-FACTUAL
        'Birds sing', or '(I see/saw) birds are/were singing.'

There is an additional type of ambiguity with verb stems which end in a vowel. In (S13), the verb is interpreted as containing the Factual: *cahno-w̌ǎ* → *cahnow*. The Absolutive form (Section 2.5) would also give the same phonemic result: *cahno-w* → *cahnow*. Thus (S13) can also be interpreted as an abstract gerund 'singing of birds' or as an evidence-less past 'Birds sang'. If further suffixes are added to the verb (not possible with the Absolutive), the ambiguity disappears. For example, the Responsive form *cahnowam* can only contain the Factual '(I see/saw) the birds are/were singing', or 'Birds sing'. With stems ending in a consonant, the ambiguity also does not exist, as the Absolutive form is quite different: In (S8), *qowá·qʰ* is the Factual form, the Absolutive would be □*qowa°q-Ø* → *qowaʔ*.

3.3 Auditory, -V̂nnǎ

The Auditory[4] suffix signifies that the speaker knows of what he speaks because he heard the sound of the action, but did not see it. It is indifferent to aspectual distinctions:

(S14)   Imperfective: □*mo-V̂°d-V̂nnǎ* → *mo·dun*.
        'I hear/heard someone running along.'

(S15)   Perfective: □*mo-ma°c-V̂nnǎ* → *momá·cin*.
        'I just heard someone run in.'

---

[4] I previously termed this suffix the Aural, which in my dialect of English is distinct in pronunciation from Oral. The conversion to Auditory is made here to avoid what are homonyms to many English speakers.

Apparent cognate suffixes are Southern Pomo (one dialect only) -*V̂nʔda* and Central Pomo -*V̂nme·*. The sound correspondences are not regular and would seem to indicate that the forms are of compound origin and that Kashaya -*V̂nnǎ* has developed -*nn*- as a simplification of a cluster of -*n*- plus some other consonant.

It is interesting to note that of the two surviving dialects of Southern Pomo only one (Mihilakawna) has an Auditory suffix and this dialect has a concomitant feature not known in the other dialect (Makahmo), nor reported for any other Pomo language: a demonstrative *no*- 'that' applying only to what is heard but not seen (for example, a mouse). Most Pomo languages do have a distinction in demonstratives between what is seen and what is not seen.

A contrast between a spontaneous remark and a response has been recorded in a natural conversation:

(S16)   (KT76:6.1)   *hayu   cáhno-n.*
        'I hear a dog barking.'

This example opens the conversation, while the following lies in a continuation.

(S17)   (KT76:6.4)   . . . *mu hayu   cáhno-nna-m̆.*
        '[. . . That's why] we hear the dog(s) barking.'

I have found no naturally occurring examples of the Negative Auditory, but elicitation shows its existence:

(S18)   □*qowa°q-tʰ-V̂nnă* → *qowáhtʰin.*
        'He is not packing, he did not pack—as indicated by a lack of the sound of packing.'

3.4   Inferential I, -qă

Most commonly *-qă,* which is indifferent to aspectual distinctions, marks an inference based on circumstances or evidence found apart, in space or time, from the actual event or state. In this use it overlaps semantically with Inferential II (Section 3.8).

(S19)   □*mu cohtoc-qă* → *mu cohtocʰqʰ.*
        'He must have left, he has left.'   (Said on discovering that the person is no longer present; the leaving itself was not seen [that would be *cohtó·y*], nor heard [*cohtocin*].)

To a certain extent *-qă* is a default category for evidence through senses other than those that have specific sensory suffixes (Visual and Auditory). Thus it is possible to say, on coming into a house and detecting an odor,

(S20)   *cuhni· muʔla-qʰ.*
        'Bread has been cooked.'

But indication of olfactory or tactile evidence by such means is fairly unspecific; greater specificity would have to be shown with a separate verb of perception:

(S21)   *cuhni· muʔla mihšew.*
        'It smells like cooked bread.'

The Kashaya Inferential suffix implies no lack of certainty, merely lack of higher ranking evidence. It appears in many situations in which English would not normally use its near equivalent 'must have':

(S22) *kalikak^h dima·   ši-qa-č-q^h.
      book   holding make-cause-self-INFER.
      'He has had a picture taken of himself holding a book.'

The existence of the picture (which is seen) is the evidence that one was taken (which act was not seen). (The verb *ši-* 'do, make' is understood in this collocation to refer to taking a photograph.)

(S23) (KT33:10.2) 'he?én   ši-n   =i-wa   ma
                   How   do-ing   =QUEST   you
                   ' "Why did you not guard [her]?"

      mace·-t^{h}i-qa-m$^˘$'   *nihced-u*   *mace·=yac-ol.*
      guard-NEG.-INF.-RESP.   say-ABS.   guard=person-OBJ.
                                [someone] said to the guard.'

The lack of guarding was not seen but is inferred to have been the case because the prisoner is gone.

Given below is an example of -*qǎ* introduced into a clause with a future tense (in a collocation that means 'not able to') by means of the Assertive (described in Section 2.4). Here the evidence comes before the predicted failure of an attempt:

(S24) (KT8:13.1) *he?én*   *ya*   *mihyáč-k^{h}e-t^{h}in*
                  How   we   win-FUT.-not

      =i-q-a·   *mu·kito   baǫo=·li.*
      =ASS.-INF.-NONFINAL   him   what=in.
      'It appears we'll never be able to beat him in anything.'

3.5 Personal Experience, -yowǎ

In narratives and in the narrative construction (Section 2.9), all of the evidentials described so far are replaced by the one suffix -*yowǎ*. As stated in Section 3.0, the final -*wǎ* is identifiable with the Factual -*ŵǎ*, added to an element -*yo-*, which occurs only with -*ŵǎ*.[5] Since the sequence is rarely final in its clause, it rarely appears without the additional suffix -*e·* that marks verbs which are not final in their clause.

---

[5] This -*yo-* is not related to the Visual suffix -*yǎ*. In the Southern Pomo language there is a cognate enclitic verb =?*yo-*, which occurs in the narrative construction but with a greater variety of evidential suffixes than the one of Kashaya: =?*yo-wa* Personal Experience, =?*yo-ka* Inferential, =?*yo-do* Quotative, etc. In Central Pomo, the apparent cognate is *yó-* 'go', which usually occurs with preposed directional adverbs: *bol yóm!* 'Go west!'

(S25)   *mul*   =*í-yow-e·*   *hayu*   *cáhno-w.*
         then   =ASS.-P.E.-NONFINAL   dog   sound-ABS.
         'Then (I saw, heard, judged) the dog barked.'

Occasionally the Responsive suffix appears in the narrative construction; that is, a form like *mulíyowam* (S33) will be used instead of *mulíyowe·*. No meaning difference has been elicitable, but one might surmise that the use of the Responsive in a story is a way of including the listener in the discourse, perhaps even inviting comments, although none need be forthcoming.

The simplification in narratives of the elaborateness of the evidential system is understandable—when one talks of events that may have happened a considerable time previously, the precise type of evidence is less important and, indeed, is often not remembered by the speaker. It is, of course, always possible to state the type of evidence through a verb of perception. The distinction of Inferential I also appears to be usually submerged in *-yowǎ,* but it is also often reintroduced through Inferential II (Section 3.8).

3.6   Remote Past, -miyǎ

The final part of this suffix is presumably the Visual suffix *-yǎ.* The element *-mi-* does not occur apart from the combination, although it does occur duplicated to *-mimiyǎ* (perhaps with an intensification of the meaning). The suffix *-miyǎ* is archaic, known only to the very oldest speakers (those born before 1910), and seldom used by them. It is not recognized by most younger speakers except in certain fixed forms. It seems to apply most often to personal experiences of the speaker in the remote past, say in the youth of an old person. In some cases it may apply to a less remote time but still to a past that is irretrievable, perhaps because the participants are dead, or because the world has changed so much over the years. In almost all of the situations in which it would seem suitable by this definition, *-yowǎ,* the more general past of personal experience, is used instead. All examples of *-miyǎ* have it suffixed to the main verb and not displaced in the narrative construction, as is usual with *-yowǎ.*

(S26)   *men*   *ši-*   *yíʔciʔ-*   *tʰi-miy.*
         thus   do-PL.HABITUAL-NEG.-REMOTE
         'They never used to do that in the old days.'

3.7   Quotative, -do

The term Quotative is a traditional one in Americanist usage for a typological feature that is widespread in the native languages of North America. In Kashaya the Quotative is the one evidential for information learned from someone else, contrasted with the many for information learned through the speaker's own experience. It does not mark a direct or indirect quote of another's words; such would be indicated by a separate verb (*nichedu* in (S23)). By far the most common use of -*do* is in the narrative construction (Section 2.9), whether in myths, traditional history, or some account the teller learned moments or years before.

(S27) *mul*   =*í-do-·*   *hayu   cáhno-w.*
       then   =ASS.-QUOT.-NONFINAL   dog   sound-ABS.
       'Then, they say, the dog barked.'

If what is being talked about has been learned from another, it can seldom refer to the present or immediate past time, unless the event takes place elsewhere. One such infrequent case is the following, from a conversation in the Responsive mode:

(S28) (KT76:19) *me?   mu   mi·   sikúhtime?* = *yach ma*
                  but   that there drinking = people

       ?i-do-m   *?ul.̓*
       be-QUOT.-RESP.   already.
       'But I was told the ones that drink are already there.'

The same conversation contains a combination of a future tense and -*do* introduced into the sentence by means of the Assertive:

(S29) (KT76:38) *qacúhse   hqamač-khe   =?-do-m ta.̓*
                  grass game   play-FUT.   =ASS.-QUOT.-RESP.
                  'I was told they'll play the grass game.'

3.8 Inferential II, -bi-

The chief difference between -*bi*- and -*qǎ* inferential I is perhaps distributional; -*bi*- is never verb-final but must be followed by some other suffix. It occurs in four irregularly fused compound suffixes that form subordinate clauses: -*bina* inference plus coreference of the agents of the subordinate and superordinate clause; -*bem* inference with different agents in the two clauses; and -*binati* and -*beti*, which add the meaning 'although' to the preceding pair. In (S30) there is a similar type of inference in each clause, but different morphemes are involved because one clause is subordinate to the other:

(S30) *du?ku-bína   cohtoch-qh.*
       finish II   leave I.
       'He must have finished and left (the work is done and he is no longer here).'

In (S31) only the subordinate clause contains an inference, which is probably based on the visual evidence in the main clause:

(S31) *du?ku-bína   cohtó·-y.*
       'He must have finished; (I just saw) he left.'

The most common nonsubordinating combination is -bi-w (where -w is probably the Absolutive), which designates evidence found after the event, and in this it overlaps the range of -qă. One difference is that -biw can be used for events or states partially perceived by any means but which become more interpretable by later evidence, a meaning captured by English 'turn out'. For example, if a woman saw a man approaching but could not recognize him until he arrived, then, in speaking of the incident, she might say

(S32)   kʰe   hí ʔbaya=ʔ-bi-w.
        My   man=ASS.-II-ABS.
        'It turned out to be my husband.'

Other occurring combinations are -bi-do (which sums the meanings of the parts) and -bi-qă (no difference has been determined for the meaning of this form versus either suffix separately). The other evidentials are not suffixed to -bi-.

4.   AUXILIARY INFORMATION

4.1   Other Sources of Information

Dreams, visions, and revelations are treated the same as ordinary waking-life happenings. Thus, what is experienced therein is reported with -yowă; what is told by some other being therein is reported with -do.

Knowledge acquired through various modern media—television, movies, radio, telephone, phonograph records, tape recordings, still pictures, writing—is reported as follows:

1.   Moving actions seen on television or in the movies: -ŵă Factual, -yă Visual, or -yowă Personal Experience, with the choice made just as for actually witnessed events and states.
2.   Speech, whether contemporaneous or recorded long earlier: -do Quotative.
3.   Nonspeech sounds of action heard but not seen (hoofbeats, etc.): -V̂nnă Auditory.
4.   Still pictures: A description of a static situation might be with -ŵă Factual or -yowă Personal Experience, but an interpretation or inference of action from a still ('The horse is running.') would be with -qă Inferential I.
5.   Writing, printed or handwritten: Most frequent is -qă Inferential I, but -do Quotative is also common. Presumably the use of -qă is an extension of its use in the interpretation of still pictures and, aboriginally, of the signs of former actions, whether conventional and deliberate (a broken branch indicating the direction a traveler has gone) or inadvertent (broken branches and matted grass left in a struggle). The use of -do is an identification of written speech with spoken.

4.2 Hierarchy

The evidentials lie in a hierarchy, and are so arranged in Table 1, such that those that precede have priority over those that follow:

Performative > Factual-Visual > Auditory > Inferential > Quotative

This order would seem to be universal, even for languages like English that must express most of the evidential concepts by separate verbs. Thus, someone speaking of an act he himself is performing, or has performed, would not normally attribute knowledge of that event to a lower type of evidence, unless, of course, he is speaking in a detached way as an observer of his own actions. The rather close relationship, in Kashaya, of the Performative and Factual-Visual is shown by their merger in other than the spontaneous mode. That visual evidence rates near the top is shown by its union in imperfective verbs, in Kashaya, with the factual of general truths. At a lower stage in the hierarchy, a speaker of any language would not normally say, 'I hear someone approaching the door' when he can see the person approaching.

Kashaya, Southern, and Central Pomo are apparently rare among the languages of the world in having an evidential for a specific nonvisual sense, the Auditory, before reaching the lower stage at which there is lumping into one class of the remaining kinds of sensory evidence. In Kashaya, this catch-all class also happens to include inference on evidence found apart from the act. Inference seems to lie at a borderline stage leading out of the domain of direct personal evidence, attested by its co-occurrence (as either Inferential I or II) with the Quotative.

It might be noted that, despite the hierarchy, all propositions with the Kashaya evidentials are presented by the speaker as certain and true. However, the evidentials themselves are at the top of a continuing hierarchy of modals expressing increasing uncertainty on the part of the speaker. These include a Suppositional suffix ('I suppose that . . .'), a Speculative ('I wonder if . . .'), an Optative ('I hope or wish that . . .'), and others.

4.3 Other Displays of Evidence

Besides the verb suffixal system, Kashaya has other ways of stating evidence. There are adverbs (for example, $p^hikaṭi$ 'visibly'), but this class is weakly developed. There are phrases, such as 'with her own eyes' (in S34). And there is a strongly developed class of verbs of perception. In certain situations, a verb of perception would have to be used to make explicit the type of evidence. For example, in the merged narrative construction, auditory evidence would have to be specified through a separate verb:

(S33) (KT42:5.1) mul =í-yowa -m ʔa· baḍo=tʰin loḍóʔ šoʔ.
then =ASS.-P.E.-RESP. I what=not move hear.
'Then I heard something moving.'

There are many features of Kashaya that help support an overt statement of evidence. In (S33), besides the word *šoʔ* 'hear', there is the verb *loq̇oʔ,* which has the particularized meaning 'move of something unseen'.

With all of the suffixes above the Quotative line in Table 1, it is the speaker, the first person, who experiences or perceives the described event or state, or the circumstantial evidence thereof. To indicate, by means of the evidential system, how a third person learned of some piece of information before passing it on to the present speaker would require giving a direct quote of that other person's message, and such a means is fairly common in stories (S23). With the Quotative, there is no way to designate the one who provided the information to the present speaker. That would have to be done through a separate sentence, and it is quite customary for a story, which may have had the *-do* suffix in almost every sentence, to end with explicit statements about the 'higher' subject of *-do:*

(S34)   (KT63:12.5)   *maʔú   ʔe·   manʔ   to   ʔama·   dič̣i·d-u   ti·*
                        this   is   she   me   thing   tell-ABS.   self
                       'This is what she told me she herself

cad-u,̌   ti-ʔkʰe   huʔú·=li   cad-u.
see-ABS,   self's   eye=with   see-ABS.
saw, saw with her own eyes.'

The Kashaya language, which is so rich in suffixes for the means by which evidence is obtained, is, in common with the other Pomoan languages, even richer in prefixes for the means by which an action is done: natural forces, body parts, types of instruments and movements. When attached to a finely graded series of roots for verbs of perception—'detect', 'detect faintly', 'be inured to the sense', plus dozens more—the prefixes can indicate the organ that senses the evidence in an intricate and discriminating way. But these prefixes constitute another story.[6]

REFERENCES

Langdon, Margaret and Shirley Silver, eds. 1976. Hokan Studies, Papers from the First Conference on Hokan Languages, held in San Diego, California, April 23–25, 1970 (Mouton).

McLendon, Sally. 1975. A Grammar of Eastern Pomo. (University of California Publications in Linguistics, 74.) Berkeley: Department of Linguistics.

Moshinsky, Julius. 1974. A Grammar of Southeastern Pomo. (University of California Publications in Linguistics, 72.) Berkeley; Department of Linguistics.

Oswalt, Robert L. 1961. A Kashaya grammar (Southwestern Pomo). University of California, Berkeley, dissertation.

---

6 A detailed semantic description of *si-* 'water, drink, tongue', only one of twenty fully productive prefixes in Kashaya, is in Oswalt (1981). The twenty prefixes are listed and defined briefly in that publication and are reconstructed for Proto-Pomo in Oswalt (1976).

———. 1964. Kashaya texts. (University of California Publications in Linguistics, 36.) Berkeley: Department of Linguistics.

———. 1976. Comparative verb morphology of Pomo. Hokan studies, ed. by Margaret Langdon and Shirley Silver. (Papers from the First Conference on Hokan Studies, San Diego, 1970.) The Hague: Mouton.

———. 1981. On the semantically interlocking nature of the Kashaya verb prefixes: The case of *si*– 'water, drink, tongue'. Proceedings of the 1980 Hokan Languages Workshop, ed. by James Redden. (Occasional Papers on Linguistics, 9.) Carbondale: Southern Illinois University.

THREE

The Origins and Deictic Nature of Wintu Evidentials

Alice Schlichter
University of California, Berkeley

Wintu is an American Indian language spoken in aboriginal times in Shasta, Trinity, and Siskiyou counties in northern California; it is now remembered by about half a dozen speakers.[1] In the 1930s and 40s Dorothy Lee published several papers describing in Whorfian terms the interrelationships of aspects of the Wintu language with the world view of its speakers, and succeeded in making the language well-known for its evidential suffixes. Relying on her work as a starting point, I will discuss and compare the evidentials in their synchronic functions as deictic elements, argue for their relatively recent origin, and show how they form a well-integrated part of the expression of Wintu concern with knowledge of the world.[2]

THE EVIDENTIALS AND THEIR ORIGINS

Knowledge is not infallible. A speaker can believe in the truth of a statement he makes but its truth does not logically follow from his belief. The only way to find out if he is right is to examine the facts. With the evidential suffixes, the Wintu speaker points to his evidence, inviting the addressee to verify it.

One of the four evidential suffixes of Wintu is the nonvisual sensorial evidential. It occurs in the shape -$nt^he\cdot$ verb-finally, before -m, the marker for du-

[1] I am grateful to Wallace Chafe for valuable comments on earlier versions of this paper.

[2] Data for this paper are from Lee (1938, 1941, 1943, 1944a, 1944b, 1950, and unpublished texts on microfilms at the Survey of California and Other Indian Languages, Department of Linguistics, University of California, Berkeley), Pitkin (1963), and my own fieldwork supported by the Survey of California and Other Indian Languages. I will be using Pitkin's terms for the evidentials unless otherwise indicated. Note that Lee never used the term 'evidential.'

bitative and third person subject,[3] and before -n, the short form of the suffix indicating second person subject; its shape is -nt^her before the interrogative suffix -i·; -nt^here before the more formal marker for second person subject -sken; and it occurs as -nt^hi before -da and -k, the suffixes for first person subject and completive, respectively. I will write this evidential morphophonemically as -nt^hEr, representing the alternation i∼e by the symbol E.[4] -nt^hEr is used if the speaker wishes to indicate that the statement he is making describes a fact known to him through one of his senses other than vision, i.e. his hearing, feeling, taste, smell, touch, or any kind of intellectual experience of 'sixth sense.' It is used when talking about the supernatural (Lee 1941), and for prophecy; for predicting future events which are somehow felt as being imminent. -nt^hEr could be called 'experiential' but I prefer to retain 'nonvisual sensorial' to distinguish it from the experiential evidentials in other languages which include visual experience.

-nt^hEr occurs most often with the imperfective aspect auxiliary bEy- (as bint^he·m in example (1), below, bint^heresken in (5), bint^hida in (8), bint^he·n in (9) and with the uninflected stem without auxiliary often translatable as present tense (daqčant^he·m in (2)); it occurs less frequently with the sequential auxiliary translatable as future wEr- (as wint^he·m in the third person in (3)), and sometimes also with the completive aspect auxiliary kir- (as kint^he·m from *kirnt^he·m in (4) and kint^heri· from *kirnt^heri· in (7).[5]

(1) Heket   wira   wača·-bint^he· m.
     someone   come   cry   IM.   DUB.
     'Someone is coming crying (I hear).'

(2) Pi   k'ilepma·   daqčant^he·m.
     it   awfully   hot   DUB.
     'It's awfully hot (I feel the heat).'

(3) Po·m   yel-hurawint^he·m.
     earth   destroy SE.   DUB.
     'The earth will be destroyed (I know, feel).'

---

[3] One of the meanings of -m is 'dubitative' but, as elaborated by Pitkin (1963:120), it is now often used as a third person subject marker, apparently in order to create a marked paradigmatic contrast between first, second, and third person subject in the verb—or perhaps to produce a form with which to translate English third person -s.

[4] This ablaut together with the alternation u∼o, represented by O, is pervasive in Wintu. In Pitkin (1963) and some of my previous papers the alternations have been represented by I and U. However, E and O seem more appropriate because Patwin has e and o wherever Wintu has the alternating vowels (Kenneth Whistler, personal communication), and there is thus reason to believe that e and o were the original Proto-Wintun sounds.

[5] Abbreviations used in the interlinear translations are: completive aspect (COM.), conditional aspect (CON.), dubitative or third person subject (DUB.) (see footnote 3), exclamation word (EX.), hortative (HO.), imperfective aspect (IM.), imperative (IMP.), interrogative (INTER.), quotative (QUOT.), sequential aspect (SE.).

(4)   *ʔUwebe·di   war   ʔunikint^he·   m.*
     don't   IMP.   QUOT.COM.DUB.
     'He said 'don't do it!' (We heard him say not to do it.)

(5)   *Q'otisa-bint^heresken.*
     strong   IM.   you
     'You're strong (I feel).' (Said while wrestling)

(6)   *T'aqiqma·-bint^he·.*
     hurt   IM.
     'It hurts (I feel the pain).'

(7)   *Henuni   mis   yi·la-kint^heri·?*
     how   you   send COM. INTER.
     'How did he instruct you (in your hearing)?'

(8)   *Č'epkal   ne·l   ba·-bint^hida.*
     bad   we   eat IM. we
     'We've been eating bad things (I sense).'

(9)   *Hida   naqalma·-bint^he·n.*
     very   pitiful   IM.   you
     'You're so pitiful! (I am emotionally affected)'

For semantic reasons *-nt^hEr* occurs most often with a third person subject. For it to occur with the first person subject marked by *-da,* the speaker has to be both the agent of what the verb stem expresses and the patient or experiencer of the sensation that goes with the action without at the same time seeing the action. This is possible in example 8 because the eating occurred prior to the sensation that what was eaten was bad. The argument against a frequent occurrence with a second person subject and its markers *-n* or *-sken* is that the speaker cannot often make a statement about an action by the addressee which he—the speaker—does not see. The nonvisual sensory experience is always that of the speaker except in the interrogative (7) where it is the hearer's.

-nt^hEr has to be added to each verb to be marked for nonvisual sensory evidence, and therefore sometimes occurs several times in the sentence. It is not enough to mark one verb per sentence if more than one verb expresses an event known to the speaker through his senses.

Evidentials are not an old Wintun trait. Only *-nt^hEr* has a cognate with similar functions in Patwin (Whistler, this volume), the only surviving related language. The other Patwin evidentials were created independently from different forms already present in the language, perhaps under the influence of drift—assuming that the development of evidentials had just begun when Proto-Wintun split up into the daughter languages—and perhaps because Patwin has neighbors with evidentials, the Pomo languages.

The easiest evidential to follow back in time is *-nt^hEr.* Since it is one of only two morphemes which begin in a consonant cluster, its origin must be in a contraction of two morphemes. A likely candidate for the second one is the passive suffix -hEr, whose allomorphy parallels that of -nt^hEr; the aspiration of the t^h is a contraction of th. A search of the Wintu vocabulary further reveals a verb root mut- 'hear, feel, sense, perceive' which echoes -nt^hEr semantically. A look at the Patwin cognate confirms that Wintu -nt^hEr is a reflex of a contraction of mut- and -hEr—Patwin has -mther or -muther. I reconstruct *mut-her for Proto–Wintun which then became Wintu *mut^her > *mt^hEr > nt^hEr. In the first person *nt^hEr(e)da became nt^hi·da (still found in Lee's texts) and then nt^hida. In final position and before -m and -n, *nt^here became nt^he·. Thus the evidential -nt^hEr arose from a passive verb form based on mut- 'hear, feel, etc.' which followed other verbs.

The second evidential indicates that the proposition expressed by the verb is known to the speaker through hearsay. The only allomorph of this morpheme, -ke·, occurs verb-finally, and before the dubitative or third person subject marker -m, and occurs most often with the conditional auxiliary kila (kilake· in (11)) and the completive auxiliary kir- (kirke· in (10)); it can also occur in the imperfective auxiliary bEy- (bike·m in example (12)), bike· in (14) and the uninflected stem, translatable as present tense (13). kirke·(m) and kilake·(m) have now come to mean simply 'past tense' because they occur most frequently in past time contexts. There are only a few examples in texts where -ke·, with or without auxiliaries, still refers to hearsay.

(10) Minel kirke· m.
     die   COM.DUB.
     'He has died (I'm told).'

(11) Le·ndada suke kilake·.
     long ago stand CON.
     'Long ago they lived (I'm told).' (Frequently used to begin a myth)

(12) Wi·ta čalit sukebike· m.
     man   good   stand IM.DUB.
     'It is said that he is a handsome man.'

(13) Čoyi·lake· ni.
     drunk   I
     'I am drunk (I hear). They tell me I'm drunk.' (Lee 1938:90 retranscribed)

(14) K'ilepma·   kuya·bike· mi.
     frightfully sick IM.   you
     'Frightfully sick you are (I hear).' (Lee, ibid., retranscribed)

In contrast to -nt^hEr, -ke· is not suffixed to every single verb of a story known through hearsay, but rather only to the verb in the first sentence, which might be the sentence in (11), establishing a frame for the whole story. Within the text other evidentials may then be used to refer to evidence adduced by participants. The hearsay evidential need not occur again at the end of a narrative, for there is a set of fixed phrases to end a story and complete the frame.

The hearsay evidential -ke· parallels the shape of the third person form of
-nt^hEr, -nt^he·, and we can assume that it was once *keCV, CV representing a
consonant-vowel sequence. A cognate morpheme in Wintu is -kEl 'maybe, must
be' which appears as -ki before first person subject -da (15), as -ke before second
person -n (16) and before hortative -di (17), and as -kele before second person
subject -sken (18).[6]

(15) Xi·na kirkida.
      sleep COM. I
      'I must have slept.'

(16) Be·di harken.
      don't go you
      'Don't go!'

(17) Yowuna·kedi   ma·let.
      worry   HO   about you two
      'He may be worried about you two.'

(18) Ho·nda   xi·na   kirkelesken.
      long time sleep   COM. you
      'I guess you overslept.'

I reconstruct *kEl- for both -ke· and -kEl, still within Wintu. Originally this
morpheme probably meant something like 'maybe, potentially, etc.' and later
changed its meaning to hearsay when it occurred in past time contexts. Since
Patwin does not have the i~e alternation but only e, the Proto-Wintun form of
pre-Wintu *kEl- was probably *kel-.

The reconstruction of -ke· as part of the same morpheme as -kEl is supported
by examples (13) and (14). In all the data available to me these were the only
examples with first and second person subjects of an action known through
hearsay. However, the appropriate subject markers -da and -sken or -n do not
occur, indicating complementary distribution of hearsay -ke· with potential -kEl.

*kEl in turn may be diachronically related to the auxiliary kila which verb-
finally translates as a conditional, e.g.:

(19) Minelkila   čala·   puke·r   ʔiye   ʔibe.
      die if   nice   would   be   is
      'It would be nice if he died.'

and as a past when combined with the hearsay evidential (as in example (11)).
Another possible remote cognate of *kEl is the completive auxiliary kir- (7, 10);

---

6 Pitkin (1963:109) analyzes -ki and -kele as allomorphs of the hearsay evidential, not of potential
-kEl. This is contradicted by his example coyilake: ni '(They tell me) I'm drunk' (cf. my example
(13)), which according to his allomorphy rules should be coyilakida ni.

there are traces in Wintu of *r* as a sound-symbolic variant of *l* indicating augmentative or iterative. All of these morphemes may ultimately go back to the predecessor of *kel-* 'long, tall, far'. Note that there is also a verb *keruma* 'to finish' and another *keruma·* 'to slaughter (cause to be finished?)' from which *kir-* may be derived instead of being traced to a sound-symbolic variant of *kil-*. The completive suffix *-k* may ultimately be related to all these suffixes and verbs.

The third evidential is *-re·*, the inferential. It may be followed only by the dubitative or third person suffix *-m*, as *-re·m*, and indicates that the speaker believes his statement to be true because of circumstantial sensory evidence. This evidence turns out to be most often visual; it is difficult to think of a situation where it is other sensory evidence and where *-nt^hEr* cannot be used.

(20)   *Heke   ma·n   hara·kire· m.*
        somewhere EX.   go   COM.DUB.
        'He must have gone somewhere (I don't see him).

(21)   *Piya   mayto·n   dekna·sto·n   piya   ma·n   biyakire·m.*
        those   feet   steps   that   EX.   be COM.DUB.
        'Those tracks of steps! That must have been him.'

(22)   *Hadi   wint^hu·h   minelbire·m.*
        why!   person   die IM.   DUB.
        'Why, a person must have died (I see or hear someone cry)!'

-re· occurs most often with the completive aspect *kir-* (20, 21) and also, less frequently, with the imperfective aspect auxiliary *bEy-* (22) and the simple stem translatable as present tense. Since the action referred to by the verb stem always has a third person subject, *-re·* is now always followed by *-m*, which has become a third person subject marker (cf. footnote 3). In Lee's older texts, *-re·* still occurs without *-m*. For example:

(23)   *Hida   k'aysare·   yo·!*
        very   hurry   EX.
        'He must be in a great hurry (I see him run, I can't catch up with him)!'

The reconstruction of *-re·* has to remain a very tentative extrapolation because of the lack of a Patwin cognate. Its form is parallel to *-ke·* (from **kele*) and *-nt^he·* (from **nt^here*), and we can assume that at one time there was an uncontracted form of *-re·* of the shape **rVCV*. We further know that in contractions of *VCV* it is often the second vowel which remains and is lengthened; cf. *buhak > ba·k*, the completive form of the durative auxiliary, while *buhak* remains uncontracted as an independent verb meaning 'he sat, remained', and *suke > se·*, the perfective aspect auxiliary; *suke* is an independent verb meaning 'to stand'. Thus *-re·* must be from **rVCe*. However, Wintu has never had any words beginning in *r* so that *r* must have been part of the preceding verb. It was probably identical with the

Wintu subordinating suffix -r which makes a verb 'syntactically dependent and semantically anterior in regard to causality or time' (Pitkin 1963:113). If -re·, like the other two evidentials reconstructed so far, is derived from a verb, it is not surprising that the preceding verb should have been subordinated to it.[7]

In our reconstruction of -re· we are now left with *verb-r + VCe. But there are no words beginning in a vowel, and I have reason to believe that there never were. There must have been an earlier stage *verb-r + CVCe. r is deleted before consonants except w, y, and ʔ. (Cf. *yaluwe(r)le > yaluwe· 'Let's quit!' and *harwe(r)le > *harwe· > hare· 'Let's go!') The reconstruction is

now *verb-$\underline{r}$ + $\begin{Bmatrix} ʔ \\ w \\ y \end{Bmatrix}$ VCe. Since the evidence left for the speaker's deductive

reasoning is most often visual, my guess is that the verb we are looking for is wine 'to see, look', so that the reconstruction, for example, of

(24) Ničay   ʔewin   sukere·.
      nephew   here   stand
      'My nephew must have been here (I see tracks).'

would be ničay ʔewin *suker wine 'my nephew's having been here (I) see'. (Note that at the time the evidentials were still verbs, verbs cannot yet have been marked for subject, or all evidentials would now be followed by the first person subject marker. The subject markers for all three persons which can follow evidentials always refer to the subject of the verb stem, not that of the evidentials. Also, the subject markers are in a position class following that containing evidentials, which implies that they became affixes later. There is other independent evidence for the late acquisition of subject markers in Wintu.)

The fourth evidential, used almost as frequently as -ntʰEr, has only one allomorph, -ʔel, a verbal suffix which is never followed by further suffixation. It denotes that the speaker believes his proposition to be true because of his experience with similar situations, regular patterns, or repeated circumstances common in human life. Pitkin's term (1963:112) for this evidential was 'experiential' but I prefer 'expectational' because of the experiential function of -ntʰEr.

(25) Tima   minelʔel,   pira·ʔel.
      cold   die   starve

---

[7] I doubt that the hearsay evidential was ever preceded by an -r subordinating the preceding verb because its predecessor was 'potential' *-kEl. An event is not causally anterior to its existence in potentiality. One would also expect –r to be unlikely before -ntʰEr (except as in example (8)) because an event is not anterior to its sensory manifestation, were it not for examples like ti·nantʰe·n 'you say (I hear)' whose indicative and infinitive is ti·n, not ti·na. If there had not been an -r it would have been *ti·n-mut-her- which should have resulted in ti·ntʰEr- from intermediate *ti·nntʰEr-, just as *kirntʰe· became kintʰe·. Perhaps -r was once a general subordinator, not implying anteriority. Reconstruction of further aspects of Wintu morphology is needed to clear up these problems.

'He might freeze to death, he might starve (it's cold and he's alone, helpless, sick).'

(26)   *ʔImto·n   nuqa·ʔel.*
        berries   ripe
        'The berries must be ripe (it's that time of year).'

My data also include several examples where *-ʔel* is used to indicate hearsay; e.g:

(27)   *Ho·nʔukin   bo·laheres   wintʰu·h   biya-kilaʔel   ʔebasp'urit   ko·t.*
        long ago   myth   people   be CON.   they   all
        'In the myths from long ago they (the animals) were all people.'

(28)   *ʔUni   ma·n   pip'urit   ʔuna·   suke-kilaʔel   ho·nto·n*
        that way   EX.   they   so   stand CON.   long ago

        wintʰu·hto·t   pip'urit.
        people   they
        'That's the way it was among the people long ago.'

This may represent a semantic change toward a single evidential for indirect evidence which includes both hearsay and expectation.

-ʔel occurs most often with the conditional *kila* (*kilaʔel*) and less frequently with the uninflected stem translatable as present tense (25, 26), the imperfective aspect auxiliary *bEy-* (*biyaʔel*), and the auxiliary *kinaha* ~ *keneha* 'maybe' (*kinahaʔel* ~ *kenehaʔel*). The experience refered to is always that of the speaker; the event or state compared to that experience is always of a second or third person. In fast speech *-ʔel* is shortened to *-·l* after a vowel, to *-el* after a consonant. There is no evidence of previous sound change in *-ʔel* so that a reconstruction cannot add anything to its present shape. Unlike the other evidentials, *-ʔel* was probably a particle, not a verb, and was never preceded by subordinating *-r* or the *ʔ* would not have been preserved. There are several morphemes in Wintu which I propose to be cognate with *-ʔel*. They may seem unrelated at first glance, but I will explain their common semantic basis after giving examples of each.

One cognate is a derivational suffix *-el* which forms stative intransitive verbs from roots; e.g. *minel* 'to be dead' (< *min–* 'nonexistence'), *silel* 'to be blind' (< *sil-* 'blindness'), *limel* 'to be sick' (< *lim-* 'sickness'). Other cognates are a nominal suffix *-ʔel* 'in, inside' (e.g. *qewelʔel* 'inside the house'); a suffix *-el* forming generic nominal stems (*qewel* 'house'); a verbal prefix *ʔel-* 'in, inside, horizontally' (e.g. *ʔel-hara·* 'to go in, enter');[8] and a suffix deriving translation

---

[8] The probable cognateness of a prefix with a suffix in this case can be explained by assuming that *ʔel* was once an independent word and occurred between nouns and verbs. It became both a suffix to the preceding noun and a prefix to the following verb, both meaning 'in, inside'.

adjectives and adverbs from verbs (*kela* 'to be long, far' + **ʔel* > *keleˑl* 'far, long', *ʔola* 'to be up, above' + **ʔel* > *ʔoleˑl* 'up, above').[9] Another cognate occurs in the negative preverb *ʔelew* which can be reconstructed as **ʔel* 'exist' + **w* 'privative'. I believe it is possible to argue that all these meanings ('in, inside, horizontal, stative, generic, exist') are expressed by cognate morphemes because the Wintu conceived of the world as flat (Du Bois 1935:75). This view is compatible with an equation of the horizontal axis with existence in the world, although no independent ethnographic evidence is available. I suggest that the evidential *-ʔel* originated as a morpheme meaning something like 'it exists', including the notions of horizontality and generic being, and it now compares an event to its existence in potentiality. Such an event is more like a state: the Wintu may know from experience that an event is possible in the world but he cannot place it in a particular stretch of time with a beginning and an end unless he witnesses it.

To summarize, a proposition is marked by an evidential if the speaker believes its content because (a) he hears, feels, senses it; (b) he heard about it from someone else; (c) he infers it from circumstantial sensory evidence; or (d) he has experienced similar situations. We could say that evidentials are used to mark indirect evidence if we specify that the only evidence accepted as direct is visual evidence whose expression is unmarked. The speaker does not claim to be absolutely sure of anything unless he sees it right then and there together with the addressee.[10] If the speaker is sure of something because he feels it, he is not imposing on the addressee by implying that his feeling 'exists' outside of himself. He states that it exists for him, leaving the addressee free to believe him or not, feel compassion or not, check the truth of the statement or not.

Before discussing the evidentials in their relation to the rest of the Wintu language, it will be necessary to summarize the most important features of Wintu morphology.

A SKETCH OF WINTU MORPHOLOGY

Wintu is an accusative-type language with a passive like English. However, in addition to the basic dichotomy between subject and object, other distinctions are

---

[9] The loss of intervocalic consonants with contraction of the preceding and following vowels is very common in Wintun; cf. the preceding reconstructions of other evidentials.

[10] Outward appearance is of primary importance, as pointed out by Lee. She discusses (1943) this Wintu preoccupation as shown in the making up of new words for items of acculturation (the word for 'car', for example, means literally 'something that moves looking like a turtle-shell'). Lee (1944b) notes such terms as 'to make one's own scalp glisten' for 'to shave the head' (p. 184).

Lee was unaware of the imperfective function of *bEy-* and believed it to be a fifth evidential for visual evidence although it occurs together with the other evidentials in the same verb. She was led to her analysis because in 'present tense' contexts the imperfective auxiliary always implies visual evidence if it is not used together with another evidential. That is, *bEy-* is a visual evidential by default in those instances.

drawn, elaborating on the nature of subjects and objects, and specifying the degree of involvement of each, as well as of the speaker if he is not identical with the subject or the object.

Many Wintu roots can be the basis for nouns, verbs, adjectives, etc., since they are unspecified as to form class except by semantic restrictions. The root, usually of the shape *CVC,* is followed by one of three derivational suffixes to form stems which can occur as complete words or be expanded through further derivation and inflection.[11] One of the suffixes, *i,* makes the root into a noun or nominal stem (including translation adjectives) which can be further derived and inflected for nominal categories. The other two derivational suffixes, *a* and *u,* express a modal dichotomy which can be called indicative versus subjunctive or realis versus irrealis if it is desired to give it a conventional, very much over-simplified name. The real difference was first described by Lee (1938). *a,* 'stem I' following Pitkin's (1963) terminology, indicates that the grammatical subject is a voluntary participant or agent of the action, process, or event described by the verb root. If the speaker is not the agent, he needs to indicate, by the use of evidentials, the source of his information. *u,* stem II, indicates that the gram-matical subject is not a free agent of the event described by the verb root. Stem II is used as the basis for inflection by means of suffixes to form imperatives, interrogatives, negative statements, causatives, passives; for statements of prob-ability, possibility, potentiality, inevitable necessary future events; to make wishes, express hopes and fears. Evidentials do not occur with this irrealis-type stem. The speaker does not claim to have any knowledge of or be an authority on what he is discussing, and thus need not indicate the source of his information. Lee (1938) called stem I 'subjective', stem II 'objective', but I will not use these terms because they are already ambiguous in several ways.

Another important thing to point out about Wintu is that the 'present' time and place, the time and place of speaking, and the speaker are not the center of discourse to which other times, places, and participants are related through the well-known deictic systems and expressions.[12] The center changes depending on who or what deserves most attention. In order to place the speaker in the center of a discourse the Wintu use an emphatic suffix *-da.* It functions as a first person subject marker (e.g. *muteda* 'I hear(d), we hear(d)'); it appears in deictic tem-poral expressions (*le·nda* 'yesterday', literally 'old in relation to the speaker'); in deictic locatives (*wayda* 'from the north', i.e. north toward the speaker); and it is used as a general emphatic suffix (*hida* 'very, too', *bohda* 'many to be sitting'). If the speaker is not the agent, the agent is always the subject.

Wintu temporal-aspectual auxiliaries are concerned primarily with rela-

---

[11] Pitkin called these derivational suffixes 'stem formants' (1963:87). They are sometimes real-ized as suffixes, in other cases as ablaut with or without suffix. The details need not concern us here, as I am giving only a simplified summary of Wintu morphology to point out features important to the discussion of evidentials.

[12] 'Center of discourse' refers to the entire activity under discussion, not just its subject.

tionships between events. For instance, the 'future', or better, 'sequential aspect', auxiliary *wEr-*, as discussed by Lee (1938:92–3), concerns itself 'not with the temporal relationship to the speaking subject, but with the sequential relationship of each event to the other.' It connects events or states whose mutual relationship is that of sequence, 'a sequence brought, or to be brought about, through the agency of the individual. Both of the two events may be in the past or in the future; or one may be present and the other future. . . . Thus it may be translated, according to context, variously as: to, so as to, with the expectation to, about to . . .' It is important to note, however, that these English translations are very poor carriers for the Wintu concept.

Similarly *kila*, the auxiliary for 'conditional aspect', translates as a past where it occurs with the hearsay evidential (recall example 11, *le·ndada suke kilake·* 'long ago they lived'), but as a conditional if verb–final; recall example (19), *minelkila čala· puke·r ʔiye ʔibe* 'it would be nice if he died', where the dying is not past with respect to the moment of speaking, but is anterior to the being nice.)

Wintu has no grammatical categories expressing past or future relative to speakers; the flow of time is analyzed as constituted of events whose temporal relations are fixed; the only thing that changes is the point of reference, the viewpoint of the speaker. The future can be known from intuition or dreams (marked by *-ntʰEr*), because it is common knowledge (*-ʔel*), or because it follows from other events (*wEr-*). The past can be known from hearsay (*-ke·*), because it was a prerequisite for other events which are directly observed (*kila*), or because its result is directly observed (*kir-*). Neither past nor future can be directly observed in the present (cf. Ayer 1958:189ff).

EVIDENTIALS AS DEICTICS

Since the speaker and his position in time and space are not the center of discourse in Wintu, it is important to state the epistemic relation of the speaker to the activity in the center, which may have happened at a different place and time; in English it is important to relate the time of the activity under discussion to the present situation, the time of discourse. English has temporal deixis (tenses) overlapping and interplaying with nondeictic aspectual distinctions. Wintu directly relates events and only secondarily assigns them a time. The time is always assigned to the event being particularized and discussed, never to the moment of knowledge. Knowledge is timeless in the case of the expectational *-ʔel;* for the other three evidentials knowledge is dependent on and unambiguously inferrable from the time of the particularized event in the center or the time of speaking. For *-re·* and *-ke·* the logic, judgment, or knowledge is always at the time of speaking, relating the event of speaking to the event under discussion with respect to evidence. Only *-ntʰEr* can refer to a feeling had at the time of the event under discussion. For *-re·* the evidence was left in the past and the speaker considers it in the present; for -nt^hEr combined with a 'past' auxiliary the feeling occurred in the past; for -nt^hEr with a 'future' auxiliary the feeling occurs at the moment of speaking, while the event will take place in the future; elsewhere the event under discussion and the feeling take place at the same time.

We are now ready to consider evidentials as a deictic phenomenon. Deixis, as I understand it, has two components: a locating component in which the speaker places the event under discussion in time and space relative to the speech act; and an interpreting component in which it is up to the addressee to correctly interpret what he hears by reversing first and second person pronominal reference and making all the adjustments necessitated by his own identity, individuality, and position in time and space as different from that of the speaker. When the speaker uses deictic expressions he organizes the information he gives with respect to himself as referent, although he may occasionally, for purposes of politeness, take the point of view of the addressee.

If we imagine the flow of time (consisting of consecutive events) as a line on which we place a particular event and a speaker, tenses in English locate the event under discussion along the flow of time as preceding, following, or coinciding with the moment of speaking. 'Aspect' usually refers to certain nondeictic verbal categories: it locates an event with respect to the flow of time, not the speaker and time and place of speaking. Both Wintu and English have deictic adverbial expressions. But Wintu has no tenses in the verb; it has only aspect, coordination, and subordination to relate events to each other. The only way in which Wintu verbs locate events with respect to speakers similar to English tense deixis is with the evidential suffixes. It must be emphasized, however, that the speaker is not the center in Wintu: the speaker places the event in the center, with himself in some relation to it, not the event in relation to himself in the center. The gap between event and speaker is bridged in Wintu by expressing the channel through which the event has come to be known to the speaker. Wintu treats the flow of time as consisting of consecutive events and locates events with respect to results, visible manifestations, and conditions which are directly observable, unlike the past or the future, or another person's mental state.

The interpretation of the relationship between events is subjective and is marked with evidentials. It is up to the addressee to interpret the evidence he is confronted with by looking at the speaker to see if he is joking or serious, looks reliable or guilty of a lie, is in pain or happy, smart or old enough to know, or just bragging. Using evidential suffixes, the speaker appeals to the hearer as a rational person who can correctly estimate the strength of evidence (cf. Ayer 1972:3). One fact may be good evidence for another in one situation, bad evidence under different circumstances. Each time a speaker makes a statement using an evidential expression, the hearer has to decide whether the evidence justifies the claim in that particular situation so that the speaker has a right to be sure.

The truth of a statement does not depend on its meaning, but on the time and place at which the event it describes is supposed to have happened. English uses tense deixis to place a statement with respect to the time its truth depends on; Wintu employs evidential deixis to place an event in the context of the other events which are entailed by it. Just as deictic terms for place, time, and person are shorter terms standing for longer descriptions (I say *I* and *you* instead of stating our names; *here* instead of stating the address; *today* instead of stating the date), so the Wintu have verbal suffixes describing the evidence, leaving it up to the hearer to supply the detailed information and interpretation.

CONCLUSIONS

I have shown that evidentials are of recent origin in Wintu. Three of the suffixes arose from independent verbs, one from a particle. The predecessors of the evidentials may have been placed after verbs by bilingual ancestors of the Wintu who had picked up the habit from neighboring languages which had evidentials.

I would like to suggest that in Wintu—and perhaps also in other languages which have evidentials and aspect, but no tense—evidential deixis is an alternative to the temporal orientation of 'Western' civilization. As elaborated by Hallowell (1955:216–235), the paramount interest in time characteristic of our own culture, with calendars and clocks dividing time into years, months, hours, etc., is based on a concept of time as a collection of hours and minutes. We think of time as an enclosed space which can be divided or filled up. But frames of reference vary from society to society, and cultures which lack our temporal orientation always have alternatives (cf. Whorf 1964, esp. pp. 57–64; Hoijer 1951). One alternative is to think of time as a sequence of events, a view which is the Wintu conceptual basis for an orientation along the lines of evidential deixis.

The Wintu evidential system, with its primary dichotomy of unmarked visible events versus nonvisible events marked according to epistemic manifestation, is by no means the only possible arrangement. Another possibility is unmarked direct perception, regardless of sensory channel, versus knowledge acquired indirectly, marked according to source: hearsay, circumstantial evidence, pure inference, etc. (cf. Chafe 1973:264–65, 277).

Languages with tense distinctions encode the link between speech act and event by stating their temporal relation;[13] languages with evidential systems do this by specifying immediacy of knowledge.

---

[13] Most Indo-European languages make a primary distinction between unmarked present and marked past. The past which cannot be directly perceived is subdivided into several tenses, just as indirect knowledge is subdivided by channel in evidential systems. As noted by Fleischman (1980), the future is always superimposed on the basic present/past distinction: the present is often used to refer to the future; languages usually have more past tenses than futures; the future is conceptually more abstract, subjective, and affective, and originates with modals.

REFERENCES

Ayer, A. J. 1958. The Problem of knowledge. London: Macmillan and Co.

———. 1972. Probability and evidence. New York: Columbia University Press.

Chafe, Wallace L. 1973. Language and memory. Language 49.261–81.

Du Bois, Cora. 1935. Wintu ethnography. (University of California Publications in America Archaeology and Ethnology, 36.) Berkeley: University of California Press.

Fillmore, Charles J. 1971. Santa Cruz Lectures on Deixis. Indiana University Linguistics Club 1975.

Fleischman, Suzanne. 1980. Futures: where do they come from and where do they go? Diachronic patterns in future reference. (Paper given at the November 11th meeting of the Berkeley Linguistics Group.)

Hallowell, A. Irving. 1955. Culture and experience. Philadelphia: University of Pennsylvania Press.

Hoijer, Harry. 1951. Cultural implications of some Navaho linguistic categories. Language 27(2).111–120.

Lee, D. Demetracopoulou. 1938. Conceptual implications of an Indian language. Philosophy of Science 5.89–102.

———. 1941. Some Indian texts dealing with the supernatural. The Review of Religion 5(4).403–11.

———. 1943. The Linguistic aspect of Wintu acculturation. American Anthropologist 45.435–40.

———. 1944a. Categories of the generic and particular in Wintu. American Anthropologist 46.362–69.

———. 1944b. Linguistic reflection of Wintu thought. International Journal of American Linguistics 10.181–87.

———. 1950. Notes on the conception of the self among the Wintu Indians. The Journal of Abnormal and Social Psychology 45.538–543.

Pitkin, Harvey. 1963. Wintu Grammar. Ph.D. dissertation, Department of Linguistics, University of California, Berkeley.

Whorf, Benjamin Lee. 1964. Language, thought, and reality. Selected writings of Benjamin Lee Whorf, ed. by John B. Carroll. Cambridge, MA: MIT Press.

FOUR

Evidentials in Patwin

Kenneth W. Whistler
University of California, Berkeley

1. INTRODUCTION

This paper is concerned with evidentials in Patwin, particularly in Hill Patwin, the best attested of the Southern Wintun languages.[1,2] The topic should be of some interest for the diachronic study of the development of evidentials, in addition to being one more synchronic description of such a system, since Patwin

[1] The research for this paper was supported, in part, by the Survey of California and Other Indian Languages, University of California, Berkeley, and by a postdoctoral fellowship from the Department of Anthropology, Smithsonian Institution. I wish to thank Oscar McDaniel (*kabalme·m* Hill Patwin), Jennie Regalado (Grimes River Patwin), and especially the late Rev. Harry Lorenzo (Rumsey Hill Patwin) for their help in teaching me about their language. I also wish to acknowledge the following people for helpful comments on the oral presentation draft of this paper: Johanna Nichols, Sally McLendon, Harvey Pitkin, Alice Schlichter, and Tony Woodbury. Of course, any omissions and/or errors of analysis are my own responsibility.

[2] The two Southern Wintun languages, Patwin and Southern Patwin, formerly spoken in Glenn, Colusa, Lake, Yolo, and Napa Counties, California, can be divided into dialects roughly as follows:

A. Patwin (2 divergent groupings of dialects)
    1. Hill Patwin (3 distinct dialects)
        a. *kabalme·m* (= WPK)
        b. *tʰebtʰi* (= WPT)
        c. Southern Hill Patwin (with subdialectal variation)
            i. Cortina
            ii. Rumsey (= WPCC)
            iii. Putah
            iv. Napa
    2. River Patwin (2 close subdialects)
            i. Colusa
            ii. Grimes
B. Southern Patwin (with several dialects)

For more details regarding this classification, see Whistler (1980). The data for this paper are taken only from the Rumsey and *tʰebtʰi* Hill Patwin dialects.

is clearly and not too distantly related to Wintu, the language which could be said to have first brought evidentials into focus as a potential grammatical category in languages.[3]

Before presenting the Patwin analysis, however, a few cautionary remarks are in order regarding the nature of the Patwin data and the scope of the analysis proposed. All of the surviving dialects of Patwin are profoundly moribund, being still spoken by only a few elderly individuals, mostly in their 80s, scattered about in different rancherias and small towns in central California. The language has been undergoing a process of rapid deacquisition over the last fifty years or so. My own work with three elderly speakers began in 1975, when the language had generally long since ceased to be used for all but the most limited functions— mostly because there was no one left to talk to. The data I was able to collect directly were mostly lexical or sentential, and what connected discourse I could record in two dialects shows little sign of the usage of evidentials. It was not until I started working with a third speaker (of a third dialect of Patwin) that I found someone whose grammatical command of Patwin seemed extensive and fresh enough to be able to give reasonable interpretations of contextually complex grammatical phenomena such as evidentials, and even then the process consisted of reeliciting and interpreting texts which had been collected twenty-five or more years earlier from other speakers and by other linguists.

Perhaps the best source of data about Patwin evidentials is a small collection of texts made by Paul Radin circa 1931 in a dialect of Patwin known as *tʰebtʰi* Hill Patwin (WPT), a dialect which I was unfortunately unable to work on directly. Radin's linguistic transcriptions are, however, phonetically abominable, and the material is very inadequately analyzed; consequently, it is somewhat unreliably translated as well. Thus, while the Radin texts are the richest source of complex, interclausal grammatical phenomena in Patwin, interpreting such constructions in the texts is a slow, bootstrapping, and somewhat speculative process.

Later Patwin linguistic corpuses gathered by two fieldworkers from the Survey of California and Other Indian Languages (University of California, Berkeley), Elizabeth Bright in 1951 and Donald Ultan in 1960/61, provide some supplementary data on Patwin grammar. But neither of these fieldworkers dealt with evidentials per se, even though by the time of their collecting, Dorothy Lee's article on evidential phenomena in the related language, Wintu, had already been published. It is only by reanalyzing and reeliciting the text material gathered by Bright and by Ultan that the evidential phenomena embedded in their data become apparent.

---

[3] Lee (1944) identifies the Wintu evidentials as 'definitive suffixes' which serve to specify the means of cognizance for a speaker when expressing beliefs about 'reality within personal cognition.' Not until later, however, were these 'definitive suffixes' actually called 'evidentials'; see, for example, Pitkin (1963).

What I have done, then, comprises a kind of textual philology to recover rather subtle distinctions in the language. Clearly, however, such data are suspect for making fine-tuned judgments about the semantics and pragmatics of evidentials in Patwin. As a result, I do not try to push the data too far. Instead, the general aim here is to provide an overall catalog and typology of the evidential-like phenomena I have discovered in Patwin. I characterize the functions of the various suffixes and clitics as well as I can, given the available data, and also provide morphological analyses where appropriate.

The most fruitful approach to take in interpreting the Patwin data is historical. Since the morphological analyses of the evidentials and evidential-like suffixes and clitics in Patwin are fairly strightforward, the pieces can be compared with cognate elements in Wintu to seek patterns of historical development of evidential functions. Which of these evidentials are old in the Wintun family? Which are innovations? And what are the semantic values of the morphological pieces which end up having evidential functions? How do the overall Wintu and Patwin systems compare? While a full answer to these questions would require a complete comparative reconstruction, I do point out the Wintu comparisons and differential developments and conclude with some general observations regarding the history of the systems.

CATEGORIZATION OF THE PATWIN PHENOMENA

Evidential qualification in Patwin discourse takes several, somewhat disparate forms. Unlike Wintu, which has been characterized as having an almost paradigmatic set of contrastive, formal evidential suffixes,[4] Patwin suffixes which qualify the evidential status of a predicate are diverse and tend to overlap functionally with other, nonevidential uses. Furthermore, a particular evidential suffix may be formally a part of a paradigmatic set of suffixes others of whose members are not especially evidential in function.

To clarify the Patwin phenomena, I have sorted the forms and their functions into three major, mode-based categories: (a) phenomena related to the quotative mode, (b) phenomena related to the declarative mode, and (c) true evidentials (and evidential-like epistemic modals), including a few suffixes apparently restricted to the irrealis mode. The analysis presented here is necessarily tentative, and subject to revision as the problems of intractable and poorly attested syntactic patterns in Patwin, such as the irrealis, are better understood through further analysis. What follows is an attempt to sort out the Patwin phenomena in such a way as to render them accessible for crosslinguistic and historical discussion of evidentials.

---

[4] See the paper by Schlichter in this volume. Also see Pitkin (1963, or 1978 revision of same) for further analysis and examples.

Table 1. Predicate modes in Patwin (WPCC)

	Modal Particle	Unmarked Tense	Definite Past	Remote Past	Definite Future
Declarative	*pi*	*-s~-Ø*	*-sa*	*-ni-sa*	*-ti-(s)*
Interrogative	*pa*	*-say*	*-ta·*	*-ni-ta·*	*-ti-(say)*
Quotative	*ʔupu*	*-m/-mu*ᵃ	—	—	—
Irrealis⁵	*ka*	*-Ø*ᵇ	—	—	—

ᵃThe unmarked tense quotative constitutes a narrative past.
ᵇThe zero-marked irrealis takes stem IVa of the verb.

PATWIN PREDICATE MODES

Patwin, or at least the Hill dialects of Patwin, has four formal modes for main clause predicates: the declarative, the interrogative, the quotative, and the irrealis. The irrealis is poorly attested in the extant data. (Imperative and hortative verb forms considered together could constitute yet another mode, but they seem to be irrelevant to the main issues of evidential status.) The four predicate modes are indicated by the presence of a clitic modal particle in the clause, often in second position, together with mutually exclusive sets of final suffixes on the verb which provide information about tense distinctions in the declarative and interrogative modes. The forms appropriate to each mode are shown in Table 1.

The declarative and interrogative modal particles are apparently optional in a given clause. They occur most often when the main verb is marked for definite future tense, as shown in (1):

(WPCC) (1a) na·me   pa   ču hara·-ti.
             last time   INTER.   I   go-FUT.
             'Shall I go one last time?'

        (1b) čo·wi pi   ču hara·-ti.
             to see   DECLAR.   I   go-FUT.
             'I'll go see.'; 'I'll go for a look.'

        (1c) po   pi   ʔele·-be čiyak-ma
             no one   DECLAR.   not-can   old man-OBJ.

---

⁵ The 'irrealis' clitic *-ka* has long posed a problem for my analysis of Patwin grammar. In earlier treatments I have listed it first as a 'suffix of uncertain function, perhaps referential' (Whistler 1977:174), and later as a ' "subjunctive" mode particle' (Whistler 1978:58). In Whistler (1981) and subsequently, however, I have reserved the term 'subjunctive' for the *-m/-mu* suffix, and have called *-ka* an 'irrealis mode clitic'. This choice is based on a partial paradigmatic parallel to the declarative and interrogative mode (clitic) particles, as well as the occurrence of *-ka* in some counterfactual constructions. However, *-ka* sometimes merely seems to indicate indefinite reference for a subject nominal in Patwin. Presumably *-ka* is cognate with the Wintu suffix *-qa-, -qat ~ -qah*, glossed 'as for . . .' by Schlichter.

>ʔut   ʔe·t-muʔu.
>that   steal-NEG.
>'Nobody can steal from that old man.'

In the quotative and irrealis modes there do not seem to be formal tense distinctions, at least as far as the available data show.

THE QUOTATIVE MODE AS EVIDENTIAL

Quotative grammatical devices serve to qualify the evidential status of a predicate by indicating that a statement has been heard from someone else and is not made on the speaker's own authority. Since in Patwin the quotative mode is grammatically distinct, I discuss its evidential functions separately from those of other evidential devices in the language.

The Patwin quotative mode serves overall as a general narrative past for stories, especially myths. It is virtually absent in the data I collected in three dialects of Patwin. This fact is presumably the result of the moribund status of the language and, perhaps more importantly, of the gradual loss of the traditional tales and the appropriate communal settings for their telling. The death of the former skilled Patwin raconteurs has left a much impoverished rhetorical structure in the more recently recorded tales. Consequently, data regarding the consistent use of the Patwin quotative mode is almost wholly derived from the manuscript mythic texts collected by Paul Radin from Anson Lowell, a Hill Patwin who spoke the *tʰebtʰi* (WPT) dialect.

I present in (2) a short excerpt from those texts which shows how the quotative operates in Hill Patwin.[6]

> (WPT) (2a) *katit-se·ktu:*   *hale-ʔum*   *pasalaʔa-m*
>   Bullethawk-Chief   I'll go-QUOT.   visit-SUBJUNCTIVE
>
>   *la·bačʉ-t.*
>   my elder brother-OBJ.
>   'Bullethawk-Chief [said]: "I think I'll go visit my older brother."'
>
>   (2b) *sedew-čiyak:*   *ʔo·-ʔum.*   *hartaro*   *wer-ʔum.*
>   Coyote-Old Man   o.k.-QUOT.   go and   come back-QUOT.
>
>   *kay-ma*   *weri-ʔum.*   *ba·se-ʔum.*
>   gopher-OBJ.   bring (ANIM.)-QUOT.   let's 2 eat-QUOT.
>
>   *du·kuru*   *weri-ʔum.*
>   beg and   bring (ANIM.)-QUOT.
>   'Coyote Old Man [Bullethawk's "grandpa"] [said]: "O.k. Have a

---

6 All *tʰebtʰi* Hill Patwin (WPT) forms cited in this paper are philologically rectified and presented in the phonemic transcription I have adopted for other Hill Patwin dialects.

good trip. [literally: Go and come back.] Bring back some
gopher[meat]. We'll eat it. Ask for [some gophermeat] and
bring it back." '

(2c) pa·l *?upu*   har-*mu*,   hartaro   di·ła   hen-*mu*.
      now   QUOT.   go-*mu*   go to and home   arrive at-*mu*
      'Now then [Bullethawk] left, travelled and arrived at [his brother's]
      home.'

(2d) piła *?upu*   *?ele··m*   tʰasi·   kayo·ro.
      there QUOT.   be gone-*m* Mink   gophering
      'There Mink was away gophering.'

This piece of text illustrates two distinct kinds of quotatives in Patwin. (2a)
and (2b) include direct quotations of lines by characters in the tale, whereas (2c)
and (2d) are narrative statements in the quotative mode. (2a) and (2b) show the
typical Patwin dramatic presentational style; the character speaking is announced
and then quoted (presumably with a distinct voice by the skillful raconteur,
although there is no audio record of such a text). An element of each directly
quoted sentence or phrase (usually the main verb, or an interjection functioning
as a minor predicate) is suffixed with -*?um*, the direct quotative suffix. Morphologically, -*?um* consists of -*?u* 'to say' + -*m*/-*mu* subjunctive (for which see
below), and could be literally glossed as 'he say. . .'.

The quotative mode illustrated in (2c) and (2d) differs somewhat. There each
narrative sentence generally exhibits the *?upu* quotative modal particle, which
could be literally glossed as 'they say' or 'I hear', and the main verb, or verbs,
each ends in the -*m*/-*mu* subjunctive suffix. 'Subjunctive' is being used here as a
catch-all label for the many functions of -*m*/-*mu*. (The two allomorphs of -*m*/-*mu*
are conditioned by the final phonological segment of the verb stem.) Among
those functions are marking of some types of negation, of main verbs in the
quotative mode, and of the subordinate purposive verbs. An example of this last
function can be seen in (2a), where *pasala?am* 'to visit' is subordinate to *hale*
'I'll go'. In the quotative mode the -*m*/-*mu* suffixed verbs correspond to what
would generally be -*s* suffixed, i.e. unmarked tense, verbs in the declarative
mode.

Another example of quotative usage from the Radin texts is given in (3):

(WPT) (3a) piła   pi·t   *?upu:*   po   *?i-say-?um*
             there then   QUOT.   who   is it-INTER. PRES.-QUOT.

             nat-panti   hama-say-*?um*,   λiktʰumas.
             me-on top of   sit-INTER. PRES.-QUOT.   make crowded.
             'There, they say, [Raven] then [said]: "Who is it sitting on top of
             me, crowding me?" '

       (3b) pi·t   *?upu:*   ču   *?i-s*   *?a·pakʰe··?um*.
             then   QUOT.   I   it is-*s* grandpa (VOC.)-QUOT.
             'Then [Bullethawk] replied]: "It's me, grandpa." '

In this example *ʔupu* indicates the quotative mode and secondarily serves as an implicit verb of saying in the absence of any overt, true verb of saying. -*ʔum* then marks the directly quoted material, as in example (2) above.

In data from other Patwin dialects there are scattered instances of the use of an apparently distinct quotative auxiliary of the shape -*bom*/-*bem*. (< -*bo* 'to be (animate locational auxiliary)', -*be* 'to be (inanimate locational auxiliary)' + -*m*/-*mu*) For example:

(WPCC) (4) *ʔele·s   ču   ʔut   win-muʔu   piʔusʔu   huymaro   bo·-<u>bom</u>   pi.*
                 not   I   her see-NEG. but   pretty   be-QUOT. she
                 'I never seen her, but they say she's pretty.'

This usage is, however, no doubt related to the full quotative mode which appears in the narrative tales.

Another miscellaneous form of note is -*mpu*, which Radin (1932) lists in his manuscript grammar and lexicon of Patwin as meaning '1. inferential perfective, 2. hearsay', and which he claims is contracted from -*mupu*. The categorical interpretations which Radin provides make it sound as if he is talking about an evidential suffix. However, what meager data there are would seem to indicate that the -*mpu* form is indeed a syntactic contraction of -*m*/-*mu* + *ʔupu* and is thus merely another manifestation of the quotative mode. This would fit with Radin's characterization of -*mpu* as a 'hearsay' suffix, but not as an 'inferential perfective'. Apparently Radin thought that -*mpu* was paradigmatically related to -*mte*, which he had termed as '1. inferential present, 2. inferential perfective'. -*mte* does in fact serve as a kind of inferential evidential, and it is discussed with the other true Patwin evidentials below.

One last suffix in Hill Patwin which is probably related to the quotatives is -*ʔunan*, morphologically comprised of -*ʔu* 'to say, to do' and -*nan* 'reflexive'. Out of context it has been literally glossed as 'he himself say', and it seems to be used in context, at least in Rumsey Hill Patwin (WPCC), to identify statements which are reported as someone else's definite assertions. For example:

(WPCC) (5) *sedew-čiyak:*   *ʔele·-ʔunana-s   pi   hen-muʔu,*
              Coyote-Old Man   not-<u>ʔunan-s</u>   he   arrive-NEG.

              nay   *tihi·tu-t.*
              I (GEN.) ask-3 SG. OBJ.
              'Coyote [said]: "He himself said he'd never been there, when I
              asked him." '

See also example (6), which shows in addition the regular quotative mode pattern:

(WPCC) (6) *hentaro   mi   ʔupu   were·-<u>m</u>; wini-ʔunana-s*
              arrived   and you QUOT. take-*m*; see-ʔunan-s

> *mit*   *pi.*
> you (OBJ.)   he
> '[I hear] you were there and took [the beads]—he himself said he
> saw you [take them].'

There is, however, a problem in interpreting this construction, since -ʔ*unan* is doubtfully distinct from another suffix -ʔ*inan,* which is glossed as 'he actually did, he himself did', and is presumably derived from the -ʔ*i* 'to do' auxiliary plus -*nan* 'reflexive'. The Rumsey Hill Patwin (WPCC) forms are consistently cited with -ʔ*unan,* but in the *t*ʰ*ebt*ʰ*i* (WPT) dialect, the functionally analogous forms seem to be cited as -ʔ*inan,* which calls into question the connection with the 'to say' sense of -ʔ*u.* Compare, for example, 5 in the Rumsey dialect with the following sentence (7), which is Anson Lowell's version of the same line in the same story.

> (WPT)   (7)   *t̓ihi·tu-t*   *nay,*   *hen-muʔu*   *ʔele·-ʔinana-sa.*
>   ask-3 SG. OBJ.   I (GEN.)   arrive-NEG.   not-ʔ*inan*-DEF. PAST
>   'I asked him (and) he never got over there he said.' [Radin's
>   translation]

Also note sentence (8), which is Lowell's version of (6):

> (WPT)   (8)   *wini·-ʔinana-sa*   *mit.*
>   see-ʔ*inan*-DEF. PAST   you (OBJ.)
>   'He saw you actually.' [Radin's translation]
>   'Look! Look! Look! The water is coming!'

Even if these forms are really quotatives, they seem to merge with the functioning of -ʔ*u* and -ʔ*i* (in their sense of 'to do') as emphatic assertives. I discuss some of these assertive uses briefly in the next section.

THE DECLARATIVE MODE AND EVIDENTIAL STATUS

Several constructions in the declarative mode in Hill Patwin function in ways that border on being true qualification of the evidentiary status of statements. (For the morphosyntax of the declarative mode, see section 3 above.) Chief among these constructions is the use of the auxiliary *bo(·)s/be(·)s,* the locational 'to be', as an equivalent to a direct sensory evidential.

bo(·)s (animate) and *be(·)s* (inanimate) function in several related senses as Patwin auxiliaries. For example, they are most commonly used to express continuative (or imperfective) aspect in a predication:

> (WPCC)   (9)   *hamtaro*   *bo·-s.*
>   sit and   be-*s*
>   'He is sitting (there).'

However, since the primary sense of *bo(·)s/be(·)s* is 'to be THERE', i.e. 'to be present in full view', in which sense it is the antonym of *ʔele·s* 'to be absent, to be away, to NOT be there', predications involving *bo(·)s/be(·)s* generally imply that the evidential basis for that predication is there in plain sight. Thus, for example, in 10:

> (WPCC)   (10)   *pi!   pi!   pi!   me·m   were·-be-s.*
>   there   there   there   water   come-be-*s*
>   'Look! Look! Look! The water is coming!'
>   [said of a world flood about to roll in on the characters of a myth]

This statement has to be construed as being asserted as true on the basis of clearly visible evidence, rather than indirect inference.

An interesting contrast can be seen in the following pair of sentences, which show a semantic minimal pair relevant to this sense of *bo(·)s/be(·)s* as a virtual direct sensory evidential:

> (WPCC)   (11a)   *behnaʔu   me·m   kʰontaro   be·-s.*
>   next morning   water   dried   be-*s*
>
>   (11b)   *behnaʔu   me·m   kʰontaro   ʔele·-s.*
>   next morning   water   dried   be gone/not be-*s*
>   'Next morning the water was dried up.'

(11a), which actually occurs a little later in the world flood myth mentioned above, can be construed approximately as 'The water has dried up, and that state of being dry now IS and is visually evident there.' (11b), however, is also perfectly grammatical Patwin, and perhaps even more elegant; it would be construed as 'The water is dried up, and is no longer there, which ABSENCE is visually evident there.'

The upshot of this discussion is that while *bo(·)s/be(·)s* used as an auxiliary does seem to carry some evidential force by virtue of its sense 'to be THERE in sight', this is not really its primary function. Furthermore, direct sensory evidence is not a hard and fast implication of use of *bo(·)s/be(·)s,* since in expressing continuative (or imperfective) aspect it is not uncommonly applied even when the affected state or action is not directly present and visible.

This analysis of Patwin *bo(·)s/be(·)s* shows an interesting functional parallel in Wintu *bEy-*, which is cognate with Patwin *be(·)-s*. Pitkin (1963) labeled *bEy-* as the Wintu visual evidential. However, as Pitkin and Schlichter have suggested,[7] *bEy-* functions primarily as an imperfective auxiliary in Wintu, and only secondarily as a visual evidential (in the absence of other, explicit evidentials).

---

[7]See especially Schlichter's article in this volume for discussion of these points.

Another class of clitics in Patwin which modify the sense of a statement in the declarative mode are what could be termed assertives. These, too, are not truly evidentials. What they do is assert the validity of a claim to knowledge.

(WPCC)   (12)   *čeme-s-ʔu   pipel.*
                have-<u>s</u>-do   they two
                'They two have got it.' (know for sure)

The certainty of knowledge in (12) contrasts with the uncertainty in (13):

(WPCC)   (13)   *čeme·-mtʰere-s   pipel.*
                have-might-<u>s</u>   they two
                'I think they two got it.' (not sure)

However, the certainty of (12) is more an assertion of truth, i.e. 'surely . . .' or 'they *do* in fact . . .', than a specification of the evidential grounds for the assertion.

A number of modals or adverbs in Patwin can also be used in epistemic senses which qualify the validity of a statement but do not directly serve to specify its evidential basis. But once again, the line is not easy to draw in Patwin. Such usages tend to fade into those of true evidentials, whose construction I take up next.

EVIDENTIALS AND VALIDATIONALS

There are five suffixes in Hill Patwin whose functioning could be analyzed as primarily evidential in character. These are summarized in (14):

(WPCC)   (14a)   *-boti/-beti*   indirect evidential
                        (knowledge based on other than direct sensory evidence requiring
                        no inference)

         (14b)   *-mtʰer/-mutʰer*   tentative inference
                        (implied insufficient grounds for certain knowledge, 'might')

         (14c)   *-mte/-mute·*   tentative inference (?)
                        (a morphological variant of b, used in the irrealis mode, 'must
                        have . . .')

         (14d)   *-mʔa/-muʔa*   confident inference
                        ('must have . . .')

         (14e)   *-monʔa*   circumstantial inference
                        (inference based on appearance, 'seems as if, appears to be')

With the possible exception of *-monʔa*, all of these suffixes seem to be connected with epistemic modal usage in one way or another.

The indirect evidential, *-boti/-beti*, is the most general evidential in Hill Patwin. It seems to encompass a number of evidential types, including hearsay, logical inference, and inference based on circumstance or appearance. What these seem to share is a disclaimer to knowledge based on direct sensory evidence whose implication is publicly obvious. In this way *-boti/-beti* contrasts with *bo(·)s/be(·)s* as analyzed above. A few examples are given in 15:

(WPCC) (15a) *likku·n   hatt^hu!   ʔilayin   berečoyi-boti.*
               quickly   pick   children   hungry-EVID.
               'Gather up [greens] quickly! [Your] children must be hungry.'

        (15b) *ma-ne·n   we·ł   tiwnana   hara·-boti.*
               your-mother   salt   to buy   go-EVID.
               'Your mother must have gone to buy salt.'

        (15c) *la·bak^he·,   sult^hi-to   pepelet   ʔi-boti.*
               elder brother (VOC.)   kill-INT.FUT.   us two (OBJ.)   do-evid.
               'Elder brother, he's trying to kill us two.'

        (15d) *he·ti   win   hene·-boti.*
               from somewhere   person   arrive-EVID.
               'Someone has come here from someplace.'

        (15e) *yirma   pi   haybaʔa-s.*
               leg (OBJ.)   he   hurt-s
               'His leg hurts.'

        (15f) *yirma   haybaʔa-boti   pi.*
               leg (OBJ.)   hurt-EVID.   he
               '[He told me] his leg hurts.'

In (15a) the children are not present. The speaker, Bear Old Lady, is fabricating an excuse to make Deer Old Lady gather greens quickly for her children. The point is that it is plausible to say that the children are (or will be) hungry, but they are not physically present to give obvious visual or aural evidence of being hungry. (15b) is similar. It is in fact a lie in the context of the narrative, but it serves as a plausible excuse for the mother's absence, in lieu of evidence to the contrary. In (15c), the inference of intent is based on a prior pattern of actions which seem lethal in aim. In (15d), the statement is in response to Bullethawk landing on top of Raven's home. There is suspicion, but not yet direct confirmation through sighting, that what Raven has heard was the arrival of someone. (15e) and (15f) show *-boti* serving as a kind of hearsay evidential not involving the quotative mode. Note that all of these uses can be glossed roughly as 'must be' or 'must have been'—the implication is that there is sufficient evidence for making a claim, but that it is not directly from vision or other senses. This evidential can be used rhetorically, as in (15a) and (15b), to make false claims, of course.

Morphologically, *-boti/-beti* is derived from the auxiliary *-bo/-be* 'to be (locational)' (without final -*s*). The -*ti* seems related to the -*ìi* definite future suffix, so that in origin these forms are the future tense of the 'to be (locational)' auxiliary, with subsequent loss of glottalization in the phonologically weak predicate-final position. (Such loss is found also in auxiliary verbs, numerals, and other suffixes.) The paradigmatic contrast of -*boti/-beti* with the unmarked tense *bo(·)s/be(·)s* thus becomes clear.

In some contexts, the original future sense of -*boti/-beti* can still be seen, as, for example, in (15a) and (15c) above, or as in (16):

(WPCC)   (16)   *hene·-kayi-boti*   *sun.*
                       arrive-be about to-EVID.   here
                       'He's about to come here.'

But -*boti/-beti* has been generalized to apply to predicates in the present or past tenses, where a claim is made in the absence of direct—usually visual—evidence, as is clear from examples (15b), (15d) and (15f).

The second Patwin evidential, -*mt^{h}er/-mut^{h}er,* indicates uncertain knowledge, in other words, an opinion rather than a claim of fact, or an assumption based on tenuous evidence rather than certain knowledge. It is often translated as 'I think . . .' or 'It looks like . . .', or 'might'. Examples are given in (17) and (18):

(WPCC)   (17)   *muhu-mt^{h}ere-s   pi.*
                       sing-might-*s*   he
                       'I think he'll sing.' 'I think he's singing.'

(WPCC)   (18)   *loti-ti-mt^{h}ere-s.*
                       storm-DEF. FUT.-might-*s*
                       'Looks like it's gonna storm.'

This Patwin suffix is cognate with the Wintu nonvisual sensory evidential -*nt^{h}er,* which has been mentioned in the various analyses of Wintu evidentials.[8] However, in Patwin the specific information about channel of sensory evidence seems to have been bleached out of the suffix—it really only entails uncertainty of speaker knowledge. In fact, its use in Patwin is in many respects not clearly distinguishable from an epistemic 'might' modal, towards which it may have been evolving. In this sense -*mt^{h}er/-mut^{h}er* verges on being a 'validational' in Patwin, indicating the relative degree of validity of an assertion, rather than functioning as a true 'evidential.'

The third Patwin suffix listed in (14), -*mte/-mute·,* seems to be a morphological variant of -*mt^{h}er/-mut^{h}er* restricted to clauses in the irrealis mode. It is quite poorly attested, but in those attestations only occurs in clauses marked with *ka:*

---

[8]See especially Schlichter's article in this volume for discussion of these points.

(WPCC) (19a) ʾalma-<u>mte</u>-ka   ču   nay-čeme·hem.
               drop-must-IRR.   I   my-belonging
               'I (must have) dropped my belonging.'

(WPCC) (19b) ʔete·ta-ka   har-mute·,   ʔele·-s   pi   sun.
               one-IRR.   go-must   be gone-s he   here
               'One of them left—he's not here.'

The translation glosses of -mte/-mute· are 'must have . . .' or 'think that probably . . .' Radin classes the tʰebtʰi Hill Patwin (WPT) suffix -mte as '1. inferential present; 2. inferential perfective' in his grammatical notes, which presumably is consistent with the general sense of -mte/-mute· as an epistemic 'must'
modal.

Use of -mte/-mute· apparently indicates an assertion based on inference or
circumstantial evidence but not direct knowledge. Thus, (19a) would be appropriate when just noticing that some belonging is missing and from that state of
affairs inferring that its missing–ness is probably the result of having dropped the
object somewhere. (19b) works similarly. The degree of certainty of inference
implied by the use of -mte/-mute· in the irrealis seems somewhat greater than that
for -mtʰer/-mutʰer, but with so few citations in the data it is difficult to be certain
that that is the case.

Historically, both -mtʰer/-mutʰer and -mte/-mute· are derived from a verb
root *mut 'to sense, to feel, to hear'. -mutʰer is derived from mut + her
'passive', whereas -mute· lacks the passive element. In both instances the loss of
the vowel -u- results from an analogic process. Originally, mut must have been a
full, subordinating verb, but at some point in the history of Wintun it was
syntagmatically reanalyzed as a verb suffix in the evidential construction. When
this happened, the mut morph fell into a verb suffix position class where it could
be confused with the -m/-mu subjunctive suffix, which shows a regular morphophonemic alternation in Patwin. That morphophonemic alternation was then
overgeneralized analogically to apply to the evidential suffixes -mutʰer and
-mute· as well. The Wintu -ntʰer is merely the result of a nasal assimilation
subsequent to syncopation of the -u- vowel at some Pre-Wintu stage.

The fourth evidential (or validational) in (14), -mʔa/-muʔa, can also be
glossed 'must have . . .' Morphologically, it is derived from the subjunctive
suffix -m/-mu plus the -ʔa 'to have' auxiliary. -mʔa/-muʔa implies certain or
near certain knowledge based on inference. Like -mte/-mute· it seems to occur
only in irrealis, ka-marked clauses and to be functioning as an epistemic modal
'must' as much as an evidential:

(WPCC) (20a) po-ka   na·no hiłi·   harme-mʔa.
               somebody-IRR.   my   beads   take-must
               'Someone must have taken my beads.'

(20b) *he·-tuka   har-muʔa   ka   tʰayču.*
where-to   go-must   IRR.   my grandson
'I wonder where my grandson could be.'

(20a) shows the basic pattern for *-mʔa/-muʔa,* where the inference is strongly asserted, i.e. 'I'm sure that . . .' In (20b), we have a more idiomatic usage in a rhetorical question, literally, 'My grandson must have gone to where (I wonder).' Such rhetorical usage may call into question the analysis of *-mʔa/-muʔa* as an evidential; the issue is whether this is basically an epistemic modal (or validational) which takes an incidental evidential function because it indicates degree of speaker certainty, or whether it is basically an inferential evidential which incidentally functions like an epistemic modal. It is not clear how the limited data regarding this suffix could resolve this question, however.

The final Patwin suffix which can be argued to have evidential function is *-monʔa* 'to seem as if, to appear to be'. *monʔa* as a full verb means 'to do like, to be like . . .' and is derived from an unclear root plus the *-ʔa* 'to have' auxiliary. *-monʔa* as an evidential suffix indicates inference based on appearance.

(WPCC) (21) *nay   čo·wi-ła   pi   čoyi-monʔa-sa.*
I (GEN.)   look at-if   he   sick-seem as if-DEF. PAST
'It seems to me that he's [gotten] sick.'

Whether this suffix is functioning as a true evidential or not is also unclear from the limited data.

GENERAL SYSTEMATIC AND HISTORICAL CONSIDERATIONS

As the discussion of the previous section should indicate, the line between evidential and nonevidential in Patwin is often hard to draw. The evidential elements overlap in function with Patwin modes, epistemic modals, and tense/aspect marking. In many instances evidential functions can be analyzed as secondary to some other function expressed by the suffix, auxiliary, or clitic in question. Thus, there is little reason to posit the category 'evidential' as constituting a formal/functional subsystem in Patwin grammar in the same sense that, for example, nominal case marking constitutes a grammatical subsystem. Rather, evidential status of the predicate is indicated by co-opting available morphological pieces of susceptible semantics (e.g. modals, auxiliary verbs 'to be', 'to say', etc.) and using them to express, by implication usually, the source of a speaker's knowledge. In this respect Patwin evidentials typologically resemble the covert evidential categories of a language like English more than the highly organized and specialized, overt and formal evidential categories of, for example, the Pomoan languages (see Oswalt, this volume).

Historically, only a few of the Patwin evidentials analyzed in this paper can be projected back to a Proto-Wintun stage. Briefly, the reconstructible forms and functions are as follows:

1. *-mut-her,* probably functioning as a nonvisual sensory or inferential evidential. The Patwin data might indicate that a form *-mut* (without the passive *-her*) was also present in Proto-Wintun functioning as an evidential of some sort.
2. *-beh/-boh,* probably functioning primarily as an imperfective auxiliary with a secondary function (or pseudo-function ?) as a visual sensory evidential.
3. *-?u* 'to say' is of Proto-Wintun age and appears in the quotative systems of both Patwin and Wintu, but the elaboration of a quotative mode based on the subjunctive *-m/-mu* seems to have been innovative in Patwin.

Other Wintu evidentials consist of morphological material which probably can be matched with some elements in Patwin, but considerable changes in form and function have occurred in both languages. No further evidentials seem to be reconstructible for Proto-Wintun. As a result, I must conclude that most of the Patwin evidentials analyzed above are recent functional developments in Patwin, and this conclusion is further supported by the morphological transparency of the forms analyzed.

REFERENCES

Lee, Dorothy Demetracopoulou. 1944. Linguistic Reflection of Wintu· Thought. IJAL 10:181–187.

Oswalt, Robert. "The Evidentials of Kashaya". [this volume]

Pitkin, Harvey. 1963. Wintu grammar. Ph.D. dissertation. University of California, Berkeley, dissertation.

Radin, Paul. 1932. Grammar and lexicon of tʰebtʰi Hill Patwin. Unpublished manuscript. Philadelphia: American Philosophical Society archives.

Schlichter, Alice. "The Origins and Deictic Nature of Wintu Evidentials." [this volume]

Whistler, Kenneth. 1977. 'Bear and Deer Children'. Northern California texts, ed. by V. Golla & S. Silver. (IJAL–NATS Vol. 2(2), 158–178.)

———. 1978. 'Mink, Bullethawk and Coyote'. Coyote stories, ed. by W. Bright. (IJAL–NATS Monograph No. 1, 51–61.)

———. 1980. Proto–Wintun kin classification: A case study in reconstruction of a complex semantic system. University of California, Berkeley, dissertation.

Whistler, Kenneth. 1981. Ablaut in Hill Patwin. Survey of California and other Indian languages, report no. 1, ed. by A. Schlichter, W. Chafe, & L. Hinton, 42–94. Berkeley: Dept. of Linguistics, Univ. of California, Berkeley.

FIVE

The Development of Evidentials in Maricopa

Lynn Gordon

Washington State University

Maricopa,[1] unlike the other languages in the Yuman family,[2] has a rather complex set of evidential suffixes which are transparently derived from independent

---

[1] An earlier version of this paper was given at the 1980 Yuman/Hokan Languages Workshop and appeared in Gordon 1981.

Maricopa is a Yuman language of the River branch, most closely related to Mojave and Yuma. The data and analysis presented in this paper come from Gordon 1980a. The data are presented in practical orthography: VV = [V:]; *ch* = [č]; *sh* = [ṣ]; *d* = [ð]; *ny* = [nʸ]; *ky* = [kʸ]; *ly* = [lʸ]; *kw* = [kʷ]; ' = [ʔ]; *h* = [x]. The abbreviations used in this paper are: 1 = first person; 2 = second person; 3 = third person; 1/2 = first person subject/second person object, etc.; ASP = neutral realis aspect; DEM = demonstrative; DU = dual; DS = different subject; HR=EV = nonsight sensory evidential; INC = incompletive; INTNS = intensifier; IRR = irrealis; NEG = negative; PERF = perfective; PL = plural; SEE=EV = sight sensory evidential; SJ = subject; SS = same subject; s.t. = something (unspecified argument).

I am grateful to my Maricopa teachers, Pollyanna Heath and Jasper Donahue, for their patience and skill. Most of the data included in this paper are from Ms. Heath. I have discussed these data at different times with Pamela Munro, Margaret Langdon, Sandra Thompson, Bonnie Glover, and Heather Hardy, and I would like to thank them for their interest and suggestions.

[2] Other Yuman languages have not been reported to have this kind of evidential system, i.e. a system which is transparently derived from a complex source and which is used to express the source of the information conveyed by the sentence. Mojave, a language very closely related to Maricopa, has a fixed construction which employs the verb *iyuu* 'see' (Pamela Munro, personal communication). The Mojave construction seems to be used to convey that the information in the sentence is self-evident; the hearer, as well as the speaker, should have been able to observe it. This is different from the Maricopa construction under discussion; in Maricopa, the sight evidential which involves the verb *yuu* 'see' is used specifically when only the speaker and not the hearer could have directly observed the event expressed in the sentence. The Mojave construction is more difficult to analyze since it is more complex: the verb 'see' is typically affixed or cliticized to an existential auxiliary and it bears a complex suffix (which has has not been unambiguously identified), as in

(i) *Utuyv-k   ido-h   m-iyuu-mpk.*
pregnant-SS be-IRR 2-see-???
'She is pregnant.'

verbs. These evidential suffixes indicate the sensory source of the informations contained in the sentence. Similarly, Maricopa has developed a reportative clitic derived from the independent verb meaning 'say'. These two sets of constructions illustrate clearly the evolution of evidential markers from independent verbs.[3]

Aspect and mood in Maricopa are marked by a complex set of suffixes, auxiliary verbs, and subordination constructions.[4] The primary aspect/mood markers are the final suffixes on main verbs. The verb has pronominal prefixes which indicate the person of its subject (and object, if the verb is transitive). The structure of the typical verb can be seen in the following:

(1)   '-iima-k.
       1-dance-ASP
       'I danced.' or 'I am dancing.'

(2)   'nym-aham-m.
       2/1-hit-ASP
       'You hit me.'

(3)   Maa-uum.
       eat-INC
       'He will eat it.'[5]

---

[3] Note that this evolution involves the change of a main verb into a suffix or clitic, not a particularly uncommon or undocumented change (cf., for example, Givón 1979). In this construction, the old main verb (the new clitic or suffix), however, is a verb which does not have the same subject as the new main verb nor does it have the new main clause as its subject. The sensory evidentials and the reportative clitic have clearly different subjects from that of the main clause and from the main clause itself. As will be demonstrated, the original subject of the original verb which developed into the evidential suffix is first person singular. The subject of the old 'say' verb of the reportative is nonspecific, but clearly it is personal, rather than clausal, and not the same as the subject of the other clause.

[4] Aspect and mood are primarily marked by final suffixes on the verb of an independent clause. More complex moods and aspects are expressed using auxiliary constructions and complex sentences. Inferential constructions include the enclitic shaa and several main and auxiliary verb constructions. The enclitic shaa indicates that the sentence to which it is attached is the belief, inference or expectation of the speaker. It is cliticized to the final verb of the main clause of a sentence which is marked with either realis -k or -m or incompletive -uum (cf. Gordon 1980a). Other inferential constructions use the sensory verbs yuu 'see' and 'av 'hear, sense' to indicate the perceptual source of the information on which the speaker bases his or her inference. Another set of inferential constructions uses the existential verbs duu 'be', wii 'do', and 'ii 'say'. These verbs are used to indicate how the event on which the speaker's inference is based is manifested.

[5] The first person subject prefix '- (intransitive and transitive with a third person object) is obligatory for most speakers on verbs with vowel-initial and glide-initial stems. With consonant-initial stems, '- is optional; thus the unmarked form is ambiguous between third person subject and first person subject.

Final suffixes can be used to indicate the source of the information presented in the sentence. *-(k)'yuu* 'sight evidential' and *-(k)'a* 'hearing and other non-visual sensory evidential' are suffixed to verbs to mark that the information expressed in the sentence is part of the first-hand knowledge of the speaker. *-(k)'yuu* is found on the final main verb of a sentence in which the speaker is asserting something which he or she knows about on the basis of having directly seen the event expressed in the sentence, as in

(4) *M-iima-'yuu.*
  2-dance-SEE=EV
  'You danced (I know because I saw it).'

(5) *Iima-'yuu.*
  dance-SEE=EV
  'He danced (I know because I saw it).'

(6) *'-iima-k'yuu.*
  1-dance-*k*=SEE=EV
  'I danced (for sure, in the past).'

In (4) and (5) the suffix clearly indicates that the speaker saw the activity expressed in the sentence. In (6), in which the subject of the sentence is first person, the evidential sense is less central: when the subject of the verb is the speaker, the evidential reading is typically redundant. (It would be uncommon for a speaker not to be present at events in which he or she is a participant.) Instead, the evidential suffix appears to indicate that the action or state has already occurred.

Similarly *-(k)'a* is also used to mark that the information in the sentence is from the speaker's first-hand knowledge, though in this case the knowledge is gained not by having seen the event, but by having otherwise sensed (usually heard) the event or state, as in

(7) *M-ashvar-'a.*
  2-sing-HR=EV
  'You sang (I know because I heard it).'

(8) *Ashvar-'a.*
  sing-HR=EV
  'He sang (I know because I heard it).'

(9) *'-ashvar-k'a.*
  1-sing-k=HR=EV
  'I sang (for sure, in the past; I heard/felt myself).'

Typically, though certainly not absolutely, *-(k)'a* is used on verbs of communication or of actions strongly associated with sound, as in (7–9).

Like *-(k)'yuu, -(k)'a* is used when the speaker is absolutely sure of the facts.

Things which are sensed, though not seen, are as real as those which are directly
seen. The use of -(k)'a does not indicate that the speaker is making an inference
based on sensory evidence. This affix indicates that the speaker is a direct
witness of the event (even if not a direct EYE-witness).

When these suffixes are used on verbs which have a first person subject, the
evidential sense is less prominent and instead they convey a strong assertiveness
about the actual occurrence of the event expressed by the sentence. -(k)'a is less
likely to be used with a first person subject (and, in general, is less common than
-(k)'yuu with any verb). Possibly the most typical place for this affix is on verbs
of 'saying' which report information addressed to the speaker, as in

(10)   Pam-sh   'i-m   nyip   ny-mhan-k   ii-'a.[6]
       Pam-SJ   say-_m_   me   3/1-like-_k_   say-HR=EV
       'Pam told me that she likes me.'

Before I can account for the distribution of the sensory evidential forms with k
and those without k, more of the structure of the verb must be examined. -k and
-m in Maricopa are used as final suffixes on independent verbs of declarative
sentences, to indicate that the clause is realis and indicative (cf. (1–2)). The
speaker presents the information as fact, not as possibility, inference, or preference, and with no hint as to its source or any doubt of its veracity. The event or
state that the verb expresses is completed if the action is punctual, as in (2) and

(11)   'iipaa-ny-sh   puy-k.
       man-DEM-SJ die-ASP
       'The man died.' or 'The man is dead.'

If the action or state is not punctual, then the verb marked with the -k or -m
expresses an action which is either completed or ongoing, as in (1) and

(12)   Mhay-ny-sh   ny-ashham-k.
       boy-DEM-SJ 3/1-beat-ASP
       'The boy beat me up.' or 'The boy is beating me up.'

If the action is punctual (like those in (2) and (11)), the verb can only have a
completed reading (since it is marked with a realis suffix). If, as in (1) and (12),
the action is durative or iterative, then it can have either a completed or ongoing

---

[6] The -k on the verb of the complement is discussed later in the paper. The verb 'ii-m 'say' varies
greatly in form: the vowel can be long or short; under certain circumstances the vowel can be lowered
and shortened or under other conditions replaced by aa; the initial ' is optional when no prefix
precedes it. (All of this variation is discussed in detail in Gordon 1980a). This accounts for the
difference in form between the two instances of 'say' in this example.

interpretation when marked with a realis suffix. This is a reasonable outcome of the fact that a punctual event is real when it is accomplished. The momentaneous nature of a punctual action entails that its onset and its accomplishment are inseparable. A progressive punctual verb is unaccomplished or irrealis or iterative. In Maricopa *puy-k* 'die' (as in (11)) and *aham-m* 'hit' (as in (2)) are punctual (non-iterative) verbs.

On the other hand, a durative event or state is to some extent accomplished when it is begun. Its onset and completion are separable; from its onset a certain amount of the event or state is real. Thus (1) and (12) can be interpreted as either completed or ongoing. All the realis suffix implies is that some portion of the event or state has held or is holding. If any portion of a punctual action holds, all of it must hold. Compare (2) and (12): the difference between them is that the verb in (12) is iterative (and, therefore, extendable over time), while in (2) the verb is only interpretable as punctual (realis and, therefore, completed). In (11) the verb is *puy-k* 'die' (death is real only when someone has died); on the other hand, in (1) the verb is *iima-k* 'dance' (the moment one has taken even one step, the dancing is real).

In Maricopa the selection of *-k* or *-m* as a final main verb suffix is lexically determined, based on the morpheme which immediately precedes the final suffix.[7] This morpheme may be the verb root, as in

(13a)   *Vtay-m.*
         big-ASP
         'It is big.' or 'It was big.'

(13b)   *Hot-k.*
         good-ASP
         'It is good.' or 'It was good'

or it can be any one of a number of nonfinal suffixes, as in

(14a)   *Vtay-haay-k.*
         big-yet-ASP
         'It is still big.'

---

[7] This is clearly not a phonologically based distribution since it is possible to find pairs of homophonous stems which differ in the assignment of final realis marker. Such pairs include:

chaa-m	'put'	*chaa-k*	'read, count'
shmaa-m	'sleep'	*shmaa-k*	'dream'
chem-m	'put'	*chem-k*	'make a mistake'

Other possible criteria for predicting the assignment of final realis suffix also fail—even verbs which are derived from nouns using the same morphological process (affixation of *-y*) may fall into different classes, e.g. *hay-m* 'damp' (from *ha* 'water') and *mthay-k* 'windy' (from *mtha* 'wind').

(14b)   *Hot-haay-k.*
        good-yet-ASP
        'It is still good'

(15a)   *Vtay-hot-m.*
        big-INTNS-ASP
        'It is very big.'

(15b)   *Hot-hot-m.*
        good-INTNS-ASP
        'It is very good.'

In (13) the verb root determines which final suffix the verb takes; in (13a) the final suffix is *-m*, while in (13b) it is *-k*. In (14) and (15) the nonfinal suffixes determine the choice of final suffix.[8]

There appears to be no feature or set of features, whether phonological, syntactic, or semantic, which distinguishes *-m* verbs (verb forms which are marked with *-m* as their final realis suffix) from *-k* verbs (verb forms which are marked with *-k* as their final realis suffix). Both sets of verbs include both active and stative, transitive and intransitive, basic and derived forms.[9]

On verbs of certain subordinate clauses of complex sentences, *-k* is used to signal that the verb has the same subject as the clause to which it is subordinate, as in

(16)   *'ayuu   nya-rav-k   yoq-k.*
        s.t.   when-hurt-SS   vomit-ASP
        'When he$_i$ was sick, he$_i$ threw up'

(17)   *Kafe   '-sish-k   pastel   '-mash-k.*
        coffee   1-drink+DU-SS   pie   1-eat+DU-ASP
        'We drank coffee and ate pie.'

-m is suffixed to a subordinate verb to indicate that the verb has a different subject from that of the clause to which it is subordinate, as in

(18)   *'ayuu   nya-rav-m   yoq-k.*
        s.t.   when-hurt-DS   vomit-ASP
        'When he$_i$ was sick, he$_j$ threw up.' (i $\neq$ j)

---

[8] Note that *hot*, the verb meaning 'good', takes *-k*, while *hot* the nonfinal intensifying suffix (which seems transparently derived from the verb) takes *-m*.

[9] This distinction shows up to a lesser extent in Yuma. In Yuma (Halpern 1947), cognates of a small subset of *-m* verbs in Maricopa are *-m* verbs, i.e. marked with *-m* as a final aspect suffix and with *-m* in both same and different subject contexts.

Munro (1981a) shows that Mojave has a more complex system which involves some of the same features as the Maricopa system, but which, for one thing, has more verb classes. Again the *-m* verbs in Mojave discovered so far are cognate to a subset of the *-m* verbs in Maricopa.

(19) *Kafe* *'-sish-m* *pastel* *mash-k.*
coffee 1-drink+DU-DS pie eat+DU-ASP
'We drank coffee and they ate pie.'

This marking of verbs of subordinate clauses as to whether their subjects are the same as or different from the subject of some other clause in the sentence is in keeping with what is to be expected from a switch reference system (cf. Jacobsen 1967), particularly the Yuman switch reference system (cf. Langdon and Munro 1979; Munro 1976a and b; Winter 1976).

-m verbs do not participate in the switch reference system. None of them can be marked with *-k* 'same subject'; they are always marked with *-m*, even when the same subject suffix might be expected, as in

(20) *Bonnie-sh* *'ayuu* *nya-maa-m* *onyor* *chaa-k.*
Bonnie-SJ s.t. when-eat-*m* book read-ASP
'Bonnie$_i$ reads while she$_{i/j}$ eats.'

Thus in (20) even though the verb of the dependent clause is marked with *-m*, the subjects of the two clauses can be interpreted as being the same or different. Such verbs must be marked with *-m* in switch-referencing contexts,[10] regardless of what the subjects of the clauses are.

In Maricopa the sensory evidential suffixes and the perfective suffixes each have two forms, one with a *-k* and one without a *-k*, as shown in Table 1. (The perfective suffixes *-(k)sh* and *-(k)sha* are used on present or past states or completed actions.)

As exemplified in (6) and (9), the sensory evidential suffixes with *k* are used when the subject is first person. In fact the constraint is stronger than this; as well as having a first person subject, the verb must also be a *-k* verb if it is to be marked with *-k'yuu* or *k'a*. The same pattern of distribution is found with the perfective suffixes as in

(21a) *'-iima-ksh.*
1-dance-1PERF
"I danced.'

(21b) *M-iima-sh.*
2-dance-PERF
"You danced.'

(21c) *Iima-sh.*
dance-PERF
'He danced.'

---

[10] Switch reference suffixes are used on verbs in dependent clauses of all types: complement clauses, adverbial clauses (temporal, causal, etc.) and certain modifying clauses. Switch reference marking is never used with case marking on the same verb.

Table 1.   Forms of Sensory Evidentials

	with -k	without -k
sight evidential	-k'yuu	-yuu
other sense evidential	-k'a	-'a

In the cases below (22a–f), the sentences contain -m verbs and therefore cannot be marked with -k'yuu or -k'a regardless of what the subject of the verb is.

(22a)   '-kyaa-'yuu.
         1-shoot-SEE=EV
         'I shot him.'

(22b)   M-kyaa-'yuu.
         2-shoot-SEE=EV
         'You shot him.'

(22c)   Kyaa-'yuu.
         shoot-SEE=EV
         'He/I shot him.'

(22d)   '-mii-'a.
         1-cry-HR=EV
         'I cried.'

(22e)   M-mii-'a.
         2-cry-HR=EV
         'You cried.'

(22f)   Mii-'a.
         cry-HR=EV
         'He/I cried.'

This association of -k'yuu and -k'a with -k verbs suggests that the k in these suffixes is segmentable and related to either the switch reference marking -k or the aspect/mood marking -k. Since the presence of k is conditioned not only by the kind of verb (-k verb or -m verb), but also by what the subject of the verb is, it seems likely that the k found in the sensory evidential suffixes is related to the switch reference system, which is also sensitive to the subject of the verb. Thus, in (23), which has a -k verb with a first person subject, the k in -k'yuu can tentatively be identified as the same subject suffix.

(23)   Nyaa   'ayuu   '-rav-k-'yuu.
        I   s.t.   1-hurt-SS-SEE=EV
        'I was sick.'

In (24), which has the same verb, but a third person subject, the *k* is not present.

(24) *Pam-sh   'ayuu   rav-'yuu.*
     Pam-SJ   s.t.   hurt-SEE=EV
     'Pam was sick.'

In (25) and (26), which both contain *-m* verbs, it does not matter what the subject is; as in the switch reference cases, these verbs cannot be marked with *k*.

(25) *Nyaa   '-wii-'yuu.*
     I   1-do-SEE=EV
     'I did it.'

(26) *Pam-sh   wii-'yuu.*
     Pam-SJ   do-SEE=EV
     'Pam did it.'

Further support for the hypothesis that the *k* in this construction is the same subject suffix comes from the remainder of the sight evidential suffix. The sight evidential suffix itself is *'yuu* which is transparently related to the verb *yuu-k* 'see' with the first person prefix *'-*; this is compatible with the semantics since this affix means that the event took place within the sight of the speaker. In other words, the sight evidential contains the morphemes for 'I see'.

In complex sentences which have a sensory verb as their main verb and a clausal object, the verb of the complement clause is marked with a switch reference suffix. In the following examples, this complex construction is shown with the sensory verb *yuu-k* 'see' with complement clauses which have the same subject (as in (27a)) and different subjects (as in (27b–c)).

(27a) *'-iima-k   '-yuu-k.*
      1-dance-SS 1-see-ASP
      'I saw myself dance.' (cf. (6))

(27b) *M-iima-m   '-yuu-k.*
      2-dance-DS 1-see-ASP
      'I saw you dance.' (cf. (4))

(27c) *Iima-m   '-yuu-k.*
      dance-DS 1-see-ASP
      'I saw him dance.' (cf. (5))

If one compared (27a–c) to the parallel evidential-marked verbs in (4), (5) and (6), it is clear that the *-k* in the evidential form is associated with *-k* 'same subject' in the complex sentence, while Ø in the evidential form is associated with *-m* 'different subject' in the complex sentnece.

Similarly, with verbs which do not participate in switch reference, *-m* on the

complement clause of the complex sentence is parallel to Ø in the evidential-
marked forms.[11] Compare (21a–c) above with (28a–c):

(28a)   *'-kyaa-m   '-yuu-k.*
        1-shoot-*m* 1-see-ASP
        'I saw myself shoot him.'

(28b)   *M-kyaa-m   '-yuu-k.*
        2-shoot-*m* 1-see-ASP
        'I saw you shoot him.'

(28c)   *Kyaa-m   '-yuu-k.*
        shoot-*m* 1-see-ASP
        'I saw him shoot him.'

Thus, *yuu-k* 'see' is a verb which takes switch-reference marked complements. Complements of *'yuu* 'I see' themselves have first person subject obligatorily marked with -*k* (if the verb of the complement is a -*k* verb). This
supports the identification of the *k* in the sight evidential with the same subject -*k*.

A parallel relationship can be traced for -*k'a* and -*'a* with respect to the verb
'av-k 'hear, sense'. The distribution of the form with *k* and that without *k* is the
same as described above for -*k'yuu* and -*'yuu*. Like *yuu-k* 'see', *'av-k* 'hear' is a
verb which takes a switch-reference marked complement clause. *'av-k* is somewhat more distant phonologically from its affixal counterpart *'a* than the first
person verb of 'seeing' is from the sight evidential. There is no explicit first
person *'*- prefix on the hearing evidential. This seems a very slight change given
the otherwise documented general process of eliminating first person *'*- on consonant-initial verb stems in maricopa. The loss of *v* is not particularly difficult to
account for; many *v*'s are lost in many contexts.[12]

The evidential forms, unlike their complex counterparts, do not have as their
main assertion that the speaker saw or heard something; instead, the main assertion is that made by the verb to which the evidential is affixed. The evidential
marking sets the verb in time and space with regard to the speaker.

The main semantic force of these affixes as directly reported by speakers is
that the clauses to which they are affixed assert something which truly happened
in the past. (An evidential is not used on a verb to express an action or state
which is presently going on within the sight or hearing of the speaker; that would
presumably also be within the sight or hearing of the person the speaker is

---

[11] Note that Ø is parallel to both the productively used different subject -*m* and the grammatically
fixed -*m*.

[12] The *v* usually lost is the medio-passive suffix. As pointed out by Munro (1981b and 1982), it
seems that 'hear' in the Yuman languages is the medio-passive form of 'say'; in Maricopa, the
transitive form of 'say' is *'aa-m* and the medio-passive form *'a(a)v* would be homophonous with *'av*
'hear, sense'.

addressing as well. Evidential suffixes are never obligatory.) More than this, of course, these suffixes reflect the actual sensory source of the information. These suffixes have a kind of hierarchy for use: if an event is both seen and heard (probably the most commonplace situation), then the sight evidential is used; the hearing evidential is used only when the event is witnessed but not seen; the direct perceptual source of the information can be hearing, feeling, or otherwise sensing (but not seeing).

Evidential marking may seem odd on first person verbs, since, of course, one is present at an event one participates in. However, we have already seen that it is possible to assert that 'I' saw or otherwise sensed 'myself' do something (cf. (27a) and (28a)). The natural inference of these evidentials is that something truly happened in the past. With a first person subject, that aspect of the meaning is central (the form of the witnessing is less important, as is the assumption of direct observation, since they are part of the natural and predictable state of affairs). When the subject is first person, the use of *-k'yuu*, in particular, marks the assertion as more emphatically true and sets the event unambiguously in the past. Neutral realis marking as in (1–2) and (15a–17b) does not necessarily imply that the action/state expressed by the verb is in the past. Compare (29a) and (29b):

(29a) *Nyaa 'ayuu '-rav-k.*
       I s.t. 1-hurt-ASP
       'I am/was sick.'

(29b) *Nyaa 'ayuu '-rav-k='=yuu.*
       I s.t. 1-hurt-SS=1=see
       'I was sick.' (same as (23))

The verb marked with an evidential suffix can be negative; one can witness something not happening, as in

(30) *Waly-marsh-ma-'=yuu.*
      NEG-win+DU-NEG-1=see
      'They didn't win.'

The evidential itself cannot be negated, since the evidential sense is presupposed, not asserted. To assert that one did not witness something requires an independent sensory verb, as in

(31) *Marsh-m waly-'-yuu-ma-k.*
      win+DU-DS NEG-1-see-NEG-ASP
      'I didn't see them win.'

The source of these evidential suffixes suggests a parallel source for *-(k)sh* 'perfective' and *'(k)sha* 'emphatic perfective' which demonstrate the same distribution of k and $\emptyset$ as the evidential suffixes. It seems likely that in the perfective suffixes as well, k is historically derived from the same subject suffix. This leaves morphemes which cannot be related to any independent verb. The perfective suffixes, if they are related to any independent verbs, are so reduced that no identification is possible. Note that as well as sharing the distribution of form with the evidentials, the perfectives also share the semantic feature of basically past time reference. Whatever the original verb was (or verbs were) in the perfective constructions, all that is historically reconstructable of them now is that they must have had first person subjects.

An interesting outcome of this grammaticization is that it gives Maricopa a set of verbal forms in with the first person subject is, in effect, marked by the shape of the suffix, rather than by a pronominal prefix or in addition to a pronominal prefix. In four different, though related, aspect/moods the presence of the k in the suffix identifies the verb as having a first person subject (though the absence of k does not suffice to mark the verb as not having a first person subject if the verb is an -m verb). This process of marking first person subject with the presence of k in the evidential/perfective suffixes has been developing concurrently with the loss of the '- as a first person prefix.

Another grammaticized evidential construction is also derived from a complex sentence. The reportative construction in Maricopa consists of a form of the verb *'ii-m* 'say', which is invariant and cliticized to the verb which precedes it; the hearing evidential is affixed to the invariant 'say' form. This form, like the sensory evidentials discussed above, is used exclusively on independent clauses. The construction is used to indicate overtly that the speaker does not vouch for the truth of the utterance, but instead is merely repeating something he or she has heard spoken of.

(32)   *Bonnie-sh   chuy-k-'ish-'a.*
       Bonnie-SJ   marry-k-say+sh-HR=EV
       '(They said, I hear tell) Bonnie got married.'

The identification of *'ish* (alternatively *ish*) as a form of 'say' is not based on the phonological similarity of the two forms alone, since this verb has many forms and this form *'ish*, resembles a number of other morphemes (*'ish* 'unspecified object, *sh* 'plural/dual suffix', *sh* 'perfective suffix', etc.). Morphosyntactic evidence exists which indicates that this construction contains the verb 'say' at some level.

'ii-m 'say', like the sensory verbs described above, is a verb which takes a complement clause. Unlike the sensory verbs, however, 'say' takes a complement whose verb is not marked with switch-reference suffixes. Instead, realis verbs of complements of *'ii-m* 'say' are marked with the neutral realis suffixes -k or -m, or with -k (which does not indicate same subject or ordinary aspect marking). Clearly the -k does not indicate same subject in (33) below, since the subjects of the two verbs are not the same under any analysis.

    (33) *Bonnie-sh   chuy-k   uu'ish-k.*
          Bonnie-SJ   marry-k   say+PL-ASP
          'They say Bonnie got married.'

Further evidence that this is not the same subject *-k* is that *-m* verbs (which are never marked with the same subject suffix *-k* or the neutral aspect suffix *-k*) can be marked with this *-k,* as in

    (34) *Pam-sh   Bonnie   tpuy-k   uu'ish-k.*
          Pam-SJ   Bonnie   kill-*k*   say+PL-ASP
          'They said that Pam killed Bonnie.'

-m verbs in such complements can also be marked with the realis *-m* suffix, as in

    (35) *Pam-sh   Bonnie   tpuy-m   uu'ish-k.*
          Pam-SJ   Bonnie   kill-ASP   say+PL-ASP
          'They said Pam killed Bonnie.'

-k verbs in such complement clauses can never be marked with *-m* (whether as different subject marker or as aspect marker). Compare (33) with

    (36) **Bonnie-sh   chuy-m   uu'ish-k.*
          Bonnie-sh   marry-*m*   say+PL-ASP

This variation between *-k* and *-m* is found on *-m* verbs followed by a reportative clitic. Compare the final suffixes on the lexical verbs in (37a) and (37b). They show parallel structure to (34) and (35) above, which are complex sentences with fullfledged 'say' verbs as the main verbs of the sentences.

    (37a) *Pam-sh   Bonnie   tpuy-k-'ish-'a.*
           Pam-SJ   Bonnie   kill-*k*-say+*sh*-HR=EV
           'Pam killed Bonnie (I hear tell).'

    (37b) *Pam-sh   Bonnie   tpuy-m-'ish-'a*
           Pam-SJ   Bonnie   kill-*m*-say+*sh*-HR=EV
           'Pam killed Bonnie (I hear tell).'

Both the sensory evidential suffixes and the hearsay construction are still quite transparent in their internal structure and both are clearly historically derived from complex sources in Maricopa. In both cases an original main verb (in fact, an original main clause with its own subject, first person in the sensory evidentials and unspecified in the reportative clitic) has been reduced to a suffix or clitic. Both constructions demonstrate parallel development of complex sentences (of different kinds) containing two clauses to simple sentences in which the main verb/clause has been reduced to being part of the verbal complex of the earlier complement clause. Both constructions illustrate the use of productive systematic morphology which has to some extent become fixed, producing a new form which does not participate in the general syntactic or morphological system. The grammatical fixing of these constructions has produced simple sentences from complex sentences; simultaneously, it has complicated the grammar by introducing new morphosyntactic categories.

REFERENCES

Givón, Talmy. 1979. On understanding grammar. New York: Academic Press.
Gordon, Lynn. 1980a. Maricopa morphology and syntax. UCLA dissertation.
————. 1980b. -*k* and -*m* in Maricopa. UCLA Papers in Linguistics, 8:119–144.
————. 1981. Evidentials in Maricopa. Proceedings of the 1980 Hokan Languages Workshop, (Occasional Papers on Linguistics 9) ed. by James Redden, 59–69. Carbondale: Department of Linguistics, Southern Illinois University.
Halpern, A. M. 1947. Yuma V: Conjugation of the verb theme. IJAL 13: 92–107
Jacobsen, William, Jr. 1967. Switch-reference in Hokan-Coahuitecan. Studies in Southwestern Ethnolinguistics, ed. by Dell Hymes and W. Bittle, 238–263. The Hague: Mouton.
Langdon, Margaret and Pamela Munro. 1979. Subject and (switch-) reference in Yuman. Folia Linguistica 13: 321–344.
Munro, Pamela. 1976a. Mojave Syntax. New York: Garland.
————. 1976b. Subject copying, auxiliarization, and predicate raising: The Mojave evidence. IJAL 42: 99–112.
————. 1981a. Mojave *k* and *m:* It ain't necessarily so. Proceedings of the 1980 Hokan Languages Workshop (Occasional Papers on Linguistics 9) ed. by James Redden, 124–129. Carbondale: Department of Linguistics, Southern Illinois University.
————. 1981b. Two notes on Yuman 'say'. Proceedings of the 1980 Hokan Languages Workshop (Occasional Papers on Linguistics 9) ed. by James Redden, 70–77. Carbondale: Department of Linguistics, Southern Illinois University.
————. 1982. On the transitivity of 'say' verbs. Studies in Transitivity (Syntax and Semantics 15) ed. by Paul J. Hopper and Sandra A. Thompson, 301–308 New York: Academic Press.
Winter, Werner. 1976. Switch reference in Yuman languages. Hokan Studies ed. by Margaret Langdon and Shirley Silver. (Janua Linguarum, series practica 181): 165–174. The Hague: Mouton.

SIX

Evidential Diachrony in Northern Iroquoian

Marianne Mithun

University of California, Santa Barbara

Over the past century, we have learned much about the mechanisms of both grammatical and lexical change.[1] Until now, however, there has been little opportunity to compare diachronic processes in these two areas of linguistic structure. Such a comparison would entail an understanding of the historical development of at least two functionally equivalent but formally distinct sets of devices, one grammatical, the other lexical. Evidential devices in the Northern Iroquoian languages present an opportunity for just such comparison. All of these languages are quite rich in both grammatical and lexical evidentials, some of them cognate across the languages, presumably reflecting a common origin and resistence to change, while others are unrelated, indicating areas of innovation.

In order to compare systems, it is necessary first to define them. Evidential markers qualify the reliability of information communicated in four primary ways. They specify the source of evidence on which statements are based, their degree of precision, their probability, and expectations concerning their probability.

The specification of the SOURCE of information communicated allows a speaker to abdicate some responsibility for its truth and permits the hearer to evaluate its reliability for him or herself. The statement may be based on inference. ('I guess he doesn't like Roquefort.' 'That dress must have been awfully expensive.') It may be based on appearance. ('He looks tired.' 'It smells like something's burning.') The source may be hearsay. ('They say he supports six former wives.' 'I hear she has twenty-seven cats.')

Another way to qualify the reliability of an utterance is to specify its DEGREE OF PRECISION OR TRUTH or the appropriateness of a category label. The speaker may be willing to take responsibility for considerable precision or truth. ('It hit

---

[1] I am grateful to Wallace Chafe and Hanni Woodbury for their helpful comments on this paper.

89

me right here.' 'We were completely exhausted.') Alternatively, the precision or
truth may be hedged, for one of several reasons. The speaker may be unsure. ('It
weighs maybe four pounds.' 'He is somewhere around fifty.') It may be difficult
to find a better label. ('He sort of crawled toward the door.' 'It was sort of
greenish.') The speaker may feel that greater precision is unnecessary and irrelevant. ('I paid around five bucks for it.' 'She's somewhere in France.') Finally,
the speaker may hedge because a specific distance from the center of a category
is the best way to label something. ('It was nearly noon.' 'She was almost
shouting.')

A third way to qualify the reliability of a statement is to specify the
PROBABILITY of its truth. ('The bakery is probably closed by now.' 'She may
decide to return.' 'It is highly improbable that Sam is our thief.') By hedging
certainty, the speaker can again abdicate some responibility for truth. If 'the
bakery' is in fact open, 'she' does return, and 'Sam' is the thief after all, the
speaker still has not lied.

Finally, a speaker may specify EXPECTATIONS concerning the probability of a
statement. 'Sure enough' can indicate that an event was in accord with some
expectation. ('Sure enough, Sam failed the lie detector test.') 'After all' can
indicate a conflict with an expectation. ('Sam escaped after all.')

In both English and the Iroquoian languages, a single marker often serves
several of these functions, either simultaneously or with disambiguation from
context. The context may be pragmatic, or linguistic, i.e. a slightly different
construction. Consider English 'seem'. It can indicate that a statement is based
on appearance. ('Sam seems tired'.) This specification of source can hedge
probability. I should not be surprised, or held to be lying if in fact Sam is not
tired at all, but rather dislikes his companion. With a slightly different construction, 'seem' can indicate hearsay. ('It seems that Sam's in the hospital.') 'Must'
can indicate both inference and high probability. If I look at your wet coat and
say 'It must be raining', I indicate both that I am convinced, and that my
conclusion is based on inference. 'Suppose' can indicate both hearsay and inference. ('It is supposed to rain tonight.' 'I suppose you won't visit your grand-
mother today.') 'Maybe' is used both to hedge precision ('He weighs maybe two
hundred pounds.') and to lower probability ('Maybe he'll return the money.').
'Sure' can be used to emphasize degree ('Sam sure likes pancakes.'), to heighten
probability ('He is sure to return the money.'), and, with 'enough', to emphasize
both reliability and accord with expectation ('Sure enough, Sam DID return the
money.'). This is a pervasive pattern among evidential markers. A given marker
will very often serve several of the four functions listed above, simultaneously,
varying with context, or with a change in the grammatical structure of which it is
a part.

Exactly the same fluidity pervades the Iroquoian evidential systems. In
Cayuga, for example, an experiential particle à:yę:' 'it seems' indicates that a
statement is based on appearance.

(1) C. _A:yẹ:'_ katsihyó:t ho'tẹ́' ne' oná'ta:'.
        it-seems knob-stands kind the bread
        'These look like homemade biscuits.'

This experiential particle is also exploited to hedge both precision and certainty.

(2) C. _A:yẹ:'_ tekayẹhstǫ́ ne' teyot'akẹhny'akǫh.
        it-seems it-is-mixed the ash-is-cut-off
        'It is sort of mixed with grey.'

(3) C. Kwe:kǫ́ akatehsrǫnihs'ǫ́ _a:yẹ:'_ ó:nẹh.
        all I-am-ready it-seems now
        'I guess I am about ready now.'

This hedging function permits _á:yẹ:'_ to serve as a marker of courtesy. It is more polite to suggest than to assert.

(4) C. Wẹhnihfri:yó _á:yǫ:'_.
        nice-day it-seems
        'It looks like a nice day.' (Said when the sun is shining brightly, the
            temperature is perfect, and there is no cloud in the sky.)

Cayuga also has an inferential particle ǫ. (The particle is currently migrating toward suffix status.)

(5) C. O:nẹ́_ǫ_ hne:' kyokhwái'.
        now this there-food-is-cooked
        'The food should be cooked by now.'

This inferential particle is also used to hedge precision and certainty.

(6) C. I:wí: ahsẹ́ nikaya:ké:'_ǫ_ a:kakwé:ni'.
        I-think 3 so-bags-many it-should-suffice
        'I think about three bags should suffice.'

(7) C. Tsisa'nikǫhẹ́'_ǫ_ kẹh?
        your-mind-settled-again?
        'Did you perhaps forget?'

A Cayuga particle _tó:kẹhs_ 'sure' can qualify degree, certainty, and expectation.

(8) C. O:nẹ́ _to:kẹhs_ akatǫhswé'tanih.
        now sure I-am-hungry
        'I'm really hungry now.'

(9) C. _To:kẹhs_ hwa' thó n'ahá:ye:'.
        sure this-time there so-he-did

'In fact, he did do it this time.' (He always promises, but never comes through. This time, he did.)

Not unrelated to this synchronic fluidity is the fact that evidential markers shift among these four functions over time. Particles which signal one distinction in one language, will be cognate to markers in other languages with different evidential functions. The particle *se'* in Cayuga, for example, indicates that a statement is true and contrary to expectation.

(10)   C.   *Hakyé: se'*.
            he-is-awake
            'He *is* awake.' (There is no need to tell her to wake him up.)

(11)   C.   *O:nẹ se' ak'ní:khọ'*.
            already   I-sewed-it
            'I already sewed it.' (So don't tell me to do it now.)

In Oneida, however, this particle emphasizes precision.

(12)   Oe.   *Yáh   se'   tha:yekwe:ní:*.
             not   could-she-do-it
             'She just could not do it at all.'

(13)   Oe.   *Nv   se'   ok   tayutáhsawv'*.
             then   just   she-began
             'She started right in.' (She began right away.)

This synchronic and diachronic fluidity indicates that these distinctions should not be treated in isolation from one another, but rather must be considered components of a single, complex system.

Now, in order to identify linguistic change, one must compare at least two stages in the development of a language or family. To compare CHANGES, it is necessary to compare comparisons, which requires more stages. As can be seen in Figure 1, the nature of the genetic relationships among the Northern Iroquoian languages permits the reconstruction of five different stages in the development of the family: Proto-Northern-Iroquoian (PNI), Proto-Lake-Iroquoian (PLI), Proto-Inner-Iroquois (PII), Proto-Western-Iroquois (PWI), and Proto-Eastern-Iroquois (PEI).[2]

In the sections which follow, the development of three formally distinct but

---

[2] For clarity, Figure 1 shows only those languages considered in this paper. Another Inner Iroquois language, Onondaga, is well documented, but, because of its relationship to the other languages, its inclusion here would not contribute to the arguments presented. Other Northern Iroquoian languages, Susquehannock, Huron, Erie, Wenro, Petun, Neutral, and Nottoway, are not sufficiently well documented textually to shed light on comparative evidentiality.

The relationship of Cayuga to the other languages is probably somewhat more complex than shown by the diagram. In particular, as shown by Wallace Chafe and Michael Foster (1981), Cayuga

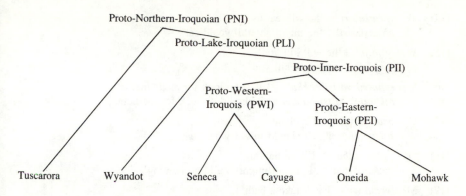

Figure 1. Genetic relationships among Northern Iroquoian languages

functionally equivalent sets of devices will be traced: evidential affixes, predicates, and particles. It will be shown that they differ significantly in their resistance to change, and that these differences may be attributed to their forms.

EVIDENTIAL AFFIXES

The Northern Iroquoian languages contain several morphological devices for indicating the reliability of predications. They appear to be quite stable over time, perhaps due to their status as members of closed sets.

All of the languages share a cognate tense system which distinguishes past punctual, future punctual, and optative punctual events. The future and optative markers also serve to distinguish the probability of events which have not yet occurred. The future prefix, PNI *ẹ- (T., Oe., M. v-, W. e-, S., C. ẹ-) indicates that an event is considered certain to happen. The optative prefix, PNI *a:-/aọ- (T. a-/ary-, W., Oe., M. a:-/aụ-, S., C. a:-/aọ-) indicates that it might, should, or could occur. (The favored reading depends upon the meaning of the verb and the context.) Compare the pairs of verbs below.[3]

---

may have separated earlier from the main branch of Northern Iroquoian, then rejoined Seneca at a later date before separating again. Since this issue does not affect the argument presented here, the representation of the relationship has been schematically simplified.

Wyandot is actually the descendant of a set of probably closely related languages, including dialects of Huron, Petun, and perhaps Neutral, Wenro, and Erie. The exact status of these last languages is unclear, due to a lack of documentation before their disappearance.

[3] The data throughout the paper are from the following sources. The Tuscarora, abbreviated T., is from the late Edith Jonathan and the late Elton Green, of Lewiston, New York. The Wyandot (W.), now extinct, is drawn from texts recorded by Marius Barbeau in 1911–1912 and published in Barbeau (1960). The Seneca (S.) is from my notes from Myrtle Peterson, of Steamburg, New York (Allegany), Sandy Crouse, of Salamanca (Allegany), Hazel Thompson, of Steamburg (Allegany), and from Chafe (1967). The Cayuga (C.) is from Reginald Henry and Jim Skye of Six Nations, Ontario. The Oneida (Oe.) is from Richard Chrisjohn of Red Hook, New York, Winnie Jacobs, of

(14) T. *vhratshù:ri'*   'he will eat'
          ahratshù:ri'   'he might/should/would eat'

(15) W. *e:ja:jú'*   'he will kill you'
          aujàjú'   'he might kill you'

(16) S. *ekhnohkwa'tsíhsakha'*   'I will go look for medicine'
          a:khnohkwá'tsihsa:kha'   'I should go look for medicine'

(17) C. *ekatekhó:ni'*   'I will eat'
          a:kate:khó:ni'   'I should/might/would eat'

(18) Oe. *vkatolátha'*   'I'll go hunting'
          a:*katolátha'*   'I should/might/would go hunting'

(19) M. *vkatá:wv*   'I will take a bath'
          a:katá:wv'   'I should take a bath'

The future prefix also occurs with events which are considered predictable because they happen so often or because they are the recognized effect of a cause.

(20) T. *vθhráhku'*   *arv́h*   *vkheyatkáhri'θ.*
          he-will-go-home   if   I-will-tell-him
          'He will go home if I tell him to.'

(21) W. *Tehstot*   *ndayémeh*   *eyò:noht*   *wá'ja'.*
          you-will-return   the-mine   I-will-give you   a-little
          'If you go back, I will give you a little of mine.'

(22) S. *Ka:nyó'*   *ewokatkanoní'he't*   *o:né*   *wa:e*   *eke'sehtá:ni:no'.*
          when   I-will-be-rich   then   before   I-will-car-buy
          'When I'm rich, I'll buy a car.'

(23) C. *Kanohskó:*   *ekhne:sé:k*   *kye:kwá'*   *eyostáoti'.*
          house-in   we-will-stay   if   it-will-rain
          'We'll stay indoors if it rains.'

(24) Oe. *Ka'ikv́*   *ná*   *yetshiyokúha'*   *kanyó*   *vhsélheke'*   *kwah*   *ikv́*
          this   they-you-child   if   you-will-want   very   it

          vhoti'nikuhlahnilúhake'   *kvh*   *thó*   *kati'*   *ni:yót*   *tsi*
          their-minds-will-be-strong   here   there   so   such   that

          vhuwatilihúni.
          they-will teach them

Oneida, New York, Georgina Nicholas of Southwold, Ontario, and texts published by Floyd Lounsbury in his *Oneida verb morphology* (1953), from a text published by Clifford Abbott and Lawrence Johns, in Mithun and Woodbury (1980), and from texts told by Georgina Nicholas and published by Karin Michelson (1981). The Mohawk (M.) is from Annette Jacobs, Rita Phillips, Josephine Horne, Carolee Jacobs, and Verna Jacobs, of Caughnawaga, Quebec, and from Mary MacDonald, of Akwesasne, New York. I am very grateful to all of these people, who so patiently and generously contributed their expertise.

'This is the way it was: if you wanted your children to have strong minds, this is the way you would teach them.'

(25) Oe. *Kwah   tsi'   nikú: vtyutlata:kó: ohwistano:lú:*
       just   so   how-many   she-will take steps   precious-metal

       ki'   thó   vkayv:táhne.
       just   there   it-will-there
       'Every step she takes there will be a silver coin.'

(26) M.   *Awvhniserakwé:ku   vkutihú:take'   nà:ku   ne   kwá:ti.*
       all-day   they-will-eat-grass   under   the   side
       'All day long, they (the cows) would graze on the east side.'

(27) M.   *Toka'   ytéhsya'ke'   sanúhkwis   nó:nv   oráhkwase'   svha*
       if   you-will-cut   your-hair   the-then   new-moon   more

       yohsnó:re'   vsewatehyá:ru'.
       it-is-fast   it-will-grow-back
       'If you cut your hair during the new moon, it will grow back much
         faster.'

The optative is used with irrealis constructions.

(28) T.   *Thaka'nyè:rvh   ayutè:nv:'.*
       I-would-do-so   it-would-be-sunny
       'I wish it were sunny.'

(29) T.   *Arvh   arvkwatsú'khu:k   akhnhsá:tya't.*
       if   I-would-be-rich   I-would-house-buy
       'If I were rich, I would buy a house.'

(30) W.   *Tą'ą   nǫ: u:saskí:tę'.*
       not   I-guess   would-you-pity-me
       'You would not have pitied me (if you had won).'

(31) C.   *A:kate:khǫ:ní   kyę:kwá'   a:yǫkékhwanǫ:t.*
       I-would-eat   if   she-would-feed-me
       'I would eat if she offered me something.'

(32) Oe. *Né: ki'   svn   usahónyake,   autú: né: ayutnutólyahte'*
       the   just   he-would-marry   it-would-be   the she would play

       ostúha   shakoyvha.
       a little bit   his-daughter
       'If he were to remarry, his daughter could play a little.'

(33) M.   *Toka'   a:yetshiwvnará:'u,   kati'   nú:wa'*
       if   you-had-addressed-a-word-to-her   perhaps   maybe

       a:yetshiyatera'swá:wi'.
       she-might-have-given-you-good-luck
       'If you had spoken to her, she might have given you good luck.

The factual could of course be considered the most certain of all, since it describes events which have already occurred.

Another prefix which reflects the speaker's knowledge about the truth of a predication is the contrastive prefix PII *th-. It can be used to indicate that a state is contrary to fact or expectation.

(34) S. *Tha'a:katkǫ:ni'*   *a:ke'sehta:ni:nǫ́'*   *nǽ:.*
          I-were-rich   I-would-car-buy   EMPHATIC-CONTRASTIVE
          'If I were rich, I would buy a car.'

(35) C. *I:'*   *a:kehfrǫ:ni'*   *kyę:kwá'*   *the'ak'yatahni:yǫh.*
          I   I-would-build   if   my-body-were-strong
          'I would build it if I were strong.'

(36) Oe. *. . . ta   thvwakna'skó:kwate.*
                 if   were-it-to-crawl-into-my-nest.
          '. . . if it were to crawl into my nest.'

(37) Oe. *Otku'*   *ki'*   *né:*   *thvtkaya:kvne'*   *yehsa:ku.*
          snake   just   it-it   so-will-it-come-out-of-there   in-her-mouth
          'A snake will come out of her mouth.' (unexpected event)

(38) M. (What are we going to do about this hole in the pipe?)

          Thvkkohò:roke'.
          'I'll just plug it up.' (contrary to all you might expect me to do, like
              calling a plumber or replacing the pipe.)

          Thvyókka'.
          'It will just leak.' (Contrary to your expectation that it will be fixed.)

This same contrastive prefix is also used to hedge the degree of truth. In Cayuga, it co-occurs with the diminutive *-ah* in this function.

(39) C. *thihaks'ako:wáhah*   'he is sort of handsome'
              (*haksa'kǫ́:wah*   'he is handsome')

(40) C. *thiha'sasté:'ah*   'he is sort of strong'
              (*ha'sáste'*   'he is strong')

(41) C. *thihawayęhǫ́:hah*   'he is sort of good at it'
              (*hawáyęhǫ:*   'he knows how')

(42) M. *tsi ne thiha'shátste'*   'he is sort of strong'
              (*ra'shátste'*   'he is strong')

(43) M. *tsi ne thihahnv́:yes*   'he is sort of tall'
              (*rahnv́:yes*   'he is tall')

The diminutive suffix, which is cognate across all of the languages, is also exploited alone in Cayuga and Seneca to hedge degree. Suffixed to stative verbs, it can add the meaning 'a little'.

(44) S. *kakę:t'ah* 'it is whitish'
          (*Kakę:ęt* 'it is white')

(45) S. *hotyánǫt'ah* 'he is kind of funny'
          (*Hotya:nǫt* 'he is funny')

(46) C. *hǫkwe'tahetkę:'ah* 'he is a little mean'
          (*Hǫkwe'táhetkę'* 'he is mean')

(47) C. *ohsno:wé:'a ǫtriho'ta:t* 'she works sort of fast'
          (*Ohsnó:we'* 'it is fast')

Finally, the plural suffix *-shǫ:'ǫh*, which is cognate within the Inner languages, is exploited in one of them, Cayuga, to hedge numbers.

(48) C. *Ha:wakyǫhǫk   kyę:'   ǫ hne:'   tekrǫ'shǫ:'ǫh.*
          I-would-arrive   it-is   I-guess   eight-ish
          'I guess I would get there by around eight o'clock.' (*tekrǫ'* 'eight')

(49) C. *O:,   hyei'shǫ:'ǫ   aotahse:'.*
          oh   six-ish   you-should-come
          'Oh, you should come around sixish.' (*hyei'* 'six')

The morphological devices which provide information about the reliability of the message are thus quite stable across the languages. The tense systems have remained intact in both form and function in all of the Northern Iroquoian languages. The contrastive prefix has remained in the Inner languages, although its function has been extended in Cayuga and Mohawk from simple contrast with expectation to a hedge on degree. The form of the diminutive and its primary function have remained the same in all of the languages, but the Western languages (Seneca and Cayuga) have innovated a secondary evidential extension of its meaning. Finally, the pluralizer, which is cognate among the Inner languages, has been extended in Cayuga to qualify numbers.

PREDICATE EVIDENTIALS

Iroquoian languages, like most, contain numerous overt predicates which specify the source and quality of the evidence on which information is based. A majority of these ('think', 'say', 'tell', 'certain', 'true,' etc.) are cognate across the languages. As throughout the rest of the lexicon, the most closely related languages share the most cognates, the most distantly related languages slightly fewer. Here are some examples of their use.

(50) T. *Kyè:rih   ú:'y   vθaka'θv̀:ya't.*
          I-think   other   I-will-hang-again
          'I think I'll hang another drape.'

(51) T. *V'nehú:'nv'   hé:snv: wehrvhv̀:weh   hè:ní:kv: tyuyè:rvh.*

it-proved-it   this   it-says-true   that   so-it-happened
'This proved that it had truly happened.'

(52) W. *Tiwa'yẹ́:'ạ'   a'yẹ̀hạọ'   de   hudú'mẹ'   daẹ' nọ́:   yawáhtsih.*
          much-likely   she-said   the   his-mother   perhaps   it-is-good
          'His mother said that it was likely that it would be good.

(53) W. *Yatù:yvh   tẹ'   unọ'tó:'ndi'.*
          it-is-certain   not   to-her-it-is-long
          'She certainly did not find it long.'

(54) W. *Kari:wáyọht   esọmá'turẹ̀:ha'.*
          matter-is-sure   he-will-find-us
          'He is sure to find us.'

(55) S. *Akẹnọhtọ́'   ẹthe'.*
          I-know   he-will-come
          'I know he is coming.'

(56) S. *Ha:wẹ̀:   ẹthe'.*
          he-said   he-will-come
          He said he would come.

(57) S. *Okwe:nyọ́:   næ:'kwá   e:yænọkẹ:ni'.*
          it-is-possible   just-really   I-will-beat-him
          'I just might beat him.'

(58) C. *Tekekahné:'   a:yẹ́:'   onahtokẹhẹkyé'   kayẹ́thwahshọ'.*
          I-am-looking   it-seems   they-are-growing   they-are-planted
          'I see your plants are growing.

(59) C. *Hẹna:tọ́   honíhẹh.*
          they-say   he-borrowed it
          'They say he borrowed it.'

(60) C. *Tka:kọ́:t   hné:'   tẹthá:yẹ'.*
          it-is-certain   this   he-will-bring-it-back
          'He is certain to bring it back.'

(61) C. *Né:'   ne'   tkaí:'   nẹ:kyẹ́   honọ́htọ'.*
          it-is   the   it-is-correct   this   he-knows
          'It is true that he knows.'

(62) C. *Kọ:tọ́   'ọ   hné:'   takwáe   kye'trọ'.*
          I-mean   INF.   this   this-side   she-lives-there
          'I suppose it is the lady over there.'

(63) Oe. *Ta: tkaye:lí: tho   yahá:yuhwe.*
          and   it-is-true   there   there-she-arrived
          'And, in fact, she did arrive there.'

(64) Oe. *Wahv́:lu   ne'n   ohkwa:lí . . .   'kwáh   olihwi:yó: ji'*
          he-said   the-one   bear   just   thing-good   that

          yukhi'shvnyú:ne' '.

they-will-beat-us
'The bear said, ''It is a sure thing that we're going to get cleaned up.'' '

(65)   Oe.   *Wé:ne'*   *wi:*   *ni:*   *ji'*   *vske' shv́:hni.*
it-is-evident   so   very   that   you-will-beat-me
'It is evident that you will get the best of me.

(66)   M.   *Wè:ne'*   *ki' wáhe'*   *tsi*   *vske' sà:ni'.*
it-is-evident   of-course   that   you-will-beat-me
'It is evident that you will get the best of me.'

(67)   M.   *Tsi*   *ní:yot*   *tsi*   <u>*yukhihró:ri*</u>   *yah*   *úhka'*   *ne*   *wv́:tu*
so   so-it-is   that   we-are-told   not   anyone   the   ever

teyotú:'u   *a:yakothró:ri'*   *ne*   *oh*   *nihaya'tò:tv'.*
it-happens   they-would-tell   the   what   so-his-body-kind-is
'And so, we are told, no one was ever able to tell what kind of body he had.'

(68)   M.   *Khè:rv*   *kv*   *tá:'a*   *tehayv́kya'ks.*
I-think   this   maybe   he-is-chopping-wood
'I believe he is out chopping wood.'

Since such predicates are often part of core vocabulary, it is not surprising that they should show a high degree of stability. Many of them have remained intact in all of the languages. (See, for example, **tkaye:ri:* 'it is correct', **-rihw-iyo:* 'certain', **-toke̯-* 'certain', **-e̯no̯tho̯'* 'know', **-ihr-/-ehr-* 'believe', 'think', **-hrori-* 'tell', **-ato̯-/-ati-/-i-* 'say'.) They do not, of course, form a closed set, and perhaps for this reason are not as static overall as the set of evidential affixes.

EVIDENTIAL PARTICLES

A third set of evidentials consists of particles, morphologically unanalyzable words usually consisting of only one or two syllables. The languages vary considerably in their repertoires of evidential particles. They are conspicuously rarer in Tuscarora than in the other languages, for example, probably totaling around half a dozen. Wyandot also seems to have had relatively few, in comparison with the rest of the family. Since all of our knowledge of Wyandot comes from texts recorded longhand, a process which often serves to eliminate particles as speakers slow down and transcribers speed up, we can of course only speculate on their frequency. Oneida and Mohawk speakers draw from a significantly larger repertoire of evidential particles, although there is considerable variation from speaker to speaker in the extent of their use. Seneca and Cayuga speakers have extremely rich sets at their disposal, which they exploit extensively in all styles of speech. Cayuga alone has well over fifty different evidential particles.

The languages vary not only in the size of their repertoires, but also in their content.[4]

Source of Information
Because of their brevity, it is generally difficult to reconstruct particles with confidence. In any case, because of their absence from Tuscarora, no evidentials qualifying the source of information can be reconstructed for Proto-Northern Iroquoian. The Lake languages Wyandot, Seneca, and Cayuga share a cognate experiential particle *a:yę:'* which indicates that information is based on observation.

(69) W.   *De   yaⁿguyomę̂   à:yę́'   uskú' taye'.*
the   it-was-bloody   it-appears   its-head-on
'His head looked bloody.'

(70) W.   *A' atijúh   tehatáka   dà:yę́'   dahstę'   ta' úh*
not-it-looks   he-talks   the-as-if   that   something

hu' diyò̧:ráçę'.
his-mind-is-troubled
'He remained silent. He seemed troubled.'

(71) W.   *Nę   ha:rǫt   dà:yę́'   du   tà:yuwáskaǫ' te.*
now   he-hears   the-it-seems   that   someone-is-walking
'It sounds as if someone is walking around.'

(72) S.   *A:yę́:'   te' o:yái   ne   kæ:né'   ahsǫh.*
it-appears   not-is-it-ripe   the   cherry   yet.
'The cherries don't look ripe yet.'

(73) C.   *A:yę́:'   wahe'   ǫ   tshǫ́:   otǫkohtǫ́   tewáhǫhte:s.*
it-appears   just   INF.   only   it-passed   two-ears-are-long
'A deer must have just passed by here.' (I see the tracks.)

(74) C.   *A:yę́:'   tewahǫhté:s   'ǫ   ętwá' waha:k.*
it-appears   two-ear-are-long   INF.   we-will-eat-meat
'We must be having venison for supper.' (I can smell it.)

(75) C.   *A:yę́:'   sahsó:kha'.*
it-appears   you-limp
'You seem to be limping.'

The Seneca particle is also used for inference based on observation of a situation.

(76) S.   *Ta: o:nę́   næ: kyǫ'ǫ   ne   haksa' tase:'a   waę'*
and   then   really   they-say   the   he-is-a-new-child   he said

---

[4] Three other papers describing particles in Northern Iroquoian languages are of note here. Two, by Wallace Chafe (1981a, 1981b), deal with Seneca particles. The third is on 'Cohesive and grammatical functions of selected Onondaga particles' (Woodbury 1980)

ky'ǫ   a:yę́:',   'Waeyajęǫskǫ:'.
they-say it-seems I-got-the-best-of-him
'Now then, it seems, the young man said, "I got the best of him." '

(77) S. *Tǫta:eyǫ́'*   *shǫ* *a:yę́:'* *kwa* *í:'*
         I-should-give-it-back-to-him only it-seems just I

         a:yǫkwaya' tákeha'.
         it-should-help-us
         'It looks like it would help us for me to give it back to him.'

Wyandot, Seneca, and perhaps Cayuga or Mohawk share an inferential particle which indicates that the information is the result of deduction.

(78) W. (Some hunters have just found some large, unusual claw marks on a tree.)
         Tą'ą *nǫ:*   *te' yawahsti* *de:* *kwaka:jatǫ'.*
         no   maybe not-is-it-safe that we-trouble-it
         'Maybe we had better not disturb it.'

(79) W. (A friend has just informed the speaker that horses do not hatch, but rather bring forth their young. He has just bought a pumpkin.)
         Nę *tu*   *i' hsę* *ne* *nǫ:*   *ahaye' diyǫha' tę'.*
         now there sure the INF. he-cheated-me
         'Then he must have cheated me!' (when I bought the horse egg)

(80) S. *Nǫ:*   *te'o:yái*   *ne kæ:ne'.*
         I-guess not-is-it-ripe the cherry
         'The cherries must not be ripe.' (because the strawberries are still out)

(81) S. *A:yę́:'*   *ni:'* *i:wí:* *hotkǫ́'* *nǫ:*   *æ:htá' k*
         it-seems I   I-think wizard I-guess too-much

         ha'te:yǫ́:   *hayęte:ih.*
         diff.-things he-knows
         'He seems to be some kind of a wizard; he knows too much.'

(82) C. *Tętha:yę́:'*   *ǫ*   *hne:'*
         he-will-bring-it-back INF. this
         'I guess he'll bring it back.'

(83) C. *Thę́'* *ǫ*   *hne:'* *t' eshe:'*   *kaya' thá'*
         not   INF. this not-you-want it-body-sets

         há:se:'.
         there-would-you-go
         'You don't want to go to the movies then, do you?'

(84) M. *Ne* *ki'* *kí:kv* *Ahkwesahshró:nu'* *thé:nv* *ki'* *nà:'a*
         the just this St.-Regis-resident something just I-guess

         yahori' wanú:tohse' *autahó:yu'*   *ne* *rahù:tsi.*
         he-asked-for he-would-give-him the he-is-black
         'I guess the St. Regis man must have asked the black fellow to hand

him something.' (Speaker infers a bridge between remembered events.)

(85)   M.   *Khe:rv   ki'nà:'a   ta'   nú:wa   akkwé:ni.*
            I-think   I-guess   maybe   perhaps   I-could
            'I guess I just might be able to do that.'

(If the particle, *ṇǫ:,* is a combination of the article *ne'* plus *ǫ:,* the Cayuga *ǫ* could be related; if not, the Mohawk *nà:'a* could be related, in accord with other observed but unsystematic correspondences between *-a'a-* and *-ǫ-* sequences.) An Oneida particle, *uhne,* resembles a compound of the Cayuga inferential plus deictic.

(86)   Oe.   *Khale'   oný   <u>uhne</u>   wahý:lu'   skvhanáksv,*
             and   now   it-seems   he-said   one-it-skin-bad

             'Tutahsanítskwak . . .'
             jump-up
             'Finally said the fox, it seems, "Jump up now."'

(87)   Oe.   *Nv   <u>uhne</u>   lotnuhtú:tu   ka'iký   skvhnáksv   kwatokv*
             now   it-seems   he-wait   this   one-it-skin-bad   really

             akawi:sátvste' lvtákne.
             it-would-ice-become-thick
             'And so it seems the fox waited for the ice to become really thick.'

Mohawk also contains another inferential particle. It usually entails a hedge on probability. The inference may be based on observation.

(88)   M.   *Oskvnú:tu   ta'   yotohétstu.*
            deer   possibly   it-has-passed
            'A deer must have passed by here.' (I see tracks.)

(89)   M.   *Khé:rv   kv   <u>tà:'a</u>   oskvnú:tu   o'wà:ru   ýtewake'*
            I-think   that   possibly   deer   meat   we-will-eat

            vyò:karahwe'.
            it-will-darken
            'I think we must be having venison tonight.' (I smelled it as we walked in.)

The Inner languages all make extensive use of quotative particles. The Cayuga, Oneida, and Mohawk particles are cognate, while the Seneca quotative is quite different in form.

(90)   C.   *Akonǫhyá'k   <u>akę'.</u>*
            she-got-hurt   they-say
            'I heard she got hurt.

(91) C. *Thayekya'khǫhá'*   *akę̨'.*
      he-went-to-chop-wood   they say
      'They say he went to chop wood.' (It seems he went to chop wood.)

(92) Oe. *Okhna'* *yakv' wí:* *wa'thatawv́li'.*
       and-so   they-say   he-traveled-around
       'And, so they say, he travelled around.'

(93) Oe. *Né:* *kati'* *yakv'* *wí: alyá:* *nv* *yah*
       it   is   they-say   that-is-why   now   not

       te'shvtáhsute' *ohkwa:li.*
       has-he-a-tail   bear
       'That's the reason, it is said, that the bear has no tail.'

(94) S. *Sǫká:'* *kyǫ'ǫ́* *te:niksa'á:* *hotiya'tahtǫ'ǫ́* *sǫ:te'. Berrino*
     someone   they-say   two-children   they-are-lost   last-night

     kyǫ'o *hiya:sǫh.* *Chickchick kyǫ'ǫ́* *koksa'ta'shǫ́'ǫh.*
     they-say   their-names   they-say   her-children
     'I heard that two kids were lost last night. Berrino I guess their names
        were. Must be Chickchick's children.' (from a conversation)

(95) S. *Ta:* *o:nę̨* *næ:* *kyǫ'ǫ́* *sę̨* *nǫ'o:tá'* *o:nę̨ kyǫ'ǫ́*
     and   then   really   they-say   3   so-days   then   they-say

     wa:ayǫ́' *né* *hǫ:kweh.*
     he-arrived   the   man
     'And then, it seems, after about three days, it seems, a man appeared.'
        (from a legend)

Precision or Degree of Truth

Particles emphasizing the degree of truth look similar in almost all of the languages. One emphatic may be traceable to Proto-Northern Iroquoian.

(96) T. *Yahwahv́'ni'*   *u'tésnakw ha' kv́'   thru'na'níhrv'.*
      there-she-threw-it   behind   the   right   there-he-was-standing
      'She threw it right back where he was standing.'

(97) W. *Kę̨* *eⁿdí'* *ahátǫme'.*
      very   much   he-is-tired
      'He is very tired.'

(98) W. *Kę̨* *nę̨'* *hatenę̨díhcę̨'.*
      just   now   he-will-be-through
      'He is almost through.'

(99) C. *Tho* *ki'* *nhǫ́:weh,* *ha'teyǫkwátatkę̨:*
      there   just   place   there-we-have-seen-each-other
      'That is just where we met.'

(100) C. *N' ethó   ki'   niyáw' ęoh.*
           the-there   just   so-it-happened
           'That is just how it happened.'

(101) Oe. *Yah   thau:tú: ki'   wi: a:yako:tá:we'.*
            not   possible   just   could-she-go-to-sleep
            'She just could not go to sleep.'

(102) M. *E'   thó   ki'   na'á:wv'ne'.*
           there   there   just   so-it-happened
           'And that is just what happened.'

(103) M. *Nv́   ki'   vkahtv́:ti'.*
           now   just   I-will-leave
           'Now, I think, I'll just start right out.'

The resemblances between the languages could represent a common Proto-
Northern-Iroquoian inheritance, but this cannot be determined rigorously. (The
difference in the vowels could indicate two original particles, *kę' > T. kv', W.
kę',* and *ki' > C.–Oe.–M. ki',* or they could be divergent realizations of a
longer sequence, such as *kai.* [PNI *a + *i > ę]. Normally initial *k is lost in
Wyandot before vowels, but the nonexistence of the expected form W. *i' could
be explained simply as avoidance of an unstable shape. In any case, the brevity
of the forms significantly raises the possibility of chance resemblance.)

The Lake languages share other emphatic particles, *kwah* and *akwah*, 'really',
'just', 'very'.

(104) W. *Dę kwa   wá'tanęsti.*
           greatly   she-is-small-and-pretty
           'She is really small and pretty.'

(105) S. *Næ: kwa: hi:kę́:   hoyá'tasha:yęh.*
           just   really   this   his-body-was-slow
           'He was really moving very slowly.'

(106) S. *Akwás   ne' hoh   niyáwę'ǫh.*
           really   that   so-it-happened
           'This is how it really happened.'

(107) C. *Thę́'   kwáhs   t'eǫkhniwayęnę́t'aǫh.*
           not   really   have-we-two-finished
           'We didn't quite finish.'

(108) C. *Thę́'   akwáhs   tho   ni:yǫ́:   t'eakhwihstáę'.*
           not   really   there   so-much   do-I-have-money
           'I don't have quite enough money.'

(109) Oe. *Nv   se'   kwah   kv'   nihv:náhse:*
            now   just   really   so   they-are-large
            'Now they are quite big.'

(110) Oe. *Wá:lelhe,*   *latkv'sé:na'*   *kwí:*   *ka'ikv*   *náhte'*   <u>*akwáh*</u>   *ka'ikv́*
he wanted   he-go-see   this   what   exactly   this

        nityotyelv́.
        so-it-happens
        'He decided he'd go and see exactly what was happening.'

(111) M. <u>*Kwah*</u>   *í:kv*   *tsi*   *rotiháhes.*
        really   it-is   so   their-road-is-long
        'Their road was truly long.' (Truly was their road long.)

(112) M. *Ka'nyuhsákta'*   *nú:we*   *nvhatikwè:tarv'*   <u>*kwáh*</u>   *se's*
        near-the-nose   place   where-they-will-cut   just   then

        yá:kv'.   *nè:ne*   *a:yohnatirúhthake'.*
        they-say   which   it-would-be-pulling
        'Near the nose, they say, is a place which is just like rubber.'

Seneca and Cayuga share a hedge *thó:ha* 'almost' from *tho* 'there', 'that' plus a diminutive.

(113) S. *O:né*   <u>*tho:há*</u>   *ękaniya:yę'.*
       now   almost   it-will-snow
       'It was about to snow.'

(114) C. *O:né*   *hne:'*   <u>*thó:ha*</u>   *hękahé:'*   *ękyahtę:ti'*
       now   this   almost   there-will-it-set   we-two-will-leave
       'It is almost time for us to leave.'

They also share an emphatic use of **tshǫ:* 'just', 'only'.

(115) S. *Hętshe:á'*   <u>*shǫ:h.*</u>
       you-will-take-her-back   just
       'You just take her right back!'

(116) C. *Tatsí:ha*   *kę́:s*   <u>*tshǫ:*</u>   *i:só'*   *atkhehtowé:nye:'.*
       short-time   customarily   just   much   I-stir-dirt
       'In just a little while I can work up the dirt (plough).'

Additional hedges exist in most of the languages, but they do not appear to be cognate across languages.

Probability

All of the languages have particles which qualify certainty, in many cases matching hedges on precision or conditionals. (As in T. *arvh* 'about', 'maybe', 'if', C. *kyę:kwa'* 'maybe', 'if', M. *toka'* 'about', 'if'.) These are generally not cognate cross the languages, although the Eastern languages Oneida and Mohawk share several.

(117) Oe. * Kv́:tho   ki'   <u>uhte</u>   wi: a:kláthv'   kalutá:ke.*
this   just   perhaps I-should-climb   tree-on
'I guess I will climb this tree here.'

(118) M.   *Rawé:ras   <u>úhte'</u>   thí:kv   ró:ne'   wa'etshí:kv'.*
he-thunders   perhaps   that   his-wife you-saw-her
'Perhaps you saw the Thunderer's wife.'

(119) M.   *Tá:ni'ts   <u>úhte'</u>   thó   yá:yv.*
might-as-well perhaps there there-she-should-go
'Well, maybe she should go.'

(120) Oe. *Ta:t   <u>nuwa'</u>   ne: tyoyánle'.*
perhaps maybe   that   it-is-good
'Maybe it would be best.'

(121) M.   *Kati'   <u>nú:wa'</u>   a:yetshyatera'swá:wi'.*
perhaps   maybe   she-might-have-given-you-luck
'She might have given you good luck.'

(122) Oe. *Nv   <u>kati'</u>   vtkatáhsawv'   vkahtahkú:ni:.*
now   maybe   I-will-begin   I-will-shoe-make
'Now, I guess, I'll start to make some shoes.'

(123) M.   *<u>Kati'</u>   né: wa'è:ru?*
perhaps   that   she-said
'Perhaps that is what she said?' ('Is that what she said?')

A Tuscarora particle resembles these but is not cognate, since *t* becomes *'n* in
Tuscarora before vowels. The cognate form is *kweniʔ* 'possible'.

(124) T.   *<u>Kweti'</u>   v'nyuríhvh   atsi'áh.*
maybe   it-will-boil   a-little-bit
'Maybe it will boil a little.'

Although all of the other languages contain additional particles which qualify the
probability of statements, they are not cognate.

Expectation

The Lake languages all contain particles indicating correspondence to expectation. One set is derived from a verb *-tokęh-* 'be certain'. It remains only as a
full predicate in Wyandot (see 53), but has spawned particles in all of the Inner
languages which indicate that a statement is both true and in accord with
expectation.

(125) S.   *<u>To:kę́s</u>   akekwe:nyǫ́:   ękǫ:ké's   ne*
sure   it-is-possible-for-me   I-will-find-for-you   the

yeksá'ko:wa:h.
she-child-large

'Yes, I will certainly be able to find a beautiful girl for you (as you suggested).'

(126)   C.   *To:kẹhs   a'akowi:yáẹta'.*
sure   she-came-to-have-a-baby
And, sure enough, she did have a baby.'

(127)   Oe.   *Tó:kvske'*
'Yes, that is true.' (in response to a tag question, such as 'isn't it?')

(128)   M.   *Tó:ske.*
'It sure is.' (in response to a tag question)

Another emphatic particle pointing to expectation can be reconstructed for the Inner languages: *wahi'/*wahe' 'in fact'.

(129)   S.   *Wai   he   niyáwẹ'ọh.*
in-fact   what   how-it-happened
'This is in fact how it happened.'

(130)   Oe.   *Wa'utu:kóhte'   ki'   wah.*
she-passed   just   in-fact
'Indeed, she kept right on going.'

(131)   Oe.   *I: wahe.*
I–EMPH.   in-fact
'In fact, I am.'

(132)   Oe.   *Nv   kwi   wa'thoyá:tahkwe'   vhatnehwahni:nú:te'   ki'*
now   just   he-body-picked-up   he-will-skin-sell   just

wahe.
in-fact
'And in fact, he did pick him up to sell his hide.'

(133)   M.   *Ó:nv   wáhi'   wa'utkáhtho'   ne   rawvhé:yu.*
then   in-fact   she-looked-at   the   he-is-dead
'Then in fact she did look at the dead man.'

(134)   M.   *Nyó: ki'   wáhe'   suke'nikúhrhv.*
gosh   just   in-fact   my-mind-set-again
'Gosh, as a matter of fact, I completely forgot.'

Otherwise, particles indicating expectation generally do not match from language to language. Wyandot and Cayuga have particles indicating contrast with expectation which may or may not be related.

(135)   W.   *Haká'tra'   ihcẹ'   hu'kiyọ:ruwá:nẹ.*
he-ventures   it-is-so   his-mind-is-great
'He is in fact daring and clever after all.' (He has just surprised us with his good performance on a test.)

(136) C. *Nę̀:,   thęnenǫkyé's   sé'*.
          look   they-are-here
          'Look, they are here after all.'

(The Wyandot *ihcę̀'* suggests a source **ihsę̀'* or **sę̀'*..)

Cayuga has another particle which indicates contrast with expectation, *nǫne:'*. This could be related to the Proto-Lake **nǫ:* plus the deictic *ne:'* 'it is this which', 'this is what . . .'.

(137) C. *Aǫsaǫtí'   nǫne:'*.
          it-rained   in-fact
          'It did too rain.'

(138) C. *Thę̀'   kyę̀:'   nǫne:'   ní:'   kwa'yǫ́'   t'ekę̀:*.
          not   this   you-know   I   rabbit   not-is-it
          'I'm no rabbit, you know.' (So stop trying to feed me lettuce.)

Other particles marking expectation of probability are not cognate from one language to the next.

Due to their brevity, tracing the source of Iroquoian particles in general can be only speculative at best. As the preceding section has shown, however, the languages vary strikingly in their repertoires of evidential particles. Tuscarora has only a handful, while Cayuga has well over fifty, and the other languages range between these extremes. Most of the evidential particles in use in the modern languages cannot be traced back to Proto-Northern-Iroquoian. Only one, **kę'/*ki'* 'just' appears possibly reconstructable for PNI. A few can be tentatively reconstructed for Proto-Lake-Iroquoian, **a:yę:'* 'it seems', the inferential **nǫ:* 'I guess', and the emphatic **kwah/*akwahs* 'really', 'very', 'just'. More evidential particles can be reconstructed for Proto-Inner-Iroquois. In addition to the experiential, inferential, and emphatic particles cited above, the quotative **yá:kę'* 'it is said', the probability marker **-tokęh-* 'sure', and the marker of expectation **wáhe'/*wáhi'* 'in fact' can be posited for PII. In addition to these, the Western languages share the qualifiers **thó:ha* 'almost' and **tshǫ:* 'just', 'only'. The Eastern languages, slightly more closely related, share as well the probability markers **úhte'* 'perhaps', **nú:wa'* 'maybe', and **káti'* 'maybe'. Each of the languages contains additional unique evidential particles which appear in none of the others.

The particles are clearly the least stable of the evidential devices. In a number of cases, changes involving particles can be observed in operation in the modern languages. Specific clusters of two or more particles have often taken on various idiomatic senses which vary from one language to the next. Languages with different internal and external sandhi rules show wavering treatment of such clusters. In Cayuga, for example, glottal stops metathesize to the left in all odd-numbered syllables except final ones. A monosyllabic particle like *ki'* 'just', for example, retains its glottal stop word–finally because the first syllable is also the last. When combined with *shęh* 'how', however, the particle retains its individual form in slow speech but exhibits metathesis in fast speech: *k'ishęh* 'perhaps'. Speakers are unsure of word boundaries in such clusters, although they tend to feel strong bonds between the elements and favor joining them in writing. Such ambivalent status of incipient clusters is apparent in the other languages as well. In addition, a number of particles, such as Cayuga *tshǫ:* 'just', and *ǫ* 'presumably' appear to be becoming ever more closely bound phonologically to the predicates they modify, pointing toward incipient morphologization.

At the same time, all of the languages exhibit synchronic loss of syllables from verbs to form particles, and from bisyllabic particles to form monosyllabic ones. Some speakers are aware of both long and short forms, while others are no longer aware of the longer ones. Such a loss can be seen in the particles derived from PII **kató:kę:* 'it is certain, true, specific, exact'. The verb remains in its full form in all of the Lake languages (W. *yatù:yę́h* S. *kato:kę:h*, C. *kató:kę:*, Oe. *kato:kv* M. *kató:kv*). In the Inner languages, however, the pronominal prefix **ka-* 'it' has also been dropped to form a particle (S. *to:kęs*, C. *tó:kęhs*, Oe. *to:kv́ske'*, M. *tó:ske/tó:kvske* 'sure enough').

THE RELATIVE STABILITY OF EVIDENTIAL AFFIXES, PREDICATES, AND PARTICLES

The three types of evidentials in Northern Iroquoian differ significantly in their stability. Nearly all of the forms of the morphological evidentials have remained intact in all of the languages, as have most of their functions.

The predicate evidentials show somewhat less stability than the affixes, although the majority have remained in most of the languages. This is not surprising. While the affixes constitute a closed set, the predicates are part of an open set, subject to the same accidents of lexical replacement as the rest of the vocabulary. Because they are generally closer to the core of the lexicon, more frequently used and less culturally sensitive than some other words, they are among the more stable of lexical items. Their patterns of retention accurately mirror the history of the family. The most closely related languages share the most evidential predicates, while the more distantly related languages share somewhat fewer.

The evidential particles, on the other hand, show much greater volatility than either the affixes or the predicates, both in form and function. Where particles appear equivalent between languages, they often do not exhibit regular sound correspondences, and apparently similar forms often differ in function from language to language. The evidential particles mirror most dramatically the different degrees of relationship among the languages in the family. The most closely related languages share many, but by no means all of their evidential particles. As degree of relationship diminishes, proportions of shared particles decrease sharply, until, in the case of the most distantly related languages, almost none are cognate. Repertoire and use of particles are in fact among the most salient ways in which the Northern Iroquoian languages differ among themselves.

It is not immediately obvious why evidential particles should be so much less stable than predicates, however, since both constitute open lexical sets. Several facts suggest an explanation. The frequent combination of evidential particles into long strings suggests that they must perform a function beyond simply specifying the degree of reliability of an utterance, which could often be neatly accomplished with a single, well chosen verb or particle. People credited with reputations as eloquent speakers tend to use more such particles, and more frequently, than less admired speakers. There is enormous speaker variation in choice and frequency of use. Furthermore, the particles seem in some ways to have low salience to speakers. If a speaker slows down for clarity or dictation, or writes out a text longhand, the particles tend to disappear. Teachers tend to omit them when teaching these languages to children or adults whose first language is English. Speakers are almost uniformly at a loss to translate most of them.

The distribution of the particles in discourse is quite interesting. As might be expected, they tend to cluster around specific statements which speakers would like to hedge, such as direct quotations or measurements. They tend to occur in very long strings particularly before shifts in topic, or around elements of high communicative value to the discourse. Their effect on the rhythm of information transmission is striking; they allow the speaker time to collect thoughts at moments of the greatest choice. In addition to facilitating the performance of the speaker, they contribute to the effectiveness of the communication. They allow the speaker to regulate the flow of information so as to be most easily and readily understood by the hearer. If too many short, highly important units of information were to occur in rapid succession, a hearer might not be able to take them in all at once with their proper force. Strings of particles permit the speaker to arrange important information such that it arrives at proper intervals.

Proper rhythm can also affect the hearer's willingness to listen. Plunging into a sentence can be considered brusque. The particles can soften the force of a communication. Consider this sentence:

(139) M. *Khé:rv   kati'   kv́   nekwá: yà:ke'.*
           I-believe maybe   there side   there-I-go
           'Well, I might as well go on over there, I guess.'

The first two words are optional as far as propositional content goes. Speakers report, however, that if one or, worse, both were removed, the sentence would suggest disgust and dissatisfaction. The same is true of this Cayuga answer to the question, 'What are you doing?'

(140)   C.   *A:yę́:'   ki'   hne:'   thę́'   kwáhs   ską́ho'tę́'*
              it-seems   just   this   not   really   anything
              'Oh, nothing much, I guess.'

The speaker knows exactly what he is doing, but the bare facts, *thę́' ską́ho'tę́'*
'nothing' would be an impolite, brusque answer.

Now in most cases, strings of evidential particles tend to be mixed with
deictic particles. The deictic particles occur, in fact, much more frequently than
is necessary to keep reference straight. Interestingly, Tuscarora, which exhibits
fewer and rarer evidential particles than the other languages, exhibits correspondingly more deictic particles in discourse.

(141)   T.   *U:nv́ha'   kayetá:kre',   vkwehv̀:weh,   kyé:ní:kv: kyè:ní:kv:*
              long-ago   they-dwell   real-people   this   this

              kv̀:ne'   kwè:ni',   kayetá:kre'   hè:ní:kv: nekaku'tikvkà:rv́hrv.
              here   near   they-dwell   that   their-minds-down
              'Long ago, the Indians living near here were depressed.'

The deictic particles in all of the languages have the same secondary function as
the evidential particles. They allow the speaker time to compose the utterance
and permit an arrangement of information so that the hearer can process it most
effectively. The use of evidential particles is thus more than a function of their
evidential role. Their diachronic behavior is also a result of their form as
particles.

The form of a linguistic marker can, then, have a significant effect on its
resistance to change over time. The hierarchy of stability of evidential devices
can be summarized as follows:

STABLE←AFFIXES————PREDICATES————PARTICLES→VOLATILE

REFERENCES

Barbeau, Marius. 1960. Huron–Wyandot traditional narratives in translations and native texts.
    (National Museum of Canada, Bulletin 165, Anthropological Series, No. 47.) Ottawa: Na-
    tional Museums of Canada.
Chafe, Wallace L. 1967. Seneca morphology and dictionary. (Smithsonian Contributions to An-
    thropology, Vol. 4.) Washington: Smithsonian Institute.
————. 1981a. Integration and involvement in speaking, writing, and oral literature. Spoken and
    written language: Exploring orality and literacy, ed. by Deborah Tannen. Norwood, NJ:
    Ablex.
————. 1981b. Differences between colloquial and ritual Seneca, or how oral literature is literary.
    Reports from the survey of California and other Indian languages, No. 1, ed. by Alice
    Schlichter, Leanne Hinton, and Berkeley: Department of Linguistics, University of
    California.
————, and Michael K. Foster. 1981. Prehistoric divergences and recontacts between Cayuga,
    Seneca, and the other Northern Iroquoian languages. *IJAL* 47:121–142.

Lounsbury, Floyd G. 1953. Oneida verb morphology. (Yale University Publications in Anthropology, No. 48.) New Haven: Yale University Press.

Michelson, Karin. 1981. Three stories in Oneida. (Canadian Ethnology Service, Paper No. 73. National Museum of Man, Mercury Series.) Ottawa: National Museums of Canada.

Mithun, Marianne, and Hanni Woodbury. 1980. Northern Iroquoian texts. (IJAL Native American Text Series, 4.) Chicago: University of Chicago Press.

Woodbury, Hanni. 1980. Cohesive and grammatical functions of selected Onondaga particles. Paper presented at the Annual Meeting of the American Anthropological Association, Washington, D.C., November, 1980.

SEVEN

Data-Source Marking in the Jaqi Languages

Martha James Hardman
University of Florida, Gainesville

The Jaqi family of languages, including Jaqaru, Kawki, and Aymara, is spoken in the Andes mountains of Peru, Bolivia, and Chile by approximately three million people. Jaqaru and Kawki are in modern contact, spoken in contiguous valleys in the Yauyos province of Lima, in Peru. Until my own work of the last quarter century there was no history of contact between the Aymara and the Kawki/Jaqaru group. The Kawki language is dying—it is not now the dominant language for anyone and no children are growing up with Kawki as a native language. Jaqaru, on the other hand, although spoken by only some five thousand, is still the first language of the children of Tupe; its demise is not imminent. Aymara, the native language of one-third of the population of Bolivia and of more than half a million in Southern Peru and Northern Chile, is expanding in absolute numbers; there are Aymara linguists, Aymara publications put out by Aymara authors, and a growing enthusiasm for bilingual education among Aymara parents.

Extensive marking of DATA-SOURCE is one of the prime characteristics of the Jaqi family of languages. However, the category was not even recognized in the first four hundred years after the conquest for the apparently simple reason that the specific marks of data-source are not directly translated within the translation tradition which quickly established itself after the conquest. With Spanish as the mediating language to English, there was no translation of the category into English either.

In 1603, Bertonio (p. 326) called the data-source markers 'ornate particles' because 'without them the sentence is perfectly fine'. In 1616, Torres Rubio says that 'some particles there are in this language which serve no other function than to adorn the sentence' (p. 244). Ellen Ross in 1963 (p. 15) calls them 'emphatic suffixes'. In 1965, Juan Enrique Ebbing (p. 360) calls them 'suffixes of adornment and emphasis'. In 1967, Wexler, in the Peace Corps grammar (p. 2), claimed that one of the data source suffixes is an 'OPTIONAL ''subject-object''

113

marker' or 'when attached to . . . a noun, conveys the meaning "to be" '
(emphasis in original). (All translations from Spanish by the author.) Where verb
tenses are involved, the Spanish translations put them into some quite irrelevant
Latin or Spanish category.

This is an amazing record, particularly in light of the talent and training of
some of the authors. This blindness to a critical category has had important
results in terms of cultural contact—to which I return toward the end of the
paper.

Data-source marking is so extensive in the Jaqi languages that it is difficult to
utter ANY sentence without indicating the source of one's information. It is so
pervasive that speakers consider the matter to be part of the nature of the uni-
verse. No informant ever explained data-source to me. As I discovered the
various markings through usage and context, and then checked with an informant, stating my hypothesis, the reaction was, inevitably and unfailingly: 'Well,
of course! Everybody knows that!'—sometimes followed by an insistence that
Spanish was equally marked for data-source information—an example of the
translation tradition leading to mutual misunderstanding.

There are cultural correlates to the grammatical category of data-source; for
this reason, data-source is recognized as a LINGUISTIC POSTULATE (Hardman
1972, 1978) of the Jaqi languages. As a linguistic postulate, data-source often
becomes critical in contact situations.

The specifics of data-source marking differ somewhat from language to language and also within the varieties of the Aymara language. For the purposes of
this paper, examples will be taken from two languages only: Aymara of La Paz,
and Jaqaru. These two are the most divergent of the extant descendants of Proto-
Jaqi. For variations in Aymara see Briggs (1976).

DATA-SOURCE CATEGORIES: AN OVERVIEW

Data-source marking in the Jaqi languages involves elements of evidential marking, of validational marking, and, to a minor degree, of certainty. There are also
elements of speaker and/or addressee involvement, although the major emphasis
is on the channel: whence the information reported in the sentence. Truth value is
not directly involved—i.e., no one data-source is seen to be more 'true' than any
other. However, accuracy on the part of the speaker is a crucial element in the
public reputation of individuals; misuse of data-source is somehow somewhat
less than human, or is insulting to the listener. Truth and certainty are byproducts
of data-source marking, rather than primary ingredients, although source and
certainty may be interwoven. Where there is an option, other postulates (Hardman 1972, 1978), such as humanness and the salience of second person, may
play a role in determining which to use, in which case speaker/addressee involvement with each other and/or the information of the sentence may play a

primary role. The category is here called DATA-SOURCE, however, because this term seems to best cover the kind of situational information first processed by the speaker in uttering any sentence—i.e. how one has knowledge of what one is saying. The term 'evidential' seems too limited given the gamut of types of information used.

In the Jaqi languages data-source is divided into three primary categories:

1.   personal knowledge
2.   knowledge-through-language
3.   nonpersonal knowledge

These categories are variously realized in different languages and within the same language with various grammatical devices.

Personal knowledge is that knowledge acquired by personal experience, through the senses—primarily, but not exclusively, visual. Thus, bodily states, such as hunger, are personal knowledge in the first person, but can never be so for other persons, because the experience is not direct. Recordings with blind persons have not shown any difference in the use of data-source markings.

The matter of direct personal experience is adhered to in what we would consider a very literal way, even to the exclusion of some types of information that we would consider general or received knowledge (these are knowledge-through-language). Courtesy demands very careful adherence, particularly in ascribing internal states to another person—hunger, thirst, pain—which are not knowable by direct observation, but only through inference or report. There are a few exceptions to such literalness; some types of general information may be conveyed as personal knowledge.[1]

(1)   Jaqaru: *Utxutxullquq aq''inw utki.*
              'Elves live in caves.'

The placement of the data-source marker on the place makes an assertion only about where elves live, not their actual existence. Older people mark personal knowledge in these circumstances less than younger people; this usage may indicate a shift under Spanish pressure. Also, future personal knolwedge sentences are used as polite commands to same-generation ritual kin (comadres and compadres), to whom it is forbidden to use an imperative. Men make personal

---

[1] All examples are given in the practical alphabets now in use by the speakers of the languages. '' marks aspiration, ' marks glottalization, *tx* is an alveopalatal stop, *cx* is a retroflex affricate, *q* is a postvelar stop, *nh* is a velar nasal. The actual examples, though collected over many years from many sources, were rechecked for accuracy for this paper with assistants at the University of Florida: Yolanda Nieves Payano Iturrizaga (Jaqaru) and Yolanda Lopez Callo (Aymara). I thank them for their help.

knowledge statements in referring to children as theirs, although they can, of course, know so only through language from women.[2]

Also, some future events can be personal knowledge, the result of looking back over one's shoulder to see what is coming from behind. The future in these languages begins immediately beyond the present moment; if I am standing in the door with one foot out and coat on, I will still use a future.

(2)   Aymara: *Sarxäwa.*
             'I'm going (home).'

Overall, however, the personal knowledge/other knowledge (metaphorically, the seen/nonseen) distinction is held to with uncanny literalness.

Knowledge-through-language is the second major category and includes all knowledge gained through the medium of language. Language is held to be THE distinguishing feature of humanness and plays a large part in the human/nonhuman linguistic postulate (Hardman 1972; Hardman et al. 1975). Hearsay is, of course, part of knowledge-through-language, but only part. All book learning, all that is gained by reading, and all that is gained from listening to speeches or conversations is also knowledge-through-language, not personal knowledge. The Jaqi people have a remarkable ability to repeat conversations verbatim. Part of this results from the standard question to children

(3)   Aymara: *kamsisa*
             'What did they say?'   *'Qué dijo?'*

in circumstances where we would ask about thoughts or feelings. That book learning is knowledge-through-language obviously has an important impact in the educational system. Knowledge-through-language will sometimes be abbreviated as 'thru-lg.'

Nonpersonal-knowledge marking is the third major category of Jaqi datasource, and is appropriate for all situations where witnesses cannot be expected. Nonpersonal knowledge is primarily a remote past and is therefore particularly appropriate for myths, legends, history, and tales of spirit encounters. These forms are also used for surprises: for suddenly encountering a situation already established.

---

[2] However, the grandmothers have a saying:

Jaqaru: *Wallmchinhn qayllp''q allchinhwa.*
         Lluqllnhan qayllp''q qachinilli.

      'Child of my daughter is my grandchild.
      Child of my son, who knows?'

thus reestablishing the primacy of personal knowledge.

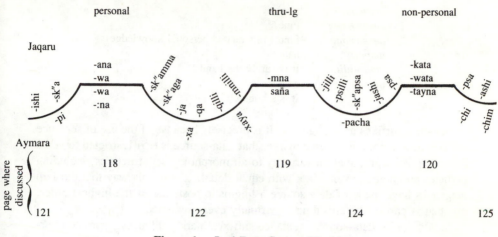

Figure 1. Jaqi Data Source Marking

There are many situations which do not fall into one of the three obligatory, major categories. The Jaqi languages make provisions for these transitional areas by using other markers, which I call WEASELS, in lieu of or in addition to the obligatory mark from one of the three majors. A speaker may opt for one of the transitional forms when (a) the situation is ambiguous, (b) the emotion involved is strong, (c) the personal interaction is the primary motive or focus, (d) there is reluctance to commit oneself, (e) there is a desire to obscure the facts without actually lying. Weasels do not translate well and are almost impossible to elicit directly; sentences with them are not ordinarily straightforward statements of fact. They vary in form and function from language to language and even from speaker to speaker.

The primary data-source categories and the weasels can be ordered on a scale progressing from personal knowledge through knowledge-through-language to nonpersonal knowledge. Figure 1 gives a schematic of the data-source scale in the Jaqi languages.

Primary data-source marking is done by (a) sentence suffixes and (b) verb tenses. The sentence itself is defined in the Jaqi languages by the use of sentence suffixes. A morphological word is a complete structure at the morphological level, and may occur as a free unit, providing the sentence in which it occurs carries a sentence suffix somewhere else. A syntactic word is a morphological word plus a sentence suffix making it possible for the word to occur alone as a sentence. Sentence suffixes may occur on any type of morphological word— noun, verb, or particle. Thus, no specific grammatical structure is required for a sentence to be well-formed, but a sentence suffix is required. Thus, a sentence is a minimum of one morphological word plus a sentence suffix:

Jaqaru:	amrucha	'fine'
	amruchawa	'Fine.'
	amruchaqa	'Fine.' (attenuated personal knowledge)
	ampara	'hand'
	amprajilli	'It is surely the hand.'
Aymara:	uta	'house'
	utawa	'It is a house.'

Sentence suffixes are obligatory. It is precisely because of the use of sentence suffixes as a major data-source marker that data-source is NOT restricted to verbs but is applied with equal universality to all morphological structures, including particles and nouns, even if not with equal detail. It is in this way that the Jaqi languages have made of data-source a linguistic postulate of the highest order, one that is part of the encoding of virtually every sentence.

In addition to data-source, sentence suffixes mark politeness, types of interrogatives, sequencing, and negations.

Within the verb system there are a number of tenses (mutually exclusive inflections involving time, data-source, mode, aspect, realization) which specifically include data-source as part of their basic function.

Other data-source marking may occur with independent suffixes, within the semantic structure, including proverbs, and also within the noun system and the derivational systems, both nominal and verbal.

GRAMMATICAL REALIZATION

Primary Categories

Personal Knowledge. The most straightforward marking of personal knowledge is through the use of the sentence suffix {-wa}, cognate in all of the languages and the primary mark of personal knowledge. {-wa} is used in a sentence without a verb or a sentence with a verb in one of the unmarked tenses.

Jaqaru:	nonverb:	yapuwa
		'It is a field.'
	present:	upaw ut'' illki
		'She sees the house.'
	past:	upaw ut'' illawi
		'She saw the house.'
	future:	upaw ut'' illani
		'She will see the house.'
Aymara:	nonverb:	yapuwa.
		'It is a field.'
	simple:	jupaw ut uñji.
		'She sees/saw the house.'

future: *jupaw ut uñjani.*
'She will see the house.'

Some of the verb tenses include data-source marking as part of their primary function. This occurs most notably in the remote tenses. These tenses are cognate, but at a deeper level, and show greater change since language separation. Examples are given below. The personal knowledge forms of the remote, outside of surprisal use (mostly in the third-to-third person), are appropriately used only by married persons over forty (Hardman 1983, Hardman et al. in press).

Knowledge-through-Language.   In ordinary discourse, these forms are no longer recognized as cognate; they are, however, historically; see below.

Jaqaru has a specific sentence suffix for 'thru-lg'; Aymara uses a quotative embedding.

Aymara: *walikiw sasaw si.*   'O.K., she said.'
                                  'Dice que está bien.'
Jaqaru: *amruchamna.*   'Bien, diciendo dijo.'

The embedding which marks all information gathered thru-lg, whether written or oral, is so frequent in Aymara that its phonological structure is subject to extreme reduction, such that the /sasaw si/ sounds more like a suffix on the quote than a subordinate clause plus a principal clause. Furthermore, {*saña*} 'to say' is the only verb in any of the languages to have irregular forms, and is also incorporated into a verbal interrogative. It is apparently rapidly on its way to either an auxiliary status (an innovation for Jaqi) or a new suffixation.

In Jaqaru, the {*-mna*} suffix marks all information gathered thru-lg, whether written or oral.

Jaqaru: *shumyaq t'ant''q palwimna.*
'They say Shumaya ate bread.'

Jaqaru does have available the embedding syntactic pattern, but does not use it for the ordinary thru-lg data-source. It may be used for a direct quote, and may itself take the {*-mna*} suffix.

(4)   Jaqaru: *Shumyaq t'ant''w paluwt'' sawi.*
'Shumaya said "I ate bread".' (said by someone who heard her say so)

(5)   Jaqaru: *Shumyaq t'ant''w paluwt'' sawimna.*
'They say Shumaya said she ate bread.' (said by someone who was told by someone who heard her say so)

The {*-mna*} suffix in Jaqaru does allow for what might be considered a type of indirect quote, but does not permit the specification of the identity of the source of the information, so that it remains primarily a data-source marker, thru-lg, without specifying the source itself. Aymara allows no indirect quote whatsoever; the option with {saña} embedding is to specify or not specify the source. Jaqaru also does not allow indirect quotes with *saja* 'to say', but only embedding of direct quotes.

In all of the languages, in referring to bodily states of a third person, thru-lg is obligatory unless a form further away on the data-source scale is opted for. Personal knowledge cannot be used.

In Jaqaru, the subordinate form {sashu} (cf. {sasaw} in Aymara) is used for logical entailment following on a statement made by another person, usually translated 'entonces', 'then', and usually occurring in the form /sashuq/. It is frequent in general conversation.

(6)   Jaqaru: *Maktkaswa sashuq.*
                'Then, I'll be going.' (on being told, e.g., that it's getting late)

The thru-lg markers are not used for traditional tales or for ancient history, only for information which could conceivably have come from a live source (including books or written materials).

Nonpersonal-knowledge.   The appropriate form in traditional tales or ancient history is the nonpersonal, which is marked primarily within the verb conjugation. The remote tenses contrast personal with nonpersonal knowledge. The forms are given here in a contrastive paradigm; the personal forms were discussed above. Spanish glosses, as given within the translation tradition of the Andes by both Spanish and Jaqi speakers, are also provided.

        Aymara: *Jupax ut uñjatayna.*
                  'She saw the house.' (nonpersonal)
                  ('Había visto la casa.')

                  Jupax ut uñjäna.
                  'She saw the house.' (personal)
                  ('Estaba viendo la casa.')

Jaqaru adds an additional distinction of relative closeness to now:

        Jaqaru: *Upaq ut'' illkata.*
                  (near nonpersonal remote)
                  'She saw the house.'
                  ('Veía la casa.')
                  (recent past, but I did not see her)

                  Upaq ut'' illwata.
                  (far nonpersonal remote)
                  'She saw the house.'
                  ('Había visto la casa.')

(far past, I did not see her, e.g., in myth or history, or, unexpectedly,
I stumbled on the knowledge)

Upaq ut'' ill<u>kna</u>.
(near personal)
'She saw the house.'
('Estaba viendo la casa.')
(I saw her see it)

Upaq ut'' ill<u>riwna</u>.
(far personal)
'She saw the house.'
('Solía ver la casa.')
(I saw her see it and I'm not young anymore)

The remotes are also used as surprisals.

Jaqaru: *Shumyaq mansan pal<u>wata</u>.*
Aymara: *Shumayax mansan manq'a<u>tayna</u>.*   'Shumaya ate an apple!'

The nonpersonal tense markers are NOT a function of truth or falsity, but a function of data-source.

Secondary Data-Source Marking or Weaseling

If the grammatical structure calls for a data-source marker, then such a marker is obligatory. In all cases, one of the major three may be used; the three obligatory markings cover every grammatical requirement. However, there are many gray areas; a skillful speaker can opt to substitute one of the attenuators in lieu of the frank, blunt, personal/thru-lg/nonpersonal markers already discussed. These weasels are indicated, in a general way, in Figure 1. The weasel markings are harder to discuss and to classify precisely because they are more involved in interaction, in personality, and in style. What follows is a general discussion.

In general, Jaqaru indulges in greater play with sentence suffixes, even to piling up several together. Aymara, on the other hand, has more inflections that can be used for such purposes.

Reconfirmation (data-source greater than -wa).
Aymara:

{*-pi*} *reconfirmational.*   This suffix is usually used when the addressee knows or ought to know, through personal knowledge, the matter referred to as well as the speaker.

(7)   Aymara: *Walik<u>pi</u>.*
              'OK, of course.'

It occurs frequently in combination with {-¨} or { -ya} for emphasis or as an exclamation.

(8) Aymara: *Ukatpiy walitätxtax.*
                'Then you got well.'
                ('Despueś te has sanado.')

Jaqaru:

{-ishi} personal remembrance.   This suffix functions somewhat like the re-confirmational of Aymara. A fact is directly within the personal knowledge of both speaker and hearer, within the personal time line.

(9) Jaqaru: *Mawtawishi.*
                'I remember that you went.'
                ('Claro que te fuiste.')

{-sk''a} contradiction.   This suffix is used to mock another's assertion of personal knowledge with contrary personal knowledge of one's own.

(10) Jaqaru: *Armask''a.*
                'Impossible that it still be night!' (e.g., it's very obviously daytime—
                the sun's up)

Attenuation.   Attenuation of personal knowledge, short of using thru-lg, is done entirely with sentence suffixes and is extremely sensitive to interpersonal interactions. It may be used, for example, to defer to a presumed greater claim to personal knowledge on the part of another. Aymara has, basically, only one sentence suffix used for this purpose, {-xa}, plus its combinations with another sentence suffix, yielding {-xaya} or {-xä}.

{-xa} attenuator.   This suffix is the most frequent in the Aymara language and, when employed with other sentence suffixes in the sentence, plays many roles other than data-source. Alone, it injects a meaning of 'surely' or 'doubt-less', as if there were a possibility of contradiction, although such is not ex-pected. It is the one means of shading within personal knowledge; it is often used when one is unsure of one's witnessing, as in the first example below, where the child speaking is not sure she does recognize the person spoken to.

(11) Aymara: *Iskuylar juttaxa.*
                'You're the one who came to school.'

(12) Aymara: *Uk''amak lurapxituxay.*
                'That's the way they treated me!' ('Así no más me han hecho (una
                maldad)') (They did not, of course, do it in my presence.)

These may be used in other combinations, and thus appear in sentences else-where on the data scale (see especially 'copping out', below).

For Jaqaru the pattern is far more complex, primarily because there are more sentence suffixes and their combinations are more easily allowed.

{-qa} attenuator.   This suffix is cognate with Aymara {*-xa*} and plays much the same role (but see next suffix).

(13)   Jaqaru: *Yanhishmashsruq mawi.*
             'She doubtless went to visit the one who helped us.'

{-ja} surprisal attenuator.   This suffix is used for situations of marginal personal knowledge. It is less definite than {*-wa*} but more than {*-qa*}. Given the distribution, it would appear that at some point in the history of Aymara, the two attenuators fell together; phonological change points in that direction.

(14)   Jaqaru: *Shumyaq t'ant''q palwija*
             'Shumaya indeed ate bread.'
             ('Shumaya sí comió pan.')

(15)   Jaqaru: *Atz'ik suylja*
             'It is doubtless cold whey.'

{-illi}.   By itself this is simply an emphatic and combines readily with the primary data-source sentence suffixes for adding additional detail to data source specification.

{-qilli}.   Personal knowledge but with an edge of doubt, as when being challenged.

(16)   Jaqaru: *Nik''aqill aruwtkasa.*
             'I already spoke earlier.'
             (you think I didn't?)

{-sk''aqa}.   Another attenuator.

(17)   Jaqaru: *Marqayawq''t''sk''aqa.*
             'We all returned (I think).'

{-sk''amna}.   Marks a contradiction of what one believed to be personal knowledge.

(18)   Jaqaru: *Waruwq''kt''sk''amna.*
             I tremble again they say.
             (I thought I was well; I hadn't noticed the return of the illness.)

{-mnilli}.   Hearsay, but with some assertion that this is only second hand rather than, say, third or fourth.

(19)   Jaqaru: *Sakimnilli.*
                 'They say they're talking.'
                 ('Dice que dice.')

Inferential.   In Aymara the inferential is part of the verb inflection, and acts
syntactically much like the remote tenses. It is used for judgments made on
indirect evidence; inferential is an accurate label.

(20)   Aymara: *Jupax ut uñjpacha.*
                 'She sees/saw the house.'
                 (I infer from, e.g. stuff left.)
                 ('Habrá visto la casa.')

The inferential may combine with the future or the remote. In combination
with the inferential the remote is {-¨*na*} and does not further specify data-source.

(21)   Aymara: *Jupax ut uñjpachani.*
                 'She will see the house.'
                 ('Verá la casa.')

(22)   Aymara: *Jupax ut uñjpachäna.*
                 'She saw the house.'
                 ('Estaba viendo la casa.')

It is the appropriate data-source indicator for the third-person bodily states where
the person has not spoken.

(23)   Aymara: *Manq'at awtjpacha.*
                 'She is hungry.'

In Jaqaru the matter is far more complicated, again with sentence suffixes.
However, conceptually, the inferential as a category is weaker and more slippery
than in Aymara. The following examples are listed in approximate order of
strength, the first being the strongest.
   {*-jilli*}.   This is an attenuated inferential, also functioning somewhat like the
Aymara inferential.

(24)   Jaqaru: *Shumyaq palwijilli t'ant''qa.*
                 'Shumaya surely ate bread.'
                 ('Shumaya debió haber comido pan.')

{*-psilli*}.   An inferential functioning much like the Aymara {*-pacha*}, but
marking the more direct side of inference.

(25)   Jaqaru: *Mawipsilli.*
                 'She doubtless left.' (e.g., her books are gone)

{-*sk''apsa*}.   An inferential usually based on past experience.

(26)   Jaqaru: *Qayllkunask''apsa.*
                   'It's most likely the children.'
                   ('A lo mejor los chicos.')

{-*jashi*}.   One more inferential.

(27)   Jaqaru: *Ut illwijashi.*
                   'She surely saw the house.'
                   ('Habrá visto la casa.')

{-*psa*}.   This is the weakest of the inferentials, and in most examples belongs on the other side of nonpersonal. However, particularly for third-person bodily states where the person referred to has not spoken, it corresponds neatly to the Aymara inferential.

(28)   Jaqaru: *Atz'ikipsa.*
                                        'She's cold.'
        Aymara: *T''aypacha.*

Copping Out or Less than Nonpersonal.   Aymara has a specific tense called the 'noninvolver' which sets the speaker outside the realm of responsibility, and thus exonerates the speaker even if there should be personal knowledge.

(29)   Aymara: *Jupaxay ut uñjchixa.*
                   'She sees/saw the house' (but I won't vouch, and don't blame me)

The noninvolver may combine with the future, both remotes, the desiderative, and the remonstrator.

(30)   Aymara: *Jupaxay ut uñjchini.*
                   'She will see the house.'
                   ('Tiene que ver la casa.')

(31)   Aymara: *Jupaxay ut uñjchitayna.*
                   'She saw the house.'
                   ('Había visto la casa.') (third hand)

(32)   Aymara: *Jupaxay ut uñjchïna.*
                   'She saw the house.'
                   ('Estaba viendo la casa.')

(33)   Aymara: *Jupaxay ut uñjchispa.*
                   'She could see the house.'
                   ('Puede ver la casa.')

(34)   Aymara: *Jupaxay ut uñjchisapana.*

'She should have seen the house.'
('Hubiera visto la casa.')

There is also one sentence suffix, which may only co-occur with {-chi}, which is used for that which cannot be known, ever, by personal knowledge.

(35)   Aymara: K''arik''arichim k''arsuskchi.
                   'Maybe the pishtaco got him.'

This suffix, today, is an extreme of nonpersonal knowledge. Not only does the speaker have no direct knowledge, but direct knowledge is, in fact, unobtainable. The 'pishtaco' of the above example is a fat-extractor never seen by his victims. The modern {-chim} appears to be a combination of the modern inflection {-chi} plus the cognate of Jaqaru {-mna} hearsay, still productive in that language (see above). For {-m} the story is reconstructable.

In Aymara, proto suffixes of the shape *-CCV normally reduced to -CV, in this case giving only {-ma}—one more of this form to add to the already half-dozen in the language. Homophony resulting from sound change is acute in Aymara; a number of structures have been affected in the apparent desire to reduce the otherwise unwieldy homophony. In this case the suffix, now reduced to simply /-m/, was enlarged with {-chi-} and simultaneously restricted in occurrence.

The loss of a thru-lg suffix, the Proto–Jaqi ancestor of Jaqaru {-mna} and Aymara {-m}, would leave a considerable gap in the data-source structure outlined for the Jaqi languages. Today there is the obligatory syntactic structure in Aymara which neatly fills the gap and is used in precisely those situations which call for {-mna} in Jaqaru (see above).

Jaqaru has two sentence suffixes which are beyond personal knowledge.

{-psa} guessing. This suffix is usually translated as 'perhaps'. It may be used as a somewhat tenuous inferential or for guesses. The matter reported has not been witnessed.

(36)   Jaqaru: Mawq''ipsa.
                   'She probably left.'
                   ('Tal vez se fué.')

(37)   Jaqaru: Tukshuwipsa.
                   'Perhaps it is done.'
                   ('Tal vez se terminó.')

{-ashi} personal conjectural. The events referred are outside the personal time line of both speaker and hearer.

(38)   Jaqaru: Wajchchawkatanhtqashi.
                   'Maybe just because I am an orphan.'

Summary of Grammatical Realization

In both languages combinations of sentence suffixes and tenses which include data-source allow further specification of data-source. These combinations are frequent, and for some sentence types obligatory.

(39) Aymara: *Jupaxay t'ant' uñjchixa.*
                'She saw the bread.'
                ('Habría visto el pan.')

(40) Aymara: *Jich''ax wajch wajchaxay uñjchïtaya.*
                'Now you'll probably miss them.'

(41) Aymara: *Jupax t'ant' manq'pacha.*
                'She probably ate the bread.'

(42) Aymara: *Shumyaq t'ant''q palwatamna.*
                'They say Shumaya ate the bread.'
                ('Dice que había comido pan.') (It is said, but no one has seen.)

(43) Aymara: *Shumyaq t'ant''q palkanmna.*
                'They say Shumaya ate the bread.'
                ('Dice que estaba comiendo pan.') (X saw, told Y, Y told me)

(44) Aymara: *Shumyaq t'ant''q palwatapsa.*
                'Shumaya doubtless ate the bread.'
                ('Había tal vez comido pan.')

The points along the data-source scale, including both major categories and transitional possibilities, common to all Jaqi languages are:

> reconfirmation of personal knowledge
> PERSONAL KNOWLEDGE
> attenuation
> KNOWLEDGE–THROUGH–LANGUAGE
> inferential
> NONPERSONAL KNOWLEDGE
> copping out

The marking is common to all sentences through the device of sentence suffixes. Markers are obligatory in the remote tenses as well as some others, and in some syntactic patterns.

Personal knowledge and nonpersonal knowledge markers are cognate; thru-lg is historically cognate with recognizably cognate patterns even today. Some elements of the transitional marking are cognate (e.g. {*-qa/-xa*}); others are specific to the language involved.

TEXT DISTRIBUTION

Data-source in the Jaqi languages is both syntactic and paradigmatic. It is syntactic in that it is distributed according to sentence, or even discourse, requirements.

This is particularly true of the additive functions of various data-source markers, in their optional selection for courtesy reasons, and particularly in the use of the secondary marks. It is paradigmatic in verb conjugations and in sentence types.

Distribution in Sentences

Data-source markers occur in both main and subordinate clauses, in all languages. In Jaqaru subordinate clauses may be inflected to mark data-source; two of the forms of subordinates in Aymara, {-sa/-sina}, may, in some varieties of Aymara, contrast on the data-source scale. In general, however, data-source in subordinate clauses is marked primarily with sentence suffixes.

(45)   (Jaqaru)   *Uknurna jayrkatapna nakshuwata.*
                  'While they were dancing inside, (the rabbit) burned them.'
                  (Both subordinate and main clauses inflected for nonpersonal.)

(46)   (Jaqaru)   *Mamchanhshqa utkinhanwa kasarwajt''a.*
                  'While I was living with my mother, I married.'
                  (personal knowledge; subordinate marked with -*wa;* main inflected for personal)

(47)   (Aymara)   *Lapis alasaw, wawar churi.*
                  'Buying a pencil, she gave it to the child.'
                  (subordinate carries -*wa,* marking entire sentence as personal)

With the exception of *saña/saja* embedding, the sentence-defining suffixes, like {-*wa*}, in all of the languages occur only once per sentence, regardless of the number of subordinate clauses. In *saña/saja* embedding the data-source marks inside the quote need not agree with those outside.

Two successive clauses may be differently marked. Where the subordinate is inflected the two clauses may be at different points on the scale, but this is generally avoided for stylistic reasons.

(48)   Jaqaru: *Disprisiwp''w yakkutu wajchchawkatanhtqashi.*
                 'They give me their scorn (personal), maybe just because I am an orphan (guessing).'

More frequently the two clauses of coordinated sentences are marked for different points on the data-source scale.

(49)   Jaqaru: *Shumyaq walnaqaw lluqaylljw, manh chujllup''mna niwnkata*
                 'Shumaya ran after the lad (personal knowledge); they say he was stealing corn.'
                 (thru-lg with nonpersonal surprisal)

The particular syntactic structure to which the mark is attached can indicate those various portions as belonging to different points on the scale.

(50) Jaqaru: *Shinkawkanmna*.
'They (A) said they (B) were drunk.' (A has personal knowledge of B but the speaker does not)

(51) Jaqaru: *Shinkawkanwa sawija*.
'They (A) must have said "they (B) were drunk"'. (A has personal knowledge of B but the speaker is not sure of the quote.)

(52) Jaqaru: *Shinkawkanwa sawimna*.
'They (A) say that they (B) said "they (C) were drunk".' (B has personal knowledge of C, but the news has traveled through several hands (at least A) before reaching the speaker.)

A few types of sentences may omit data-source marks, e.g. flat imperatives to someone that one has the right to order about (parent to child, for example).

(53) Jaqaru: *Ujtma.*
                   'Come!'
Aymara: *Jutam.*

Paradigmatic Distribution

Data-source is paradigmatic in verb conjugations, as is most clearly seen in 3 → 3 person.

Jaqaru:	*paluwi*	'ate'	('comió')
	palkna	'ate'	('estaba comiendo')
	palkata	'ate'	('comía')
	palwata	'ate'	('había comido')
Aymara:	*manq'i*	'eats/ate'	('come/comió')
	manq'äna	'ate'	('estaba comiendo')
	manq'pacha	'ate/eats'	('está comiendo')
	manq'atayna	'ate'	('había comido')
	manq'chi	'ate/eats'	('habrá comido')

Data-source is also paradigmatic in that it participates in the sentence suffixes that occur once per sentence, and that form a paradigm of contrasting sentence types.

Jaqaru:			
Qamishasa.	'How is X?'	('¿Cómo está?')	(information interrogative)
Amruchatxi.	'Is X well?'	('¿Está bien?')	(yes/no interrogative)
Amruchawa	'X is well.'	('Está bien.')	(personal knowledge)
Amruchamna	'X is well, they say.'	('Dizque está bien.')	(thru-lg.)
Aymara:			
Kamisasa.	'How is X?'	('¿Cómo está?')	(information interrogative)

Walikiti̱.	'Is X well?'	('¿Está bien?')	(yes/no interrogative)
Walikiwa̱.	'X is well.'	('Está bien.')	(personal knowledge)

Sentences referring to body states also form a paradigm by person. (In all cases the grammatical form is body state as subject, human as object, the grammatical persons being 3→1, 3→2, 3→3.)

	Jaqaru	*Aymara*	
1st person	*Yamkutuwa̱.*	*Manq'at awtjituwa̱.*	'I'm hungry'
2nd person	*Yamktamtxi̱.*	*Manq'at awtjtamti̱.*	'Are you hungry?'
3rd person	*Yamkimna̱.*	*Manq'at awtjit si̱w.*	'She said she's hungry.'
3rd person	*Yamkipsa̱.*	*Manq'at awtjpacha̱.*	'She's hungry.'

The last two contrast as to whether the person has spoken or not, or can; the last one is used, for example, with babies. Person may occur with a marker further to the right on Figure 1 than those illustrated above, but NOT with one further to the left.

Since interrogatives are marked by their own sentence suffixes, as seen in the paradigms above, they may be said to be part of the data-source paradigm in that they state specifically that the speaker does not have the information.

Discourse and Narrative Distribution

No discourse or narration is free from the obligation of data-source marking, not even written materials.

Placement of data-source mark within the sentence may indicate which item is being specifically linked to preceding textual material. For example, the placement of {-*wa*} will indicate the specific new piece of information being asserted, in answer to the question, underlying or explicit.

Jaqaru	*Aymara*	
Na̱w linkwistawt''qa.	*Na̱w linkwistätxa.*	'I̱ am a linguist.'
Na̱q linkwistawt''wa	*Nax linkwistätwa̱.*	'I am a linguisṯ.'

Interrogatives may not contain a second sentence-defining suffix, such as {-*wa*}. However, data source may be marked in interrogatives by (a) use of data-source verb inflections, (b) use of *saña* embedding, (c) use of attenuation, (d) use of inferentials. Because interrogatives may also be used to soften an otherwise blunt situation, such combinations are not rare (Hardman 1966; Hardman et al. in press).

The remote tenses are used, frequently, as surprisals. For obvious reasons, the nonpersonal remotes are by far the most frequent. The personal are only appropriate if one stumbles over something one has known before but forgotten, e.g. where one put one's lunch. There are no restrictions on the persons that may occur in surprisals. The usage has influenced Andean Spanish (see below),

(54)   Aymara: *Akankaskataynaw.*
                        'So here they are!'

(55)   Jaqaru: *Antz laqwatawa.*
                        'This is ugly!'

The skillful and accurate use of the data-source discourse devices at their command is highly esteemed by the Jaqi peoples; minimum competent use is a prerequisite to a claim to human status. Full study of discourse use will also entail a critical literary study.

DATA-SOURCE IN OTHER SUBSYSTEMS

A full study of data-source marking would require a full study of the entire grammar, including style, discourse, and oratory, all in great detail. Some allusions were made earlier to various aspects of the interplay of other features with data source and of the pervasiveness of this category in the Jaqi languages.

Subordinate verb inflections agree in part and/or may mark an entire sentence by data-source.

(56)   Jaqaru: *Wakir utkatapna, wakap" ik"arpaypanqa, wakaq jayptawi.*
                        'When she was a cowherder, when she was out herding her cows, the cows got
                            lost.' (remote nonpersonal, marked in subordinate)

In Aymara verb derivationals, the beneficiary is personal knowledge; the 'victimary' (or maleficiary) is nonpersonal.

(57)   (Aymara)   *T'ant' churarapiwa.*
                        'She gave her bread for him.'

(58)   (Aymara)   *T'ant'ap churaraqiwa.*
                        'She gave his bread to her.' (he didn't know about it, and is thus victimized)

Other verbal derivationals may alter to some degree the data-source marks involved. In causatives the agent is marked partially in accord with data-source.

The independent suffixes in Aymara are heavily involved in data-source nuances, in some ways acting like some of the Jaqaru sentence suffixes. For example, {-raki} as an objector resembles {-sk"a} in its use.

(59)   Aymara: *Parlxaraktasä.*
                        'But you already speak Aymara!' (even if you say you don't)

In all verb conjugations, second person, which is characteristically over-marked, interplays with data-source. Some noun root subclasses have data-source implications. Some noun suffixes reinforce personal knowledge, others negate it. Particularly important is the suffix {-jama} 'like', which may, when acting as a data-source marker, even behave as an independent suffix or a sentence suffix, co-occurring with verbs in a limited way.

(60) Aymara: *Asnux t'aqshuchjamarakitaynasa.*
         'It looks like that donkey broke loose from the stake.'

(61) Jaqaru: *Cxunhk watjama.*
         'I believe around ten years.' (noun sentence)

         Ujtwatjamaqa.
         'I believe she has arrived.' (verb sentence)

A number of particles have functions primarily associated with data-source, e.g. Jaqaru {*jalli*} 'I don't know', Aymara {*inasa*} 'maybe' when occurring with the noninvolver, Aymara {*chiqat*} acting as reinforcer, Jaqaru {*ichaqa*} also acting as a reinforcer.

(62) Jaqaru: *Jaqit'' arw ichaq laqaq.*
         'To talk about people is ugly indeed.'

Aymara verbalizes forms far more extensively than does Jaqaru; this is directly related to the greater involvement in data-source of verbal inflections in Aymara and of sentence suffixes in Jaqaru.

(63) Aymara: *Qaläpacha.*
                                         'It must be a rock.'
(64) Jaqaru: *Qalajilli.*

Both languages have many other tenses involving mode, aspect, realization, etc. Two tenses, contrary-to-fact present and past, could also be considered to be part of the data-source chain. I have not done so, however, because (a) their primary functions are for wishing (desiderative) and scolding (remonstrative), and (b) they co-occur with sentence suffixes which may reflect any point on the data-source scale.

Some Aymara speaking students of linguistics are now beginning their own studies of some of these aspects of Aymara. Those are indeed studies to look forward to if we are to understand the scope of data-source marking in the Jaqi languages.

CULTURAL CORRELATES

The pervasiveness of data-source in the language is paralleled by a similar pervasiveness in the culture. Children are corrected immediately if they make a data-source error. There are even relevant proverbs with which they are taught:

Aymara: *Uñjasaw ⟨uñjt⟩ sañax, jan uñjasax jani ⟨uñjt⟩ sañakiti.*

'Seeing, one can say "I have seen", without seeing one must not say "I have seen".'

Jaqaru: *Illush arma, ish illshuq jan artatxi.*
'Seeing, speak; without seeing, do not speak.'

These proverbs are also used in disputes, to impugn the statements of the adversary.

Those who come into the community from outside and state as personal knowledge (i.e. with unmarked verbs and {-*wa*} or in Spanish with tenses corresponding to the simple and future) facts which they know only through language (e.g. things they have read in books) are immediately categorized as cads, as people who behave more like animals than humans and, therefore, ought to be treated like animals, specifically, through the loss of linguistic interchange. Language is that which is most characteristically human, that which makes people human, and that which is NOT extended to animals.

Outside helping agencies have run into this barrier in a big way. It is extremely difficult for Jaqi speakers to believe that it is possible to have a language without data-source, a fact that has helped to contribute to the universal blindness spoken of earlier. Why tell someone something they already know, and are just too animal-like to wish to observe? Every Aymara assistant we have had at the University of Florida has insisted that surely English speakers do mark data-source; if it is not overt, then at least it must be 'understood' somehow. It always takes a good deal of persuasion and illustration to lead to the belief that we really are not lying when we use an unmarked sentence to relate material we have not personally experienced. (As when I might say, 'Whorf was the student of Sapir'—'No, I did not know them,—but no, I am not lying,—and no, I don't have to say that I read it.' Sometimes I think we never quite succeed in the endeavor. Even when the point is intellectually grasped, it is still difficult to act upon at all times. To some degree we find ourselves having to adjust our English.)

Contact and Translation

The details of the influence of this linguistic postulate of the Jaqi languages on the Quechua languages are still being worked out and will be most significant in the reconstruction of Andean prehistory. On the contemporary scene, the influences on the Spanish of La Paz specifically, and the Andes in general, are clear indeed (Martin 1981a, 1981b; Laprade 1976, 1981). The verbal tense markings have had more influence than the sentence suffixes, although the latter influence is not lacking. The apparently 'empty' (for the Jaqi) pluperfect has simply been co-opted as the nonpersonal-knowledge marker.

(65)   *Había visto la casa.*
'She saw the house.' (nonpersonal or surprisal)

(66)   _Vió la casa._
         'She saw the house (and I saw her see it).'

The translation tradition itself gives the following paradigm:

English	_ate_	_was eating_	_had eaten_
Spanish	_comió_	_comía_	_había comido_
Jaqaru	_paluwi_	_palkna_	_palwata_
Aymara	_manq'i_	_manq'äna_	_manq'atayna_
	(personal knowledge)	(remote personal knowledge)	(nonpersonal knowledge)

The use of the pluperfect is the most clear case of direct influence and the most startling for Spanish speakers of other areas (Martin 1981). In addition, however, another data-source distinction which exists, perhaps somewhat tenuously, in other areas is made clear, and cut and dried, in the Andes.

(67)   _Vendré._
         'I will come (maybe, but don't wait for me).' (nonpersonal)

(68)   _Voy a venir._
         'I will come (and do wait).' (personal)

The inflected future is frozen as a dubitative; the syntactic future is a committed, personal knowledge future. This contrast also causes misunderstanding for outsiders who think they know Spanish.

These equivalences have become part and parcel of what I call the 'translation tradition' of the Andes, and are felt to be, by both sides, the 'true' translation, thus contributing to a thorough obscuring of the actual grammatical structure involved in the contact situation. Even Spanish speakers from the Andes react with disbelief when Spanish grammarians from other areas explain the 'real' meaning of, e.g., the pluperfect.

Metaphors

In Jaqaru 'to understand' is _ishapa_ 'to hear'; 'to lie' is _yanhqañ arki_ 'to speak in vain'. In Aymara 'to understand' is _amuyaña_ 'to sense, to have in mind'. In both languages to observe data-source is to speak well. It may be noted that lying and truth are not moral issues but aesthetic ones. The metaphors given are related to personal knowledge in that the latter is wider than 'to see'. Indeed, 'to see' _illa_, _uñjaña_ is used itself metaphorically for 'to care for, to look after'. 'To believe' in Aymara is 'to say OK' _iyaw saña;_ Jaqaru has no equivalent. The Aymara construction is mostly found in Protestant texts and may have been a construction developed for that purpose.

Other Observations

Many aspects of Spanish have been influenced in addition to its verb forms. For example, in many areas there has been a retention of the now archaic form *dizque* 'they say' even by Spanish monolinguals. The syntactic correlate is that the Spanish sentence *Shumaya dice que comió pan* is nowhere ambiguous in the Andes; it always means 'it is said that Shumaya ate bread', never what would be the more usual reading elsewhere, 'Shumaya says she ate bread'. Also influenced has been the use of Spanish particles, particularly *pero, siempre,* and *pues,* so that they act like sentence suffixes interacting with data-source (Laprade 1976).

The judgment of the character of an individual rests in part (in large part, at first meeting) on data-source use. For example, if missionaries claims as personal knowledge that Adam ate an apple, then they are seen as trying to put one over on the listeners—claiming to have been present in the garden of Eden. Or, if a Peace Corps volunteer, reading out of a book, claims as personal knowledge that a certain seed will give a good crop, the perception, again, is one of someone trying to deceive. The matter is not one of truth or falsity, but of misuse; not one of morality, but accuracy. By misuse, the misuser is seen as trying to put something over on the listener.

Misunderstanding goes both ways. When a Jaqi speaker is told 'I am from California' and replies, in Andean Spanish or Jaqi, 'You say you are from California', many an outsider feels accused of lying.

There is no weakening of data-source in contact with Spanish, although there are some shifts; rather it is spreading and imposing itself on Spanish, and even on the English of people who work long with Jaqi speakers.

Implications

Because data-source is a linguistic postulate of the highest order in the Jaqi languages and therefore one which they will attempt to impose on those with whom they come in contact, because it is assumed to be part of the natural order (much as Indo-Europeans treat number and gender in contact situations), the spread of data-source marking can be one more tool for the reconstruction of the prehistory of the Andes. Of particular interest is its use in the Quechua languages as a method for detailing the contact between the Jaqi and the Quechua, of prime importance in Andean prehistory.

In applied projects, data-source within the Jaqi languages must be seriously taken into account in the preparation of all bilingual materials and in the preparation of all materials providing information (e.g. agricultural bulletins). As I mentioned in the Introduction, informational materials have been prepared almost entirely without such consideration, leading to their general rejection. I saw one example of this in a primer prepared in summer 1980 by a German linguistic team; the problem is still acute.

In addition to applied projects aimed at the indigenous populations, the influence of this postulate on the Spanish of the area must also be taken into account. Materials prepared for Mexico or Puerto Rico, for example, cannot be used without change. Either the writers will be seen as trying to put one over on the readers, or the material will simply not be understood. One Spanish literature professor, a student of mine in Bolivia, found that after understanding the matters explained in this paper he was, for the first time, able to lead his Bolivian university students to an understanding of peninsular literature by explaining the difference between their Spanish and that of the material they were reading— literature they had formerly despised or rejected.

Data-source marking in Jaqi is not an extension or derivative of any other system but is as close to a primitive as we get in language. Some of the markings today are clearly derived from or extensions of forms having other functions, diachronically and/or synchronically. Data-source marking is, however, pervasive and uncompromising, an integral part of the Jaqi world view.

REFERENCES

Bertonio, Ludovico. 1603. Arte y grammatica muy copiosa de la lengua aymara. Rome: Luis Zannetti.
Briggs, Luch. 1976. Dialectical variation in the Aymara language of Bolivia and Peru. Doctoral dissertation, University of Florida.
Ebbing, Juan Enrique. 1965. Gramatica y diccionario aymara. La Paz: Don Bosco.
Hardman, M. J. 1966. Jaqaru outline of phonological and morphological structure. The Hague: Mouton.
————. 1972. Postulado lingüísticos del idioma Aymara. El reto del multilingüísmo en el Peru, edited by Alberto Escobar. Lima, Peru: Instituto de Estudios Peruanos.
————. 1978. Linguistic postulates and applied anthropological linguistics. Memorial volume in honor of Ruth Hirsch Weir. The Hague: Mouton.
————. 1983. Jaqaru: Comendio de la estructura morfológica y fonológica, traducido por Dimas Bautista Iturrizaga. Lima, Peru: Instituto de Estudios Peruanos.
————, ed. 1981. The Aymara Language in its social and cultural context. Gainesville: Florida University Press, Social Science Series.
Hardman, M. J., Juan de Dios Yapita Moya, Juana Vasquez, with Laura Martin, Lucy T. Briggs, Nora England. in press. Compendio de estructura fonologica y gramatical del idioma Aymara ILCA (Instituto de Lenguaje y Cultura Aymara). (not available in English)
Laprade, Richard A. 1976. Some salient dialectal features for La Paz Spanish. M.A. thesis, University of Florida.
————. 1981. Some cases of Aymara influence on La Paz Spanish. In Hardman ed., 1981.
Martin, Eusebia Herminia.
————. 1981a. Data source in La Paz Spanish verb tenses. In Hardman ed., 1981.
————. 1981b. Effect of Spanish tense versus Aymara tense on natural attitudes. In Hardman ed., 1981.
Ross, Ellen M. 1963. Rudimento de gramática Aymara, 2nd Edition. La Paz: Canadian Baptist Mission.
Torres Rubio, Diego de. 1616. Arte de la lengua Aymara. Lima.
Wexler, Paul, ed. 1967. Beginning Aymara: A course for English speakers. Seattle: University of Washington.

EIGHT

Information Perspective, Profile, and Patterns in Quechua

David J. Weber
Huanuco, Peru

The Quechua languages[1] of central Peru generally have three evidential suffixes *-mi, -shi,* and *-chi;* these will be glossed 'direct' (DIR), 'indirect' (IND), and 'conjecture' (CNJ) respectively.[2] The goal of this paper is to raise and possibly answer some questions concerning *-mi, -shi,* and *-chi,* or at least provide descriptive material which makes the questions and answers meaningful. Three major points will be made:

1. *-mi/shi/chi* give a *perspective* on the information of a sentence.[3] By "perspective" I mean such things as how the speaker came by the information (*evidential,* e.g., first hand or second hand), what the speaker's attitude is toward the information (*validational,* e.g., does he regard it as fact/fiction/conjecture . . .), what the speaker intends the hearer to do with the information (e.g., believe it, act on it, doubt it, etc.). The question whether *-mi/shi/chi* are basically evidential or validational is addressed.

2. The relative positions of the so-called "topic" marker *-qa, -mi/shi/chi,* and the verb define a pattern. This pattern gives an *information profile* to the information of the sentence, roughly characterizing the sentence's progres-

---

[1] Quechua is a family of languages widely spoken in western South America. Primary attention is given here to three dialects of the department of Huanuco (in central Peru) represented by the following speakers: Amador Tucto Ramirez (*ATR*) of Marias (province of Dos de Mayo), Lorenzo Albino Moreno (*LAM*) of Matihuaca (province of Ambo), and Teodoro Cayco Villar (*TCV*) and Anastacia Nasario de Figuieredo (*ANF*) of Llacon (province of Huanuco).

[2] These have sometimes combined with other suffixes or postpositions to yield variants (e.g., *-mari* from *-mi+ari*); such combinations are not considered in this paper.

[3] An assumption made here is that the primary unit into which information (to be communicated by speech) is packaged is the *sentence,* where "sentence" is roughly defined as "a finite verb and its subordinates." This covers all sentences except those whose main verb is an implicit copula.

sion from theme (topic, old information) to rheme (comment, focus, new information).
3. Deviating from the normal pattern is a rhetorical device.

INFORMATION PERSPECTIVE

The evidential suffixes are testimony to the caution a Quechua speaker exercises with respect to information. The following are, I believe, true of Quechua culture:[4]

1. (Only) one's own experience is reliable.
2. Avoid unnecessary risk, as by assuming responsibility for information of which one is not absolutely certain.
3. Don't be gullible. (Witness the many Quechua folktales in which the villain is foiled because of his gullibility.)
4. Assume responsibility only if it is safe to do so. (The successful assumption of responsibility builds stature in the community.)

The utility of -mi/shi/chi lies in allowing the Quechua speaker to handily assume or defer responsibility for the information he conveys, thus minimizing his risks while building his stature in the community. With -mi the speaker assumes responsibility, with -shi he defers it (to someone else), and with -chi he indicates that it is not the sort of information for which anyone should be held responsible.

What do -mi, -shi, and -chi mean? For Tarma Quechua, Adelaar (1979:79) says that -mi/shi/chi "indicate the validity of the information supplied by the speaker" and that

-mi "indicates that the speaker is convinced about what he is saying,"
-shi "indicates that the speaker has obtained the information that he is supplying through hearsay,"
-chi "indicates that the speaker's statement is a conjecture."

This characterization is consonant with the majority of cases found in a wide range of dialects. Examples follow from Huanuco Quechua. The gloss sometimes includes the situation (ST) in which the example would be appropriate and the rhetorical force (RF) it would have in this situation.

(1) TCV

Wañu-nqa-paq- $\left\{ \begin{matrix} \text{mi} & \text{(a)} \\ \text{shi} & \text{(b)} \\ \text{chi} & \text{(c)} \end{matrix} \right\}$
die-3FUT-FUT
'It will die.'

ST: a diviner has chewed coca and predicts death

---

[4] Perhaps they are to some extent cultural universals?

(a) said by the diviner
     RF: (I assert that) it will die.
(b) said by someone who brings the diviner's prediction
     RF: (I was told that) it will die.
(c) said in response to the diviner or to the messenger
     RF: (Perhaps) it will die.

(2) TCV

$$\text{Noqa-} \left\{ \begin{array}{l} \text{mi (a)} \\ \text{shi (b)} \\ \text{chi (c)} \end{array} \right\} \text{chaya-:-man} \quad \text{aywar-qa}$$
I   arrive-1-COND   if:I:go-TOP
'I would/could/might arrive, if I were to go.'

(a) ST: In response to person(s) who have expressed doubt as to the speaker's
          ability to make it (e.g. to the top of a mountain)
     RF: (I assert that) I would make it if I were to go.
(b) ST: The speaker knows that someone has said he should able to make it
     RF: (It is said that) I would make it if I were to go.
(c) ST: In response to expressed confidence that the speaker *can* make it,
          when the speaker wants to hedge
     RF: I *might* make it.

(3) TCV

Qam-pis   maqa-ma-shka-nki- $\left\{ \begin{array}{l} \text{mi (a)} \\ \text{shi (b)} \\ \text{chi (c)} \end{array} \right\}$
you-also hit-1OBJ-PERF-2
'You also hit me.'

(a) ST: I saw/felt you hit me (and was conscious)
(b) ST: I was drunk when you hit me, and someone has informed me that you
          hit me
(c) ST: A group of people beat me up, and I think you might have been one
          of them

These examples are consistent with the characterization of *-mi* as information
about which the speaker is convinced, *-shi* as information gained by hearsay, and
-chi as conjecture. I will now consider an alternative analysis.

-mi and -shi are evidentials. The characterization given above has the pecu-
liar property that *-mi* and *-chi* are *validational* (indicating commitment to the
truth of the proposition) while *-shi* is *evidential* (indicating the source of the
information). This gives rise to certain problems: for example, what about information the speaker learns by hearsay but about which he is convinced; would *-mi*
or- *shi* be used? If *-mi* and *-shi* were both of the same type (i.e., either both
evidential or both validational) such problems would not arise. I will argue that
-mi and *-shi* are basically evidential: *-mi* means 'learned by direct experience'

and *-shi* means 'learned by indirect experience (hearsay).' A validational interpretation for *-mi* is often appropriate because of the axiom that direct experience is reliable (and thus one is convinced about it). (4) summarizes these relationships (where the arrow indicates the force of the just-mentioned axiom):

(4)

	EVIDENTIAL	VALIDATIONAL	RESPONSIBILITY
-mi	direct ⟶	convinced	speaker
-shi	indirect	unconvinced	other than speaker

There are various data which support this view:

1: -mi where direct experience is unlikely. According to TCV, 'My mother's grandfather's name was John' is natural with *-shi* but not with *-mi*, even if the speaker is convinced that it is true. This is because with *-mi* it implies that the speaker has met his great grandfather. What is basic for *-mi* is the source of the information (direct experience), not commitment to the truth of what his name was. The same result obtains for a sentence that the speaker does not believe, e.g. 'The moon is made of cheese.' According to TCV this is natural with *-shi,* indicating that the speaker has been informed that the moon is made of cheese. With *-mi,* says TCV, it implies that the speaker has been to the moon.

2: -shi to escape the implication of direct experience. A speaker may use *-shi* when he wishes to escape the implication that he has had direct experience. For example, descriptions of cultural practices and institutions are generally told either with *-mi* or with no marker, but *-shi* is used if the speaker wishes to make explicit that he has not had direct experience. This *-shi* has nothing to do with whether the speaker really believes the information. For example, TCV believes the following but, since he has not experienced it (he seldom chews coca), he uses *-shi*:[5]

(5) TCV (from a description he wrote of coca use)

```
. . . mana   kuka-ta     chaqcha-r    puñu-y-lla-ta-shi          munan
      not    coca-ACC    chew-ADV     sleep-INF-JUST-ACC-IND     they:want

. . . kuka-ta      chaqcharkuptin    balur-nin-pis         sumaq-shi    yurirkun
      coca-ACC     chewing           strength-3P-EVEN      well-IND     it:arises
```

---

[5] For Huaraz (Ancash) Quechua Pantoja gives a similar example in his text on coca chewing (1974:254). In his text on avoiding conception and abortion (number 25), he uses *-shi* throughout except in statements like 'They told me that about them' (line 26) in which *-mi* is used. In Pantoja's eighth text (p. 132) he uses *-mi* for the descriptive parts but *-shi* in cases where he wants to disclaim responsibility for the information, e.g. (line 60–61): '. . . they say that those who do the fiestas (i.e., those who sponsor them) are really good. It takes away their guilt . . .'

'. . . if they don't chew coca, they just want to sleep.
. . . having chewed coca, their strength comes to them.'

The same results obtain where the information is not believed; for example, TCV
has not witnessed nor does he believe the following:

(6) TCV (from a description of burial practice)

Kikin	kasta	armaptin-qa	fiyu	nin.
themselves	family	if:they:bathe-TOP	bad	they:say

Llapan-shi	chay kasta	kaq-qa	wañun.
all:of:them-IND	that family	which:are-TOP	they:die

'They say it is bad for a relative to bathe it (corpse).
All of that family dies (if they do so).'

3: -shi when scope of information is too large. In some cases where *-mi* would
be expected, *-shi* occurs if what would have to be experienced is impossibly
large. For example, in Cayco 1975b (a booklet on Peruvian history) 'Their tools
and things are found throughout Peru' has *-shi* because the author could not
possibly have seen all those things found in all those places.

4: -shi is inappropriate as a direct response. *-shi* is never appropriate when
repeating some information back to the speaker. If *-shi* were basically validational (meaning 'unconvinced'), one might expect it to be used to indicate doubt
concerning what was just said. On the evidential view one would not expect it to
be used in this way, since there is no reason to inform one's interlocutor that
what he has just said was heard second hand.[6]

5: where -mi may be absent. Whereas many speakers use *-mi* in telling
personal narratives, describing procedures, institutions, etc., TCV does not. He
uses *-mi* only where there is some question about the source of the information.
When he reports events in which he was obviously a participant (e.g., a trip to
Lima, an amusing mishap that occurred to him and a cousin, etc.), he regards it
as unnecessary to indicate (by *-mi*) his direct experience.[7] Other speakers demonstrate this tendency to varying degrees. For example, ATR, in telling of going to
see a football game, did not use *-mi* in the parts describing his getting to and from
the game (told in the first person), but he did use *-mi* in describing the events of
other people (companions, players, referees).

Further, TCV does not use *-mi* for "non-events," i.e., happenings not somehow embedded in time. (This is not to be taken as "irrealis" because he does use
-mi with the future tense.) He does not use *-mi* in "how-to-make" texts (how to

---

[6] Note that *-chi* may be used to repeat information back to one's interlocutor.

[7] The only exception is a description of a trip which concludes with *Chaynawllami Limata aywar
imatapis rikashkaakuna* 'In that way-DIR having gone to Lima we saw whatever'; this is the only *-mi*
in the text.

make a basket, weave a poncho, build a house, butcher a sheep), in descriptions of static objects (buildings, pictures), in descriptions of culture (coca chewing, bathing, curing, fiesta administration), or in more narrative descriptions (Holy Week happenings, engagement practice). These have in common that they do not concern actual events (either past, present, or future) but rather hypothetical instances of events. He is speaking/writing on these matters from direct experience (and would defend the accuracy of his descriptions); his non-use of *-mi* in these cases is not because of a lack of commitment to the truth of his claims, but because these are not actual, but hypothetical events.

6: -shi may also be interpreted validationally. *-mi* is often interpreted validationally because one is generally convinced of his own (direct) experience. *-shi* may sometimes be interpreted validationally (meaning 'unconvinced') because one believes much of what he learns indirectly. For example, a speaker (from a dialect in northern Junin) wrote a pamphlet on cultivating pastures. His source of information was an agricultural engineer with whom he had talked at length; consequently the author used *-shi* throughout his pamphlet. Readers apparently interpreted this as the author's lack of commitment to the idea: no one was moved by it to plant a pasture. Such evidence is insufficient justification for analyzing *-shi* validationally. In the same way, one should not, just on the basis of some cases in which *-mi* is interpreted validationally, analyze it in that way since these cases can be explained from an evidential analysis in terms of the axiom that one's own experience is reliable.

These cases support the claim that the fundamental distinction is evidential: what is at issue is not whether the author is convinced that what he is communicating is true or not, but whether or not he learned it by direct or indirect experience.

A word must be said in defence of Adelaar's claim for Tarma Quechua that *-mi* means 'convinced.' In all Ignacio Zarate Mayma's texts in Adelaar (1977:308–407) and in Puente (1972), I have not found a single case of *-shi*. Even though much of the material is far beyond the realm of the teller's experience (including folktales about the fox and the condor), he uses *-mi* throughout. This is because he believes the stories he is telling; for example, he says, 'Even the fox, being very powerful and very clever, died eventually. In the same way today we are very clever and powerful . . . (319).' These facts justify Adelaar's claims for Tarma.[8]

---

[8] To the Huanuco Quechua ear, Zarate's use of *-mi* seems exceedingly incautious with respect to the information he conveys. This suggests that perhaps he is not a member of a Quechua speaking community which values his stature? Such cases are not unknown. For example, TCV knows a man (referred to by his neighbors as "loko") who constantly uses *-mi*. TCV reports that no one believes what he says because he "always speaks as though he had witnessed what he is telling about." (At best he is an argumentative braggart and from TCV's description I would guess that he is mentally ill.)

More on -*chi*. Given 'conjecture' as the meaning of -*chi*, one would expect it to be an appropriate way to say 'Perhaps it needs to be wound' in response to 'Why is your clock not working?' Such is not the case. One could respond with (7a) but not (7b):

(7)
Mana   musya-:-chu
not   know-l-NEG

(a) Kapas   pishi-n   millu-na-n.
    perhaps   lack-3   wind-SUB-3

(b) *Pishi-n-chi   millu-na-n.
    lack-3-CNJ   wind-SUB-3

'I don't know. Perhaps it needs to be wound.'

Why is (b) not acceptable? It is grammatical.[9] Perhaps the answer lies with one of the rhetorical effects of -*chi* now to be discussed.

In conversion, -*chi* is useful as a way to respond to a statement without commitment to its truth—a way to avoid being taken as gullible. We will now see that -*chi* achieves a wide range of rhetorical effects, based on its use as a way to avoid commitment to the truth of a statement, a consequence of its marking information for which no one should be held responsible.

-*chi cannot initiate conversation.* One may not initiate a conversation with (1c) above; it must be said in response to a statement like (1a) or (1b). To say 'Perhaps it will die' *not* following a statement like (1a) or (1b), one uses the Spanish loan *kapas* 'perhaps.'[10]

-*chi as a query.* In some cases, -*chi* results in a query, a sort of challenge to answer. For example, if someone's boss is reading a list of those who are to go, and the person is not sure whether his name was called he could say (8) to his boss. It has the force of the question 'Am I to go?'

(8) TCV
Noqa-chi   aywa-shaq-paq
I-CNJ   go-lFUT-FUT
'I will go.'

---

[9] For example, in response to 'Your clock needs to be wound' (*Relohuyki pishin millunan*) one could respond:

Pishi-n-chi   millu-na-n.   Millu-y   ari!
lack-3-CNJ   wind-SUB-3   wind-IMP   emphatic
'It needs winding (you say; well go ahead and) wind it!'

[10] For example, one could say

Kapas   wañunqa
perhaps   it:will:die
'Perhaps it will die.'

In response to 'John killed his son,' (9) would be a challenge to respond, roughly, 'If you could give an adequate reason why he would do such a thing, then I might believe what you say.'

> (9) TCV
> Wamra-n-ta-chi   wañuchi-ra-n   ima-pita-(taq)
> child-3p-ACC-CNJ   kill-PAST-3   what-ABL-(?)
> 'He killed his son because of what?'

In Cayco (1975a:18) the cat says 'You are going to play (music)' with -chi, to which the dog and the donkey answer 'Yes, yes!' The fact that it is answered shows that the rhetorical force of the sentence is a query.

-chi as a negative. In some cases the rhetorical force is equivalent to a negative. For example, the following sentence conveys something like 'So you think I know? I don't know a thing about it!'

> (10) TCV
> Chay-ta   musya-yka-:-chi
> that-ACC   know-IMPFV-1-CNJ
> 'I know that.'

Suppose two peoples' paths converge, and after walking a short distance together they take a rest. One gets up and, on the assumption that the other is continuing in the same direction, says, 'Let's go.' The other, who was not planning to go further, might reply:

> (11) TCV
> Noqa aywa-yka-:-chi   qam-paq-qa
> I   go-IMPFV-l-CNJ   you-PUR-TOP
> 'I am going (on your behalf).'

The rhetorical force is roughly 'you might have thought I was going (there), but I'm not.' It is a curt/abrupt way to respond, definitely not polite. It could comfortably be followed by an emphatic denial like *noqa aywaykaataqchu* 'I'm *not* going!'

-chi as flippant, sarcastic, or haughty. In Cayco (1974) the fox, while prancing about showing off, accidentally steps on a frog, and says:[11]

> (12) TCV
> Sapu-ta-chi   ima-chi   haru-riyku-:   hahaa hahahaha
> frog-ACC-CNJ what-CNJ   step-ASP-:   (laughs)
> 'It seems I've stepped on a frog, haha hahahaha!'

---

[11] In (12) *ima-chi* has either become frozen, or *ima* 'what' is present simply to support an added *-chi*.

To conclude, -chi has various special restrictions and rhetorical effects (question, negation, sarcasm, etc.) which do not obviously follow from its evidential or conjectural function. Further research may yield more refined explanations for them.

INFORMATION PROFILE

What determines where -mi/shi/chi occur in a sentence? Perhaps in some dialects they are directly associated with a pragmatic function. For Tarma Quechua, both Creider (1979:16f) and Adelaar (1977:80) identify the element to which -mi/shi/chi is attached as "focus." This is not true generally for Huanuco Quechua (although it sometimes is the case), as shown by (13). Note that in the second sentence 'having tied me' is not the focus (being thematic) and yet bears -mi.

(13) LAM
Hatratruu-*mi*   wataraykaa.   Wataykamar-*mi*   aywamusha.
on:bush-DIR   I:am:tied   tying:me-DIR   she:went
'I am tied on a bush. Having tied me (here), she went.'

The pattern in Huanuco Quechua. The evidentials, -qa 'TOP(IC)', and the verb generally pattern in Huanuco Quechua as in (14). ($(X)^j_i$ means "between i and j cases of X," < means "precedes but not necessarily contiguously," and <= means "precedes (not necessarily contiguously) or coincides with".)

(14) $(X\text{-}qa)^n_0 < (Y\text{-EVD})^1_0 <= \text{VERB} (\{OBJ\text{-}qa, SUBJ\text{-}qa\}^2_0$

This means that there may be any number of elements bearing -qa, followed by the element bearing the -mi/shi/chi, which must either precede the main verb or be the main verb itself; this may be followed by one or two -qa-bearing elements, which must be the subject or object.

The practical limit on the number of occurrences of -qa is probably five. For example, (15), an extreme case, has five -qa's.[12]

(15) LAM
Chawrana-*qa*   puntatruu-*qa*   trayaruptin-*qa*   wamrata-*qa*   mayna-*shi*
so:already-TOP   at:the:peak-TOP   arriving-TOP   child-TOP   already-IND

Diosninchi-*qa*   heqarkaykachisha   syelutana-*shi*
our:God-TOP   had:taken:her:up   to:heaven:already-IND
'When she (the witch) reached the peak, God had already taken the child up into heaven.'

---

[12] (15) violates (14) in that the evidential-bearing element follows the verb.

To what extent is (14) followed? Counts made on written folktales by three Huanuco authors (from the three different dialects considered) yielded the following results:[13]

(16)   (1)   (2)   (3)   (4)   (5)

	(1)	(2)	(3)	(4)	(5)
LAM	.67	.57	12%	5%	293
ATR	.30	.27	6%	3%	387
TCV	.13	.54	5%	1%	575

(1) = number of -*qa* per sentence
(2) = number of evidential suffixes per sentence
(3) = percentage of sentences not conforming to (14)
(4) = percentage of sentences having a post-verbal subject or object
(5) = approximate number of sentences counted

Note that the number of pattern-deviating sentences (3) and the number of postverbal subjects and objects bearing -*qa* is very closely proportional to the frequency of -*qa* (1). That is, the more frequently -*qa* occurs, the greater the frequency of sentences deviating from (14) and sentences having a postverbal subject or object which bears -*qa*. These figures amply demonstrate that there is a pattern, with deviations (for various authors) running from 5% to 12%.

The pattern as information profile. The image of sentence in terms of which this discussion is framed is roughly that which has evolved in the Prague school (Firbas 1971): a sentence is seen as a crescendo of communication-advancing material. It builds from elements which relate it to the context (theme, old information, topical material) and material which sets the stage for the communication-advancing material, to the material which advances the communication (rheme, new information). A few disclaimers are in order: admittedly, the notions of theme, rheme, old information, new information, topic, focus, etc., are very difficult ones to define or convincingly impose on text. And the boundary between thematic and rhematic material is not a discrete one. Despite these problems, the theme-rheme distinction captures, in my opinion, something real about sentences.

---

[13] Sentence-initial *chayshi* or *chaymi* was not counted as *chay* 'that' followed by an evidential because it has become a single word (a sentence-initial conjunction meaning 'then' or 'because of that'). Evidence for this is that an evidential suffix may occur elsewhere in the sentence. The actual number of sentences counted was slightly larger than the counts given since sentences without finite verbs were generally not counted.

I suggest that the pattern of (14) serves roughly to characterize a sentence's progression from thematic to rhematic material. I call this progression an "information profile." That is, with fair accuracy one can tell what parts are thematic and what parts are rhematic simply from the pattern of -*qa*(s), the evidential, and the verb. This should not be construed as identifying the evidential suffix with any particular element, e.g., the first rhematic or the last thematic one. The strongest claim that can be made is apparently that in "ordinary" sentences, the thematic material occurs to the left of the evidential suffix and the rhematic material follows the last preverbal -*qa*.

As a first justification for information profile consider the conclusion to Weber (1980): "-*qa* marks those constituents of a sentence which, in the speaker's view, are most responsible for that sentence being relevant to its context." If this is correct, then the initial -*qa*-bearing elements contain material which is thematic, while the rhematic material follows.

The following examples further support the information profile explanation. Consider (17), the beginning of a text. In (a), the rhematic information is that there was a famine. This becomes thematic in (b); the rhematic information is that the famine was long ago. In (c) the thematic part sums up (a) and (b) 'so when there was a famine.' Note how in (b) and (c) the pattern of -*qa*'s and -*shi*'s relates to the progression from thematic to rhematic material:

(17) ANF
(a) Chayshi   karan   muchuy.
     so   there:was   famine

(b) Muchuy-shi   karan   unay.
     famine-IND   there:was   long:ago

(c) Chawra-qa   muchuy   kaptin-qa   pasaypa   mana-shi   imapis   karanchu
     So-TOP   famine   being-TOP   really   not-IND   anything   there:was

     mikunanpaq.
     to:eat

'There was a famine.
The famine was long ago.
So there being a famine, there really was not anything to eat.'

In (18), note that the thematic material in (b) is a repetition of the rhematic material of (a):

(18) ANF
(a) Machka   papata-shi   qaran   wamrata-qa.
     mealy   potato-IND   she:gives   child-TOP

(b) Chawra   machka   papata   qaraptin-qa   wamra-qa
     so   mealy   potato   when:she:hands-TOP   child-TOP

aptarkun-shi
she:grasps:it-IND

'She (the witch) gives the child mealy potatos.
So when she gives her a mealy potato, the child grasps it.'

In (19), note the repeated interjection that there were many children (too many to feed). When it is repeated in the last sentence, it is much more thematic than on its first mention (in the second sentence), and thus it bears the *-qa* and *-shi*. Note the thematic clause of the third sentence repeating the rhematic material of the first:

(19) ANF
Chawra   utkupa   murullanta-shi   tarimun.
So   cotton   just:seed-IND   she:finds

Wamra   achka   kasha.
child   many   there were

Chayshi utkupa   murullanta   tarirkamur-qa   ankaq-shi.
so   of:cotton its:seed   finding-TOP   she:fried-IND

Wamra-qa   achka-shi   kasha.
child-TOP many-IND   there:were

'So she found only some cotton seeds.
There were many children.
So finding just some cotton seeds, she fried them.
There were many children.'

Example (20) (Albino 1980c) shows that the thematic element may reach back across background material. The second and third sentences (with verbs in the past perfect) are not on the event line. The thematic adverbial clause in the last sentence picks up from the first sentence.[14]

(20) LAM
Y   trayachin   markaman {mayman-mi   hipash qeshpisha} chayman.
And   it:brings:him to:the:town {to:where-DIR girl she:escaped} to:there

Hipash-qa   willakushana kasha   kaynuy   paasanqanta.
girl-TOP   had:already:been:told like:this what:had:happened

Chaynuy   willaakuptin   iglesyaman   witrapaakush kash.
like:that being:told   into:church   she:had:been:shut:in

Chawra-qa   iglesya   punkuman   trayarur-qa   kondenadu-qa   nin-shi . . .
so-TOP   church   to:door   arriving-TOP   condemned-TOP   says-IND

'And it brings him to the town, to the place where the girl had fled.
The girl had been told what had happened.

---

[14] The braces mark off a correlative relative clause.

When she had been told that, she was shut into the church.
So arriving to the door of the church, the condemned one says . . .'

To conclude, these examples show that the pattern in which the -*qa*'s, the evidential, and the verb occur characterize (in a loose way) a sentence's progression from thematic to rhematic material.

Other dialects. *Huaraz (Ancash) Quechua (HQ).* The pattern in HQ seems to be (21):[15]

(21) $(\text{X-EVD})_0^1 < (\text{Y-}qa)_0^n < \text{VERB} < (\{\text{OBJ-}qa, \text{SUBJ-}qa\})_0^2$

Examples like (22) (from Larsen 1974) suggest that this pattern is used to indicate the progression from thematic to rhematic elements. However, unlike Huanuco Quechua, in HQ the thematic element is the initial, evidential-bearing constituent and the following -*qa*-bearing element may be rhematic. (The last sentence contains the first mention of a dove, which bears -*qa*.)

(22)
Porfin	tsaynoo	kaykaayaptin-na-shi	gallu	kantaykun.
finally	like:that	they:being-NOW-IND	rooster	he:crows

Kantaykuptin-na-shi	mas	lluqan	lluqan.
when:he:crows-NOW-IND . . .	more	he:climbs	he:climbs

Tsay	lluqaykaptin-na-shi	paluma-qa	lapapapap	ayukun.
that	climbing-NOW-IND	dove-TOP	flapping	he:goes

'Finally as they were like that, a rooster crowed.
When it crowed, he climbed higher and higher.
As he was climbing, a dove went flapping off.'

Tarma (Junin) Quechua (TQ). Ignacio Zarate Mallma's texts in Adelaar (1977) and Puente (1975) strongly evidence the pattern in (21) given above. However, whereas in HQ the evidential-bearing element may be a conjunction, a noun, an adverbial clause, etc., in Zarate's texts it is virtually always *chay* 'that.'[16]

---

[15] The practical limit on *n* (the number of occurrences of pre-verbal -*qa*'s) is perhaps 3; I have yet to see more.

[16] Sometimes this *chay* is followed by a case marker (e.g., *Chay-pita-mi* 'After that' *Chay-nuypa-mi* 'In that way' . . .) or forms a definite noun phrase (e.g., *Chay atoqyupay-mi* 'like that fox'). Also possible is *chinarkur-mi* 'then' (from *chay nirkur?*). Rarely *kay* 'this' is used rather than *chay*. In rare cases the evidential-bearing element is some longer, thematic material; e.g., in (b) (from a text by Ignacio Zarate Mallma in Adelaar 1977:309):

(a)	Chinarkur	atoqta	qipikura	washanman.
	then	fox:ACC	he:took:him	onto:his:back

In TQ the pattern also seems to characterize roughly the progression from thematic to rhematic material. As in Huanuco, the thematic material will bear *-qa* (Adelaar 1977:71). However, in TQ the evidential suffix will also be on thematic material. For example, consider (23) (from Adelaar 1977:310). The preceding text describes the setting for a wedding, so 'in that wedding' is thematic in (a). In (b) *chaytruu* is thematic since (a) has told the reader that they arrived "there." The evidential in both sentences is attached to the sentence-initial element linking the sentence to its context.

(23) IZM

(a) Chay-mi   chay   kasamintutruu-qa   naa   trarunaq   lapan
    that-DIR   that   wedding:at-TOP   now   they:arrived all

    pishqukuna   kay   pampa   pachapita   altu   pachaman
    birds   this   ground   place:from   high   place:to

(b) Chay-mi   chaytruu-qa   kanaq   montikuna
    that-DIR   there:at   there:were   woods

'(a) And so, for the occasion of that wedding, all the birds had arrived in heaven from the earth.
 (b) There were woods in that place.'

Cajamarca Quechua (CQ). This section is included to show that similar patterns hold for very different dialects, while speakers of the same dialect differ considerably in their use of *-qa* and evidentials. CQ is a northern Peruvian dialect. It is unique among Quechua languages in *commonly* allowing both *-qa* and an evidential to occur on the same word. (Other dialects *rarely* allow it; see Weber 1980, example 7 from Huanuco Quechua.) Folktales were counted for two speakers: Cruz Landa Quito (*CLQ*) (roughly 315 sentences) and Blanca Ortiz Ch. (*BOC*) (roughly 381 sentences). They are faithful to the following patterns to the degree indicated (discounting post-verbal subjects and objects bearing *-qa*, and evidentials on main verbs, both of which are allowed):

CLQ: (X-(qa)-EVD) < (Y-qa) < VERB [97%]

BOC: (X-EVD) < (Y-qa) < (Z-qa) < VERB [98%]

Both allowed two pre-verbal *-qa*'s, but BOC never (with one exception) placed *-qa* on the evidential-bearing word, while CLQ used only one pre-verbal *-qa* other than the *-qa* co-occurring with the evidential. The frequency of *-qa* was remarkably similar for the two speakers (.36 and .39 *-qa*'s per sentence for BOC

(b) Chinarkur   washanman   qipikurkur-mi   paariyta   qalayura.
    then   onto:his:back   having:taken:him-DIR   to:fly   he:began

'Then he took the fox upon his back.
Then, after taking him upon his back, he started to fly.'

and CLQ, respectively), but BOC used significantly fewer evidentials than CLQ (.20 vs. .71 evidentials per sentence). Despite these differences, it is evident that the evidential, -*qa,* and the verb occur in a pattern. A cursory look suggests that, in CQ as well, this pattern roughly characterizes the sentence's progression from thematic to rhematic material.

PATTERN DEVIATIONS AS A RHETORICAL DEVICE

There is a basic pattern for the occurrence(s) of -*qa,* the evidential, and the verb, with few deviations from this pattern (5–15%). These deviations are not randomly distributed in a text, but constitute a rhetorical device for marking crucial points in a narrative.[17] Three kinds of deviation have been noted.

First, pattern deviations occur at textual boundaries, e.g., sentences like 'So the three of them go on their way' which concludes an episode, like 'And then there appears a hawk' which begins an episode, and like (24) which implies a change of scene:[18]

(24) TCV
Chaypita   atoq   chayan   runaman-shi
after:that   fox   he:arrives   to:man-IND
'After that the fox arrives at the man's place.'

Second, deviations sometimes flag a theme on which tension is built in the narrative. For example, a tension running through one text is a girl's ignorance of what the witch has done with her brother (particularly since her ignorance puts her in considerable danger). The girl asks about her brother and does not get a satisfactory answer. She asks a second time, and her question is set by 'Again the girl asks . . .' where X-*shi* < Y-*qa* < verb. The danger she is in is brought home by a sentence saying that the witch *had cut* her brother up and put him in a pot to boil, in which X-*shi* < Y-*qa* < verb. After some intervening events, the tension builds with 'And she asks the witch about her brother' in which verb-*shi* < Y-*qa*. The girl's preoccupation with her brother, and the reader's concern that she realize her dangerous situation, are resolved when the bird and frog inform her, where W-*qa* < X-*qa* < Y-*qa* < verb < Z-*shi.*)[19] This illustrates a tension woven into the narrative which is flagged by pattern deviations.

---

[17] Not all pattern deviations are crucial points, and conversely, not all crucial points involve a deviation from the pattern.

[18] This accords well with the observation that *chaypita* 'thereafter, then' is a very "loose connective," the sort which initiates paragraphs.

[19]Chawra-qa   yukish-qa   sapu-qa   asta   willan   wamrata-sh
then-TOP   bird sp.-TOP   frog-TOP   even   they:tell   to:the:child-IND

'So the yukish and the frog tell the child.'

Third, two intertwined themes may be kept distinct by making the sentences of one strand conform to the pattern, while making those of the other strand deviate from it. For example, in Cayco (1975b) two elements are intertwined: (1) that which happened or was long ago, and (2) the basis on which we know such things. Very consistently, the 1-sentences have past verbs (tense marker -ra/rqa) and -shi on some constituent *following* the verb, thus deviating from (14), and the 2-sentences have present tense verbs, have -na 'now' somewhere in the sentence, and do not violate (14).[20]

To conclude, deviation from the pattern (14) is a rhetorical device which can be used to mark boundaries, to signal a theme of concern, and to interweave two themes. There may well be many further uses various speakers make of this rhetorical device.

OTHER USES OF -mi AND -shi

For the sake of completeness, four non-evidential uses of -mi and -shi are presented.

-mi as a question marker. -mi is sometimes used in the formation of content questions.[21] Far more common for this is -taq (or -raq, see Diana Weber 1979). For example,

(25)

$$\text{Pi} \left\{ \begin{matrix} \text{-mi} & \text{(a)} \\ \text{-taq} & \text{(b)} \end{matrix} \right\} \quad \text{chayamusha}$$

'Who arrived?'

-mi in correlatives. -mi is a structural feature of correlative relative clauses. It co-occurs with other evidentials, and is -mi regardless of whether the other is -mi, -shi, or -chi. One example is in (20) and another is (26) (where the correlative is enclosed in braces):

(26)

Kondenaa	karkamur-qa	chay runa-qa	{maytruu-mi	haqiran}
condemned	having:been-TOP	that man-TOP	where-DIR	he:left

chayman-shi	trayan.
to:there-IND	he:arrives

'Having been condemned, that man arrives to where he had left her.'

---

[20] Generally the 2-sentences do not have an evidential suffix, but when they do, they conform to (14).

[21] Cerron (1976:108) states that a question with -mi is less polite than a question with -taq or -raq, and indicates that the speaker has much confidence in his interlocutor.

-shi **with complements.** There is a rather restricted sort of complement in which (1) the superordinate verb is a verb of perception (e.g., *rika-* 'see') or of cognition (*reqsi-* 'be acquainted with'); (2) the verb of the complement is finite (all other complements have a non-finite verb); and (3) the complement contains a WH word with *-shi*. Examples are (with the complement bracketed):

(27) TCV
[Ima-shi   kaykan   chaychaw]   rikaykamunki
what-IND   there:is   there   go see!
'Go and see what is there!'

(28) TCV
Chaynawpa   musyashun   [mayqanchii-shi   mas   kalpa-yoq   kanchi]
like:that   we:will:know   which:of:us-IND   more   strength-have   we:are
'In that way we'll know which of us is the stronger.'

-chush = *-chu-shi?* *-chush* is probably derived from *-chu* 'yes/no question' followed by *-shi* 'reportative.' It is used to form yes/no questions in the same way as *-chu,* with slightly different semantic/rhetorical effect (which I am not able to state precisely). An example from Adelaar (1977:83) follows:

(29)
Maa   tupayuy,   kuyurinaq-chush
let's:see   push:it!   it:turns:out:to:move-CHUSH
'Why don't you give it a push, to find out whether it moves or not!'

Adelaar also reports the use of *-chuch* (from *-chu+chi* -Y/N-CNJ) for Tarma Quechua.

CONCLUSIONS

1.   *-mi/shi/chi* allow the Quechua speaker to exercise caution in the amount of responsibility he assumes for information. With *-mi* the speaker assumes responsibility, with *-shi* he defers it to someone else, and with *-chi* he indicates that it is not the sort of information for which anyone should be held responsible.

2.   *-mi* and *-shi* are evidential, but because of axioms like ''one's own (direct) experience is reliable,'' a validational interpretation is sometimes appropriate for *-mi.*

3.   *-chi* has rhetorical effects which have a basis in its use as a way to avoid commitment to the truth of a proposition.

4.   The relative positions of one or more *-qa*'s, the evidential suffix, and the main verb form a pattern which grossly characterizes the sentence's progression from thematic to rhematic material. In ''ordinary'' sentences, the the-

matic material occurs to the left of the evidential suffix and the rhematic material follows the last pre-verbal -*qa*.

5. Deviations from this pattern serve as a rhetorical device. Three uses of this device were identified: occurrence at textual boundaries, for flagging high tension themes in the narrative, and for intertwining two thematic strands.

I conclude by suggesting that information profiling and the use of pattern deviations as a rhetorical device naturally follow from the status of -*mi*/*shi*/*chi* as indicators of information perspective. A marker of information perspective (be it evidential or validational) accompanies the new information more naturally than material which simply "paves the way" for it; thus, evidentials naturally occur with the rhematic part of a sentence (provided they are free to do so). In conjunction with a marker of thematic material like -*qa* 'relevance to context,' this naturally gives rise to a profile along theme-rheme lines. In addition, it is natural that the speaker/author should tamper with the information profile for rhetorical effect, since that goes to the very heart of rhetorical "punches": unsettling the listener to make him take note. Information profiling and pattern deviations for rhetorical effect are thus natural outgrowths of the states of -*mi*/*shi*/*chi* as indicators of information perspective.

REFERENCES

Linguistic Sources

Adelaar, Willem F. H. 1977. *Tarma Quechua* Lisse: The Peter de Ridder Press.

Burns, Donald and P. Alcocer H. 1975. "Un analisis preliminar del discurso en quechua: Estudio lexico y grammatical del cuento *Taklluscha y Benedicto* en el quechua de Ayacucho" Documento de Trabajo No. 6, Yarinacocha: Instituto Linguistico de Verano.

Cerron-Palomino, Rodolfo. 1976. *Gramatica quechua: Junin-Huanca* Lima: Ministerio de Educacion.

Creider, Chet. 1979. "On the Explanation of Transformations" in T. Givon *Discourse and Syntax,* pg. 3–21.

Firbas, Jan. 1971. "On the Concept of Communicative Dynamism in the Theory of Functional Sentence Perspective" *Studia minora facultatis philosophicae universitatis brunensis.*

Givon, Talmy. 1979. *Discourse and Syntax,* Syntax and Semantics, Vol. 12, New York: Academic Press.

Keenan, Edward and E. Ochs. 1979. "Becoming a Competent Speaker of Malagasy" in T. Shopen *Languages and Their Speakers* Cambridge: Winthrop pg. 113–158.

Larsen, Hellen. 1974. "Some Grammatical Features of Legendary Narrative in Ancash Quechua" in R. Brend *Advances in Tagmemics* The Hague: Mouton pg. 419–440.

Longacre, Robert. 1980, "Peak as a Zone of Turbulence" manuscript.

Puente B., Blas. 1972. *Quechua Tarmeño I: Textos,* Documento de Trabajo No. 2, Lima: Centro de Investigacion de la Linguistica Aplicada.

Weber, David. 1980. "On the So-called "Topic Marker" -QA in Huallaga (Huanuco) Quechua" manuscript.

Weber, Diana Dahlin de. 1976. "Presuposiciones de Preguntas en el Quechua de Huanuco" Documento de Trabajo No. 8, Yarinacocha: Instituto Linguistico de Verano.

Material Written by Quechua Speakers

Albino Mendoza, Lorenzo. 1980a. "Ishkay Ukushpa" Tercer Seminario de Autores Quechua Hablantes, Huanuco.

———. 1980b. "Ishkay Kwentukuna" Tercer Seminario de Autores Quechua Hablantes, Huanuco.

———. 1980c. "Kondenaado Y Hipash" manuscript.

Cayco Villar, Teodoro. 1974. "Cuento Atoq Waychaw y Sapo" Llacon.

———. 1975a. "Libro de Cuentos en Quechua" Llacon.

———. 1975b. "Peru Marcanchichu Unay Awilunchicuna Tiyashan" Llacon.

——— (editor). 1975c. "Unay Runacuna Parlashan" Llacon.

Landa Quito, Cruz. 1980a. "Chayqam Wañuy" Tercer Seminario de Autores Quechua Hablantes, Huanuco.

———. 1980b. "Shumaq Kwintukuna" Tercer Seminario de Autores Quechua Hablantes, Huanuco.

Ortiz Ch., Blanca M. 1980a. "Pinkichu Prinsesawan" Tercer Seminario de Autores Quechua Hablantes, Huanuco.

———. 1980b. "Suq Sapatiru Warminwan" Tercer Seminario de Autores Quechua Hablantes, Huanuco.

Pantoja Ramos, Santiago, J. Ripkens and G. Swisshelm. 1974. *Cuentos y Relatos in el Quechua de Huaraz* Volumes I and II, Estudios Culturales Benedictinos No. 3, Huaraz: Priorato de San Benito.

Tucto Ramirez, Amador. 1980a. "Kimsa Konchukanukuna" Tercer Seminario de Autores Quechua Hablantes, Huanuco.

———. 1980b, "Unay Achakaypa Kwentu" Tercer Seminario de Autores Quechua Hablantes, Huanuco.

PART TWO

EVIDENTIALITY ELSEWHERE IN THE WORLD

NINE

A Psychological Account of the Development and Use of Evidentials in Turkish

Ayhan A. Aksu-Koç
Boğaziçi University, Istanbul

Dan I. Slobin
University of California, Berkeley

For all past tense expressions in Turkish there is an obligatory choice between one of two verb suffixes: (a) direct experience *-dI* (realized as *-di/-dı/-dü/-du/-ti/tı/-tü/-tu*) and (b) indirect experience *-mIş* [-mIš] realized as *-miş/-mış/-müş/-muş*). This paper concerns itself with the second form, which encodes events to which the speaker was not a direct or fully conscious participant.[1]

The basic functions of the *-mIş* form are to convey inference and hearsay. For example:

(1) *Ahmet gel-   miş.*
     Ahmet come   mIş
     'Ahmet came / must have come.'
     (a) inference: The speaker sees Ahmet's coat hanging in the front hall, but has not yet seen Ahmet.
     (b) hearsay: The speaker has been told that Ahmet has arrived, but has not yet seen Ahmet.

---

[1] This paper is based on Slobin and Aksu 1982. The reader is referred to that paper for full details of the argument summarized here. We would like to thank Francesco Antinucci for lengthy and enlightening discussions on some of the topics considered here. D. I. Slobin expresses gratitude to Hubert Dreyfus, who will hopefully detect some aspect of his skillful presentation of the ideas of Merleau-Ponty. We acknowledge support from the William T. Grant Foundation to the Institute of Human Learning and from NIMH to the Language-Behavior Research Laboratory, both at the University of California at Berkeley, and from the American Research Institute in Turkey to A. A. Aksu-Koç.

159

In addition to the everyday hearsay function, *-mIş* has a special narrative function, limited to accounts of unreal events outside the regular experience of the speech community such as myths, folktales, dreams, and jokes. (However, generally familiar events, such as those related in historical accounts and realistic fiction, are usually reported in the past of direct experience, *-dI*.)

Our task is to characterize the PSYCHOLOGICAL underpinnings of the *-mIş* form in Turkish. In this regard it is necessary to consider pragmatic extensions of the form, as well as its historical origins and its course of development in modern child language. First, however, let us consider the psychological grounds of the "core" uses of the *-mIş* form in Turkish—the expressions of inference and hearsay.

EXPERIENCE AND INFERENTIALITY

Unlike some of the other evidential systems considered in this volume, the inferences encoded by *-mIş* can be based on any kind of sensory evidence of resultant state, with the provision that no aspect of the antecedent process itself has been present in the speaker's consciousness. In psychological terms, the use of *-mIş* represents an experience of which the speaker has had no PREMONITORY AWARENESS. Thus we are dealing not only with sensory evidence as grounds for an assertion, but with an inference from sensory evidence which follows and is not temporally coexistential with the process referred to. For example, (1) *Ahmet gelmiş* 'Ahmet must have come', is appropriate in the context of encountering Ahmet's coat, but not in the context of hearing the approach of Ahmet's car, because, in the latter case, the auditory sensory experience is part of the process of Ahmet's arrival. Having heard the approach of the car, the speaker's consciousness was involved in the process which led to the end state.

The *-mIş* form encodes a lack of CONSCIOUS involvement, rather than simply lack of speaker involvement, as shown in expressions such as

(2) *Uyu-   -muş-   um.*
     sleep   *mlş*   1SG.[2]
     'I must have fallen asleep.'

said upon awakening over one's books, or

(3) *El-   im-   i   kes-   miş-   im.*
     hand   1SG.POSS.   ACC.   cut   *mlş*   1SG.
     'I must have cut my hand.'

---

[2] The following abbreviations are used in this paper: ACC = accusative, FUT = future, HAB = habitual, LOC = locative, NEG.EXIS = negative existential, PRES = present, POSS = possessive, SG = singular.

said upon noticing a cut in one's hand. Such events, although predicated of the speaker, occurred outside of the speaker's awareness. We wish to argue that this externality of the process to awareness is at the core of all uses of the *-mIş* particle.

INFERENCE VERSUS HEARSAY

In the inferential uses of *-mIş*, only the process leading to the end state is external to consciousness, while in the hearsay uses, both process and end state are external. In an inferential statement, the speaker's assertion presupposes the reported event and the *-mIş* particle indicates that the grounds of the assertion do not come from direct experience of the event itself. Note that this usage is limited to inference of completed processes from end states. Thus, as an inferential statement, one cannot say, on seeing a cloudy sky,

(4) *Yağmur   yağ-   acak- mış.*
     rain [NOUN]   rain [VERB] FUT.   *mIş*

An inferred expectancy must be expressed in modal terms, as, for example, the equivalent of 'It will probably rain'. However, (4) is both grammatical and appropriate in predicting rain on the basis of hearsay, such as a weather forecast, carrying the meaning 'It is reported that it will rain'. Here the speaker's assertion presupposes the report of the event, and the *-mIş* particle indicates the grounds for the speech act—namely, that the speaker is conveying information received in verbal form.

When suffixed to a verb root, as in (1), *-mIş* can convey either inference or hearsay, because a past process can be apprehended indirectly either through perception of its results or through verbal report. However, an inferential reading is not possible when *-mIş* is suffixed to a stative or existential expression or to verb complexes conveying iterative, habitual, or durative notions. For example,

(5) *İskender bura- da-   ymış*
     İskender   here   LOC. *mIş*
     'İskender is here.'

cannot represent an inference, since Turkish limits inference to the predication of processes, and (5) is stative. On hearing an utterance such as (5), the listener knows that the speaker is conveying hearsay (or perhaps surprise, as discussed below). In similar fashion, sentences such as the following, because of their aspectual-modal forms, cannot be interpreted as inferential:

(6) *Her   gün   koş-   uyor- muş.*
     every day   run   PRES. *mIş*
     '(It is said that) he jogs every day.'

(7) *Küçük köpeğ- im-   i   çok   sev-   er-   miş- im.*
    little   dog   1SG.POSS.   ACC.   much   love   HAB.   *mİş*   1SG.
    '(It is said that) I used to love my little dog a lot.'

(8) *Ev-   i   yok-   muş.*
    house   POSS   NEG.EXIS.   *mİş*
    '(It is said that) he doesn't have a house.'

Utterances of these sentences naturally are given a hearsay interpretation (or may, in some contexts, be interpreted as pragmatic extensions, to which we now turn).

PRAGMATIC EXTENSIONS

Beyond the traditionally described functions of *-mİş* to convey inference and hearsay, the form has several interesting pragmatic extensions. What these have in common is that the speaker was, in some sense, not quite prepared for the event in question. Our first example *Ahmet gelmiş* 'Ahmet came', could also be an expression of surprise, even if the speaker has had full sensory information of Ahmet's arrival. For example, (1) could be uttered in a situation in which the speaker hears someone approach from outside, opens the door, and sees Ahmet, provided that Ahmet is a totally unexpected visitor. Normally, upon opening a door to a visitor, one would say to the others in the room, *Ahmet geldi,* using the past of direct experience. Surprise, however, is not normal, since the event is somehow NOT CONSONANT WITH THE CURRENT STATE OF MIND OF THE SPEAKER. Similarly, statives like (5) *İskender buradaymış* 'Iskender is here', can be uttered on directly experiencing Iskender's presence if the speaker had no mental preparation for that situation. In using *-mİş* to convey surprise, the speaker seems to be saying: 'I have just become aware of something for which I had no premonitory consciousness'.

In some contexts, surprise itself can be pragmatically extended, expressing degrees of "metaphorical" or "feigned surprise." When uttered with the appropriate intonation, in the appropriate context, an utterance like (6) ('He reportedly jogs every day'), can convey not only hearsay, but doubting scorn when predicated of a well-known exercise hater. Kononov (1956:232) has discussed such uses as expressing 'an ironical attitude toward the carrying out of an action ("Ah, so you think we went!")'.

Curiously, in other contexts, an expression of surprise can function as a compliment, conveying not scorn or irony, but a pleasant experience of surpassed expectations. For example, one can compliment a proud mother at the conclusion of her daughter's piano recital by saying:

(9) *Kız-   ınız   çok   iyi   piyano çal-   ıyor-   muş.*
    daughter   2PL.POSS.   very   good   piano   play   PRES.   *mİş*
    'Your daugher plays [*-mİş*] the piano very well!'

Again, the speaker conveys a lack of preparation for the experienced event—in this case, a lack of preparation for the high quality of the event.

The various pragmatic extensions of *-mış* to surprise, scorn, irony, and compliments share a psychological feature with the inference and hearsay functions. In every use of *-mış,* speakers present events as states of affairs which they were not fully prepared to experience—situations on the fringe of consciousness, learned of indirectly, or not immediately assimilable to the mental sets of the moment. An apparent violation of the normal hearsay use of *-mış* clearly points up the central role of mental preparedness in the use of this form. When the speaker is well prepared for an event, even hearsay can be reported as direct experience. For example, in 1974, during an early phase of investigating these issues, events of the day increasingly prepared us to expect Richard Nixon's resignation. When we finally learned of the resignation through the news media—certainly a channel of indirect experience—it was quite natural to report the event in the past of direct experience, *-dI: Nixon istifa etti* 'Nixon resigned'. During the same time period, the Turkish premier, Bülent Ecevit, suddenly and unexpectedly resigned. There was no way to report this event except in the *-mış* form, although the identical source of indirect evidence was involved: *Ecevit istifa etmiş* '(It is reported that) Ecevit resigned'. Again, the use of *-mış* implies that the speaker's mind was unprepared for the event in question.

Consistent with this interpretation is the curious fact that the use of *-mış* to convey hearsay is no longer obligatory as the event recedes in time from the moment of speech. That which is reported as *-mış* today may be reported as *-dI* next week or next month (the length of time varying with personal characteristics of the speaker and general knowledge of the event). What is important communicatively in the use of *-mış* is an indication to the listener of the source of currently relevant information. It is well known in psychology that information that has been stored for some time becomes assimilated to one's own stock of knowledge, while the source of information often fades from memory. Such information becomes part of one's general world knowledge, and can no longer be reported as something that has entered an unprepared mind. Thus as Ecevit's resignation became familiar recent history, it came to be reported in the *-dI* form. Indeed, all history is reported in this manner in Turkish.

UNPREPARED MINDS AND INDIRECT EXPERIENCE

The reader will note that we have moved from defining the *-mış* form as a marker of 'indirect experience' to the use of terms such as 'outside of the speaker's awareness', 'external to consciousness', and 'lack of preparation for the experienced event'. Clearly, pragmatic extensions to surprise, irony, and compliments go well beyond the feature of the speaker's direct or indirect experience of the event. A general psychological or phenomenological stance towards experience seems to underlie the entire range of functions of the two past tense forms in

Turkish, -dI and -mIş. The neutral expectation, encoded by -dI, is that experienced events can be assimilated to a network of existing assumptions and expectations. Normal experience is characterized by premonitory consciousness of the
contents of coming moments. We refer to this neutral, background mental set as
a 'prepared mind'. An observed process arouses premonitory consciousness of
its consequences, and can later be encoded in the past of direct experience, -dI.
Hearsay assimilable to a prepared mind, as in the case of Nixon's resignation, is
not really hearsay, because the recipient has had premonitory consciousness of
the state of affairs leading up to the reported event. Such reports are conveyed as
'direct experience'.

When a mind is unprepared, however, events cannot be assimilated at once.
The speaker stands back, saying, in effect, by use of the -mIş form: 'It seems that
I am experiencing such–and–such' or 'It seems that such–and–such must have
taken place'. An unprepared mind has not had normal premonitory consciousness of the event in question. The event has become apparent through its
consequences, or through verbal report; or the experienced event is radically
different from the consciousness that preceded the experience. The speaker feels
distanced from the situation he or she is describing. Events which enter unprepared minds are encoded by -mIş.

In some psychological sense, there are classes of events for which one can
never be quite prepared, events which are always somehow distant from one's
normal mental set. These are events which partake of a quality of unreality or
otherworldliness, and they are the special domain of -mIş in Turkish. Thus, -mIş
is always used in such narratives as myths, folktales, and fairy tales; and it is the
form used for recounting those parts of dreams that seem most alien to everyday
experience. In broadest terms, then, we may summarize by stating that the -dI
form represents the realities of moment-to-moment, consciously involved experience, while the -mIş form represents intrusions into consciousness from psychologically more distant, less directly apprehended worlds of thought and experience. Both the historical and ontogenetic courses of development of the uses of
-mIş seem to reflect an increasing distancing from the encoding of ongoing,
immediately apprehended experience.

A BRIEF HISTORICAL NOTE

Both historically (Grunina 1976) and ontogenetically (Aksu 1978), there is evidence that inferential forms develop from forms expressing the perfect. As
Comrie has pointed out (1976:110): "the semantic similarity . . . between perfect and inferential lies in the fact that both categories present an event not in
itself, but via its results." A crucial conceptual bridge between perfect and
inferential thus can be found in an attention to resultant states, and it is no
accident that -mIş also functions to form stative participles derived from process
verbs. In this adjectival function the element of indirect experience is not present. Compare, for example, 10 and 11:

(10) *Çiçek   kuru-   muş.*
      flower   dry   *mlş*
      'The flower dried (apparently, reportedly).'

(11) *kuru-   muş   çiçek*
      dry   *mlş*   flower
      'dried flower'/'flower which has become dry'

The participial form in (11) can only be used to encode resultant states—that is, it focuses on an end state achieved by a patient. (See Slobin and Aksu 1982 for details.) It is thus completive in meaning, embracing both process and resultant state in its scope. The participle may well have provided the historical point of departure for the inferential past tense form, which goes from resultant state to the inference of antecedent process. Both the participial and past tense functions of *-mlş*, however, are present in writing on the earliest monuments of the eighth century A.D. (Tekin 1968). It has been suggested by some scholars (e.g. Baskakov 1971) that the participial function was prior, having been extended to indicate past tense because of its focus on both process and end state. In historically attested time, *-mlş* has moved from an early period of functioning as a perfect, to later take on the modal distinctions described above, while the range of the *-dl* past tense became limited to the domain of direct experience (Grunina 1976, described for Turkish and related forms in other Western Turkic languages). The *-mlş* form thus seems to have moved from participle, through perfect, to past tense—presumably facilitated by the fact that observed end states result from past processes. The ultimate movement of the form to the modality of indirect experience was probably facilitated by (a) the cognitive fact that nonwitnessed processes can be inferred from observation of resultant states, and (b) the linguistic fact that the verbal system already provided a potentially contrasting past tense form (*-dl*) that was neutral in regard to source of experience.

ONTOGENETIC PARALLELS

What we take to be the historical sequence bears striking similarity to the contemporary Turkish child's acquisition of the semantic functions of the *-mlş* particle (Aksu 1978; Aksu-Koç and Slobin 1985). The particle emerges around the age of two, several months later than the *-dl* particle. At first, *-dl* is used simply to comment on immediately preceding changes of state with perceptible results, without regard to the child's direct or indirect experience of the process in question. The form is hardly a past tense, but more a sort of completive-resultant aspect. When *-mlş* emerges, it is at first limited to picture descriptions and story telling, and to the encoding of a small range of states (e.g. locative states and physical experiential states such as hunger and pain). Interestingly, adult utterances in the *-mlş* mode are imitated only when they occur with stative verbs, being replaced by *-dl* in children's imitations when they occur with process verbs. Thus, in the child's system, the *-dl* and *-mlş* inflections at first serve to indicate different types of events in the here-and-now—dynamic and static, respectively. Neither form serves to order events in time in relation to the moment of speech.

After this early period, -*dI* is extended from its completive aspectual use to a general past tense function. At the same time, -*mI§* begins to be used as a past tense with change of state verbs in situations where an object is perceived in a state or location different from its canonical state, although the child has not perceived the preceding process. Thus, in the earliest inferential uses of -*mI§,* a resultant state serves as perceptible evidence for the inference of a precipitating event in the past. The cognitive process underlying the acquisition of the two past tense inflections is the same, namely that of coordinating a present perceived state with a past process. As Piaget has pointed out (1927 [1969:284]), the very young child's notion of temporality is characterized by "living purely in the present and assessing the past exclusively by its results." The observed time lag in the order of emergence of the two forms in Turkish child speech is presumably due to the further complexity of making an inference (-*mI§*) as compared to simply accessing an experienced event from memory (-*dI*).

By age three or so, the two verb particles have become general past tense forms, dividing up the field in terms of witnessed and nonwitnessed modalities. The -*mI§* form comes to be used to encode inferred past events and to differentiate pretense from "real" activity, but has not yet taken on the hearsay and pragmatic extensions described above. It may well be that, in the child's world, adult utterances have the force of direct experience, and do not partake of the psychological distancing from events inherent in the -*mI§* form. One can also argue that, on the cognitive level, the hearsay function is more complex than the inferential, since it involves the use of another person's utterance, rather than one's own experience, as evidence for one's assertion. In any case, the hearsay function is not primary in development.

Experimental investigation also suggests that children gradually extend the definition of events qualifying as "nonwitnessed" and "indirectly experienced." Aksu (1978) presented children with pictured sequences of events, eliciting judgments as to which characters would be in a position to report events in the evidential modality. The characters varied in terms of direct experience of the events in question. It was found that young children express the belief that one must directly experience or perceive an event in order to be able to talk about it at all. Older children recognize the relevance of the physical results of a past event as an indirect source of information and thus as the basis for an assertion about the event. Only after the age of four do they accept the legitimacy of assertions made on the basis of other people's reports.

Thus, the factors we have considered in discussing the psychological bases of adult usage of Turkish evidentials—psychological distance or degree of externality of an event from consciousness—seem to play a role in children's developing understanding about who can talk about what and in what way. While the historical evidence is not certain, it is at least clear on ontogenetic grounds that: (a) perception of results leads to inferences about their antecedents; (b) linguistic forms describing end states can evolve into past tense forms; (c) the marking of indirect experience on the basis of physical evidence of results antedates the marking of indirect experience on the basis of hearsay. Although we have not carried out detailed investigation of children's use of the pragmatic extensions of -mlş for expressions of surprise, scorn, irony, and compliments, it is our impression that these functions develop considerably later than the inference and hearsay functions described above.

To conclude, we suggest that every language embodies an implicit theory of conscious experience, such as the one we have proposed for Turkish. Languages differ in the particular distinctions which come to form the habitual background of grammatical choice. The Turkish speaker must implicitly take account of the degree to which his or her mind has been prepared to assimilate a given event prior to forming an utterance about that event. The Turkish child must implicitly elaborate the phenomenological theory underlying the language. Finally, the researcher seeking universals must determine the range and variability of such theories, along with investigating their acquisition and use.

REFERENCES

Aksu, Ayhan A. 1978. Aspect and modality in the child's acquisition of the Turkish past tense. Berkeley: University of California dissertation.

Aksu-Koç, Ayhan A., and Dan I. Slobin. 1985. Acquisition of Turkish. The crosslinguistic study of language acquisition, ed. by Dan I. Slobin. Hillsdale, NJ: Lawrence Erlbaum Associates.

Baskakov, N. A. 1971. O kategorijax naklonenija i vremeni v tjurkski jazykax, 71–80. Moscow: Nauka.

Comrie, Bernard. 1976. Aspect. Cambridge: Cambridge University Press.

Grunina, E. A. 1976. K istorii semantičeskogo razvitija perfekta –miš. Sovetskaja tjurkologija 7(1).12–26.

Kononov, A. N. 1956. Grammatika sovremennogo tureckogo literaturnogo jazyka. Leningrad: Izdatel'stvo Akademii Nauk SSSR.

Piaget, Jean. 1927. Le développement de la notion de temps chez l'enfant. Paris: Presses Universitaires de France. (1969. The child's conception of time, trans. by A. J. Pomerans. New York: Routledge and Kegan Paul.)

Slobin, Dan I., and Ayhan A. Aksu. 1982. Tense, aspect, modality and more in Turkish evidentials. Tense–aspect: Between semantics and pragmatics, ed. by Paul Hopper. Amsterdam: John Benjamins.

Tekin, Talât. 1968. A grammar of Orkhon Turkic. Bloomington: Indiana University Publications (Ural and Altaic Series Vol. 69).

TEN

Evidentiality in the Balkans: Bulgarian, Macedonian, and Albanian*

Victor A. Friedman

University of North Carolina, Chapel Hill

INTRODUCTION

Jakobson (1957:4) uses the term EVIDENTIAL as a tentative label for a verbal category which indicates the source of the information on which the speaker's statement is based. He offers a distinction between 'direct narration' and 'indirect narration' in Bulgarian (*prjako izkazvane* and *preizkazvane,* cf. Andrejčin 1944:§281–285) as his chief example and also refers to a 'vouched for' vs 'distanced' distinction in Macedonian (cf. Lunt 1952:93). Similar accounts of Bulgarian are to be found in various survey works, e.g. those of Comrie (1976:108–110), Haarman (1970:33–35), and Serebrennikov (1974:208), and these follow descriptions in traditional grammars. All these works state or imply that Bulgarian (with Jakobson including Macedonian) possesses a separate set of forms which necessarily denote that the speaker is basing the statement on reported information. When the facts of these languages are examined in greater detail, however, it can be seen that this picture is greatly oversimplified and not, strictly speaking, accurate.

It will be shown that evidentiality, which in the languages discussed here actually involves the speaker's ATTITUDE toward the information—source being

* I wish to thank the National Endowment for the Humanities for a Category A grant for the year 1980–81 and the American Philosophical Society for a grant from the Penrose Fund for Summer 1979 which allowed me to conduct much of the research on which this article is based. I also wish to thank the Center for Bulgaristics of the Bulgarian Academy of Sciences, the Macedonian Academy of Arts and Sciences, the Secretariat of Information of the Socialist Republic of Macedonia, and both the Academy of Arts and Sciences and the Secretariat of Information of the Socialist Autonomous Region of Kosovo for providing me with materials which were essential to my research.

an implication derived from that attitude—is the chief contextual variant meaning (HAUPTBEDEUTUNG) in the Balkan Slavic (i.e. Bulgarian and Macedonian) forms which are usually cited as exemplary, namely the descendants of the Common Slavic perfect. These forms still retain their older nonevidential perfect meanings and have developed simple preterite uses as well; thus, evidentiality cannot be said to function as the invariant meaning (GESAMTBEDEUTUNG) in these forms. This distinction between Hauptbedeutung and Gesamtbedeutung is crucial in understanding the structure of the Balkan Slavic (or any language's) verbal system. Although the forms in question can be used evidentially and often are, the fact that this is not always the case means that evidentiality is not inherent in these forms but results from a combination of whatever meaning is always present when the form is used (which meaning must then be sought) and the surrounding context. These forms are thus not special evidential forms but rather forms contextually capable of expressing evidentiality. In pluperfect forms which developed later, during or after the rise of evidentiality, it appears that an evidential meaning can be treated as invariant, though it need not be treated as a separate grammatical category.

This is to say that in the languages under discussion, evidentiality does not constitute a generic grammatical category on a level with, for example, mood, tense or aspect. Rather, evidentiality is a meaning, whether contextual or invariant, expressed by the generic grammatical category which indicates the speaker's attitude toward the narrated event. In Jakobsonian and traditional terms this category is labeled MOOD. Aronson (1977:13–15), however, has argued convincingly that Jakobson's (1957) definitions of mood and status be reversed, in which case the category in question should be labeled STATUS. The question of the precise label for the generic category to which evidentiality belongs, however, is not at issue here. The investigation of such a question is the task of a separate study of generic grammatical categories. The purpose of this article is to describe how evidentiality is expressed and how these expressions developed in the languages under consideration.

The term EVIDENTIALITY will be used in the paper as a convenient label for the meanings to be discussed, but with the understanding that it is not to be taken as literally descriptive. Comparable but nonetheless strikingly different developments in Albanian, where the inverted perfect developed into a separate set of paradigms with a Gesamtbedeutung very much like the Hauptbedeutung of the Balkan Slavic descendents of the Common Slavic perfect, will also be discussed in view of the light they shed on the synchronic and diachronic facts of Balkan evidentiality.[1]

Table 1 illustrates the maximum number of past tense indicative paradigms

---

[1] Unless otherwise specified, this article will discuss the modern literary forms of these languages, i.e. the speech and writing of educated native speakers since the appropriate dates of codification. All examples whose sources are not specified were checked with native speakers.

Table 1.   1SG and 3SG of "Do" in Bulgarian and Macedonian

	Bulgarian		
	Definite Past	**Indefinite Past**	**'Reported'**
AORIST	pravix	sŭm pravil	sŭm pravil
	pravi	e pravil	pravil
IMPERFECT	pravex	/sŭm pravel/	sŭm pravel
	praveše	/ e pravel/	pravel
PLUPERFECT	bjax pravil	[sŭm bil pravil]	sŭm bil pravil
(aorist)	beše pravil	[e bil pravil]	bil pravil
PLUPERFECT	(bjax pravel)	(sŭm bil pravel)	sŭm bil pravel
(imperfect)	(beše pravel)	(e bil pravel)	bil pravel

	Macedonian		
	Definite Past	**Indefinite Past**	**Pluperfect**
AORIST	praviv	sum pravil	bev pravil
	pravi	pravil	beše pravil
IMPERFECT	pravev	sum pravel	bev pravel
	praveše	pravel	beše pravel
PLUPERFECT	imav praveno	sum imal praveno	{beše sum/bev imal praveno}
	imaše praveno	imal praveno	{ beše imal praveno}

Key
Slashes: Forms excluded from the most conservative norm but now generally recognized as part of the literary language.
Square brackets: Forms not mentioned in the grammars but discussed in linguistic literature with examples.
Parentheses: Forms not mentioned in the grammars or linguistic literature but acceptable to some educated speakers and occurring in dialects.
Braces: Forms which either are not truly paradigmatic or do not occur in the literary language although they are mentioned in grammars and handbooks.

which are not totally homonymous in Bulgarian and Macedonian.[2] The aorist/imperfect opposition is an aspectual one similar to but clearly distinct from perfective/imperfective, and will not be relevant to this discussion.[3] The terms DEFINITE PAST and INDEFINITE PAST (Macedonian *minato opredeleno, minato*

---

[2] Macedonian also possesses a present perfect of the type *imam praveno, ima praveno* which refers to the present results of past actions. For the purposes of this article, i.e. in terms of evidentiality, these forms are neutral and pattern like the unmarked present tense forms (cf. Friedman 1977:82–99), and so they will not be considered.

[3] At one time it was claimed that the imperfect *l*-participle could only occur in evidential forms (cf. Andrejčin 1944:§295). This was an artificial distinction and was not even observed by those who

neopredeleno, Bulgarian *minalo opredeleno, minalo neopredeleno*) are traditionally applied to the forms above the dashed lines. Here the label will be used
for the entire column. While 'definiteness' and 'indefiniteness' cannot be taken
as the basic meanings of these forms, as will be seen below, the terms will be
used here because they are convenient, well established, and widely recognized
labels for the paradigmatic sets to which they are applied.

The following explanations of the forms in Table 1 are given to orient the
reader unfamiliar with Slavic languages. The root which carries the meaning 'do'
is *prav-*; the stem vowels *-i-* and *-e-* indicate aorist and imperfect aspect, respectively (in this conjugation). The form in *-l* is descended from a Common Slavic
resultative participle and can still be used participially in Bulgarian but not in
Macedonian, where it can only be used in the formation of compound tenses.
The auxiliaries *sŭm/sum* and *e* are the first and third persons of the present tense
of 'be'; *bjax/bev* and *beše* are the definite past and *sŭm/sum bil* and (*e*) *bil* are the
indefinite past forms of the same persons of the verb.[4] Macedonian also has
grammaticalized (paradigmatic) pluperfects using the definite and indefinite
pasts of *ima* 'have' and the neuter form of the verbal adjective in *-n-*, which is
descended from the Common Slavic past passive participle.[5] These forms can be
translated literally by the English 'had done'.

BALKAN SLAVIC DEFINITE PAST

The definite past in both Macedonian and Bulgarian specifies the speaker's
personal confirmation of the truth of the statement. As the source of this conviction is generally the speaker's direct experience of the event, the forms are
frequently described as marked for witnessing, but numerous examples show that
this definition is too narrow (see, e.g. Aronson 1967:87; Friedman 1977:40).
Thus, for example, a Bulgarian colleague of mine, discussing which of his
colleagues had attended a conference in America which he had not been able to
attend, said of one of them:

(1)   *Beše   tamo.*
       '(She) was there.'

---

prescribed it (see Aronson 1967:91 n.12). It is now generally recognized that the imperfect *l*-
participle has at least some of the same nonevidential uses as the aorist *l*-participle (see, e.g. Penčev
1967; Stankov 1967).

[4] The second person either is identical to the third person or patterns like the first person, and the
plural patterns like the singular, so these forms have been omitted to save space and increase ease of
comparison.

[5] Bulgarian has similar constructions but they are considered dialectal or marginal, and they are
nonparadigmatic (see Georgiev 1957; Teodorov-Balan 1957). In the Bulgarian constructions the
subject must be animate and the participle usually agrees with the direct object, and cannot be formed
from intransitive verbs; it is still a true past passive participle (see Penčev 1968; V. Kostov
1972:378). It should be observed for the sake of completeness that this adjective or participle is
occasionally formed using *-t-* instead of *-n-*; the rules are of no concern to this article.

This despite the fact that his only source of information was a report. Consider also the following Macedonian sentence, based on, but not translated from, the Watergate Tapes (p. 188), which appeared in the daily newspaper *Nova Makedonija* (June 19, 1974, p. 5). Ehrlichman is suggesting what Nixon could say to clean out the 'cancer growing about the Presidency':

> (2) *No   podočna   se slučija   raboti   za   koi   ne   znaev.*
>   but   later   happened   things   about   which   not   (I) knew
>   'But later things happened that I didn't know about.'

The definite past verb *se slučija* refers to actions which the President is specifically denying having known about, much less having seen, at the time they occurred, but whose actual occurrence he must confirm. Hence, the term 'witnessed' does not capture the meaning of these forms.

The definite past can also be used, in both Macedonian and Bulgarian, in sentences which do not actually refer to a definite past time, as in the following Macedonian example:

> (3) *Od   najstarite   vreminja   luǵeto   veruvaa   deka*
>   From   oldest   times   the-people   believed   (past def.)   that
>
> *mesčina   vlijae   vrz   životot   na   zemjata.*
> moon   influences   on   the-life   on   the-earth
>
> (*Nova Makedonija*, November 12, 1972).
> 'Since most ancient times people have believed that the moon influences life
>   on earth.'

Sentences of the type *Ne znaja kogato/kato* (Bulgarian) /*Ne znam koga/kako* (Macedonian) 'I don't know when/how' with a subordinated clause in the definite past also show that 'definiteness', while frequently present as a contextual variant meaning, cannot be taken as the invariant meaning of these forms (cf. Friedman 1977:38–39, 148–149). The one restriction on the occurrence of the definite past is in subordination to clauses which directly contradict the meaning of personal confirmation, as in the following example:

> (4) **Toj   ne   veruva   deka   taa   go   napravi   toa.* (Macedonian)
>   **Toj   ne   vjarva   če   tja   napravi   tova.* (Bulgarian)
>   he   not   believe   that   she   it   did   it
>   *'He doesn't believe that she did it.'

This sentence is ordinarily understood by native speakers as ungrammatical due to the logical impossibility of both disbelieving and confirming something at the same time. The one possible grammatical reading of (4) is if the speaker is actually confirming that she did it despite his disbelief. Similarly, if the subject of the main clause is changed to the first person—*Jas ne veruvan/Az ne vjar-*

vam—the sentence is acceptable only if the speaker actually does believe that she did it, but is displaying extreme surprise at this fact by a nonliteral expression of disbelief, much as in the English *I can't believe she really did it.*

The same type of restrictions apply to the Bulgarian definite pluperfect, i.e. the one contextual restriction is that of anticonfirmation:

(5) *Kaza,   če   bjaxa   xodili   na   plaž.* (Conversation)
    (he) said that   (they) were   gone   to   beach
    He said that they had gone to the beach.'

(6) **Ivan me   kaza,   če   Petŭr   beše   došŭl,   no   az*
    Ivan   to-me said   that Peter   was   come   but I

    ne   vjarvam (Stankov 1967:342).
    not   believe
    * 'Ivan told me that Peter arrived, but I don't believe it.'

Similar restrictions also apply to the Macedonian definite pluperfect, but with an additional sharpening of the confirmative/nonconfirmative opposition from privative to equipollent, and with an unmarked form in between. There also appears to be some sharpening of the opposition in Bulgarian, but this will become clearer after consideration of the indefinite pasts. The main point here is that 'confirmative' functions as the Gesamtbedeutung of the definite past forms.

MACEDONIAN INDEFINITE PAST

Due to questions of auxiliary usage, the Macedonian and Bulgarian indefinite pasts will be examined separately. In Macedonian, this form, which is descended from the Common Slavic perfect, can still be used as a perfect, as an unmarked or indefinite past, and also in definite past contexts. As it is impossible to assign a single meaning which is present in all uses of the indefinite past, i.e. as there is no specific type of restriction on its occurrence as there is for the definite past, it must be treated as unmarked with respect to the definite past. This can be seen from the following examples:

(6) *Dosta   sme   rabotele.* (Conversation)
    enough   (we) are   worked
    'We've worked enough.' (One retired man commenting to another on their right to a pension)

(7) *Tatko   mi   bil   mnogu   meraklija   za   cveḱa.* (Conversation)
    father to-me   was   very   fond   for   flowers
    'My father was very fond of flowers.'

(8) *Sum   stanal   noḱeska   vo   eden.* (Koneski 1967:462)
    (I) am   got up   last night at   one
    'I got up at one this morning.'

Despite the fact that the indefinite past has these nonevidential uses, however, it will ordinarily be assumed that the speaker is using this form in order to avoid personal confirmation of the information, e.g. due to its being based on a report, in the absence of contextual specification to the contrary. Thus, for example, if the dative-possessive pronoun *mi* 'my' were changed to *mu* 'his' in example (7), it would normally be assumed that the speaker was basing the statement on indirect information, since there would be nothing in the context such as a first person reference to indicate otherwise.

The opposition between the nonpluperfect definite and indefinite pasts in Macedonian can be explained in the following manner. The definite past is marked for the speaker's confirmation of the information, as indicated by the fact that the one type of context in which a definite past cannot occur is one which specifically excludes the possibility of such confirmation (4–5). The indefinite past cannot be restricted to a single invariant meaning because it has retained its old perfect uses (6) while at the same time it has developed into an unmarked past (7–8; as in the other Slavic languages, this is indicated by its use with definite past time adverbs and in situations not focusing on present results). Concurrently the indefinite past has also developed a chief contextual variant meaning of nonconfirmativity, reportedness, or evidentiality, due to its contrast with the markedly confirmative definite past.[6] Thus despite the fact that the indefinite past is statistically less frequent than the definite past, it is unmarked because it is also semantically less restricted.[7]

BULGARIAN INDEFINITE PAST

The facts of Bulgarian are essentially the same as those of Macedonian, with one difference: the auxiliary is always absent from the third person of the literary

---

[6] It should be noted that even the meaning 'distanced' suggested by Lunt (1952:92; cf. also Aksu and Slobin 1981 on Turkish) cannot cover all the uses of the Macedonian indefinite past. The indefinite past in the following sentence specifically contradicts such a meaning:

(i) *Jas sum go <u>skršil</u> šišeto namerno vo dva saatot.*
     I   am   it   broke   the-bottle purposefully at two the-hour
     'I broke the bottle on purpose at two o'clock.'

See Friedman (1977:36–37) for further discussion of this point.

[7] Some scholars have proposed that the Macedonian verbal system possesses two totally homonymous sets of forms: one nonevidential indefinite past and the other markedly evidential or reported. From a diachronic viewpoint it is clear that additional meanings have accrued to a single form, the indefinite past, and that these meanings resulted from or were at least influenced by the actual shift of meaning in the definite past to marked confirmativity. Also, given the fact that the meaning of the indefinite past can only be determined from the context in which it is used, an analysis relying on total homonymy must often employ arbitrary decisions in order to determine which 'paradigm' a given form represents. One could even propose defining as many paradigms as there are contexts. In view of all this, I consider the indefinite past to be a single form with several meanings or uses.

Macedonian indefinite past (as it is in the west-central dialects on which the literary language is primarily based), but in literary Bulgarian (as in some Bulgarian and Macedonian dialects), it is possible for the third person auxiliary to be present or absent. Due to this alternation, all traditional Bulgarian grammars and linguistic studies published in the last four decades have set up two sets of paradigms which are always homonymous in the first two persons—one with and one without the auxiliary in the third person. The form with the auxiliary, like the Macedonian indefinite past, can be used in all types of contexts and is treated as unmarked (cf. Aronson 1967:89–92). The form without the auxiliary, however, is treated as marked for reportedness, and it is this form which is cited by Jakobson (1957:4) as marked for evidentiality.

As was indicated at the beginning of this chapter, if an invariant meaning is assigned to a given form and the form is said to be marked for a certain grammatical category, then that meaning must be present in every occurrence of the form in question. However, such is not always the case in the Bulgarian third person indefinite past without an auxiliary, which is said to be marked for reportedness. This can be seen from the following examples, which use the indefinite past without auxiliary but do not carry the meaning of reportedness:

(9) *Sto na sto bili*   *pokaneni.* (Conversation)
     100%   (they) were   invited
     'Absolutely, they were invited.'

(10) *Togava čak se ogledaxme*   i   *vidjaxme, če   sestra*
     then   just (we) looked around   and   saw   that sister

     mu   izbjagala. (Dejanova 1970:847)
     to-him   ran away
     'Just then we looked around and saw that his sister had run away.'

(11) *. . . podigna malko oči—   i   v   ottatŭšnija sokak, i   v*
     (he) raised   a little eyes   and   in   the-next   street   and   in

     po-ottatŭšnija . . . plŭznali bežanici kato mravunjak.
     the-more-next   swarmed   refugees like   anthill

     'He looked up a little (and saw that) both in the next street and the one after
        that refugees swarmed like (ants on) an anthill.'
                                                        (Dejanova 1970:847).

Example (9) requires a clarifying context: it was uttered by a colleague of mine in Sofia during the course of a discussion as to whether a certain delegation had been invited to a congress. My colleague was convinced that they had been invited, although his conviction was not based on any kind of direct or indirect evidence, i.e. the statement was not based on a report or even a deduction, but only on the speaker's assumptions and expectations regarding the normal conduct of such matters. It is clear from their own contexts that (10) and (11) also do not involve reported actions.

The data from a recent study by Roth (1979) can be added to these examples. Among other things, this study contains fourteen pages of transcribed narratives based on reported information which document what I myself have observed in Sofia and elsewhere in Bulgaria: different speakers will omit or include the third person auxiliary to varying degrees, but reportedness (or any other form of evidentiality) cannot be said to function as the determining factor. Thus, in Roth's texts the speakers switch back and forth between forms with and without the auxiliary in the same narrative, based on the same information, as in the following examples:[8]

(12) *I*   *se sŭbrali*   *momčeta* *pokraj* *njakakŭv*   *ogŭn*   *i*
      and   gathered   lads   by   some kind of   fire   and

      sa   *započvali*   *razni*   *istorii*   *za*   *samodivi*   *i*   *za*
      (they) are   began   various   stories   about   fairies   and   about

      takiva. (Roth 1979:177)
      such
      'And the lads gathered around a fire and began stories about fairies and the
          like.'

(13) *Toj*   *si*   *ja*   *e*   *viždal*   *tam*   *i*   *nakraja*   *se zapoznali*
      he   to-himself   her   is   saw   there   and   in-the-end   (they) met

      na   *ski*   —*bili sa*   *na*   *ski*. (Roth 1979:179)
      on   ski   (they) were on   ski
      'He saw her there and finally they met one another skiing—they were on a
          ski trip.'

(14) *Tja*   *stojala*   *po*   *cjal*   *den*   *na*   *izložbata*   —*i*   *sled*
      she   stood   for   whole   day   at   the-exhibition   and   after

      tova   *večer*   *se e*   *razxoždala*. (Roth 1979:180)
      that   evening   (she) is   strolled
      'She would stand (on duty) at the exhibition all day, and in the evenings she
          would go out for a walk.'

In each of these examples forms with and without the auxiliary are used for events which are identical in terms of evidentiality.

On the basis of data such as these, supported by the historical and dialectological facts given immediately below, I would propose that omission of the auxiliary in the third person of the Bulgarian indefinite past is not the marker of a separate evidential paradigm but rather part of the process of total auxiliary loss in the third person. This process is well attested in numerous Slavic languages and dialects (e.g. Russian, where the auxiliary was lost in all three persons,

---

[8] For those unfamiliar with Bulgarian, it should be noted that *se* is an enclitic marker of intransitivity (as it is in Macedonian) and does not affect the occurrence of the auxiliary. The 3PL.auxiliary of the indefinite past is *sa*.

beginning with the third [Buslaev 1959:363]; and the Macedonian dialect of Kumanovo, about 50 kilometers from the Bulgarian border, where the third person auxiliary is entirely facultative [Vidoeski 1962:218, 234]). The question can be raised as to whether auxiliary omission in Bulgarian can be treated as semantically distinctive in any systematic fashion such as, for example, signaling a difference between backgrounding and foregrounding or between scene–setting or stative events and plot–advancing actions. The data do not appear to support such a distinction, but the question of the semantics and degree of systematicity of third person auxiliary loss in Bulgarian is in need of a special study which has yet to be undertaken. It is clear, however, that the traditional explanation based on evidentiality is contradicted by the data presented here.[9] For the purposes of this article, two observations are sufficient: (a) omission of the auxiliary in the third person of the Bulgarian indefinite past is a syntactic phenomenon which does not justify the establishment of independent paradigms: (b) whatever the semantic value or conditioning contexts of auxiliary omission, if any, it cannot be treated as a signal of marking for evidentiality.[10] Thus the opposition between the nonpluperfect definite and indefinite pasts in Bulgarian is of essentially the same type as in Macedonian; the definite past is marked for confirmativity while the indefinite past, with or without its auxiliary in the third person, is unmarked and therefore implies, but does not specify, nonconfirmativity.

BALKAN SLAVIC PLUPERFECTS

The situation in the pluperfects seems to involve the sharpening of the privative confirmative/nonconfirmative opposition to equipollent oppositions. Of the forms labeled pluperfect in Table 1, only those using the definite past of 'be' and the aorist *l*-participle (3SG *beše pravil*) were inherited from the older system; the others are all later developments. Aside from the spread of the aorist/imperfect aspectual opposition, which need not concern us here, Macedonian has two new pluperfects using the definite and indefinite pasts of 'have' (3SG *imaše praveno, imal praveno*) while Bulgarian has new pluperfects using the indefinite past of 'be' with and without its own auxiliary (3SG *e bil pravil, bil pravil*).

The equipollent sharpening of the confirmative/nonconfirmative opposition in the pluperfects results in a set of restrictions which are truly evidential in

---

[9] As was observed in note 1, the term 'literary language' is used here to refer to actual usage rather than the prescriptions of standard grammars. If a literary language is defined as being whatever the standard grammars say it is, then any counterexamples to those prescriptions are, by definition, merely mistakes.

[10] Cf. Aronson (1967:93, especially n. 14) on the neutralization of evidentiality in Bulgarian. The type of analysis which employs a theory of total homonymy such as that mentioned in note 7 with regard to Macedonian has been carried even further in most Bulgarian grammars and other works, but essentially the same arguments apply against it.

nature—witnessed/nonwitnessed in Macedonian and confirmative/nonwitnessed in Bulgarian. Thus in Macedonian the definite pluperfect cannot be subordinated to verbs of reporting, while the indefinite pluperfect cannot be subordinated to verbs of witnessing and direct perception but can only be used for reports and, rarely, deductions and suppositions. The third type of pluperfect, the original one (3SG *beše pravil*), is neutral with respect to these distinctions in the speech of most younger and some older speakers.[11] So, for example, sentences (15) and (16) are unacceptable because they violate these restrictions, while sentences of the type illustrated by (6), mutatis mutandis, are acceptable (see also example ii, note 11):

(15) **Toj reče deka tie   ja   imaa svršeno rabotata.* (definite
        he   said that they it   had   finished the-job   pluperfect)
        *'He said that they had finished the job.'

(16) **Jas vidov kako/deka toj go   imal napraveno toa.* (indefinite
        I   saw   how/that   he   it   had   done   that pluperfect)
        *'I saw how/that he had done it.'

In Bulgarian the sharpening of these distinctions is not as rigid, insofar as the definite pluperfect (which in Bulgarian is the inherited form) can be used for reported actions just as the definite past can (example 5). The key issue here is the significance of the omission of the present auxiliary in the third person indefinite pluperfect. It appears that while the form with the present auxiliary is neutral, that without the present auxiliary may actually be limited to reports,

---

[11] The Macedonian pluperfect with the definite past of 'be' (3SG *beše*) is felt by some older speakers to have the same restrictions as that with the definite past of 'have' (3SG *imaše*) due to the fact that both use definite past auxiliaries. Younger speakers and other older speakers, however, will accept sentences such as the following:

(ii) *Ivan reče deka tie   ja   bea   svršile   rabotata pred da   stasav*
        Ivan said that they it   were   finished the-job   before that arrived

       jas, no   ne   veruvam vo   toa.
        I   but not believe in   that
        'Ivan said that they had finished the job before I arrived, but I don't believe it.'

The picture is further complicated by the fact that the forms using 'have' are not native to the dialects spoken east and north of the river Vardar, which runs from northwest to southeast roughly through the middle of Macedonia, while forms with the *l*-participle become increasingly rare as one moves southwest of the Vardar and eventually disappear altogether in southwestern Aegean (Greek) Macedonia. Since the establishment of the literary language in 1944, the spread of education has been leveling these dialectal distinctions within Yugoslavia, but they still influence usage and judgments, especially in older speakers. In terms of tense form usage, the literary language follows the dialect of the west-central town of Prilep most closely, but even here speakers differ in their judgments on the acceptability of sentences such as (ii).

deductions, statements of doubt and disbelief, etc. This phenomenon can be analyzed as a stricter semantic-syntactic conditioning of auxiliary loss, however, rather than as the basis for a separate paradigm.

The question of syntactic rules vs. grammatical categories is particularly vexed in instances such as Bulgarian auxiliary loss. The fact that evidentiality does seem to serve as a conditioning factor for auxiliary loss in the pluperfects but clearly cannot do so in the nonpluperfect indefinite pasts suggests that the difference between rule conditions and grammatical categories is one of degree rather than kind.[12] A more detailed study of conditioning factors must be conducted, however, before any definite conclusions can be reached in this area.

DIACHRONIC EXPLANATION

The Balkan Slavic synchronic situation which has been described here—a marked confirmative definite past, an unmarked indefinite past whose Hauptbedeutung is nonconfirmative, and a series of pluperfects in which this nonconfirmative Hauptbedeutung becomes a type of Gesamtbedeutung in opposition to marked confirmative and unmarked forms—has two possible diachronic explanations, which are themselves not mutually exclusive. The first possibility is that as the semantic field of the definite past became restricted to contexts in which the speaker personally confirmed the information being conveyed, the semantic field of the old perfect expanded to include nonconfirmed, nonperfect contexts. The second possibility is that the current situation resulted from the fact that the perfect, due to its indefiniteness and its focus on the results of a past action rather than on the past action itself, has a natural tendency to be used for conveying reported and other nonwitnessed information (Lohmann 1937:43); it also has a tendency to develop into an unmarked past, as it did in all the other Slavic languages, where it has completely replaced the synthetic (definite) pasts (except in Lusatian and some varieties of Serbo-Croatian, where the synthetic pasts survive as marked forms).

Regardless of whether one or both of these explanations apply to the nonpluperfect developments, it is clear that the pluperfect forms have become paradigmatically more complex since the dissolution of Common Slavic (during the same period in which the indefinite past developed its evidential Hauptbedeutung) and have sharpened the confirmative/nonconfirmative opposition from privative to equipollent. Those pluperfects which arose during the period when the meanings associated with evidentiality also developed have more rigid marking restrictions than earlier pluperfects. Thus the newer and more highly marked forms reflect a sharpened, more extreme semantic-syntactic development than the older, less marked forms.

---

[12] Suggested to me by Johanna Nichols (personal communication).

Table 2.   1SG Indicative of 'Have' in Albanian[a]

	Nonadmirative	Admirative
Present	*kam*	*paskam*
Perfect	*kam pasur*	*paskam pasur*
Imperfect	*kisha*	*paskësha*
Pluperfect (impf.)	*kisha pasur*	*paskësha pasur*
Aorist	*pata*	—
2nd Pluperfect (aor.)	*pata pasur*	—

[a]Excluded from this table are the compound pasts using the Geg short participle as these are marginal in the modern literary language.

THE ALBANIAN ADMIRATIVE

The Albanian verbal system provides an instructive contrast to Balkan Slavic in its treatment of evidentiality. Albanian possesses two series of indicative tense forms, traditionally labeled *mënyrë dëftore* 'indicative mood' and *mënyrë habitore* 'admirative mood', which will be referred to by the labels NONADMIRATIVE and ADMIRATIVE.[13] Historically, the admirative is derived from an inverted perfect with a truncated participle (Demiraj 1971:32), as can be seen in Table 2, which gives the lsg of *kam* 'have' in its nonadmirative and admirative indicative forms by way of illustration.

Although the admirative is traditionally defined as a mood expressing surprise, it is also used to express irony, doubt, reportedness, etc. In all its uses the admirative somehow refers to the speaker's present or past nonconfirmation of the truth of the statement.[14] This is obvious when the admirative is used to express irony or doubt (as in example 18), but it is also the case when the admirative is used for surprise (as in examples iii and iv, note 14) or reported speech (as in example 17). Surprise results from a past state during which the speaker would not have accepted the truth of some subsequently discovered fact or event. In this manner, doubt/irony and surprise are two facets of the same type of noncommitment; one refers to a state continuing into the moment of speech, the other refers to the real or hypothetical existence of such a state rejected at the moment of speech. It should be noted that surprise is not to be limited to

---

[13] It has been argued by Sytov (1979:110–111) and Friedman (1981) that the admirative is not a nonindicative mood for a number of reasons: (a) it refers to ontologically real events (cf. Aronson 1977:13); (b) it ordinarily takes the indicative negators *nuk* and *s'* rather than the modal negator *mos*, (c) when functioning modally it is subordinated to the special modal particle *të*. Sytov suggests that a Jakobsonian category such as 'evidential' might provide a better label. Following Aronson (1977:13), I suggest that it is marked for a form of status (Friedman 1981). Regardless of the concrete solution, it is clear that the admirative is not a mood like the optative, subjunctive, or conditional, but is opposed to them, together with the nonadmirative indicative, as unmarked for such modality.

[14] For more detailed discussion see Friedman (1981).

expressions of strong amazement. Any expressive relation of the speaker to the speech event in which there is some nuance of the unexpected can be included in this use of surprise (cf. the use of terms such as 'unprepared mind' in Aksu and Slobin, this volume, 'new information' in Akatsuka 1981, and also Lunt's 'distanced').[15]

Albanian has a rule of sequence of tenses for ordinary reported speech very much like that of English, so that if a report is rendered using the admirative the speaker is expressing noncommitment to the truth of the information, either due to uncertainty or disbelief, or because it is somehow surprising. In addition to examples (iii) and (iv) of note 14, the first of which expresses disbelieving surprise and the second of which expresses pure, or believing, surprise, the following examples illustrate the use of the admirative to express doubt and reportedness:

(17) *Një   farë   prifti   nga   Trikalla,   i quajtur   Dionis,   u vu*
        one   kind   of-priest   from   Trikalla   called   Dionis   put-himself

---

[15] Akatsuka's argument that 'new information' is, in a sense, unreal for the speaker, creates a bridge between the category evaluating ontological reality ('mood' in Aronson's terms) and the category expressing speaker attitude ('status' in Aronson's terms). While this description of the admirative makes it sound very similar to the Turkish forms in *-miş* (see Aksu and Slobin 1981), there are significant differences in their uses, as can be seen from comparing the following sentences taken from Albanian and Turkish translations of the Bulgarian novel *Baj Ganjo:*

(iii) *Nga   e   paske   marrë   vesh   ti   që   unë   jam*
      whence   it   have   gotten   ear   you   that   I   am

     liberal? (Albanian; Konstantinov 1975:118)
     liberal

     Liberallerden   olduğumu   sana   kim   söyledi? (Turkish; Konstantinov 1972:182)
     From-liberals   my-being   to-you   who   said
     'Where did you hear that I am a liberal?' or 'Who told you that I am liberal?'

(iv) *Çudi   qysh   e   hëngërki   ju   gjellën,   fare   pa   bukë!—tha*
    wonder   that   it   eat   you   the-soup   completely   without   bread   said

     baj   Ganua   i çuditur. (Turkish; Konstantinov 1975:58)
     Mr.   Gano   amazed

     Siz   ekmeksiz   mi   içiyorsunuz   şu   çorbayı   yahu?   diye   de
     you   breadless   ?   are-drinking   this   soup   !   saying   and

     şaşar   Bay   Ganü. (Albanian; Konstantinov 1972:79)
     wonders   Mr.   Ganü
     '"My goodness, why you're drinking the soup without bread!" said Baj Ganjo in amazement.'

In both examples Albanian uses admiratives, but Turkish does not use *-miş* forms in either. Cf. also example (18) where the Turkish equivalent of the Albanian present admirative *u pritka* 'is met, awaited, treated' is the so-called aorist (*geniş zaman*) *karşılanp ağırlanır* 'be met and treated as a guest' (Konstantinov 1972:84).

në   krye   të   masës   së   fshatarëve,   duke   thirrur   se
at   head   of   mass   of   peasants   while   shouting   that

në   trupin   e tij   <u>paskej</u>   <u>hyrë</u>   fryma   e shenjtë. (Godo 1972:57)
into   body   his   had   entered   spirit   holy

'Some priest from Trikalla called Dionis put himself at the head of the
peasant masses shouting that the holy spirit had entered his body.'

    (18)   *E   na   i   <u>dashka</u>   bullgarët . . .   Ai   ë! . . .   E   pse,*
           and   to-us   them   loves   Bulgarians   He   hah!   And   why

           kështu   <u>u pritka</u>   një   Bullgar? (Konstantinov 1975:61)
           thus   is met   a   Bulgarian

           'And he (said he) likes us Bulgarians. Him? Hah! After all, is that how you
           treat a Bulgarian?'

In example (17), the author is casting doubt on Dionis's claim, while in (18) the
form *dashka* is a mocking report of what someone else has said, while *u pritka*
expresses surprise at the actual treatment. Thus, the three major uses of the
Albanian admirative—surprise, disbelief, and reportedness—correspond to the
three major types of nonconfirmative use of the indefinite past in Balkan
Slavic.[16]

COMPARISON OF ALBANIAN AND BALKAN SLAVIC

In some contexts, these nonconfirmative uses of the Balkan Slavic indefinite past
appear to have a present meaning, and this has sometimes been taken as evidence
that the nonconfirmative uses of these forms constitute a separate, tenseless
paradigm marked only for evidentiality. As will be seen, however, all such uses
in Balkan Slavic have some type of past reference. Since Weigand's (1923/4)
comparison of the Bulgarian indefinite past with the Albanian present admirative, which he erroneously treats as a synchronic inverted perfect, it has been
commonly assumed that there is a one-to-one correspondence between the Albanian admirative and the nonconfirmative uses of the Balkan Slavic indefinite
past. In actuality, as can be seen from comparisons of translations (See Friedman
1982), the vast majority of Albanian present admiratives correspond to Balkan
Slavic simple presents, while most Balkan Slavic indefinite pasts correspond to
Albanian nonadmirative past tense forms. Thus, for example, the Balkan Slavic
equivalent of present admirative *hëngërki* 'you eat' in example (iv) of note 14 is
the present tense form *jadete* (Konstantinov 1973:58, 1967:50), while that of
present admirative *u pritka* 'is met' in example (18) is Bulgarian *se posrešta* and

---

[16] As was indicated earlier, the Bulgarian indefinite past generally lacks the third singular
auxiliary in these usages, but this is not always the case (see, e.g., Stojanov 1964:§407, Demina
1959:322–323 n. 36).

Macedonian *se prečekuva* (Konstantinov 1973:60, 1967:54), which are also present tense forms.

Those few examples in which an Albanian present admirative corresponds in translation to a Balkan Slavic indefinite past refer to some ontologically past state or event and usually employ the verbs 'be' or 'have'. Thus the form *dashka* 'loves' in example (18) corresponds to the Bulgarian indefinite past *običăl* and the Macedonian *sakal* (Konstantinov 1973,60, 1967:54), but the speech event being mocked by these words took place in the past. It is impossible to use an indefinite past with a present reported meaning unless there is a past speech event to which it refers, as can be seen from the following example:

(19)   *Ivan   šte   kaže   če   ne   znael. (Bulgarian)
       *Jovan   ḱe   reče   deka ne   znael. (Macedonian)
        John   will   say   that not   knew
       *'John will say that he doesn't know.'

The form *ne znael* cannot report the speaker's anticipation that John will say *Ne znam* 'I don't know', because in such a context there is no past event—neither the saying nor the knowing—for *znael* to refer to. Hence the indefinite past cannot replace a present tense form, i.e. it cannot have a 'present' meaning, unless it actually has some type of concrete past reference. Sentence (19) could be used to mean 'John will say he didn't know', but in that case *ne znael* must refer to a time in the past when, as John will claim, he did not know. Thus the use of the indefinite past to render reported speech events with an apparently present meaning (as in the Slavic translations of 18) actually represents a type of sequence of tense usage similar to the English *He said he loved Bulgarians* as a report of *I love Bulgarians*.

Most Balkan Slavic examples with 'be' and 'have' corresponding to an Albanian present admirative represent a use of the indefinite past to refer to a state which has been true before but was only discovered by the speaker at the moment of speech:

(20) *Ama   če   si bil*   *prost   čovek.* (Bulgarian; Konstantinov
                                                      1967:83)
       Ama   si bil   *prost   čovek.* (Macedonian; Konstantinov
                                                      1967:87)
       but   that (you) have been simple   person
       'My, what a simpleton you are!'

Here the statement refers to a state which existed before the moment of speech but only became apparent to the speaker at the time of speaking, so it has the force of 'as it turns out, it has been true all along that . . .'. English normally uses a present tense in such contexts, and Albanian could use the present admirative *qenke* '(you) are' as the translation of the Balkan Slavic *si bil,* but the

Balkan Slavic usage can still be said to refer to the past time during which the state was in existence but unsuspected by the speaker.[17] The actual translation of (20) in the Albanian version of *Baj Ganjo* illustrates the difference between this type of usage and ordinary Albanian admirative usage, for it is in precisely such contexts, with the verbs 'be' and 'have' referring to states which existed for some time before the speech event, that Albanian can also use an admirative perfect, as well as a nonadmirative perfect or an admirative imperfect or pluperfect. All these possibilities are illustrated in the Albanian translation of *Baj Ganjo,* but the actual translation of sentence (20) used a perfect admirative:

(21) *Ama,   i humbur   fare   paske   qenë.* (Konstantinov 1975:92)
      but   lost   completely (you) have been

These facts show that the Balkan Slavic admirative phenomenon, which is a special use of a past tense form of 'be' or 'have' to refer to a pre-existent but unsuspected state discovered at the moment of speech, actually corresponds to a phenomenon of exactly the same type in Albanian and cannot be equated with the Albanian series of admirative paradigms. The Balkan Slavic and Albanian construction with 'be' and 'have' is a type of usage, while the Albanian admirative is a morphologically distinct set of grammatically marked paradigms.

Although the Balkan Slavic system does not correspond exactly to the Albanian system, the comparison is instructive insofar as the new nonconfirmative meanings which became associated with the Balkan Slavic indefinite past are very similar to those which became associated with the Albanian inverted perfect, which subsequently developed into a paradigmatically distinct set of marked forms.

CONCLUSIONS

On the basis of the material presented here, the following statements can be made about evidentiality in the Balkans.[18] First of all, the forms under consideration

---

[17] Cf. the Turkish version, which uses the enclitic *miş*-form of 'be':

(v) *Amma   da   akılsız   şeymişsin   be!* (Konstantinov 1972:134)
     but   and   mindless   thing-you–are hey

[18] Of the other languages of the Balkans, Greek and the Romance languages do not have any type of grammaticalized evidential distinction, and Turkish is treated elsewhere in this volume (see Aksu and Slobin), although there may be significant differences between standard Turkish usage and the Rumelian dialects and Gagauz. A study of such differences has yet to be undertaken, but the subjective impression of some informants is that Turks from the Balkans do use the relevant forms differently. It is reported that the Sliven dialect of Romani also has an evidential distinction based on an invariant particle and modeled on the Bulgarian use of the *l*-participle (K. Kostov 1973:108). It is

do not mark the source of information or evidence, but rather the speaker's attitude toward it. The question of whether the source of information was a report, deduction, direct experience, or something else is answered by the context in which the speaker's choice of form occurs. Thus terms such as 'evidential' or 'inferential' do not really define the grammatical category expressed by these forms. Rather, these terms describe specific meanings associated with a generic category.

As was indicated at the beginning of this article, the relevant category is that which expresses the speaker's attitude toward the narrated event. Jakobson (1957), following Vinogradov and traditional opinion, labels this category MOOD. Aronson (1977:13–15), however, follows Gołąb's (1964:1) definition of mood as the ontological (objective) evaluation of the narrated event (modal = nonreal/indicative = real; see also Kuryłowicz 1956:26; Janakiev 1962; Lyons 1969:304ff.) and uses Jakobson's term 'status' to refer to the subjective evaluation of the narrated event of the type which has been considered in this article. Of particular relevance to Aronson's arguments are similarities and relationships between mood and aspect (cf., e.g., *He would eat lox and bagel every Monday* (a) *if he could afford it.* (b) *when he was in graduate school.*), and distinctions between ontological evaluations such as negation and interrogation, which Jakobson gives as examples of status, and subjective evaluations such as the English assertive *dó* (e.g., *He díd go.*), which Jakobson also gives as an example of status, but which Aronson compares to the Balkan Slavic phenomena discussed here. These arguments, and the entire question of labeling the category expressing the speaker's attitude, however, are beyond the scope of this article. Such a task requires the complete re-evaluation of the nature of modality. The goal here has been to distinguish the relevant paradigms, define the meanings they express, and indicate their routes of development.

In Balkan Slavic the Common Slavic aorist and imperfect developed into the definite past with an invariant marking for the speaker's confirmation of the information being conveyed. At the same time the Common Slavic perfect developed into the indefinite past with a chief contextual variant meaning of nonconfirmation. (During the course of its development into an indefinite past, the perfect, which could only be formed on the basis of the aorist stem in Common Slavic, developed an imperfect/aorist opposition parallel to that of the definite past.) The most common reason for the speaker's choosing the form which can express the meaning of nonconfirmation is that the source of information is a report or deduction, but it is the speaker's attitude toward the reliability of the truth-value of the information, and not the evidence on which it is based, that is

---

sometimes claimed that Serbo-Croatian possesses a witnessed/nonwitnessed distinction based on the forms which correspond to the Balkan Slavic definite and indefinite past, but there is much disagreement on this point, and the arguments for it do not seem particularly convincing (see Friedman 1977:34, 123).

crucial in determining the choice of forms, as was seen in examples (1), (2), and (4). The perfect, however, also retained its old resultative nuances while expanding into contexts vacated by the definite past. Thus, as in the rest of Slavic, the perfect has become the unmarked past in Balkan Slavic by virtue of the fact that it cannot be assigned a single invariant meaning and applies to the widest range of contexts.

In the pluperfects, however, the development of the confirmative/ nonconfirmative opposition coincided with the development of new forms. Here the opposition became equipollent rather than privative, with new forms being both markedly confirmative and markedly nonconfirmative. This is to say that what was added on to an existing form as its Hauptbedeutung could become the Gesamtbedeutung of newly developed forms. The implication that the speaker's attitude is based on the source of the information has been virtually grammaticalized in these newer forms, as seen in examples (15) and (16).

In Albanian, the type of nonconfirmative meanings which appear as the chief contextual variant meanings of the Balkan Slavic descendants of the old perfect became attached to an inverted perfect which then broke off and formed a separate set of paradigms without the development of any marked confirmative forms.[19]

Thus, evidentiality in the Balkans actually involves the speaker's attitude toward the truth of the statement. The languages considered here display a pattern in which nonconfirmative evidential meaning appears as invariant only in newly developed forms, i.e. those which developed during the rise of evidentiality itself, while confirmative meaning occurs where nonconfirmativity is also present as a chief contextual variant meaning.

REFERENCES

Akatsuka, Noriko, 1981. Conditionals. Unpublished paper.

Andrejčin, Ljubomir. 1944. Osnovna bŭlgarska gramatika. Sofia: Hemus.

Aronson, Howard I. 1967. The grammatical categories of the indicative in the contemporary Bulgarian literary language. To honor Roman Jakobson, vol. 1, 82–98. The Hague: Mouton.

———. 1977. Interrelationships between aspect and mood in Bulgarian. Folia Slavica 1,1.9–32.

Buslaev, F. 1959. Istoričeskaja grammatika russkogo jazyka. Moscow: Akademija nauk SSSR.

Comrie, Bernard. 1976. Aspect. Cambridge: Cambridge University.

Dejanova, Marija. 1970. Izjavitelnijat perfekt bez spomogatelen glagol v bŭlgarski ezik v sravnenie sŭs sŭrboxŭrvatski. Bŭlgarski ezik 19.843–853.

Demina, Evgenija I. 1959. Pereskazyvatel'nye formy v sovremmenom bolgarskom literaturnom jazyke. Voprosy grammatiki bolgarskogo literaturnogo jazyka, ed. by Samuil B. Bernštejn, 313–378. Moscow: Akademija nauk SSSR.

Demiraj, Shaban. 1971. Habitorja dhe mosha e saj. Studime filologjike 8,3.31–49.

Dodi, Anastas, 1968. Për vlerën e së kryerës së dëftorës në gjuhën shqipe. Studime filologjike 5,1.60–74.

---

[19] The nonadmirative perfect has become or is becoming the unmarked past in Albanian (cf. Dodi 1968).

Friedman, Victor A. 1977. The grammatical categories of the Macedonian indicative. Columbus: Slavica.

————. 1981. Admirativity and confirmativity. Zeitschrift für Balkanologie 17.12–28.

————. 1982. Admirativity in Bulgarian compared with Albanian and Turkish. Bulgaria past and present, vol. 1, 63–67. Sofia: Bulgarian Academy of Sciences.

Georgiev, Vladimir. 1957. Vŭznikvane na novi složni glagolni formi sŭs spomogatelen glagol *imam*. Izvestija na Instituta za bŭlgarski ezik 5.31–59.

Godo, Sabri. 1972. Ali Pashë Tepelena. Prishtina: Rilindja.

Gołąb, Zbigniew, 1964. The problem of verbal moods in Slavic languages. International Journal of Slavic Linguistics and Poetics 8.1–36.

Haarman, Harald. 1970. Die indirekte Erlebnisform als grammatische Kategorie. Eine eurasische Isoglosse. Wiesbaden: Harrassowitz.

Jakobson, Roman. 1957. Shifters, verbal categories, and the Russian verb. Cambridge: Harvard University.

Janakiev, Miroslav. 1962. Za gramemite naričani v bŭlgarska gramatika 'segašno vreme' i 'bŭdešte vreme'. Izvestija na Instituta za bŭlgarski ezik 8.420–432.

Koneski, Blaže. 1967. Gramatika na makedonskiot literaturen jazik. Skopje: Kultura.

Konstantinov, Aleko. 1973. Baj Ganjo. Sofia: Bŭlgarski pisatel. (1st ed. 1895).

————. 1967. Baj Ganjo. Skopje: Kultura. (Macedonian translation by Ǵorǵi Caca).

————. 1972. Bay Ganü. Istanbul: Milliyet. (Turkish translation by İsmail B. Ağlagül).

————. 1975. Baj Gano. Prishtina: Rilindja. (Albanian translation by Dhurata Xoxa).

Kostov, Kiril. 1973. Zur Bedeutung des Zigeunerischen für die Erforschung Grammatischer Interferenzerscheinungen. Balkansko ezikoznanie 16.99–113.

Kostov, V. 1972. Semantische Beobachtung über die Verbindung von *imam* mit dem Partizipium Perfecti Passivi im Bulgarischen. Zeitschrift für Slawistik 17.371–379.

Kuryłowicz, Jerzy. 1956. L'Apophonie en indo-européen. Wrocław: Polska Akademija Nauk.

Lohmann, Johannes. 1937. Ist das Idg. Perfektum nominalen Ursprungs? Kunst Zeitschrift 64.42–61.

Lunt, Horace. 1952. A grammar of the Macedonian literary language. Skopje: Državno knigoizdatelstvo.

Lyons, John. 1969. Introduction to theoretical linguistics. Cambridge: Cambridge University.

Nova Makedonija. (Daily newspaper published in Skopje.)

Penčev, Jordan. 1967. Kŭm vŭprosa za vremenata v sŭvremennija bŭlgarski ezik. Bŭlgarski ezik 17.131–143.

————. 1968. Konstrukcii s glagola *imam*. Slavističen sbornik, ed. by Lj. Andrejčin and St. Stojkov, 173–177. Sofia: Bŭlgarska akademija na naukite.

Roth, Juliana. 1979. Die indirekten Erlebnisformen im Bulgarischen: Eine Untersuchung zu ihrem Gebrauch in der Umgangssprache. (Slavistische Beiträge 130). Wiesbaden: Sagner.

Serebrennikov, Boris A. 1974. Verojatnostnye obosnovanija v komparativisktike. Moscow: Nauka.

Stankov, Valentin. 1967. Kategorii na indikativa v sŭvremennija bŭlgarski ezik. Bŭlgarski ezik 1967:330–344.

Stojanov, Stojan. 1964. Gramatika na bŭlgarskija knižoven ezik. Sofia: Nauka i izkustvo.

Sytov, A. P. 1979. Kategorija admirativa v albanskom jazyke i ee balkanskie sootvetsvija. Problemy sintaksisa balkanskogo areala, ed. by A. V. Desnickaja, 90–124. Leningrad: Nauka.

Teodorov–Balan, Aleksandŭr. 1957. Osobit sŭstav s glagola *imam*. Izvestija na Instituta za bŭlgarski ezik 5.23–29.

Vidoeski, Božidar. 1962. Kumanovskiot govor. Skopje: Institut za makedonski jazik.

Weigand, Gustav. 1923/4. The admirative in Bulgarian. The Slavonic Review 2.567–568.

The White House Transcripts. 1974. Ed. by Irwin Horowitz *et al.* New York: Bantam.

ELEVEN

Interactions of Tense and Evidentiality: A Study of Sherpa and English*

Anthony C. Woodbury
University of Texas at Austin

INTRODUCTION

The hypothesis of this paper is that when grammatical categories occur together their semantic content limits the ways they can interact. If we understand in general terms how the semantic content of two grammatical categories combines (or fails to combine) when they occur together in a proposition, we can predict how the surface inflectional forms that express them will interact with each other. Such an approach promises to narrow the range of possible inflectional systems predicted by a universal grammar, and to motivate many as yet unexplained semantic and distributional patterns appearing in inflectional systems in language after language. To a degree, of course, this hypothesis is already implicitly accepted by linguists in order to explain some of the more obvious interactions of grammatical categories. For example, in a language with an optative mood the co-occurrence of the optative with inflection for second person subject is generally expected to yield an imperative of some kind, and this expectation is based on the semantic content of the categories 'optative' and 'second person'. As a second example, in a language distinguishing animate vs. inanimate natural gender among its nouns, the gender opposition is generally expected to neutralize in first and second person pronouns. In this case too, the expectation is based on the semantic content of the categories involved, and their meaning in combination.

---

* Many thanks to Konchhok Lama, who served as informant on Sherpa, and to Orin Gensler, Mary Haas, John Kingston, James Matisoff, Johanna Nichols, Michael Silverstein, Henry Thompson, and Kenneth Whistler for comments on earlier versions of the material presented here. Funds for fieldwork in 1975 and 1976 were provided by the Department of Linguistics, University of California, Berkeley.

Here I will take up a decidedly nonobvious categorial interaction which can nevertheless be explained in terms of the hypothesis discussed above. It is the interaction of some EVIDENTIAL oppositions with some TENSE oppositions. I will begin by discussing this interaction in the verb inflection system of Sherpa, where I first became aware of it. Sherpa is a member of the Tibeto-Burman family related very closely to Tibetan, and it is spoken in the Solu-Khumbu district of Nepal in the Himalayas south of Mt. Everest.[1] In Sherpa, evidential and tense(-aspect) categories are the principal categories expressed in verb inflection. The morphemes signaling evidential categories are peculiarly skewed: what marks a particular category in one tense takes on a different meaning in another tense; there, a different morpheme expresses the meaning of the first category. I will argue that this interaction is a consequence of how the evidential and tense categories involved combine semantically. If this is correct, it makes testable predictions about the interactions of the same categories when they show up in other languages. I will show that the correct predictions are made for English, which expresses the relevant categories in part inflectionally, but in part syntactically and lexically. Since English makes a few more distinctions than Sherpa does, it sheds light on the Sherpa system. Finally, I will briefly discuss what significance should be attached to the fact that Sherpa expresses the tense-evidential interaction in its inflectional system, while English does so in other parts of its structure.[2]

---

[1] Data from Sherpa is from Konchhok Jangbu Lama, born around 1950 and abbot of Tākshindhu Monastery, Solu-Khumbu District, Nepal. Members of the Summer Institute of Linguistics (SIL) are responsible for most of the published work on Sherpa (B. Schöttelndreyer 1975, 1980a, 1980b; B. and H. Schöttelndreyer 1973). Their work was done in—or with speakers from—Kerung, near Solleri, approximately forty air miles south of Tākshindhu. Dialect differences are noticeable. The Schöttelndreyers' published work so far contains little on the semantics of verb inflection, and it is hoped that this work will supplement this aspect of the effort to make grammatically analyzed material on Sherpa available.

Transcription is phonemic. The consonants are /p, ph, b, m, t, th, d, n, ts, tsh, dz, ṭ, ṭh, ḍ, c, ch, j, ɲ, k, kh, g, ŋ, s, š, h, w, r, ṛ, l, ḷ, y/ and the vowels are /a, aa, i, u, e, o/. There are four phonemic tones, working at the word level rather than the syllable level. Tone is transcribed following the SIL's system, using word-initial apostrophe and word final q, as follows:

$$'\cdots\cdot q \;=\; \text{high rising}$$

$$\cdots\cdot q \;=\; \text{high falling}$$

$$'\cdots\cdot \;=\; \text{low rising}$$

$$\cdots\cdot \;=\; \text{low falling}$$

In some examples, recorded early in my field work, tone transcription is omitted.

[2] For a comprehensive treatment of category interaction in the Sherpa inflectional system and a fuller demonstration of the hypothesis of the present paper, see Woodbury 1982. The tense-evidential interaction discussed here is just one among many.

INTERACTIONS OF EVIDENTIAL AND TENSE CATEGORIES IN SHERPA

Sherpa has three main tense categories, present, future, and past. The first two are formed from nonpast verb stems, and the last from past verb stems. (The present, and to an extent the future, has several contrasting aspectual forms. We will consider here only the habitual, which is least marked formally, and by far the most common in available texts. All present tense aspects behave similarly with respect to evidential categories.) Table 1 shows the inflections schematically, in morphophonemic representation, and Table 2 illustrates them for the verb *'duŋ-/'du-* 'hit'. The evidential meanings of the forms in Table 2 are given in parentheses.

In what follows, the surface evidential contrasts in each tense are presented, showing how tense skews both evidential meaning and the distribution of evidential forms. In the course of the exposition an explanation for the skewing is developed based on the semantic content of the categories involved.

Evidential Contrasts in the Present Tense (Habitual Aspect)
The principal evidential opposition in the present tense is carried in the habitual aspect by the HABITUAL EXPERIENTIAL (HE; *nP + ki/+i +nok*) vs. the GNOMIC (GN; nP *+ki/+i +wi*). The habitual experiential indicates that the speaker ports to see or have seen the present tense narrated event taking place, or to perceive it in some other direct way, e.g. by hearing or feeling it take place. By contrast, the gnomic indicates either that the speaker does NOT purport to have such evidence, or else (in some contexts) that he purports NOT to have it. Consider these minimal pairs:

Table 1.   Schematic Representations of Some Major Sherpa Verbal Inflections

Name of Inflection	Abbr.	Stem	(Nominalizer)	(Aux.)	Evidential
			Morphological Composition		
Non-past stem inflections					
Gnomic	GN	nP		*+ki/+i*	*+wi*
Habitual experiential	HE	nP		*+ki/+i*	*+nok*
Future first person	FF	nP	(*+wa*)		*+in*
Future inferential	FI	nP	*+up/+wap*		*+nok*
Past stem inflections					
Past experiential	PE	P			*+suŋ*
Past inferential	PI	P			*+nok*

Note: nP = nonpast stem; P = past stem

Table 2. Illustration of Major Sherpa Verbal Inflections with <u>'duŋ</u>–(nP)/<u>'du</u>–(P) 'hit'

GN	*'duŋ–gu–wi*	'(someone) hits, is hitting' (It is known . . .); (someone) will hit'
HE	*'duŋ–gi–nok*	'(someone) hits, is hitting' (I see, have seen . . .)
FF	*'duŋ–in*	'(I) will hit' (I think . . .)
FI	*'duŋ–gum–nok*	'(I) will hit' (I can tell you right now . . .)
PE	*du–suŋ*	'(someone) hit' (I saw . . .)
PI	*du–nok*	'(someone) hit' (I infer . . .; I hear . . .)

(1a) *'ti   'gi -nok*
     he   come-HE
     'he comes, is coming' (I see, have seen . . .)

(1b) *'ti   'gi -wi*
     he   come-GN
     'he comes, is coming' (It is known . . .); 'he will come'

(2a) *ḍaa   saa-p   mi   ti   yembur-laa   de -ki-nok.*
     rice   eat-NOMNLZR   man   he   Katmandu-DAT   stay-HE
     'The man who is eating rice lives in Katmandu.' (I see, have seen . . .)

(2b) *ḍaa   saa-p   mi   ti   yembur-laa   de -ki-wi.*
     rice   eat-NOMNLZR   man   he   Katmandu-DAT   stay-HE
     'The man who is eating rice lives in Katmandu.' (It is known . . .)

With (1a), the speaker indicates that he sees or has seen the man on his way, whereas with (1b), this is left open. The same holds for (2a) and (2b). I will represent the evidential value of the habitual experiential as +EXPERIENTIAL, and that of the gnomic as −EXPERIENTIAL. (Both inflections indicate that the speaker purports to be certain of the proposition, and a fuller treatment would reflect this too with an appropriate feature.) The future use of the gnomic shown in (1b) will be discussed below.

    The nature of the +/− EXPERIENTIAL opposition is further revealed by the distribution of the habitual experiential and gnomic inflections in the presence of first person experiencers or actors. In (3) *ŋa* 'I' (nominative case) has the role of experiencer, and in (4) *ŋe* 'I' (ergative case) has the role of actor:

(3a) *ŋa   ne -nok (<na +i +nok)*
     I   sick-HE
     'I am sick.'

(3b) *ŋa   ne -wi.*
     I   sick-GN
     *'I am sick.' (But grammatical for 'I will be sick'.)

(4a) *ɲe   ca   ɲimi   dyeŋ   thuŋ -ki-nok.
       I (ERG) tea day   every drink-HE
      'I drink tea every day.'

(4b) ɲe   ca   ɲimi   dyeŋ   thuŋ -gu-wi.
       I (ERG) tea day   every drink-GN
      'I drink tea every day.'

In both pairs the habitual experiential vs. gnomic opposition is neutralized, apparently reflecting the fact that in reports by a speaker of his own internal experiences or his own actions, the +/− EXPERIENTIAL opposition usually raises a moot question. It is interesting that the habitual experiential is required when the first person is an experiencer, so that the speaker's own internal experiences must be reported as having been directly perceived while they occurred. On the other hand the selection of the gnomic in clauses with first person actors is not so clearly motivated semantically. The gnomic may occur with first person actors only by default, reserving the habitual experiential for first person experiencer subjects, where it is especially appropriate.[3]

It is clear from the morphology of the habitual experiential and the gnomic that their common tense-aspect meaning lies in the stem-plus-auxiliary assembly that they share, $nP +ki/+i-$, and that their evidential values are carried by the final suffixes $+nok$ and $+wi$, respectively. Etymologically, $+nok$ is the uninflectable linking verb 'nok, and $+wi$ the uninflectable linking verb 'wayi. Like the habitual experiential and the gnomic, 'nok and 'wayi have the evidential values +EXPERIENTIAL and −EXPERIENTIAL, respectively:

(5a) di   khaŋb-i   naŋ   -laa pye nok.
       this house-GEN inside-DAT rat LINK
      'This house has rats.' (I see, have seen . . .)

(5b) di   khaŋb-i   naŋ   -laa pye wayi.
       this house-GEN inside-DAT rat LINK.
      'This house has rats.' (It is known . . .)

---

[3] The first person vs. nonfirst person distinction is widespread in Sherpa, but the term 'first person' is something of a misnomer. In the interrogative all so-called first person phenomena are associated with second person. This is because second person forms in questions anticipate the use of first person in the answer: compare the following with (3a-b)

(i)   khyeruŋ   na -nok?
       you   sick-HE (INT)
      'Are you sick?'

(ii) *khyeruŋ   na -wi?
        you   sick-GN (INT)
       'Are you sick?'

Clearly, the habitual experiential in (i) anticipates the evidential value of (3a).

Uses of these linking verbs are always present tense. To express linked propositions in the past and future suppletive verbs that DO inflect are used. This is
significant because, as we shall see in following sections, the association of
+*nok* with +EXPERIENTIAL evidential value is a PECULIARITY of the present
tense.

Evidential Contrasts in the Past Tense

All past tense inflections are formed from the past stem of the verb. The principal
evidential distinction is carried by the past experiential (PE; *P* +*suŋ*) vs. the past
inferential (PI; *P* +*nok*). (A third form, the past first person, substitutes for the
past experiential when the actor is first person. It will not be considered here.)
The past experiential indicates that the speaker purports to have seen or otherwise
directly perceived the narrated event taking place. It can be marked as
+EXPERIENTIAL in the sense that the term was used for the habitual experiential. The past inferential, by contrast, is −EXPERIENTIAL. Most importantly,
however, the past inferential indicates that the speaker purports to base the truth
of the narrated event on indirect evidence obtained in the present, or in the past
after the narrated event had been completed. The evidence may be a tangible
result of the narrated event from which the speaker has inferred its truth, or else
hearsay. The specification +INFERENTIAL will be used to indicate this entire
range. (In many evidential systems QUOTATIVES marking hearsay are kept distinct from true inferentials. Sherpa too has a specifically quotative inflection that
occurs in some contexts, but which is not discussed here.) In contrast, the past
experiential will be marked −INFERENTIAL. The following illustrate the past
tense contrasts:

(6a)   *'jon-ki   'ti   'kuršiŋq   'ti   dzo -suŋ.*
      John-ERG   the   chair   it   build-PE
      'John built the chair.' (I saw . . .)

(6b)   *'jon-ki   'ti   'kuršiŋq   'ti   dzo -nok.*
      John-ERG   the   chair   it   build-PI
      'John built the chair.' (I infer . . .; I hear . . .)

Informant's comment: *dzosuŋ* means 'I saw John build it'; *dzonok* means' I saw the
finished chair', or 'I heard that he built it'.

(7a)   *bil-ki   iki   'ti -suŋ.*
      Bill-ERG   letter   write-PE
      'Bill wrote a letter.' (I saw . . .)

(7b)   *bil-ki   iki   'ti -nok.*
      Bill-ERG   letter   write-PI
      'Bill wrote a letter.' (I infer . . .; I hear . . .)

Informant's comment: '*ţisuŋ* means 'I saw Bill write it'; '*ţinok* means 'I see or saw the letter and recognize Bill's handwriting', or 'I heard that he wrote it'.

The informant's comments on the past inferential (b) forms should be taken as suggestions for contexts in which the sentences would be appropriate, but seeing a chair or recognizing Bill's handwriting are clearly not the only possible bases for the conclusions expressed in (6b) and (7b).

The evidential contrast carried by these inflections is further illustrated by clauses with an NP bearing the semantic role of experiencer. When the experiencer is first person the past experiential is favored over the past inferential, but when it is nonfirst person, the reverse is the case:

(8a) ?*ŋa   naa -nok.*
       I   sick-PI
       'I was sick.' (I infer . . .)

(8b) *ŋa   naa -suŋ.*
       I   sick-PE
       'I was sick.' (I felt . . ., perceived directly . . .)

(9a) '*ti   naa -nok.*
       he   sick-PI
       'He was sick.' (I infer . . .)

(9b) ?'*ti   naa -suŋ.*
       he   sick-PE
       'He was sick.' (I saw . . .)

The speaker perceives his own internal states directly as they occur, motivating the past experiential in (8b); someone else's internal states are usually inferred from tangible evidence, or known by hearsay, motivating the past inferential in (9a). Notice that the past experiential and the habitual experiential both are favored in clauses with first person experiencer NPs. (In the present tense, as noted above for examples (3–4), the habitual experiential is favored to the exclusion of the gnomic.) This supports the claim that the evidential value +EXPERIENTIAL is carried by both inflections.

To conclude this section, note that the morphology of the past inferential and the past experiential is straightforward: the past stem signals their common tense meaning, while their contrasting evidential values are carried by the final suffixes +*nok* and +*suŋ*.

Evidential Skewing in the Present and Past Tenses
The evidential value of +*nok* in the past inferential may seem surprising when compared with its evidential value in the habitual experiential, as shown in Table 3, which summarizes the findings so far. Note that +*nok* has the value +EXPERIENTIAL in the present, but −EXPERIENTIAL in the past. In the

Table 3.   Evidential Values Carried by the Morphemes +*wi*, +*nok*, **and** +*suŋ* **in Some Principal Sherpa Present and Past Tense Inflections.**

	+wi	+nok	+suŋ
Present tense (gnomic and habitual experiential)	−EXPERIENTIAL	+EXPERIENTIAL	——
Past tense (past inferential and past experiential)	——	−EXPERIENTIAL +INFERENTIAL	+EXPERIENTIAL −INFERENTIAL

past +*nok* also has the value +INFERENTIAL. Thus the evidential value of +*nok* is skewed by tense.

A Theory of Sherpa Evidential Skewing and Its Cross-Linguistic Implications

I propose to treat +*nok* as having a single basic evidential value which I will call IMMEDIATE EVIDENCE. With a marker of immediate evidence the speaker purports to have evidence for the truth of the proposition, and to have gotten it in the present. (I mean PRESENT in the sense of the present tense, and include evidence obtained at the moment of utterance, as well as evidence obtained in the past but continuing to be available in the present, or expected still to be available in the future.) The category of immediate evidence combines with different tenses to give more specialized evidential values. When the proposition as a whole is in the past tense, the evidence immediately perceived cannot be the event itself since it is already complete at the time of speaking. Thus an immediate evidence marker cannot have the value +EXPERIENTIAL with past tense propositions. Accordingly, when the Sherpa immediate evidence marker +*nok* occurs with past tense propositions in the past inferential, it indicates perception of a RESULT —either tangible evidence or hearsay—of the past tense narrated event. When the Sherpa immediate evidence marker occurs with present tense propositions in the habitual experiential it does have the value +EXPERIENTIAL. (Logically speaking, there is no reason why it could not also have the value +INFERENTIAL, since it is possible to make inferences in the present about something going on in the present.)

The foregoing account, uniting inferential meaning in the past with experiential meaning in the present appeals to the following general principle concerning the combination of evidential and tense meaning:

(10)   When the time reference of an evidential category is different from that of the proposition with which it occurs, the resulting evidential value will be nonexperiential.

The immediate evidence category has present tense time reference, and thus has different evidential values with past and present tense propositions.[4]

(10) makes testable cross-linguistic predictions. It is based on the semantic content of the categories involved, and it limits the ways they are expected to interact. The fact that inferential and quotative (hearsay) are commonly attested nonexperiential evidential values adds to its predictive power: it should be common to find inferential and experiential categories signaled by the same morphological or syntactic devices in different tense contexts. Note that (10) leaves open whether an experiential will result when the time reference of evidential and proposition coincide, since it is possible to make inferences about something at the same time that it is going on.

Finally, if (10) is correct, then the time reference of +*suŋ* in the past experiential must coincide with that of the past tense propositions with which it occurs. I know of no evidence disputing this.

Theory of Evidential Skewing Applied to Evidential Contrasts in the Sherpa Future Tense

The principal marker of future tense is the gnomic. A future reading of it is shown in (1b) and (3b). However when a first person actor NP is present, the gnomic is joined by two more inflections, the future first person (FF; *nP (+wa) +in*) and the future inferential (FI; *nP +up/+wap- +nok*). The inflections differ from each other in evidential value. I will show that the evidential value of the future inferential is accounted for by the analysis of +*nok* as an immediate evidence marker, and the princple in (10). (The evidential value of the gnomic with first person actors will not be taken up here.)

As a first approximation, the future first person indicates that the speaker purports to be guessing about the truth of the future proposition, while the future inferential indicates a stronger commitment:

> (11a) *ɲe*   *'ti-laa   salaa   'sir-um-nok.*
>   I (ERG)   he-DAT   tomorrow   say -FI
>   'I will say (it) to him tomorrow.' (I can tell you right now . . .)
>
> (11b) *ɲe*   *'ti-laa   salaa   'sir-in.*
>   I (ERG)   he-DAT   tomorrow   say -FF
>   'I will say (it) to him tomorrow.' (I think . . .)

---

[4] The immediate evidence analysis of +*nok* does not account for uses of the past inferential in which the evidence was obtained in the past, after the completion of the narrated event. I retain the immediate evidence analysis, but in doing so commit myself to claiming that the meaning of the past inferential has EXTENDED to cover instances where the evidence was not obtained in the present. In effect then, I claim that the past inferential is lexicalized, since its meaning is not strictly predictable from the meaning of its parts. This issue is discussed again in another section.

(12a) ŋa 'khyeruŋ 'duŋ-gum-nok.
I you hit-FI
'I will hit you.' (I can tell you right now . . .)

(12b) ŋa 'khyeruŋ 'duŋ-in.
I you hit -FF
'I will hit you.' (I think . . .)

In (11a) the future inferential has the force of a commitment, and in (12a) the force of a threat or bluff. They contrast with (11b) and (12b), which indicate no extraordinary commitment on the speaker's part. The following is a textual example of the future inferential to illustrate it further:

(13) 'ti iki -ki 'len "khyeruŋ dye
the letter-GEN answer you here

'phye -wup 'si-nok 'si-siŋ, ɲe-ki lo
come:HONRFC-NOMNLZR CONDITIONAL I -ERG year

cik-kiq 'dosuŋ 'yomo puraq 'toŋ -gum-nokq' 'si-nok.
one-GEN expense any all handle-FI say-PI
'The answer to the letter said, "If you wish to come here I will take care of all of your expenses for one year".'

Had the future first person been used in place of the future inferential, the offer would have seemed only lukewarm.

If +nok in the future inferential is an immediate evidence marker, and the stem plus auxiliary complex nP +up/+wap- marks future tense, then (10) predicts that its evidential value must be nonexperiential. This much is clearly the case, since in using the future inferential the speaker does not purport to directly experience the narrated event in the future! But I suggest further that the future inferential has the evidential value +INFERENTIAL. It is an inferential in the sense that the speaker purports to have direct evidence in the present which allows him to predict with certainty the actions he is going to take in the future. In principle, future inferentials need not be restricted to propositions with first person actors (compare the English future inferential expression *It looks like it's going to rain*). To account for the restriction in Sherpa we may surmise that the immediate evidence meaning of +nok is narrowed in the future inferential to include only the speaker's internal perceptions. (Other examples where +nok marks internal perceptions are (3a), (4a), (8a), and (9a).) By this hypothesis, we must attribute some lexicalization to the future inferential since it is not quite the semantic sum of its parts.

THE INTERACTION OF EVIDENTIALITY AND TENSE IN ENGLISH

I will show here that English displays the same categorial interactions as those discussed for Sherpa, that is, that it follows the predictions made by the principle in (10). English illustrates the interactions in a very productive part of its grammar, its syntax, and for this reason makes clear the ways in which the Sherpa system is NOT productive. This in turn will explain why an obvious system in English corresponds to a nonobvious system in Sherpa.

Let us take *I see [S]* as our marker of immediate evidence (with respect to the complement [S]) in English. It should correspond to Sherpa +*nok,* and behave with respect to tense as the principle in (10) would predict. (+*nok,* however, has a broader meaning than *I see [S]* since it includes nonvisual perceptions.) The following examples show that when the complement in the English construction is in tenses other than the present, nonexperiential evidential value is the result:

(14)   *I see (that) Jack was drinking.*

(15)   *I see (that) Jack will be drinking.*

In fact, (14) and (15) are not only nonexperiential, but inferential in particular. Thus (14) might indicate that the speaker sees an empty bottle, and (15) a full bottle. In this way both English and Sherpa not only follow (10), but both narrow the evidential value from nonexperiential to inferential. (One difference, however, is that the Sherpa past inferential has inferential and quotative evidential value, while (14) has only the former.)

When the complement in English *I see [S]* is in the present tense, the evidential value is broadened:

(16)   *I see (that) Jack is drinking.*

In (16) the evidential (*I see [S]*) and the proposition itself (*Jack is drinking*) have the same time reference (present). In this situation (10) does not explicitly rule out either experiential or nonexperiential readings and, in fact (16) may be read both as an experiential, in which I see Jack in the act, and as a nonexperiential (inferential), in which, for example, I see a liquor bottle. Notice that the Sherpa habitual experiential, which also involves an immediate evidence marker (+*nok*) and present tense on the proposition, is ONLY an experiential, and not an inferential. This restriction is a specific fact of Sherpa, and is not a consequence of (10). (However, a more refined analysis of the categories involved in English and Sherpa would perhaps motivate this difference in cross-linguistically valid semantic terms.)

English does, in fact, have a complementizer which, when it marks the complement in *I see [S]* constructions, explicitly signals experiential evidential value:

(17)   *I see Jack drinking.*

Here the complementizer is zero rather than *that* (with the subject of the complement verb appearing as an accusative), and the past vs. nonpast tense opposition in the complement is neutralized. The time reference of *I see [S]* and the complement are the same (in spite of the neutralization), so that according to (10) an experiential reading is possible. (17) is like the Sherpa habitual experiential but unlike (16) in that it never has non–experiential evidential value.

So far we have seen English patterns which are remarkably similar to those of Sherpa, and which bear out the notion of immediate evidence as well as the principle in (10). But (14–17) are selected entirely in terms of Sherpa. When we pursue English a little further on its OWN terms, we find that the patterns glimpsed in (14–17) further confirm (10) and shed new light on the Sherpa evidential system.

English provides additional support for (10) because when *I saw [S]* is substituted for *I see [S]*, (10) is validated for evidentials with other-than-present time reference. Consider these past evidential versions of English sentences already discussed (tenses are adjusted in the lower clause to preserve evidential value):

(18)   *I saw Jack drinking.* (Cf. (17) *I see Jack drinking.*)

(19)   *I saw (that) Jack had been drinking.* (Cf. (14) *I see that Jack was drinking.*)

(20)   *I saw (that) Jack was drinking.* (Cf. (16) *I see that Jack is drinking.*)

These sentences show that in English it is a combination of complement type and tense SEQUENCE that determines evidential value, regardless of the tense of the evidential marker. In (17) and (18) the complement type indicates simultaneity of the main and complement clauses. As a consequence, tense is not overtly marked in the latter. This simultaneity makes possible the experiential evidential value in both (17) and (18), just as (10) would predict.

Sentences (14–16) and (19–20) have *that*-complements. In contrast to the complement type in (17–18), *that*-complements are not necessarily simultaneous with the main clause, and both clauses carry their own tense marking. When main and complement clauses have different time reference, a nonexperiential evidential value results, as (10) predicts. This is so whether the evidential marker is *I see [S]* as in (14), or *I saw [S]* as in (19). When main clause and complement clause have the same or overlapping time reference, experiential evidential value becomes possible (but not obligatory), again, regardless of the particular tense of the main clause (cf. (16) and (20)).

The English facts thus show that (10) applies to nonpresent evidential markers as well as to present ones.

We have seen that English—unlike Sherpa—can INFLECT its evidential marker *I see [S]* for tense, and that it uses contrasting complement types, as well as tense sequencing, to indicate simultaneity and nonsimultaneity. This productivity in English allows us some insights into the less productive, more lexicalized Sherpa system, which does not independently signal dimensions like simultaneity. For instance, notice that when the English sentences just discussed are set beside Sherpa inflections with corresponding evidential values, shown in Table 4, there is an interesting asymmetry. In (17) and (18), Sherpa distinguishes

Table 4. English Sentences and Sherpa Inflections with Similar Evidential Values

English Sentence	(Example Number)		Sherpa Inflection	
I see Jack drinking.	(17)	=	nP+*ki/*+*i-* +*nok*	Habitual experiential
I saw Jack drinking.	(18)	=	P +*suŋ*	Past experiential
I see (that) Jack was drinking.	(14)	=	P +*nok*	Past inferential
I saw (that) Jack had been drinking.	(20)	=	P +*nok*	Past inferential

the *I see [S]* and *I saw [S]* forms, but in (14) and (20) it does not. Now, *I see* in (17) and *I saw* in (18) correspond to +*nok* and +*suŋ* in the Sherpa forms. (The rest of the Sherpa forms, nP +*ki/*+*i-* vs. P-, marks the tense of the proposition to which the inflection attaches.) There is no clear morphological relationship between +*nok* and +*suŋ*, as there is between *I see* vs. *I saw,* but the English parallel suggests the possibility of a suppletive tense opposition carried by the two Sherpa evidentials: +*nok* 'immediate evidence' vs. +*suŋ* 'past evidence'. Some support for the suppletion hypothesis comes from the fact that +*nok* is not itself inflectable for tense. Furthermore the linking verb '*nok,* from which it comes, is expressed in the past tense with a suppletive stem.

As noted, the Sherpa past inferential covers the tense-evidential values of both (14) and (20). Given the analysis of +*nok* as an immediate evidential, it SHOULD only cover (14). (In note 4 I proposed that the past inferential has been extended to cover inferences based on evidence obtained in the past, and is thus lexicalized.) Now, if Sherpa were to distinguish the evidential value of (20) from that of (14) in a way that follows the English pattern, it might (i) use a past tense form of +*nok* and (ii) indicate somehow that the past act of evidence-getting that it signals is not simultaneous with the past tense narrated event. This is the type of solution that Sherpa gives to the problem of distinguishing the evidential values of (17) and (18). (The past tense form is suppletive there, in my view.) But Sherpa does not give such a solution in this case. Rather, the past inferential is extended to cover the evidential value of (20), with the result that it is not distinguished formally from the evidential value of (14).

Because they are formally and semantically finite, inflectional systems cannot make as many distinctions as productive syntactic systems. In Sherpa the inflectional system cuts corners where it might be cumbersome to carry out the logic of its own categories. A case in point is the extension of the past inferential to cover the evidential value of (20). Comparing the Sherpa inflectional system with a semantically equivalent syntactic system in English helped show where the corners were cut, as well as suggest how forms like +*nok* and +*suŋ* were related. In fact, it is precisely phenomena like the alternation of +*nok* and +*suŋ* in the experiential forms and the extension of the meaning of the past inferential that make the Sherpa tense-evidential system so inscrutable: they head one away from a consistent, comprehensive analysis.

LINGUISTIC EXPRESSION OF TENSE-EVIDENTIAL INTERACTIONS, AND THE NATIVE SPEAKER'S ANALYSIS

Tense-evidential interactions in Sherpa and English follow the principle in (10), and the evidential values of Sherpa and English forms can often be equated directly. In spite of this, the differences in formal means for expressing tense and evidential categories in the two languages lead to important differences in how speakers discuss their meanings. The following generalizations about my Sherpa informant Konchhok Lama's translation practices illustrate this.

First, in translating from Sherpa to English, there was not a single instance when Konchhok Lama included the Sherpa evidential value in his English translation. (Notice that my own glosses of Sherpa sentences in this chapter reflect this fact.) The only time he elucidated evidential value was when given minimal pairs, as is specifically indicated in examples (6) and (7). Even then the evidential value is ascribed to the whole inflected verb, rather than to the contrasting evidential suffixes, that is, to *dzosuŋ* vs. *dzonok*, and *'ṭisuŋ* vs. *'ṭinok*, rather than to +*suŋ* vs. +*nok*. In fact, the question 'What does +*nok* mean?' was not answerable in the terms in which Konchhok Lama understood his language: it did not make sense to him.

Second, in giving Sherpa translations in English sentences containing *I saw . . .* , *someone said . . .* , and so on, Konchhok Lama always rendered these expressions lexically, as *ŋe . . . thoŋsuŋ* 'I saw . . .', *'sinok* 'someone said . . .', and the like, and never only inflectionally, as past experiential or past inferential. On repeated occasions this happened even when we had just arrived at 'I saw . . .' or 'someone said . . .', etc., as (clumsy) glosses for members of minimal pairs like (6) and (7)![5]

One difference between the English and Sherpa forms that accounts for this is that in English *I see [S]* and similar evidentials occupy the main clause in the sentence, and are the main assertion. In Sherpa the evidential value is not the main assertion, so that the negation of (6a), for example, means 'I saw John not building the chair', rather than 'I did not see John building the chair'. This may explain Konchhok Lama's reluctance to translate English lexical items with Sherpa evidential inflections, and vice versa.

But why is it difficult to give +*nok* and other evidentials any gloss at all? It

---

[5] It is of course very likely that Sherpa *thoŋ-* 'see' works much like *see* in English. If so, many of the points in the preceding sections could be made without reference to English.

appears generally to be the case that IF some part of a linguistic system is going to be inaccessible to speakers' conscious reflection, it is likely to involve bound (or discontinuous or suprasegmental) morphemes more so than free lexical items, members of sporadic alternations moreso than productive ones, and obligatory more so than optional categories. (For a general theory of what speakers are likely to be conscious of in their languages, see Silverstein 1979, 1981). Comparing +*nok* and *I see* on these points, we find that +*nok* is bound and *I see* is free; +*nok* alternates sporadically with +*suŋ* and +*wi,* while *I see* alternates not only with *I saw,* but also with *you saw* and with *I hear,* among many others; and +*nok* and the other evidential morphemes are obligatory in Sherpa inflection, while framing English utterances with *I see [S]* and similar evidentials is a matter left entirely up to the speaker. It should be clear from these structural facts that the English speaker has greater opportunity to reflect on the meaning of *I see* than the Sherpa speaker does on +*nok.*

We have seen, then, that the form that categories take has nothing to do with their behavior with respect to principles like (10), but a great deal to do with how speakers reflect on them. This first point is important for universal grammar, and the second is important for the linguistic fieldworker, as well as for an understanding of how grammar is made conscious by individuals and by societies.

REFERENCES

Schöttelndreyer, Burkhard. 1975. Clause patterns in Sherpa. Collected papers in Sherpa—Jirel, 1–57. (Nepal Studies in Linguistics II.) Kirtipur, Nepal: Summer Institute of Linguistics, Institute of Nepal and Asian Studies.

————. 1980a. Glides in Sherpa. Papers in Southeast Asian linguistics, 7, ed. by Ronald L. Trail et al., 107–112. (Pacific Linguistics A:53.) Canberra: Australian National University, Research School of Pacific Studies.

————. 1980b. Vowel and tone patterns in the Sherpa verb. Papers in Southeast Asian linguistics, 7, ed. by Ronald L. Trail et al., 113–123. (Pacific Linguistics A:53.) Canberra: Australian National University, Research School of Pacific Studies.

————, and Heiderose Schöttelndreyer. 1973. Sherpa texts. Clause, sentence, and discourse, patterns in selected languages of Nepal, III, ed. by Austin Hale. (Summer Institute of Linguistics Publications in Linguistics and Related Fields, 40:3.) Norman, OK: Summer Institute of Linguistics.

Silverstein, Michael. 1979. Language structure and linguistic ideology. The elements: A parasession on linguistic units and levels, ed. by Paul R. Clyne, et al., 193–247. Chicago: Chicago Linguistic Society.

————. 1981. The limits of awareness. Texas Working Papers in Sociolinguistics.

Woodbury, Anthony C. 1982. Evidentiality in Sherpa verbal categories and its implications for universal grammar. MS.

TWELVE

Evidentiality and Volitionality in Tibetan

Scott DeLancey
University of Oregon

INTRODUCTION

My purpose in this chapter is to describe a rather unusual evidential-like category in Lhasa Tibetan and its interaction with a more typical evidential distinction and with the category of agentivity or volitionality. I will also suggest an explanatory account of these three semantic-morphosyntactic categories based on a general approach to transitivity and agentivity proposed in DeLancey 1981a, 1982a, in terms of which the pattern of interaction which they manifest in Tibetan is entirely natural.

I will begin by describing and exemplifying the less common evidential-like distinction, which I will refer to (rather clumsily) as the 'old/new knowledge' distinction, and its morphosyntactic interaction with the category of volitionality. I will then briefly describe the Tibetan manifestation of more typical (inferential) evidentiality, which is marked only in the perfective system, and which makes use of some of the same morphological material as the old/new distinction. Finally I will argue that this morphosyntactic congruence and the interaction of both evidential categories with volitionality provide useful insights into the se-mantic/cognitive structure of both evidentiality and the old/new knowledge distinction.

THE NONPERFECTIVE SYSTEM: VOLITIONALITY AND SPEAKER'S KNOWLEDGE

In Standard Tibetan,[1] as in many if not all other Tibetan dialects, we find a rather complicated tense/aspect/modality system which incorporates some evidential

[1] Most of the data presented here was elicited from or checked with Mr. Thubten Tsering Dalor Anyetsang. A few examples are taken from Goldstein and Nornang (1970) or Jin (1979) without checking. All examples are in a transcription of standard Tibetan spelling; misspellings or other errors are my responsibility.

categories. Most of the forms of the Standard Tibetan system are built on one of four existential/copular verbs, *yod, 'dug, yin,* and *red.* Of these, the copulas *yin* and *red* have the same tense/aspect value, marking future and some perfective forms, and the existentials *yod* and *'dug* likewise have the same value, marking present forms. Our interest here is in the other distinction marked by the choice of otherwise equivalent auxiliary, i.e. the choice of *yod* or *yin* vs. *'dug* or *red.*

The Old/New Knowledge Distinction

All four of these verbs have main verb uses: *yin* and *red* are copular 'be' verbs, which equate two NPs:

> (1a) Ḍa   slab-gra-ba   <u>yin</u>.
>   I   student   be
>   'I am a student.'

> (1b) K'oŋ   slab-gra-ba   <u>red</u>.
>   s/he   student   be
>   'S/he is a student.'

Yod and *'dug* are 'have' verbs which indicate possession, location, or existence:

> (2a) Ḍa   la   śa-mo   <u>yod</u>.
>   I   LOC. hat   exist
>   'I have a hat.'

> (2b) Dorje   la   śa-mo   <u>'dug</u>.
>   D.   LOC. hat   exist
>   'Dorje has a hat.'

> (3a) Ḍa   k'aŋ–ba   la <u>yod</u>.
>   I   house   LOC. exist
>   'I am in the house.'

> (3b) Dorje k'aŋ–ba la   <u>'dug</u>.
>   house   LOC exist
>   'Dorje is in the house.'

> (4a) Bod   la   gyag   <u>yod</u>.
>   Tibet LOC. yak   exist
>   'There are yaks in Tibet.'

The difference between *yin* and *yod* on the one hand and *red* and *'dug* on the other constitutes the core of the Tibetan evidential system. A rough approximation of the difference which is often presented by (native) teachers of Tibetan, and which is made plausible by pairs such as (1), (2), and (3), has it as an incipient personal agreement system, with *yin* and *yod* used with first person subjects and *red* and *'dug* with nonfirst persons. It is, however, easy to find examples such as (4a) which show that person is not the determining factor in the choice at least of *yod* vs. *'dug*.[2]

A more satisfactory approach is implied in Goldstein and Nornang's statement that '[*'dug*] constructions imply <u>actual visual</u> knowledge' (1970:23), which correctly suggests that a sentence like (4a) could be appropriately spoken by someone who has never seen a yak. Note that examples like (2a) and (3a) show that this formulation must be based on visual and not simply first-hand knowledge. However, a sentence like (2a) is perfectly acceptable even if the speaker has the hat in his hand and thus can visually verify his statement.

The actual distinction (suggested by Goldstein 1973 and Jin 1979) is even farther from the usual notion of evidentiality. Goldstein and Nornang's earlier account correctly predicts that along with (4a), (4b) should be grammatical,

(4b)   *Bod   la   gyag   <u>'dug</u>*.
          Tibet LOC. yak   exist
          'There are yaks in Tibet.'

but fails to account for the fact that no Tibetan could ever say (4b), although informants will accept it with the understanding that it was spoken by a non-Tibetan. This fact makes it clear that eyewitness knowledge is not the relevant criterion, since a Tibetan, who has actual visual knowledge of the presence of yaks in Tibet, cannot use *'dug* to report this fact. However, either (4a), with *yod*, or (4b), with *'dug*, could conceivably be spoken by a non-Tibetan. The distinction represented here is not, as in more typical evidential systems, the source of the speaker's knowledge, but rather its relative novelty or the degree to which it has been integrated into the speaker's overall scheme of knowledge of the world. (4a) would be the appropriate form both for a Tibetan, who knows of the existence of yaks in Tibet through daily experience, and for someone like me, who knows the fact only by hearsay, but has known it for years. I could use (4a) in describing what I know of the distribution of yaks, while (4b) might be the response of someone who was fascinated with yaks but knew nothing of where they existed until visiting Tibet and encountering one.

Yod, 'dug, and the Chain of Causality

The characterization of 'old' and 'new' knowledge which I will suggest later, and the relationship between this distinction and true evidentiality, will be clarified by consideration of a somewhat different sort of example:

---

[2] It is clear that in their auxiliary use *yin* patterns with *yod*, and *red* with *'dug*. Jin (1979) states that the distinction between *yin* and *red* as main verbs also parallels that between *yod* and *'dug*, but my own data is not sufficient for me to exemplify this.

(5a) *Gza-spen-ba*   *la*   *tsog-'du*   <u>*yod*</u>.
      Saturday   LOC.   meeting   exist
      'We have a meeting on Saturday.'

(5b) *Gza-spen-ba*   *la*   *tsog-'du*   <u>*'dug*</u>
      Saturday   LOC.   meeting   exist
      'There's a meeting on Saturday.'

The difference between (5a) and (5b), suggested but not really captured by my glosses, is that (5a) would be appropriate in case the speaker was involved in organizing the meeting, while (5b) would be spoken by someone who, for example, had seen a notice posted announcing the meeting. The relevant point is not that one mode of knowledge is necessarily more certain than the other; (5b) does not express any particular doubt that there will actually be a meeting. Neither represents a category of eyewitness knowledge as opposed to inference; although (5b) is reminiscent of the 'hearsay' category marked in some languages, we have seen in our discussion of (4a–b) that such an account is inadequate.

To begin an attempt to describe the values of *yod* and *'dug,* let us consider the meeting as the terminus of a causal chain of events. In order for a meeting to take place, someone has to decide that there should be one, arrange a time and place, take steps to inform those who should attend, and so on. The meeting is realized only as the outcome of such a chain of events. Let us simplify matters a bit, and consider a two-event causal chain—the meeting is planned, and as a result it occurs. This can be diagrammed with a simple vector representation:

(6) PLANNING ─────────────→ MEETING

where 'PLANNING' and 'MEETING' are specific instances of the general categories CAUSE and EFFECT. In this case I would suggest that the choice of *yod* or *'dug* depends on where in this chain the speaker comes in, or, in other words, on what portion of the vector he actually perceives and makes the basis of his statement. The use of *yod* indicates an assertion made on the basis of direct knowledge of the entire vector, while *'dug* indicates direct knowledge of the result, but not of the cause.

Person and Volition in the Auxiliary System
When the four verbs which we have been discussing are used as auxiliaries, two new dimensions become relevant to the choice of *yod/yin* or *'dug/red:* the person of the actor(s) and the volitional or nonvolitional nature of the verb. Ordinarily verbs with nonfirst person subjects take the *'dug/red* forms:[3]

---

[3] *Yin* and *yod* are also used in yes/no questions with second person subject.

(7) *K'oŋ   las-ka   byed-gi-'dug*[4]
s/he   work   do -IMPF
'He's working/he works.'

(8) *K'oŋ   las-ka   byed-gi-red.*
s/he   work   do -FUT
'He'll work/be working.'

(9) *K'oŋ   na-gi-'dug.*
s/he   sick-IMPF
'He's sick.'

First person subjects, on the other hand, distinguish verbs which require some degree of control on the part of the subject from those which are beyond control; the former take the *yod/yin* auxiliaries, the latter the *'dug/red:*

(10) *Ŋa   las-ka   byed-gi-yod.*
I   work   do-IMPF
'I'm working.'

(11) *Ŋa   na-gi-'dug.*
I   sick-IMPF
'I'm sick.'

(12) *Ŋa za-k'aŋ   la   p'yin-pa-yin*
restaurant   in   went-PERF.
'I went into a restaurant.'

The old/new knowledge distinction remains relevant, however, so that auxiliary *yod,* ordinarily occurring with first person, can occur with nonfirst in a sentence like (13) (taken from Jin 1979):

(13) *Da-ltar   k'oŋ   slob-grwa   nas   bod-pa'i   skad-yig   bslab-gi-yod.*
now   s/he   school   from   Tibet-GEN. language   study-IMPF.
'He's now studying Tibetan at school.'

if the speaker knows that the subject has been doing so for a while.

Among the details of the distribution of *yod* and *'dug* are a few apparently anomalous patterns (several are exemplified in Jin 1979). One which will be of

---

[4] The subjects of most transitive and active intransitive verbs are marked with ergative case in perfective aspect, and sometimes in imperfective and future constructions (where it affects the meaning of the clause in ways which I do not entirely understand). See Goldstein and Nornang (1970), Chang and Chang (1980), and DeLancey (1982b, 1984) for available details. A preliminary account of the semantic interaction between ergative case marking and volitionality as reflected in choice of auxiliary is given in DeLancey (to appear).

interest in developing a model of the phenomena discussed here is the fact that we find the *yod/yin* forms used with volitional verbs having nonfirst person agents if the action is somehow directed toward first person. 'Directed toward first person' includes transitives with first person patients and dative and motional verbs with first person goals:

(14) *K'oŋ   gis   de   la   'k'ryid-gi-yin.*
      he   ERG.   there to   convey-FUT.
      'He'll take [me] there.'

(15) *K'oŋ   gis   bod nas yi-ge   gtoŋ-gi-yod.*
      he   ERG.   Tibet   from letter send-IMPF.
      'He writes [me] letters from Tibet.'

(16) *K'oŋ   gis   ŋa dbyin-ji'i   skad   bslab-gi-yod.*
      he   ERG.   I   English   language   teach-IMPF
      'He's teaching me English.'

(17) *Dmag-mi   'di-r   yoŋ-gi-yod.*
      soldier   here-to come-IMPF.
      'The soldier is coming this way.'

Volition and Causality

The distribution of the auxiliaries described here can be assimilated to the causal chain representation suggested above. Let us first consider the first-person subject forms, where we find the auxiliaries marking a distinction between volitional and nonvolitional verbs. The immediate causal origin of a volitional event is a conscious decision on the part of the agent to perform an action; the difference between volitional and nonvolitional events is precisely the presence or absence of such a conscious decision leading to the actual event. Thus we can represent any volitional act as a CAUSE-EFFECT vector parallel to (6), as in (18), where INTENTION and REALIZATION represent subcategories of the more general categories of cause and effect:

(18) INTENTION —————————→ REALIZATION (ACT)

When, on the other hand, one enters into a state or commits an act involuntarily, the causal origin of the vector is at least inaccessible to the actor's consciousness, and often simply indescribable in principle. Thus the distinction between (10), with a volitional verb and auxiliary *yod,* and (11), with a nonvolitional verb and auxiliary *'dug,* precisely parallels that between (5a) and (5b):

(10) *Ŋa   las-ka   byed-gi-yod.*
      I   work   do-IMPF.
      'I'm working.'

(11)   Ḍa   na-gi-'dug.
       I   sick-IMPF.
       'I'm sick.'

(5a)   Gza-spen-ba   la   tsogs-'du yod.
       Saturday   LOC.   meeting   exist
       'We're having a meeting Saturday (I was there when it was planned).'

(5b)   Gza-spen-ba   la   tsogs-'du 'dug.
       Saturday   LOC.   meeting   exist
       'There's a meeting on Saturday (I have reliable information to that effect).'

(10) and (5a), with *yod*, represent situations which the speaker is able to track from their inception, while (11) and (5b), with *'dug*, represent situations to which the speaker has access only as the results of a causal chain begin to appear.

By describing these facts in terms of the speaker's perceptions we can predict that the volitional/nonvolitional distinction will be neutralized in nonfirst person subject sentences, which we have seen to be the case. For any situation which does not involve a first person, a decision on the part of the actor is inaccessible to the speaker's perception until such time as it is manifested by an observable event. Thus any action by another person, volitional or not, is always 'new knowledge' to the speaker.

We have seen one exception to the predicted pattern, that exemplified in (21–24), in which nonfirst person actions with first person goal take the 'old knowledge' auxiliaries. An analysis of this pattern provides strong confirmation for the validity (as opposed to heuristic utility) of the vector representations which we have been using, and is evidence for the place of such representations in a general account of linguistic structure (other evidence along these lines is presented in DeLancey 1981a). Note that, as implied by my description in terms of first person 'goal', all such events are representable as vectors with much more concrete end points than those discussed hitherto:[5]

(16)   K'oŋ   gis   ŋa   dbyin-ji'i   skad   bslab-gi-yod.
       he   ERG. I   English   language   teach-IMPF
       'He's teaching me English.'

(19)   he ——————————————→ I
                (English)

(17)   Dmag-mi   'di-r   yoŋ-gi-yod.
       soldier   here-to   come-IMPF.
       'The soldier is coming this way.'

---

[5] These examples are taken from Jin 1979. Some Tibetan informants whom I have worked with since writing this paper find these unacceptable, although their perfective equivalents do take the first-person goal auxiliary *byuŋ*.

(20)   elsewhere ——————————————→ here
                        (soldier)

We have seen that in terms of a vector representing volitionality/causality, only the terminal point—the action manifested in the external world—is accessible to a speaker who is not also the actor. Thus if the choice of auxiliaries were being determined in terms of such a vector in examples (14–17), we should expect *red/'dug* rather than the *yin/yod* which occur. However, if we suppose that in these cases the choice of auxiliary is made in terms of more concrete vectors like (19) and (20), then we would predict exactly the pattern which we find. For the entirety of this vector is accessible to the speaker: the overt act on the part of the nonfirst person actor, as well as the goal, which is the speaker himself or his location.

TRUE EVIDENTIALITY: THE TIBETAN PERFECTIVE SYSTEM

In the perfective system Tibetan does mark a more typical evidential category, rather than the old/new knowledge distinction. Person and volitionality are tracked separately. There are four perfective auxiliary forms: two, *pa-yin* and *pa-red*, which use members of the auxiliary set we have been discussing, and two others, *byuŋ* and *soŋ*, which are etymologically derived from motion verbs. As we might expect, the *pa-yin* form is associated with first-person volitional verbs:

(21a)   *ŋa-s   yi-ge   bri-pa-yin.*
        I-ERG.   letter   write-PERF.
        'I wrote a letter.'

The *pa-red* form, however, does not have the range of use the *'dug/red* forms in the present and future, but rather has a clearly inferential sense (and thus, of course, is restricted to nonfirst person). Thus sentence (21b)

(21b)   *K'oŋ   gis   yi-ge   bri-pa-red.*
        s/he   ERG.   letter   write-PERF
        'S/he wrote a letter (it seems).'

reports a fact which the speaker knows only by inference, e.g., from the existence of the letter.

   A sentence reporting firsthand knowledge of an event not involving the speaker uses the auxiliary *soŋ*, etymologically a perfective form of a verb meaning *go*, as in (21c) and (22a). Note that, as in other tense/aspects, no volitionality distinction is made for nonfirst person:

(21c)   *K'oŋ   gis   yi-ge   bri-soŋ.*
        s/he   ERG.   letter   write-PERF
        'S/he wrote a letter (I saw it happen).'

(22a)   *K'oŋ   na-soŋ.*
        s/he   sick-PERF
        'S/he got sick.'

The final perfective auxiliary, *byuŋ,* which is etymologically a perfective form of a verb meaning 'to arrive, appear, come into view', marks first person nonvolitional verbs:

(22b)   *ŋa   na-byuŋ.*
        I   sick-PERF
        'I got sick.'

A comparison of the perfective with the nonpast system suggests an interesting parallelism between the evidential and the old/new knowledge categories. Of the four perfective forms the *pa-yin* first person volitional form has exactly the same function as the *yod/yin* forms have in the other tense/aspects: as I have already suggested, it marks an event which the speaker has tracked from its first cause to fruition, and the only type of event for which such complete knowledge is typically possible—a volitional event with first person actor. For present purposes we will consider the *soŋ* and *byuŋ* forms as equivalent in marking an event which the speaker knows first-hand only from the effect end of the cause-effect vector.

Now the last perfective category, the *pa-red* form, marks an event of which the speaker has no first-hand knowledge at all. But, of course, any statement reflects first-hand knowledge of something; in this case it is of evidence of the event—aspects of the world which exist because of the occurrence of the event. This configuration can likewise be represented as a cause-effect vector, labeled as in (23), of which the speaker has direct knowledge of only one end—that labeled evidence:

(23)   EVENT ─────────────▶ EVIDENCE

EVENT and EVIDENCE, like intention and realization (example 18) are subcategories of cause and effect, thus our description of the evidential category is precisely parallel to our description of the choice of *yod/yin* or *'dug/red* in other constructions: the *'dug/red* forms, including the evidential perfective *pa-red,* mark a sentence as reporting an event of which the speaker has direct knowledge only of the effect end of a cause-effect vector, while the *yod/yin* forms indicate the speaker's direct apprehension of the entire cause-effect sequence.

OLD AND NEW KNOWLEDGE REVISITED

My argument so far can be summed up as follows: a number of semantic/cognitive categories can be described in terms of a simple vector representation, among them spatial SOURCE-GOAL (cf. examples 15 and 17), AGENT-PATIENT (14), and various manifestations of cause and effect (e.g. intention-realization and event-evidence). The linguistic relevance of this representation is shown by the fact that the choice in Tibetan of *yod/yin* or *'dug/red* is made in terms of it. (Considerable evidence from other languages is described in De-Lancey 1981a,b, 1982a).

The category which I have referred to as 'old/new knowledge' does not obviously fit into this scheme (but cf. the discussion of Turkish *miş* in Aksu and Slobin, this volume, and the brief discussion of their findings in DeLancey 1981a). The distribution of *yod/yin* and *'dug/red* with respect to person which we saw in the Tibetan examples (1–3) is consistent with my model since if I have a hat, or am in a house, I presumably know how I came to have it or to be there, while I cannot count on having such knowledge with respect to someone else. That the category of person *per se* does not govern here either is easily demonstrated:

(24a) ŋa'i   k'aŋ   la   si-mi   yod.
       I-GEN.   house   LOC.   cat   exist
       'There's a cat in my house.'

(24b) ŋa'i   k'aŋ   la   si-mi   'dug.
       I-GEN.   house   LOC.   cat   exist
       'There's a cat in my house.'

In (24a) the cat is presumably mine, or one that for some reason I expect to find in my house, while (24b) requires that I have no reason to expect there to be a cat in my house—the most likely context for the sentence being if I come home and unexpectedly find a strange cat wandering about. Thus it is not the presence of a first person which requires *yod*, but rather a situation whose origins the speaker understands.

However, cases such as (4a–b), which represent one of the major distinctions marked by the *yod* vs. *'dug* contrast, do not fit the model so neatly. The choice of verb here has nothing to do with whether the speaker knows how or when yaks came to be in Tibet, or how he knows, or anything of the sort. The distinction, as I understand it, is rather whether or not the fact reported is an integrated part of the speaker's knowledge of the world. 'New' knowledge is knowledge which has yet to be assimilated into one's representation of the world, while 'old' knowledge is that which has been made part of the consistent world view which all human beings attempt to maintain. 'New' knowledge may require some modification of one's world view (or of the newly acquired fact) in order to maintain consistency. When we describe it in these terms, it becomes easy to see how this semantic category could develop out of the various manifestations of the cause-effect category. Events and situations fit into a consistent world view only to the extent that they can be assigned causes, and the thought processes which are manifested in semantic categories such as inferentiality or evidentiality arise from the need to assign cases to perceived events and situations. Thus an event or situation whose causal origin is known fits into a rational world view without difficulty, while one whose causal origin is not directly accessible to cognition requires cognitive manipulation before it can be integrated.

There is, then, sufficient conceptual overlap between the old/new distinction and evidentiality on the one hand, and between evidentiality and volitionality on the other, to explain the overall pattern of use of the *yod/yin* and *'dug/red* forms. The use of the same grammatical distinction to encode the old/new knowledge distinction as well as evidentiality and volitionality is consistent with, and counts as evidence for, the model which I have suggested for the categories of evidentiality and volitionality.

REFERENCES

Chang, Betty Shefts, and Kun Chang. 1980. Ergativity in spoken Tibetan. Bulletin of the Institute of History and Philology, Academia Sinica 51.1:15–32.

DeLancey, Scott. 1981a. An interpretation of split ergativity and related patterns. Language 57.3:626–57.

———. 1981b. Parameters of empathy. Journal of Linguistic Research 1.3:41–9.

———. 1982a. Aspect, transitivity, and viewpoint. Tense-aspect: Between semantics and pragmatics, ed. by Paul Hopper, pp. 167–83. Amsterdam: John Benjamins.

———. 1982b. Lhasa Tibetan: A case study in ergative typology. Journal of Linguistic Research 2.1:21–31.

———. 1984. Transitivity and ergative case in Lhasa Tibetan. Proceedings of the tenth annual meeting of the Berkeley Linguistics Society.

———. to appear. On active typology and the nature of agentivity. Typology of language structures: Nominatival, ergatival, actival, ed. by Frans Plank. Berlin: Mouton.

Goldstein, Melvyn. 1973. Modern Literary Tibetan. Urbana, IL: Center for Asian Studies, University of Illinois. (Occasional Papers of the Wolfenden Society on Tibeto-Burman Linguistics, vol. 5.)

———, and Nawang Nornang. 1970. Modern Spoken Tibetan. Seattle: University of Washington Press.

Jin, Peng. 1979. Lun Zang-yu Lasa-ko dungci-de tedian yu yufa jiegou-de guanxi. (On the relations between the characteristics of the verb and syntactic structure in spoken Lhasa Tibetan). Minzu Yuwen (Beijing) 1979.3:173–81.

THIRTEEN

The Nature and Origins of the Akha Evidentials System*

Graham Thurgood

California State University, Fresno

INTRODUCTION[1]

In Akha, evidentiality is overtly and obligatorily expressed through an elaborate system of sentence final particles which indicate 'the alleged source of information about the narrated event' (Jakobson 1971:135). The following examples, all reporting nonpast, nonexpected events, differ only in evidential marking (Egerod 1974:10):[2]

(1) *Nɔ-màq   àjɔq-áŋ   dì-é.*
    you-PL.   he-OBJ.   beat NONSENSORIAL
    'You (plural) will beat him.'

(2) *Nɔ-màq   àjɔq-áŋ   dì-ŋá.*
    you-PL.   he-OBJ.   beat VISUAL
    'You (plural) are beating him (I see it now).'

(3) *Nɔ-màq   àjɔaq-áŋ   dì-nja.*
    you-PL.   he-OBJ.   beat NONVISUAL
    'You (plural) are beating him (e.g. I guess so from the sound of beating).'

---

* This paper, a thoroughly revised and modified version of Thurgood (1981b), has benefited enormously from the substantive and stylistic comments of Johanna Nichols. The Akha data comes largely out of the works of Egerod and Hansson (especially 1974), supplemented by Lewis (1968). The diachronic analysis is my own.

The speculative and somewhat preliminary nature of this paper is due in part to the fact that there are no handbooks or etymological dictionaries or comparative grammars for the languages treated; for my tentativeness I offer no apology. However, to those whose papers I have read and may to some degree have misunderstood, I do apologize, with the hope that errors will be gently pointed out.

[1] This introduction owes a debt to Woodbury 1981 (this volume), which is also my source for the reference to Jakobson (1957) 1971.

[2] Akha forms are cited in the notation used in Egerod and Hansson (1974).

In the first example the speaker's source of evidence is nonsensory, while in the second it is visual and in the third it is nonvisual sensory evidence, e.g. auditory evidence.

The foundations for a historical look at the origins of the Akha evidentials are found in the works of Egerod and Hansson, in which the synchronic system is explicitly laid out. Using their synchronic work as a base, I will trace the particles that make up the modern evidential system back to earlier etyma with fuller meanings and more precise functions. I discuss paths of historical change emphasizing evolution in the meanings and functions of these forms.

Akha Sentence Particles

The centrality of evidentiality to the elaborate system of Akha sentential particles is implicit in the fact that after treating the ubiquitous -ə separately, Egerod and Hansson (1974:227–8) begin by dividing the sentential particles into two evidential sets: the 'sensorial' particles, which specify how the speaker's knowledge was arrived at, and the 'nonsensorial' particles, which do not. Although other manifestations of evidentiality can be found elsewhere in the grammar, these sentential particles contain the essence and core of the system.

The Ubiquitous -ə: *Synchronic Grammar.*   The ubiquitous -ə is the most frequently used particle in Akha. Its functions include: subordinating one noun to another in possessive, genitive, and other noun-modifying constructions; subordinating verbs to nouns in relative clause constructions; marking the citation form of the verb; and terminating utterances, most typically in the declarative mood. As with many Akha particles, tense is marked tonally, with the low-toned variant -ə̀ indicating past tense and the high-toned variant -ə́ indicating non-past.

In Egerod and Hansson's analysis -ə̀ and -ə́ are analyzed as differing only in tense and tone, but Lewis' dictionary suggests an evidential distinction in its three entries under -ə:

- -ə́   used in the following statements: declarative positive, declarative negative, and in questions demanding an explanation (it tends to be a bit scoldy in the latter)
- -ə̀   this signifies STRONG ASSERTION THAT WHAT IS SAID IS TRUE [emphasis mine]
- -ə̀   much the same as -ə́, but tends to be used more with: 1. negative statements 2. about something in the past

It is the variant -ə̀, marked as past tense by the low tone, that carries with it the 'strong assertion that what is said is true'. However, what Lewis saw as its strong assertive flavor may be nothing more than a predictable consequence of two pragmatic factors: the past tense marking and the LACK of an evidentiality marker. Reference to events in the past has its own consequence: our knowledge of the present and future is perceived as less certain than our knowledge of the past. This would give a more 'assertive' flavor to any statement about the past. The second pragmatic factor involves the very fact of qualification of a statement. It is only statements which need attestation that are qualified; consequently, implicit in a totally unqualified statement is a greater degree of certainty than in a qualified one (cf. *Bill is male* with *It is true that Bill is male*). Thus, Lewis' perception of an assertive flavor may have originated from a combination of our perception of sureness about past events and the 'certainty' implicit in unqualified statements.

The Ubiquitous -ə: *Diachronic Origins.*   The Akha -ə is reconstructed successively at the Proto-Loloish (PL) level as *way³ (Bradley 1979:254), at the Proto-Lolo-Burmese level as *wəy (=*wiy) (Thurgood 1977, 1981a, 1982), and at the Proto-Sino-Tibetan level as *wəy (Thurgood 1982). Regular correspondences within Lolo-Burmese (ibid.) demonstrate the cognacy of the -ə of Akha with the *ve* of Black Lahu, and the *rgh⁵/rgh³* of Fraser's Lisu (1922); the same correspondences also indicate that the Burmish *rai/rai'* of Written Burmese is not cognate and reflects a distinct etymon (cf. Kachin *we* versus *rē, rai*). Outside of Lolo-Burmese, reflexes are found in other Tibeto-Burman languages such as Khaling and Sherpa, as well as in Karen and in Archaic Chinese. In several of these languages the reflexes have an evidential meaning, but it does not seem necessary to reconstruct the distinction back to the proto-stage.

For Proto-Loloish, Bradley (1979:254) describes the functions of *way³ thus:

> There is one particle, probably of considerable antiquity, which occurs both after nouns and after verbs. This particle, 'declarative'/'genitive' *way³, occurs in every language for which there are any significant data available on particles. Its functions include the subordinating of one noun to another, . . . ; the subordinating of verbs to nouns, in a relative-clause-type relationship; and the termination of an utterance in a declarative mood.

This characterization is virtually identical to the functions of its modern Loloish reflexes Black Lahu *ve* and Akha -ə. However, in other languages it is a particle other than the phonological cognate which is the functional counterpart of Black Lahu *ve* and Akha -ə. The phonologically cognate form in Fraser's Lisu is *rgh³/rgh⁵*, but this is in no sense a functional counterpart to either particle. In the *tai/tai'* of Written Burmese we have a functional counterpart which subordinates one noun to another in possessive, genitive, and other noun-modifying constructions; subordinates verbs to nouns in relative clause constructions; marks the citation form of the verb; and terminates utterances, most typically in the declarative mood; however, this is clearly not a phonological cognate. In short, although a functional counterpart to the Akha -ə often exists, except in the case of Black Lahu *ve* it is not the particle which is phonologically cognate. And, in fact, this exemplifies the independence in the evolution of form and function typified throughout Lolo-Burmese.

The Sentential Particles.   Egerod and Hansson divide the remaining particles into sensorial and nonsensorial. These show category intersections with both tense and a notion they describe as expected/nonexpected. With the sensorial particles, their category labeled expected/nonexpected often shifts meaning to other related dimensions (1974:228):

expected	nonexpected
nonsurprise	surprise
all the time	intermittently
luckily	unfortunately

Common to the notions in the first column is predictability and hence good fortune; common to the notions in the second column is unpredictability and hence misfortune. The category labeled past/nonpast is also reported as sometimes undergoing a shift of meaning to indirect/direct. This may be a consequence of the fact that the past but not the present is inaccessible to direct knowledge.

The sensorial particles.   The sensorial particles, which specify how the speaker's knowledge was arrived at, distinguish between visual and nonvisual sources of evidence.

The core of the four visual evidential particles (Table 1) is the morpheme *ŋa*. The two 'nonexpected' particles are variants of *ŋa* marked by tone for tense, and the two 'expected' particles are composite forms containing *ŋa* i.e. *ŋá* + -*a* > *ŋáa* and *ŋà* + -*á* > *ŋàá*.[3] The *ŋa* itself descends historically from the first person singular pronoun found throughout Tibeto-Burman, PTB *ŋa*. In this specific sentence-final environment, the Akha evidential sense of *ŋa* arose from one of two sources: either it came from the reinterpretation of a first person agreement marker—a conclusion that in one sense simply begs the question of where it ultimately came from—or it arose out of the semantics and syntax of embedding a clause under *ŋa* 'I' plus a verb of perception or cognition, i.e. arose out of the semantics and syntax of a structure like *[ₛSOV]ₛ + ŋa + verb,* which is the Tibeto-Burman equivalent of a structure such as *I see that . . .* or *I know that . . .*

The four nonvisual sensorial evidentials are divided into an 'expected' pair *mía* and *mìá* and a 'nonexpected' pair *nja* and *njà* (Table 2). Like their visual counterparts, the two 'expected' particles are composite forms i.e. *mí* + -*a* > *mía* and *mì* + -*á* > *mìá*, with the tonal variation marking tense. The *mi*-segment, the essence of the marker, has a direct cognate in Lisu *mi*[4], a concessive particle found with both nouns and verbs in Lisu; in addition, it has

---

[3] The *a* of the these two composite forms and of the two composite forms *mía* and *mìá* (discussed below) is a sentence final particle which serves to mark the sentence as 'expected'. Ultimately, this *a* appears to descend from the third person pronoun *a* of Tibeto-Burman, but its path of development from this origin to a sentence final particle remains unclear.

[4] See footnote 3.

Table 1. Akha Sensorial Evidential
Particles (Visual) (Adapted from Egerod and
Hansson 1974:227–8)

	Expected	Nonexpected
nonpast	ŋáa	ŋá
past	ŋàá	ŋà

another possible cognate in the Burmese *-mai'-* of the phrasal conjunction *pei mai'(lui')* 'although, in spite of . . .' (Okell 1969:381). The Lisu evidence suggests the reconstruction of an earlier concessive for *mi-*, a particle that now indicates a nonvisual source of evidence.

Putting aside discussion of *nja* and *njá* for a moment, the modern distinction between the four visual and the two nonvisual expected particles, which now distinguish between visual and nonvisual sensorily attained knowledge, reflects an earlier distinction between knowledge obtained through personal experience, the forms with *ŋa* from **ŋa* 'I', and what was assumed to be true, the forms with *mi-* from a concessive particle.

The final pair of particles *nja* and *njá*, both monomorphemic, are related to the auxiliary verb *nja* 'able to' and to the sentence-final particle *njá* 'will'. In fact, the initial member of this pair, *nja*, indicating a nonpast, nonexpected event, is indistinguishable from *nja* 'able to'; not only does *nja* lack the anticipated high tone associated elsewhere with the nonpast and not only is it phonologically identical to *nja* 'able to', but the identity is also supported by the semantics. A comparison with the pragmatics of English *can*, used here not to argue for the semantics of Akha but only as a more familiar parallel, illustrates the point about semantics: an assertion that something 'can be' implies both that it is the result of nonvisual knowledge and unexpected. *njá*, the second member of the pair, is a tonal variant of *nja* 'able to' with the expected low tone designating past tense. The semantics again support this analysis: an assertion that something 'could be' implies both that it is the result of nonvisual knowledge and that it is unexpected. In the case of both members of this opposition, the

Table 2. Akha Sensorial Evidential
Particles (Nonvisual) (Adapted from Egerod
and Hansson 1974:227–8)

	Expected	Nonexpected
nonpast	mía	nja
past	mìá	njá

Table 3.   Akha Nonsensorial Particles (Positive and Negative)
(Adapted from Egerod and Hansson 1974:227–8)

	Expected X · Y			Nonexpected X · Y	
positive:					
nonpast	*má* · *mé*			*é* · *á*	
past	*mà* · *mè*			*è* · *à*	
negative: (mà . . . 'hot')					
nonpast	*mà . . . má* ·	*mà . . . mé*	*mà . . .*	·	*mà . . . a*
past		*mà . . . à*			

earlier, fuller, more precise meanings have given way to less restricted, more abstract evidential meanings.[5]

The non-sensorial particles.   The nonsensorial particles, which do not indicate the source of evidence for a statement, also show category intersections with both tense and the notion of expected/nonexpected. There is, in addition, a person distinction shown in Table 3 and indicated by the labels x and y. For example, in a declarative statement, if the subject is first person, the pertinent particle from set x is used; otherwise, the particle is chosen from set y. (Examples from Egerod 1974: 8, 10, 13.)

(4)   Ɖá   nɔ̀-áŋ   dì-è.
       I   you-OBJ.   beat-*è* (X)
       'I beat you.'

(5)   Nɔ-màq   àjɔ̀q-áŋ   dì-mé.
       you-PL.   he-OBJ.   beat-*mé* (Y)
       'Yes, you (PL.) beat him.'

(6)   Àkhỳ   tsèq-à.
       dog   bark-*à (Y)*
       'The dog barked.'

On the other hand, for a question, it is with the second person subjects that the pertinent particle from set x is used; otherwise, the particle is chosen from set Y.[6] (Examples from Egerod 1974:12.)

---

[5] Related to this pair is *njé*, glossed as 'will' by Egerod and Hansson and described as indicating one's immediate intention or purpose by Lewis. This *njá*, which functions as a marker of predications of the future, carries the high tone associated elsewhere with the nonpast. Intriguingly, but inexplicably, this particle is cognate to the topic marker in Lisu that marks new topics.

[6] Egerod and Hansson also note the existence of a third pattern for 'indirect reference' in which the particle is chosen from set X for third person subjects but from set Y otherwise.

(7) *Nɔ́   ŋà-áŋ   dì-é-ló.*
     you   I-OBJ.   beat = *é* (X) = QUESTION
     'Will you beat me?'

(8) *Na-màq   nɔ̀-áŋ   dì-á-ló.*
     I-PL.   you-OBJ.   beat = *á* (Y) = QUESTION
     'Will we (exclusive) beat you?'

(9) *Àjɔq   nɔ̀-áŋ   dì-á-ló.*
     he   you-OBJ.   beat = *à* (Y) = QUESTION
     'Will he beat you?'

The above Akha person distinction is paralleled in distantly related Sherpa (Woodbury this volume, p. 192, note 3):

> The first person vs. nonfirst person distinction is widespread in Sherpa, but the term 'first person' is something of a misnomer. In the interrogative all so-called first person phenomena are associated with second person. This is because second person forms in questions anticipate the use of first person in the answer . . .

As a consequence of this, questions carry an evidential value which is appropriate to the anticipated response.

This person distinction is the remnant of much earlier co-occurrence constraints within the Proto-Tibeto-Burman verbal paradigm. An examination of the paired particles *-e*(X) and *-a*(Y) illustrates this well. This restriction of Akha *-e* to first person is paralled by a similar restriction on its Tibetan cognate *yin* and on its Sherpa cognate *'in*.[7] On the other hand, the particle paired with *-e* is *-a*, whose person restrictions relate to its ultimate origin as a third person pronoun.[8] Akha *mɛ* also shows traces of earlier co-occurrence constraints. Throughout Tibeto-Burman *mɛ* and its cognates favor nonfirst person environments. However, the particle *ma*—paired with *mɛ*—is part of a different system; it originated as a full verb. The person restrictions on its Akha distribution are the result of its pairing with *mɛ*, a particle with its own co-occurrence restrictions, rather than being the result of inherited constraints. In any case, the person distinction found with the nonsensorial particles is a residue of co-occurrence constraints present in the verbal paradigm of Proto-Tibeto-Burman and has had little effect on the semantics of the modern Akha particles.

The morphemes *ma* and *mɛ* are the core of the 'expected' nonsensorial particles. Contra Thurgood 1981b, the particle *ma* is related to the Akha full verb *má* 'be real, true' and the adverb *má má* 'really, surely', an origin which fits nicely with particle's meaning 'I know by experience that this is true' (Inga-Lill Hans-

---

[7] In addition, the Sherpa cognate has an evidential function (Woodbury 1981:11): *'in* 'entails that the speaker is unsure of the proposition, and found out perhaps by hearsay'.

[8] This PTB *a appears to be the same *a* found in the composite sensorial particles *ŋa-a* and *mi-a* (see note 3).

son, personal communication). The low-toned variant *mà* is due to the same historical mechanism that imposed a tonally-marked past/nonpast distinction on all the Akha particles. The other member of the expected, nonsensorial pair is *mε*, which developed out of a copula and is still realized as such in the *mè* of Karen. Within Lolo-Burmese, it has a number of excellent cognates, including the sentence-final aspectual particle of Burmese *mai/mai* 'future, or as-sumptive' (Okell 1969:354). The assumptive aspect is compatible with the modern Akha evidential meaning of nonsensorial, expected.

The morphemes *e* and *a* are the core of the 'nonexpected' nonsensorial particles. The *e* is, as mentioned above, cognate with the copulas *yin* of Tibetan and *'in* of Sherpa. This appears to have represented a 'speculative' future contrasting with the 'assumptive' future of *mε*. This distinction might be illustrated by the contrast between *He could go to Fresno tomorrow* and *He is going to Fresno tomorrow*. The other member of this pair is *a*. Etymologically its various manifestations are reflexes of the Proto-Tibeto-Burman third person pronoun **a*, which subsequently developed into a relatively neutral sentence-final particle (see the person distinction discussed above and note 3). Any additional meaning it may have acquired is due more to its opposition to *e* than to any originally inherent meaning of its own.

The Quotative

The quotative is the last evidential particle to be discussed in this paper. It is illustrated in the following examples (from Egerod 1974:10):

(10)   *Nɔ-màq   àjɔq-áŋ   dì-mé.*
       you-PL.   he-OBJ.   beat = *mé*
       'You (PL.) will beat me.'

(11)   *Nɔ-màq   àjɔq-áŋ   dì-mé   djé.*
       you-PL.   he-OBJ.   beat = *mé*   QUOT.
       'He told me that your group will beat him.'

The Akha quotative is cognate with Phunoi *cè*, Bisu *kyì/tsì*, and Mpi *tçe¹*. It derives from a verb meaning 'to speak' and can be used either to report indirect knowledge or to indicate the hearsay nature of the knowledge.

CONCLUSION

The Akha evidential particles evolved from a variety of sources with a number of different functions: (a) Full verbs: the quotative *djé* descended from a full verb meaning 'to speak, say', under which full clauses were originally embedded. *má* came from another full verb meaning 'be true'. (b) Modal *nja* originated as a modal verb meaning 'be able'. (c) Copulas: Both *mε* and *e* evolved from copulas with future meanings, the first an 'assumptive' future and the second a 'speculative' future. (d) Particle: *mi-* derives from a concessive particle. (e) Pronouns: *ŋa* came from a first person pronoun, which was original either an agreement marker or part of a matrix sentence under which clauses were embedded. It may also have gone through a stage in which it was a sentence-final particle. *a* started as a third person pronoun and went through a stage in which it was a neutral sentence-final particle.[9]

Despite the variety of sources and despite the gaps in our knowledge of historical developments, an outline has emerged. Through the reconstruction and examination of earlier forms and functions, a general picture of the evolution of the Akha evidentials has been drawn, tracing them from their ultimate origins in the grammatical and semantic roots present in the language family as far back as Proto-Tibeto-Burman through to their development into the complex system of the modern language.

REFERENCES

Bradley, David. 1979. Proto-Loloish. London and Malmö: Curzon Press.

Egerod, Søren. 1974. Further notes on Akha sentence particles. Seventh International Sino-Tibetan Conference, Atlanta.

Egerod, Søren and Inga–Lill Hansson. 1974. An Akha conversation on death and funeral. Acta Orientalia 36.225–84.

Fraser, J. O. 1922. Handbook of the Lisu (Yawyin) language. Rangoon: Government Printing Office.

Jakobson, Roman. (1957) 1971. Shifters, verbal categories, and the Russian verb. Selected Writings II, 130–47. The Hague: Mouton.

Lewis, Paul. 1968. Akha–English dictionary. (Data paper no. 70, Southeast Asia Program, Cornell.) Ithaca: Cornell University Press.

Okell, John. 1969. A reference grammar of colloquial Burmese. Two volumes. London: Oxford University Press.

Thurgood, Graham. 1977. Lisu and Proto-Lolo-Burmese. Acta Orientalia 38.147–207.

———. 1981a. Notes on the origins of Burmese creaky tone. Monumenta Serindica no. 9. Institute for the Study of Languages and Cultures of Asia and Africa. Tokyo.

———. 1981b. The historical development of the Akha evidentials system. BLS 7.295–302.

———. 1982. The Sino-Tibetan copula *wəy. Cahier de linguistique Asie orientale 11.1:65–82.

Woodbury, Anthony C. 1981. Evidentiality in Sherpa. Manuscript.

---

[9] With the exception of *djé*, a still not understood historical development has imposed a tonal split on particles, doubling their number. Each now has a low tone variant designating past tense and a high tone variant designating nonpast.

FOURTEEN

Evidentials in Japanese

Haruo Aoki*
University of California, Berkeley

This paper discusses three areas of meaning associated with Japanese evidentials. The first area involves expressions which deal with sensation and make a syntactic distinction between the description of a sensation experienced by the speaker and a sensation experienced by a nonspeaker, the latter description being marked by *gar*. The second area of meaning is expressed by *no* or *n,* which makes nonspecific evidential statements, sometimes from restricted or inaccessible information. The third area is expressed by a group of forms which make hearsay or inferential statements, such as *soo, yoo,* and *rasi* meaning 'they say', 'appear', or 'seem'. It is this last area which Japanese linguists have traditionally treated as the area of Japanese evidentials.[1] However, evidentials in Japanese can be considered to range over three types of meaning: the speaker communicates (a) that he has, of necessity, only indirect evidence, as in *gar,* (b) that he has generally valid evidence as in the case of *no* or *n,* and (c) that he cannot say that he is in complete possession of information because of the nature of the evidence, as in the cases of hearsay and inferential forms.

Japanese evidentials are not grammaticized and belong to various word or morpheme classes: morphologically *gar* is a verb, *no, n, soo,* and *yoo* are nouns, and *rasi* is an adjective.

The organization of this paper is as follows: first, I will discuss four types of evidentials which occur in the verb phrase; next, evidential adverbial phrases; then, evidentials and politeness; and last, the historical development of evidentials.

---

* In the preparation of this paper I received many valuable comments from Noriko Akacuka, Patricia Clancy, Kiici Iitoyo, Huzio Minami, Hideo Teramura and have particularly benefited from thoughtful comments from Wallace Chafe and Johanna Nichols. Any errors that remain are my own.

[1] For example, Martin labeled *soo* as 'the' evidential in Japanese (1975:991).

VERBAL PHRASES

Four types of verb phrase evidentials will be discussed. They are (a) descriptions of sensation, (b) *no* or *n*, (c) hearsay, and (d) inference.

Inferences Regarding Feelings of Others

Sensations such as being hot, cold, or lonely are expressed in Japanese sentences such as (1), (2), and (3) when the experiencer is the speaker:

(1) *Atu   -i.*
     hot -NP.[2]
     'I am hot.'

(2) *Samu -i.*
     cold -NP.
     'I am cold.'

(3) *Sabisi -i.*
     lonely -NP.
     'I am lonely.'

However, sentences (4), (5), and (6) in which the experiencer is a third person are ungrammatical:

(4) **Kare   wa   atu -i.*
     he   T.M.[3] hot -NP.
     'He is hot.'

(5) **Kare   wa   samu -i.*
     he   T.M.   cold -NP.
     'He is cold.'

(6) **Kare   wa   sabisi -i.*
     he   T.M.   lonely -NP.
     'He is lonely.'

The sentences (4–6) may be made grammatical by addition of *gar* and *te-i-ru*. *Atu* 'hot' is a state. The addition of *gar* turns it into a nonstate. *Te-i-ru* is added to turn it back into a state:

(7) *Kare   wa   atu -gatteiru.*[4]
     he   T.M.   hot
     'He is hot.'

---

[2] NP = nonpast suffix. The form is *-ru* after a verb and *-i* after an adjective.

[3] T.M. = topic marker.

[4] gatteiru = *gar* + *-te* (gerundive suffix) + *-i* verb stem meaning 'be' or 'exist') + *-ru* (nonpast suffix).

(8)   *Kare   wa   samu   -gatteiru.*
      'He is cold.'

(9)   *Kare   wa   sabisi   -gatteiru.*
      'He is lonely'

The speaker's wishes and desires are expressed in sentences such as (10). When the wishing is done by a third person, addition of *gar* and *te-i-ru* produces grammatical sentences as in (12). When the sentence ends in an adjective, which has the suffix *-i* in the nonpast tense, the object is marked by *ga* as in (10).[5] Otherwise, the object is marked by *o* as in (12):

(10)   *Watasi   wa   mizu   ga   nom   ita   -i.*
        I   T.M.   water S.M.[6] drink DESID.   -NP.
        'I want to drink water.'

(11)   **Kare   wa   mizu   ga   nom   ita   -i.*
        he   T.M.   water S.M.   drink DESID.   -NP.
        'He wants to drink water.'

(12)   *Kare   wa   mizu   o   nom   ita   -gatteiru.*
        he   T.M.   water O.M.[7] drink -DESID.
        'He wants to drink water.'

Sentences like (1–3) and (10) occur without *gar* since they directly express the first person experiencer's sensations and desires. The testimony of the first person experiencer is considered self-evident. The sentences involving third person experiencers are ungrammatical without *gar,* as in (11). *Gar* converts inner sensations and desires into a verb which expresses externally observable changes. The verb derived by the addition of *gar* receives the further addition of *te-i-ru* to express a state. *Gar* has the function of expressing inference rather than direct experience, from which a further inference can be made about person, which is often left unexpressed in Japanese. For example, without *gar,* a hearer infers that (13) is about the speaker and that (14), with *gar,* is about a third person:

(13)   *Atu   -i.*
        hot   -NP.
        'I am hot.'

(14)   *Atu-gatteiru*

---

   [5] Kuno gives a more detailed list of sentence types in which objects are marked by *ga* (1973:90–91).
   [6] S.M. = subject marker.
   [7] O.M. = object marker.

       hot
       'He is hot.'

Commenting on *gar* Kuno (1973:84) states that it adds the meaning of 'to show a sign of, behave like *-ing*'. Martin's words for the meaning of *gar* are 'display symptoms of being . . .' (1975:359). For this reason, use of *gar* to express one's own inner feeling is superfluous, making a sentence like (15) unacceptably circuitous:

    (15)   *Watasi   wa   atu -gatteiru.*
          I   T.M.   hot
          'I am hot.'

The ungrammatical (15) becomes grammatical when there is a shift in time away from the time of speaking:

    (16)   *Sono   koro   watasi   wa   taihen   sabisi-gattei-ta.*
          that   time   I   T.M.   very   lonely   -PAST
          'I was very lonely at that time.'

    (17)   *So   nar   -eba   watasi   wa   taihen   saisi-garu[8]-daroo.*
          so   become   -if   I   T.M.   very   lonely   -CONJ.
          'If that happened I would be very lonely.'

Gar, then, might be called an indirect evidence marker used to describe internal feelings and sensations of an experiencer removed in time and space.

    (18)   *Kare   wa   atu -i.*
          he   T.M.   hot -NP.
          'He is hot.'

    (19)   *Kare   wa   samu -i.*
          he   T.M.   cold   -NP.
          'He is cold.'

    (20)   *Kare   wa   sabisi -i.*
          he   T.M.   lonely -NP.
          'He is lonely.'

Sentences such as (18), (19), and (20) without *gar* become grammatical in exceptional cases when the speaker is not subject to the usual physiological constraints, such as having a direct neural connection to sensation in someone else's body. For example, a narrator may adopt a position which enables him to process sensations as though he has privileged direct access to the sensing areas which are inaccessible under ordinary circumstances. Kuroda called a style pro-

---

[8] garu = *gar* + *-ru* (nonpast suffix).

duced by such an omniscient narrator a nonreportive style (1973:381). Sentences such as (18), (19), and (20) are examples of those which are acceptable in the nonreportive style.

On the other hand, if one wishes to ask about the way (s)he appears to others, (21) and (22) are possible:

(21) *Watasi   wa   atu-gatteiru   yooni   mie   -ru   ka?*
     I   T.M.   hot   COMP.   appear -NP.   Q.P.[9]
     'Do I look hot?'

(22) *Kare   ni   wa   watasi   ga   atu-gatteiru   yooni   mie*
     him   to   T.M.   I   S.M.   hot   COMP.   appear

     -ru   rasi   -i.
     -NP.   seem   -NP.
     'He seems to think I am showing a sign of being hot.'

Besides the basic evidential meaning, *gar* also means 'to act in a certain way, not necessarily with good reason.' For example (7), repeated here as (23), also has a second meaning:

(23) *Kare   wa   atu   -gatteiru.*
     'He   is   hot.'   or
     'He shows signs of being hot (but he may not be hot at all).'

In other words, *gar* indicates that what is being presented is inferred from evidence, and not necessarily a fact. The questionable status of the inference expressed by *gar* may be seen in sentences such as (24):

(24) *Sonnani   atu   -garu   na.*
     so much   hot   NEG.-IMP.
     'Do not act so hot (it cannot be that hot).'

Mimetic words in Japanese are of three types: auditory (phonomimes), visual (phenomimes), and affective (psychomimes) (Hirose 1981:3). Concerning the third type Kindaici states that there is a predominance of adverbs which describe irritation or disturbing feelings (1978:19). In addition, there are adverbs which describe different kinds of pain: *cikuciku* 'pricking', *gangan* 'pounding (of head-ache)', *sikusiku* 'throbbing (of toothache and stomachache)' and *zukizuki* 'throbbing (of headache and surface wound)'. Both irritation and pain are sensations which can be reported first hand only by the feeler, or the first-person.

Pain may be perceived as something a person feels directly, as in *ita-i* 'I am in pain', or as sensation caused by a part of the body, as in *itam-u* 'it hurts'. In the first case *ita* is an adjective stem followed by the nonpast adjectival suffix-*i;* in

---

[9] Q.P. = question particle.

the latter *itam* is a verb stem followed by the nonpast verb suffix-*u*. Pain of the first person is expressed as in 25:

> (25) *Zukizuki   ita   -i.*
>   throbbing pain -NP.
>   'I have a throbbing pain.'

> (26) **Kare   wa   zukizuki   ita   -gatteiru.*
>   he   T.M.   throbbing pain
>   'He has a throbbing pain.'

However, when one wishes to describe a painful condition of a non–first-person, use of mimetic adverbs as in (26) is strange, probably due to *zukuzuki* being a word used in direct-evidence statements and *gar* being an indirect-evidence marker.[10]

First-person irritation is expressed by a combination of a mimetic word and a verb such as *suru* 'do': *iraira suru*. For a nonfirst-person, *no* or *rasi*, discussed below, is used: *iraira site iru rasii* 'he/she seems to be irritated'.

No *or* N *as Markers of Fact*

An evidential *no,* or more informal *n,* may be used to state that the speaker is convinced that for some reason what is ordinarily directly unknowable is nevertheless true.

We saw earlier that a sentence such as (27) was ungrammatical and that the use of *gar* made it grammatical:

> (27) **Kare   wa   atu   -i.*
>   he   T.M.   hot   -NP.
>   'He is hot.'

It is also possible to use *no* or *n* as in (28), which means 'it is a fact that he is hot'.

> (28) *Kare   wa   atu -i   <u>no</u> da.*
>   he   T.M.   hot -NP.   be
>   'I know that he is hot. It is a fact that he is hot.'

---

[10] A non–first-person's painful condition is expressed by use of *no* or *rasi,* to be discussed later:

> (i) *Kitto   zukizuki   itam-u   no   da   yo.*
>   surely throbbing hurt-NP   be   FP
>   'He/she must have a throbbing pain.'

> (ii) *zukizuki   itam-u   rasi-i.*
>   throbbing hurt-NP appear-NP
>   'He/she seems to have a throbbing pain.'

(29) *Ase   o   kai   -teiru   kara   kare wa   atu*
     sweat O.M.   perspire -PROG.   because   he   T.M.   hot

     -i   no   da.
     -NP.   be
     'Because he is sweating I know that he is hot.'

For this reason sentences with *no* or *n* are often used as the main clause of a
complex sentence in which the subordinate clause indicates reasons, as in (29).
Grammatically *no* or *n* nominalizes the preceding phrase. Semantically it removes the statement from the realm of a particular experience and makes it into
a timeless object. The concept thereby becomes nonspecific and detached.

We saw that pain-related mimetic words occur with adjectives such as *ita* 'be
painful'. There are a large number of mimetic words which are not related to
pain. They do not cooccur with adjectives such as *ita* but cooccur with the
semantically colorless verb *suru* 'do'. (30) is an example:

(30) *Mukamuka suru.*
       'I feel sick to my stomach. I have a nauseated feeling.'

When we want to say 'he feels sick to his stomach', however, (31) is as ungrammatical as (27).[11]

(31) **Kare   wa   mukamuka   suru.*[12]
     he   T.M.   sick   do
     'He feels sick.'

Other mimetic words which are found in direct evidence statements are those
expressive (a) of an itching sensation, such as *muzumuzu, uzuuzu;* (b) of an
irritating or frustrating sensation, such as *ziriziri, iraira;* (c) of a fainting sensation, such as *kurakura;* (d) of depressed feelings, such as *musyakusya,
kusyakusya;* (e) of relief from anxiety: *hotto;* (f) of pleasant and serene feelings,

---

[11] A similar phenomenon is also found in Korean:

(i) *na   nin   sok   i   nikilnikil   ha   -ta.*
    I   T.M.   inside S.M.   nauseating   do   -NP.
    'I feel sick to my stomach.'

However, the following sentence is ungrammatical.

(ii) **ki   saram   in   sok   i   nikilnikil   ha   -ta.*
    this man   T.M.   inside S.M.   nauseating   do   -NP.
    'He feels sick to his stomach.'

[12] Again, (31) is not ungrammatical in Kuroda's nonreportive style.

such as *sabasaba, sappari;* (g) of fear or chill sending a shiver through one, as in
zokuzoku; (h) of palpitation from excitement or fear: *dokidoki* (about oneself) and
harahara (about someone else); (i) of comforting warmth—*hokahoka,
pokapoka;* and (j) of a sudden feeling of sympathy and caring for someone, such
as *horotto*. In all these cases *gar* cannot be used since it is suffixed only to an
adjectival stem. It is *no* or *n* which makes sentences dealing with the sensation of
a nonfirst person grammatical, as in:

(32) *Kare   wa   mukamuka   si   -teiru   no   da.*
      he   T.M.   sick   do -PROG.   be
      'It is a fact that he feels sick to his stomach.'

In contrast with *gar,* which is an indirect evidence marker, *no* or *n* is a marker
which converts a statement for which ordinarily no direct knowledge is possible
into a statement which is asserted as a fact.

Hearsay

Hearsay evidence is expressed most commonly by the use of a special nomi-
nalizer *soo* followed by a copula *da* as in (33). There are also the more collo-
quial-*tte* as in (34), and the archaic and literary *gena*. There are another dozen or
so alternative expressions.

(33) *Ame   ga   hutteiru   -soo   da.*[13]
      rain   S.M.   fall
      'They say it is raining.'

(34) *Ame   ga   hutteiru   -tte.*
      'They say   it   is raining.'

-*soo* occurs with verbs as in (35) and (36), with adjectives as in (37) and (38),
and with noun predication sentences (39) and (40):

(35) *Ame   ga   hutta   (=hur + -ta)   -soo   da.*
      rain   S.M.   fall-PAST
      'They say it rained.'

(36) *Ame   ga   hur   -u   -soo da.*
      rain   S.M.   fall -NP.
      'They say it is going to rain.'

(37) *Kaze   ga   cuyokatta   (cuyo + -katta)   -soo da.*
      wind   S.M.   strong-PAST
      'They say the wind was strong.'

---

[13] hutteiru = hur + -te (gerundive suffix) + -i (verb stem meaning 'be' or 'exist') + -ru (nonpast
suffix).

(38) *Kaze   ga   cuyo   -i   -<u>soo</u> da.*
     wind   S.M.   strong -NP.
     'They say the wind is strong.'

(39) *Kare   wa   daigakusei   da   -tta   -<u>soo</u> da.*
     he   T.M.   university   student   be   -PAST
     'They say he was a university student.'

(40) *Kare   wa   daigakusei   da   -<u>soo</u> da.*
     he   T.M.   university   student   be
     'They say he is a university student.'

Phonologically the hearsay-*soo* is high pitched in the first mora, and the high pitch stays when the preceding verbals are atonic; when the preceding verbals are tonic, -*soo* is pronounced with a low pitch throughout.

Properly Evidential Forms

There are three inferential forms which may be translated 'seem', 'look like', 'appear', or left untranslated. Of these-*yoo da* is used when the speaker has some visible, tangible, or audible evidence collected through his own senses to make an inference. Sentence (41) from *Takasebune* by Oogai Mori bears this out:

(41) *Soreni   omae   no   yoosu   o   mi   -reba   doomo   sima*
     further   you   P.M.[14]   behavior O.M.   see -when   at all   island

     e   iku   no   o   kunisi   -te-i   -nai   -<u>yoo</u> da.
     to go   NOM.   O.M.   be troubled -PROG. -NEG.
     'Besides, as I watch you I get the feeling that you are not at all bothered by
        the prospect of exile.'

The second is *rasi -i,* which is used when the evidence is circumstantial or gathered through sources other than one's own senses. Tamako Kasioka (1980:172) points out that (42) is inappropriate when the speaker is looking at the blue sky.

(42) *Hare   te-i-ru   <u>rasi</u> -i.*
     clear   result
     'It seems to be clear.'

(42) is appropriate when the speaker is unable to see the sky directly, but can make a guess about the weather condition on the basis of brightness of the room and so on. Kasioka's pair of (43) and (44) clarifies the difference between *yoo da* and *rasi -i:*

---

[14] P.M. = possessive marker.

(43) *Kono   kusuri   wa   yoku kiku   yoo da.*
      this   medicine T.M. well work
      'I infer from my own experience that this medicine works well.'

(44) *Kono   kusuri   wa   yoku kiku   rasi -i.*
      this   medicine T.M. well work
      'I infer from what I heard that this medicine works well.'

The third is *soo da,* which differs from *yoo da* and *rasi -i* in two respects. *Soo da* does not express inference about what occurred in the past. For example, (45) and (46) are grammatical but (47) is not:

(45) *Kare   wa   soo si   -ta   yoo da.*
      he   T.M. so   do   -PAST
      'I infer from my own experience that he did so.'

(46) *Kare   wa   soo si   -ta   rasi -i.*
      he   T.M. so   do   -PAST.
      'I infer from what I heard that he did so.'

(47) **Kare wa soo si -ta soo da.*
      'I infer that he did so.'

Second, *soo da* is used when the speaker believes in what he is making an inference about. For example, (48) is ungrammatical:

(48) **Ame ga   huri soo da ga   hur -ru   to   wa*
      rain   S.M. fall   but   fall -NP.   Q.M.[15] T.M.

      omowa -na   -i.
      think   -NEG. -NP.
      'It seems that it is going to rain but I don't think it will.'

In contrast to (49) and (50), (51) is used when the speaker judges that the event is imminent:

(49) *Ame   ga   hur -u   yoo da.*
      rain   S.M. fall -NP.
      'It seems that it is going to rain (for example observing increasingly dark skies).'

(50) *Ame   ga   hur -u   rasi -i.*
      rain   S.M. fall -NP.
      'It seems that it is going to rain (for example, overhearing talking about rain).'

---

[15] Q.M. = quotative marker. For this special use of the quotative marker, see Martin (1975:1009–1010).

(51) *Ame   ga   huri   soo da.*
      rain   S.M.   fall
      'It looks like it is going to rain (any minute).'

Phonologically the inferential *soo* is high pitched throughout when the preceding verbals are atonic; when the preceding verbals are tonic, *soo* is high pitched in the first mora and low in the second. The phonological contrasts of forms with hearsay and inferential *soo* may be seen in the following examples:

Stems	+ Hearsay *soo da*	+ Inferential *soo da*
yob (atonic)	yo|buso|oda	yo|bisooda
yom (tonic)	yo|musooda	yo|miso|oda

Compared to the *soo da* which expresses hearsay, the inferential *soo da* is much more restricted in terms of the verbals which precede it. The inferential *soo da* occurs with only one tense form and does not occur with noun predication sentences. For this reason the inferential *soo da* precedes the hearsay *soo da:*

(52) *Asita   wa   gohan   ga   tabe-rare   soo da soo   da.*
      tomorrow T.M.   rice   S.M.   eat -possible INF.   hearsay
      'I hear that he is likely to be able to have rice tomorrow.'

Yoo da, rasi-i, and *soo da* have similar restrictions in first person present tense:

(53) *Kare   wa   hatarai   -teiru.*
      he   T.M.   work   -PROG.
      'He is working.'

(54) *Kare wa hatarai -teiru yoo da.*
      'It seems that he is working.'

(55) *Watasi wa hatarai -teiru.*
      'I am working.'

(56) **Watasi wa hatarai -teiru yoo da.*
      'I seem to be working.'

Yoo da and *rasi-i* occur after a past tense marker not only with a third person subject but also with a first person subject:

(57) *Sono   koro   watasi   wa   mazimeni   hatarai   -te-i   -ta*
      that   time   I   T.M.   seriously   work   -PROG.   -PAST
      yoo da.
      'I seem to have been working seriously at that time.'

Here again, as in the case of *gar* above, the evidential meaning is clearest in the present tense.

ADVERBIAL PHRASES

A subclass of adverbs dealing with the speaker's attitude toward the truth value of a statement was recognized by Yosio Yamada in 1908, and is not unlike what Quirk, Greenbaum, et al. call disjuncts (1972:508). The examples of adverbs of this subclass cited by Yamada (1908:503ff.) are the classical forms *kedasi* 'probably', *osaosa* 'in any way', and *yomo* 'ever (with negative)'.

Modern Japanese forms expressing conviction include *matigainaku* 'unmistakably', *utagainaku* 'undoubtedly', *tasika(ni)* 'certainly', *kanarazu* 'infallibly', *sadamesi* 'presumably', *kitto* and *sazo* 'surely'. Forms expressing some degree of doubt are *tabun, osoraku, dooyara* 'probably'. Those expressing a greater degree of doubt are *mosikasuruto, hyottosite* 'possibly'. Adverbs such as *masaka* 'surely (not)' and the somewhat formal *yomoya* '(not) by any possibility' express negative conviction.

At one extreme there are the adverbs which express the speaker's certainty about the statement which is being made. These do not necessarily require overt evidential elements in the verb system. (58) and (59) are examples:

(58) *Matigainaku   kare   wa   hon   o   yon-de-iru.*
     unmistakably   he   T.M.   book   O.M.   read-PROG.
     'I am sure he is reading the book.'

(59) *Anata   no   okamisan   wa   kitto   yakimotiyaki*
     you   P.M.   wife   T.M.   certainly jealous

     nanda   yo.
     be   F.P.[16]
     'Your wife must be the jealous type.' (from Tooson Simazaki, *Yoakemae*)

Further down the continuum there are adverbs indicating lesser degrees of certainty. These often require that the verb system indicate a corresponding degree of certainty.

(60) *Dooyara   kare   wa   hon   o   yon-de-iru   rasi -i.*
     likely   he   T.M.   book   O.M.   read-PROG.
     'He seems to be reading the book.'

(61), which lacks the inferential *rasi-i*, sounds strange:

---

[16] F.P. = final particle.

(61) *_Dooyara_ kare wa hon o yon -de-iru.
      'He is likely to be reading a book.'

The adverb _masaka_ requires both inferential and negative elements. For this reason (62) and (63) are ungrammatical.

(62) *_Masaka_ kare wa sono hon o yon-de-iru.
      'He could not possibly be reading the book.'

(63) *_Masaka_ kare wa sono hon o yon-de-iru _rasi-i_.
      'He could not possibly be reading the book.'

Instead, either a combination of conjectural and negative suffixes separately, as in (64), or a lexicalized _mai,_ a combination of inferential and negative, as in (65), is required:

(64) _Masaka_ kare wa sono hon o yonde (wa) i-_nai daroo_.
                                        -NEG. CONJ.
      'I doubt that he is reading the book.'

(65) _Masaka_ kare wa sono hon o yonde (wa) i-_mai_.
      'I doubt that he is reading the book.'

The correspondence between the adverbs and the verb suffixes is so predictable that an answer consisting of just the adverb (66A) is sufficient in a discourse to provide the full evidential information expected of a question such as (66Q):

(66Q) _Kare wa sono hon o yonde-iru ka._
       'Is he reading the book?'

(66A) _Masaka._
       'I doubt it.'

Here (66A) is an equivalent of (64) or (65).

EVIDENTIALS AND POLITENESS

Most of the evidential expressions can be used to make polite sentences.

-Gar

-Gar is used with sensation and desiderative adjectives, and has the meaning of 'to show a sign of' in reference to a person other than the speaker. For this reason sentences such as (67) are used to express the speaker's appreciation of a gift by including a third person for whom _gar_ can be used to indicate that (s)he would show externally observable appreciation of it.

(67) *Kitto   haha   mo   uresi   -gar-imasu.*
      surely   mother   too   be glad   -POLITE-SUFFIX
      'I am sure mother will be happy too.'

No, *or* n

This is a despecifying evidential, and is used to minimize the speaker's involvement. For example, it may be used to tone down the harshness of a request (68), to soften the expression of desire (69), or to cite a statement as something for which the speaker cannot be held responsible (70):

(68) *Satoo-san   ga   soo   yuu   no   desu.*
      Mr. Sato   S.M.   so   say   POLITE COP.
      'Mr. Sato says so (I am not requesting this, he is).'

(69) *Watasi   mo   mairi   -tai   no   desu.*
      I   too   go   -DESID.   POLITE COP.
      'I would like to come along also.'

(70) *Kore   ga   kimari   na   no   desu.*
      this   S.M.   rule   COP.   POLITE COP.
      'This is the rule.'

The hearsay soo.

Soo is often used when the speaker does not wish to reveal the source of information and wants to minimize the problems which result from such knowledge. For example, (71) is less direct and less harsh than (72):

(71) *Yamada   wa   sir   -anai   soo da.*
      Yamada   T.M.   know   -NEG.
      'They say that Yamada does not know.'

(72) *Satoo   ga   Yamada   wa   sir   -anai   to*
      Sato   S.M.   Yamada   T.M.   know   -NEG.   QM

      itta.
      said (*iw* 'say' + *ta* 'past')
      'Sato said that Yamada doesn't know.'

The inferential forms may be used when one has definite information but wants to produce a softer impact as in:

(73) *Wakai   koibito   ga   deki   -ta   rasi -i.*
      young   lover   S.M.   come to have   -PAST
      '(S)he now has a young lover.'

Note that the original meaning of *rasi -i* adds the implication that the speaker is not directly responsible for the news but came across indirect clues. *Yoo* is also used to muffle a pointed statement:

(74) Dokoka   de   omenikakat -ta   <u>yoo</u> desu ne.
      somewhere   at   meet   -PAST   F.P.
      'I met you somewhere, didn't I?'

HISTORICAL DEVELOPMENT

Of the evidential forms, *gar* and *rasi-i* are native Japanese words. *Gar* has been known since the eleventh century. The earliest record of *rasii* is found in the eighth century in the form of *rasi*. In the written language, after a hiatus which starts in the twelfth century, it reappears in the eighteenth century with the modern suffix *-i* and in the form *rasi -i*.

As for *soo* and *yoo*, Masaru Nagano, Kanehiko Yosida, and Daizi Siraisi are among those who consider them to be Chinese loans. However, there is a chance that at least *yoo* is not a loan in the usual sense. There was a native Japanese form *sama* which meant 'appearance' and there is a chance that *sama* was translated into Chinese *yang* of comparable meaning. *Yang,* when it undergoes regular sound changes in Japanese, after the intermediate stages of [yaū], [yau], [yɔ·] would become [yo·] or *yoo*. The source of *soo* is explained in at least two ways: one is that it derives from Chinese *xiang* which, among other things, means 'shape', 'appearance', 'aspect' (Yosida 1971:404), and the other is that it derives from Japanese *sama* (Oono 1978:131). If *soo* is from Chinese *xiang,* then both *soo* and *yoo* provide examples of indigenous linguistic elements translated into prestigious foreign languages.

Background for a more systematic treatment of Japanese evidentials will be created as studies such as those in this volume become available. In the meantime it seemed useful to point out that there is no consensus as to what Japanese evidentials are; to adopt a scope wider than, for example, Martin's; and to suggest that, though some of the morphemes involved in evidential statements appear to be Chinese on the surface, they might actually be indigenous. I hope other studies based on new theories, others presenting suggestive typological and genetic comparisons, and still others exploring biological and psycho-linguistic significance will be forthcoming. Meanwhile this is a nondefinitive look at what might be called Japanese evidentials.

REFERENCES

Hirose, Masayosi. 1981. Japanese and English comparative lexicology: The role of Japanese 'mimetic adverbs'. Ph.D. dissertation, University of California, Berkeley.

Kasioka, Tamako. 1980. *Yoo da* to *rasi–i* ni kansuru iti koosatu. Nihongo kyooiku 41.169–78.

Kindaici, Haruhiko. 1978. Giongo gitaigo kaisecu. Giongo gitaigo ziten, ed. by Curuko Asano. Tokyo: Kadokawa syoten.

Kuno, Susumu. 1973. The structure of the Japanese language. Cambridge, MA: MIT Press.

Kuroda, S.–Y. 1973. Where epistemology, style, and grammar meet: a case study from Japanese. A

Festschrift for Morris Halle, ed. by Stephen R. Anderson and Paul Kiparsky, 377–91. New York, NY: Holt, Rinehart and Winston, Inc.

Martin, Samuel E. 1975. A reference grammar of Japanese. New Haven, CT: Yale University Press.

Nagano, Masaru. 1964. Yoo da. Kokubungaku 9.13.177–9.

Oono, Susumu. 1978. Nihongo no bunpoo o kangaeru. Tokyo: Iwanami Syoten.

Quirk, Randolph, Sidney Greenbaum, Geoffrey Leech, and Jan Svartvik. 1972. A grammar of contemporary English. New York and London: Seminar Press.

Siraisi, Daizi. 1969. Soo da. Bunpoo 1.8.50–1.

Yamada, Yosio. 1908. Nihon bunpooron. Tokyo: Hoobunkan.

Yosida, Kanehiko. 1971. Gendaigo zyodoosi no siteki kenkyuu. Tokyo. Meizi Syoin.

FIFTEEN

The Bottom Line: Chinese Pidgin Russian

Johanna Nichols
University of California, Berkeley

One of the recurrent concerns in the study of evidentiality is the problem of grammaticalization: which evidential meanings are most prone to become incorporated into inflectional paradigms of verbs? which are most likely to become fused into obligatory paradigmatic oppositions, so that the speaker must decide and mark, for every predicate or every sentence or every paragraph, whether or not it carries the given meaning? The end result of such work will be a cross-linguistic implicational ranking of evidential meanings, giving at least some attention to category intersections with tense-aspect and person. For such an endeavor, languages with minimal grammatical systems provide crucial evidence for the first entries on the implicational hierarchy. We have seen examples of minimal evidential systems embedded in well-developed tense-aspect systems, in the form of Turkish (Aksu and Slobin, this volume) and Balkan Slavic (Friedman, this volume). These languages probably give us good evidence for first-ranked evidential oppositions, although we cannot be sure that the information they yield is information about evidentiality alone rather than about category intersections: do they tell us about the least marked evidential meaning, or about the first evidential meaning to arise from among tense-aspect meanings?

Chinese pidgin Russian gives every indication of providing the crucial example. It is a pidgin, thus its system of verbal categories is minimal by definition. Most important, its pared-down system of verbal inflection consists of a single opposition, namely one of evidentiality. In what follows I will show that the presence of this evidentiality opposition may be due to substratal influence and therefore cannot be taken at face value as proof that evidentiality is the universal unmarked verbal category. Nor can this single instance prove that the particular evidential meaning coded in Chinese pidgin Russian is universally unmarked. What it does show is that a language can survive, and fairly sophisticated communication can be undertaken, on the basis of a single evidential opposition alone; and that, relative to the fully developed tense-aspect systems of the source languages, evidentiality was viewed as indispensable by at least one speaker. Furthermore, comparison to other languages does support the hierarchization of this particular evidential category as cross-linguistically unmarked among evidentials.

BACKGROUND

Chinese pidgin Russian arose when the Russians and the Chinese began regular trading in 1768 in Kjaxta, located on the present Russian–Mongolian border south of Lake Baikal. The little information we have on the structure and origin of this Kjaxta variant indicates that it was heavily Chinese-influenced and that much of its original impetus may have come from the Chinese side.[1] The pidgin continued to be used for almost two centuries, spreading eastward to Manchuria and the Far East as the Russians built railroads to Vladivostok and Xabarovsk. In its twentieth-century form the pidgin bears greater resemblance to Russian than to Chinese. There are two sources of information on the twentieth-century pidgin: it is remembered by the (mostly emigrated) remnants of the Russian community of Harbin (Manchuria); and it is well attested in ethnographic, geographic, and popularizing travel literature from the Russian Far East. This literature shows that the native population of Sikhote-Alin area and the Ussuri and Amur basins used (or were perceived as using) a variant of the pidgin when speaking with Russians. The native population spoke Tungusic languages, of which primarily Nanai and also Udehe and Oroch underlie attestations of the pidgin.[2]

It is this Far Eastern variant, which I call the Ussuri dialect, that will concern us here. Only the Ussuri dialect grammaticalizes evidentiality. (The others occasionally use optional tense distinctions, marked with tense forms of an auxiliary verb 'be'.) The Ussuri dialect is attested in a number of sources of varying length and quality. The corpus for this study comes almost entirely from the works of the ethnographer-explorer-writer V. K. Arsen'ev, who depicts his Tungusic guides as speaking the pidgin in their interactions with him. It is a corpus of some three hundred utterances of up to several sentences in length, which yields a consistent, high-quality, and apparently faithful rendition of the pidgin.

---

[1] Sources of information on the Kjaxta dialect are Čerepanov (1853), Timkovski (1827) (fragmentary passages only), Maksimov (1864:485ff). The first two are reproduced by Neumann (1966), who does not mention the Maksimov texts. Despite evidence that the pidgin arose as the result of imperfect learning of Russian by Chinese traders, there is also indication of an active Russian role in its formation: it bears similarities to (White Sea) Russenorsk that can only be considered genetic; and it can be viewed as just one extreme of a continuum of simplified, foreign, and broken Russian depicted in literature. For the Russenorsk connection see Fox MS; for the organic connection to literary stereotypes see Nichols (1980).

[2] These are members of the Amur subgroup of Tungusic, a branch of Manchu-Tungus. The family extends from the Urals through Siberia to the Pacific coast and Sakhalin island. It is a substock of Altaic.

The corpus presents some problems of interpretation which must be mentioned at the outset. First, the pidgin lacks inflection other than for evidentiality, although readers who know Russian will observe that forms in the examples reflect Russian inflected forms. The pidgin simply uses one or another frozen inflectional form, rather than an artificial bare stem, as its unvarying lexeme. (Nouns usually reflect Russian nominatives, although masculines often reflect the genitive, probably because of its vocalic ending. Verbs often reflect imperatives, but some are past or present indicatives.) Second, all recorders of the pidgin, including Arsen'ev, lapse into correct Russian on occasion. The beginnings of utterances tend to be more nearly pure pidgin than the final phrases, which show more lapses into Russian. The more oblique a syntactic relation, the greater the likelihood that it will be marked by correct use of Russian cases.

A third problem is the question of just whose linguistic competence the corpus represents. Arsen'ev depicts only Tungusic speakers, never Russians or Chinese, as speaking the pidgin. Yet he himself must have known the pidgin, or he could not have recorded it as accurately as he did. (His corpus differs markedly from the literary stereotypes produced by writers who do not know the pigdin, and from ordinary broken Russian as portrayed in literature set in Siberia. Some of these stereotypes are surveyed in Nichols 1980.) Does the corpus then represent Arsen'ev's competence, or that of his guides? The lapses into standard Russian are clearly Arsen'ev's. The clear Tungusic influence would seem to argue that it is the Tungusic speakers' competence that is depicted; but Arsen'ev himself did know at least Udehe and Oroch well enough to make himself understood in those languages when necessary. That the pidgin is never put into the mouths of Chinese speakers is evidently due to the fact that Arsen'ev knew Chinese and used that language with its speakers in preference to the pidgin; this indicates that Arsen'ev portrays speech acts from his own perspective, and thus indirectly suggests that the pidgin represents his own competence. The most compelling evidence in favor of regarding the pidgin utterances as reflecting Tungusic speakers' competence comes from the occasional misunderstandings inadvertently recorded by Arsen'ev himself. For instance, the Ussurian dialect uses the form *ljudi*, standard Russian 'people', to substantivize adjectives: *bol'šoj* 'big', *bol'šoj ljudi* 'the/a big one'; *xudoj* 'bad', *xudoj ljudi* 'bad one'. On nearly every occasion when a pidgin speaker uses one of these constructions with *ljudi*, Arsen'ev misunderstands the utterance as referring to people. When it becomes clear that the pidgin speaker is not referring to a person, Arsen'ev then muses (in print) on the anthropomorphizing world view of the natives.[3] The fact that

---

[3] E.g. UK 20–21:

. . . —Boars!—I shouted. . . .
—*Odin   ljudi   šibko   bol'šoj,*—whispered Dersu.
   one   SUBST.   very   big
   'One of them is really big' [Arsen'ev understands: 'One man/guy is really big'.]

Arsen'ev can fail to understand a point of grammar and yet record it correctly, speaks in favor of interpreting the entire corpus as reflecting the actual competence of those who are portrayed as speaking the pidgin.

Another problem of interpretation is presented by the Tungusic influence mentioned above. Since for the great part of the corpus, and for all examples cited here, the speaker is Arsen'ev's Nanai guide Dersu Uzala, I will restrict this comparison to Nanai. Aside from the evidentiality, Nanai influence on the Ussuri pidgin dialect makes itself felt in three areas. One is the consistent sov word order and the consequent preference for postverbal auxiliaries (in contrast, the pidgin of the Harbin Russian community uses svo order and preverbal auxiliaries for the most part). This is especially conspicuous in the Ussuri use of postverbal, tonic *netu* (in standard Russian, 'there isn't', 'there aren't') for verbal negation, in contrast to Harbin dialect preverbal, atonic *ne,* used as in standard Russian:

(1) Ussuri: *ponimaj   netu*
           understand   NEG.
           'don't/doesn't/didn't understand'

(2) Harbin: *ne ponimaj*
           NEG understand
           'don't/doesn't/didn't understand'

Another Nanai influence is lexical: in Dersu's speech a number of proper and common nouns, especially animal and divinity names, are Tungusic.[4] The third area of influence is two distinctly Nanai functions of whole-word reduplication. In the Ussuri dialect, as in Nanai, reduplication forms indefinites from interrogatives, e.g.:

I did not understand what 'person' he was talking about, and looked at him, disbelieving. . . . The boar Dersu had killed turned out to be a two-year-old. I asked him why he had not shot the mature male.

—*Ego   staryj   ljudi. . . . Ego   xudo   kušaj,   mjaso   malo-malo   paxnet.*
  him   old   SUBST. him   bad   eat   meat   sort of   smells
'He was old. . . . They're bad to eat; their meat sort of smells.'

I was surprised that Dersu called the boars 'people'. I asked him about it. [Dersu engages in some folk etymology on the substantivizer.]

Then it became clear to me. This primitive man's world view was animistic, therefore he anthropomorphized all his surroundings.

4 Not all of the lexical material is identifiably Nanai. For instance, 'star', recorded twice as *uikta,* is like Udehe, and unlike Nanai, in lacking intervocalic -*s*- (Nanai dialects have *osikta,* etc.). It is impossible to tell whether this represents Udehe influence on Dersu's dialect of Nanai (he was from a peripheral area adjacent to Udehe, and seems to have also spoken Udehe) or Arsen'ev's spelling of a Nanai word in its Udehe form (since he knew Udehe but apparently not Nanai).

> čego   'what'
> kakoj   'what (kind)', 'which'
> kakoj ljudi   'who', 'what'   (with substantivizer ljudi)
> čego-čego   'something, anything'
> kakoj-kakoj   'some, any'
> kakoj-kakoj ljudi   'someone, anyone', 'something, anything'

Also as in Nanai, reduplication forms distributives from various quantifiers, e.g. *odin* 'one', *odin-odin* 'one each'.

Reduplication of either sort is unknown to pidgin speakers from Manchuria. (For reduplication in Nanai see Avrorin 1959:219, 273–6.) In view of such pervasive grammatical and lexical influences, it is possible that the evidentiality in the Ussuri pidgin dialect reflects substratal influence rather than simply reduction of Chinese and Russian grammar.

I submit that the most conservative approach to all the problems of interpretation is—having mentioned them for the sake of honesty—to disregard them. Regardless of whose competence the corpus reflects, and regardless of whether the evidentiality is substratal or a natural result of reduction, the corpus is language, and the system is a genuinely minimal one.

INFLECTIONAL EVIDENTIALITY

Evidentiality in the pidgin is signaled with postverbal *est'*,[5] which is existential, locative, or emphatic 'is/are' in standard Russian (never used as a verbal auxiliary or inflectional marker), and corresponds typologically to Tungusic forms of 'be' used postverbally as various auxiliaries, including that forming the Tungusic inferential evidential.[6] The particular meaning added by *est'* depends on the lexical aspect class of the verb stem and the tense of the clause, both of which must therefore be briefly described.

Lexical aspect of pidgin verbs is not overtly marked. Like most pidgins and basal creoles,[7] the Ussurian pidgin divides its lexical stock of verbs into two classes which I term PUNCTUAL and NON-PUNCTUAL. Examples are:

punctual:	najdi	'find; arrive'
	pomiraj	'die'
	pojmaj	'catch'
	končaj	'finish'

---

[5] *est'* is pronounced /jesí/ in Harbin. Since Arsen'ev uses standard Russian spellings, it is never clear what pronunciation underlies them.

[6] The evidentials of Tungusic are not always mentioned in grammars, and are virtually never described as evidentials. My analysis of their form and meaning is based on text examples.

[7] In the framework of Bickerton (1975) (who uses the terms 'stative' and 'non-stative' where I use, respectively, 'non-punctual' and 'punctual').

| *načinaj* | 'start' |
| *ponimaj*[8] | 'understand' |

non-punctual:	*xodi*	'come, go; walk'
	pribavljaj	'add, increase; rise (of water)'
	rabotaj	'work'
	posmotri	'look; see'
	dumaj	'think'
	kriči	'cry, call; make noise'

These lexical classes have nothing to do with the inflectional aspect of standard Russian. Each class contains forms derived from Russian perfectives and forms derived from Russian imperfectives. (Etymologically perfective punctuals are *najdi, pomiraj, pojmaj;* the others are from imperfectives. Of the non-punctuals, *posmotri* is etymologically perfective, the others imperfective.) The classification of verbs as punctual vs. non-punctual is not based on form or etymology, then. It is based on two criteria: the array of tense-aspect meanings that the verb has in text examples, and the kind of evidential meaning given to it by addition of *est'*. The most conspicuous tense-aspect patterning is the fact that the punctual verbs never have present-tense meaning, while the non-punctual ones frequently do. The intersection with evidentiality is described below.

The punctual verbs tend to denote changes of state, culminative processes, and bounded events or processes; the non-punctuals denote states, durative actions, non-culminative processes. This is then a (presumably reduced, pidginized) two-way system corresponding to the more elaborate lexical aspect classes proposed by e.g. Vendler (1967). While the opposition here is not comparable to the Russian inflectional opposition of perfective and imperfective aspect, it is comparable to the system of lexical classes that must be established before the semantic effects of Russian lexical aspect can be described (see Forsyth 1970:46 ff.).

Tense, with one exception, is never overtly marked but must be inferred from context. The sole exception is the verb 'be', which has tense forms as in standard Russian:

past: *byl*
present: { Ø (copula)
{ *est'* (existential)
future: *budet*

Example (3) shows the existence of two verb classes. It contains two instances of the nonpunctual (-P) verb *xodi* 'come, go' and one instance of punctual (+P)

---

[8] It is interesting that this punctual main verb 'understand' is homophonous with the auxiliary 'know how', which is non–punctual.

najdi 'find; come to, arrive'. The tense and evidentiality context is one and the same: Dersu describes a planned journey in terms of departures and arrivals; he knows the route and predicts with confidence. In this uniform context the non-punctual verbs have no auxiliary and the punctual verb has the auxiliary *est'*. The formal difference in the same semantic context demonstrates the existence of the two covert lexical classes.

(3)   *Zavtra   moja   prjamo   xodi.*
       tomorrow   I   straight go   (-P)

      Četyre   solnce   xodi,
      four   sun   go

      Daubixe   naidi   est',   potom   Ulaxe   xodi . . .
                come   (+P)   AUX.   then   go (-P)
      'Tomorrow I'LL GO straight (east). After four days' walk I'LL COME to the
      Daubixe, the I'LL COME to the Ulaxe . . .' (UK 46)

Evidentiality is the only arguably inflectional category in the pidgin. It is the only category for which the speaker must decide, in every utterance, whether to mark it or not. (This definition takes obligatoriness, and hence the Boasian notion of grammatical meaning as explicated by Jakobson [1944] 1971, as criterial for inflectional status.) The pidgin makes use of a number of other ad-verbal elements which may be described as auxiliaries. These display word-order preferences which are suggestive of position class and thus of formal gram-maticalization; but their content is clearly lexical. There are three position types:

Strictly postverbal:
    xoču   'want to'
    končaj   'finish'[9]
    netu   (negation)
Postverbal or preverbal:
    ponimaj   'know how'
    mogu   'can, may'
    načinaj   'start'[9]
Clause-initial:
    nado   'must, have to' (imperative)
    možno   'may; possible'

Negation is with postverbal *netu* for most verbs. A small set of verbs takes preverbal *ne*: auxiliaries *mogu* 'can, may', *nado* 'have to', *xoču* 'want to' and main verbs *znaju* 'know' and *videl* 'see'. Some examples of verb phrases:

---

[9] That 'finish' is strictly postverbal while 'start' may also be preverbal is suspicious, and probably due to accidental skewing in the corpus.

(4)   *xodi*
      go
      'goes', 'went', 'will come', etc.

(5)   *xodi   netu*
      go   NEG.
      'isn't coming', 'won't go', etc.

(6)   *xodi   končaj*
      go   finish
      'stopped walking', 'passed by', 'had gone'

(7)   *nacinaj   kriči*
      start   cry
      'will start to make noise'

(8)   *posmotri   ne   mogu*
      look/see   NEG.   can
      'can't see'

(9)   *ubej   ne   xoču*
      kill   NEG.   want
      'don't want to kill'

(10) *rybu   lovi   ponimaj   tože   netu*
      fish   catch   know how   also   NEG.
      'don't know how to fish, either'

The marker *est'* of inflectional evidentiality patterns formally with the strictly postverbal auxiliaries:

(11) *xodi   est'*
      go   EVID.
      'Here he comes', 'There he goes'

(12) *pomiraj   est'*
      die   EVID.
      'must have died'

The only possible cooccurrence among auxiliaries is that the negative may cooccur with others (as in (8), (9), (10), above). The negative does not, however, occur together with the evidential *est'*. This is undoubtedly due not only to semantic incompatibility but to formal incompatibility: the productive negative auxiliary *netu* is simply the negative of the copula and existential verb *est'* which is itself used as the evidential auxiliary.

The evidential marker *est'* shows another distributional constraint: it occurs in main clauses only. Non-main clauses (one hesitates to make a claim for actual syntactic subordination) are mostly *if, since,* and *when* clauses; these can contain lexical auxiliaries but never contain evidential *est'*.

The evidential marker *est'* contributes uniformly evidential meaning to the verb stem, although the exact character of the evidential meaning depends on the lexical aspect class of the verb and the tense meaning of the sentence. For punctual verbs *est'* is attested in both past and future tense contexts (recall that punctual verbs cannot have present-tense meanings). For nonpunctual verbs, it occurs only in the present tense. *Est'*, then, shows complementary distribution by tense. This distribution is shown graphically below; the varying meanings contributed by *est'* are shown by the labels 'inferential', 'immediate', and 'predictive'. These terms will be defined for each tense-aspect category below.

Functions of evidential marker *est'*:

	Punctual	Nonpunctual
Past	inferential (3rd pers.)	
	immediate (1st pers.)	(∅)[a]
Present	—[b]	immediate
Future	predictive	(∅)

  [a](∅): the tense-aspect category does occur and does appear to bear evidential meanings, but no such evidential meanings are marked with *est'*.
  [b]—: the tense-aspect category does not occur.

One clear generalization can be made: *est'* is never used for events which are witnessed, i.e. seen by speaker and/or hearer. It is used for nonwitnessed events which are asserted on the basis of evidence.

For punctual verbs in the past tense, *est'* contributes one of two evidential meanings, depending on the person of the subject. If the subject is third person, a verb marked with *est'* has INFERENTIAL meaning: the speaker perceives the evidence and infers the event or action that produced the evidence. (13–14) are a minimal pair. (13) is a neutral, nonevidential statement: Dersu reports what happened to his family long ago. There is no evidence and no inference: he knows the facts because he witnessed them directly.

(13) *Vse   davno   pomiraj* . . . *Ospa   vse   ljudi   končaj.*
      all   long ago die   small-pox all   people   kill
      'They've all long since died. Smallpox killed everyone.' (UK 12)

(14) *A-a! Ljudi   pomiraj   est'.*
            person die
      'Oh! The man's died.' '. . . must have died.' (DU 183)

(14) is inferential. Arsen'ev's group is following the tracks of an obviously sick person. As they round a bend, they startle two crows and Dersu utters (14). The presence of carrion-eating birds is the evidence from which he infers that the man has died. And, in fact, a few paces later the group comes on the man's corpse.

With first-person subjects, past punctuals with *est'* do not have inferential meaning—predictably, since (for the psychological verbs which are the only examples for this category in the corpus) a speaker need not infer but knows his own psychological states. Rather, *est'* contributes IMMEDIATE meaning: the speaker uses it in a more or less spontaneous reaction to a new, salient, often surprising event just as it happens. (15–16) are a minimal pair for immediate meaning. (15) is nonimmediate: Dersu reports a past instance of coming to understand. (16) is immediate: he sees a railroad for the first time and suddenly now understands what he has heard people talking about on past occasions.

(15) *Segodnja   odin   ljudi   posmotri,   togda   vse   <u>ponimaj</u>.*
      today   one   person   see   then   all   understand
      'Today when I saw (that) one man, I UNDERSTOOD everything.' '. . . then
      everything BECAME CLEAR' (UK 161)

(16) *Hm!   Moja   èto   slyxal.   Krugom   ljudi   govori.*
      I   this   heard   around   people   talk

      Teper'   <u>ponimaj est'</u>.
      now   understand
      'Hm! I've heard of this [railroad]. Everybody has been talking about it. Now
      I UNDERSTAND.' '. . . now everything's CLEAR' (UK 45)

Further examples are the two instances of *najdi* 'find' used in the sense 'smell' with *est'*. Both have first-person subjects.

(17) *Moja   zapax   dyma   <u>najdi</u>   <u>est'</u>.*
      I   odor   smoke   find
      'I smell smoke!' (UK 282)

Actually, third-person examples may also be said to have immediate meaning, since all of them reflect not just inference but a spontaneous reaction to just-perceived evidence. This is further discussed below.

In the future tense, punctual verbs with *est'* have what I will call PREDICTIVE force: the speaker confidently infers a future event from present evidence or intentionality plus understanding of the forces of nature. (3), cited above (p. 245), is an example of a predictive future: Dersu is about to set off on a journey, knows the route and the location of major landforms, and predicts arrivals and departures. (3) shows that the predictive future of punctual verbs is marked with *est'*. (It also shows that the predictive future of nonpunctuals is not overtly marked.) (18–19) show other predictive future punctuals. In (18), Dersu predicts, from his knowledge of the route and the group's rate of progress, that they will soon come to a cabin. In (19) he predicts, on the basis of his (to Arsen'ev) uncanny understanding of nature, a change in weather.

(18) *Naša   skoro   balagan   najdi   est'.*
      we   soon   cabin   find
      'We're ABOUT TO COME to a cabin.' (UK 169, UK 16)

(19) *Moja   dumaj,   polovina   solnca   končaj,   drugoj   veter   najdi   est'.*
      I   think   half   sun   finish   other   wind   find
      'I'd say by mid-day the wind WILL CHANGE.' (UK 37)

(20) shows a different punctual verb in the future. It is the rutting season for deer, and Dersu and Arsen'ev are listening to the bucks bellowing. Dersu points out that one voice is actually that of a Siberian tiger, who decoys the herd to make a kill. Based on this knowledge, he predicts a kill for the tiger.

(20) *Izjubr   teper'   ponimaj   netu,   kokoj ljudi   kriči,   Amba   skoro*
      deer   now   understand NEG.   who   cry   tiger   soon

      matka   pojmaj   est'.
      doe   catch
      'The deer don't know who (what animal) that is bellowing, and the tiger WILL CATCH himself a doe pretty soon.' (UK 219)

(21) provides a subtle minimal contrast. The verb is punctual; it names an imminent event, yet lacks *est'*. This is not a predictive future in the technical sense defined above: the speaker does not predict a particular future event, but simply warns of an oncoming event. The utterance is based not on evidence and understanding of it, which is the shared factor in the above examples, but on the fact that all participants see an ice floe bearing down on them. This is then a witnessed future.

(21) *Led   skoro   lodku   lomaj!   Skorej   nado   xodi!*
      ice   soon   boat   break   right now have to go
      'The ice is about to wreck the boat! Hurry up!' (UK 270)

(18–21) show that the predictive future is the converse of the inferential past: in both cases the speaker reasons from evidence and knowledge of it to a particular event. *Est'* is not used in promises or threats, to judge from the single example of each in the corpus. This shows that knowledge, inference, and evidence, and not just certainly or vouching, are the relevant semantic parameters for use of *est'*.

Non-punctual verbs in the past tense never take *est'*. (22) is an example of a past non-punctual which could be said to have inferential meaning: Dersu looks at some tracks and infers past events from them. Yet the verb does not have *est'*.

(22) *Davno   odin   ljudi   <u>xodi</u>.*
      long ago   one   person   go
      'A long time ago one person went by here.' (UK 16)

In the present tense, non-punctual verbs take *est'* for immediate meaning.
(23–24) are a minimal pair. In (23) Dersu, backtracking briefly, comes on fresh
tiger tracks and reports that they are being followed by a tiger. This example does
not have immediate meaning, and there is no *est'*.

(23) *Posmotri,   kapitan,   èto   Amba.   Ego   szadi   naša   <u>xodi</u>.*
      look   captain   this   tiger   he   behind   us   go
      'Look, captain, this is a tiger. He's FOLLOWING us.' (UK 16)

(24) *<u>Xodi</u>   est'*.
      go
      'Here he comes.' ' There, he's walking.' 'Hear that? He's coming.'
          (DU 43)

But in (24) there is immediate reaction. It is night; the group hears a large animal
approaching, then silence. As stealthy footsteps resume, Dersu utters (24). This
is immediate reaction to an event or, more specifically, to the perceptual evidence directly connected with it. Again, the evidence plays a crucial role and,
since the tense is present, the meaning which triggers *est'* is immediate.
   (22–23) share another generalization: they have to do with reading tracks.
There are eleven examples which have to do with tracking, at least three of them
punctual. None of them contain evidential *est'*, despite the fact that reading
tracks clearly involves crucial use of evidence. But the tracking examples differ
from the *est'*-marked immediates and inferentials in that the latter are spontaneous, immediate reactions to evidence while the tracking examples involve
systematic reading of evidence, often given as a lesson in track-reading or as an
explanation of how the tracker knows what happened. Such examples, then,
show that immediacy is also involved in the inferential function of *est'*. (They
also suggest that the evidential is appropriate when the inference is presupposed,
but not when it is asserted, in that the tracking examples more or less assert the
inference and lack *est'*.)
   (25–26) are another minimal pair. (25), with *est'*, has immediate meaning.
Dersu, standing at a riverbank as a storm approaches, notices the high water and
remarks on it.

(25) *Voda   pribavljaj   est'*.
      water   rise
      'The water's RISING.' (UK 42)

(26) *Kamni   smotrju: voda   pribavljaj.*
      rocks   look   water   rise
      'I'm looking at the rocks: the water's RISING.' (DU 47)

(26) lacks *est'* and lacks the immediate force. Dersu utters (26) during a rainstorm, when asked where he is going. This is not an immediate reaction on initial perception of a situation: Dersu has been aware for some time that a flood might take place (although the context does not make it clear whether the water is actually high yet).[10]

Future nonpunctuals lack *est'* even when their meaning is predictive, as shown in (3).

In summary, *est'* contributes evidential meaning to punctual verbs in both of the tenses which they take, and to non-punctuals in the present tense. The nature of the evidential meaning is contingent on tense and person. Non-punctuals appear to have evidential meanings in the past and future, but those meanings are never marked with *est'*.

There are only three apparent counterexamples to this analysis, none of them compelling. One involves *est'* used for contrastive stress. Another, (27), shows *est'* with a punctual verb which is not inferential:

(27)   *Tam   pomiraj   est'   moja   žena   i   moi   deti.*
       there   die   my   wife   and   my   children
       'There's where my wife and children died.' 'My wife and children died
          there.' (UK 178)

Dersu says this while pointing to the place in question. There is no inference; there is no evidence, the event happened long ago, and he knows it because he witnessed it. This example differs from (13) above, which has the same verb (without *est'*) referring to the same event, in that (27) contains the place adverbial *tam* 'there', is spoken in view of the place and as an expression of the grief triggered by seeing it (while (13) is spoken in answer to a question), and lacks the time adverbial *davno* 'long ago' found in (13). In (27) there is some kind of reaction to evidence, but the sense is neither immediate nor inferential as those terms have been defined here.

(28) may be a counterexample to the claim that evidentials occur only in main clauses.

(28)   *Net,   moja   xorošo   ponimaj,   tebe   ubej   est'.*
       No   I   well   understand   you   kill
       'No, I understood perfectly well that you (had) killed him.' (UK 185)

---

[10] Since all examples of *pribavljaj* 'increase, add; rise (water)' are ambiguous as to aspect, is possible that it is punctual. If so, the interpretation of (25–26) must be adjusted. (25) then represents the deviant construction shown in (17); (26) means 'the water may rise' and has no *est'* because it is conjecture rather than prediction. I prefer the analysis as nonpunctual because immediate meaning is more plausible for (25) than inferential, and because context following (26) makes it clear that, if it is to be interpreted as a future, it is a prediction: a flood does materialize, and Dersu's advance warning saves the group.

It is a counterexample if the clause *tebe ubej est'* 'you('ve) killed (him)' is subordinated to *ponimaj* 'understand/understood'. Since there is no clear evidence for subordination in the pidgin, the clause *moja xorošo ponimaj* 'I understood (perfectly) well' can be regarded either as the main clause with a subordinate or as a parenthetical or paratactic introductory clause. Leaving aside the insoluble question of syntactic subordination, (28) may be described as showing semantic subordination: the evidential is used in a statement of reported inference, rather than, as with previous examples, in the actual statement of inference. The context for (28) is this: Arsen'ev has shot and killed a boar far from camp. As he is dressing it Dersu appears and offers to help carry the meat. Arsen'ev is amazed: how did Dersu know from the sound of gunshots alone that he had killed the animal rather than missed it? Dersu utters (28) and explains how the spacing between gunshots indicated a kill rather than a miss or wounding. When hearing the gunshots Dersu could have uttered (29):

(29)   *Ubej   est'*.
       kill
       'He's killed (him/it/them/something/. . .), 'He got him'
       (The asterisk marks nonattestation.)

(28), with shifted pronoun and introductory or main-clause *ponimaj* 'understand/understood', simply reports (29), but preserves its evidential.

In summary, both (27) and (28) support the connection of *est'* to evidentiality, although they depart from the usual grammatical patterning of evidentiality in the pidgin.

LEXICAL EVIDENTIALITY

The corpus contains examples of two lexical means of indicating inference. One is *moja dumaj* 'I'd say; in my opinion', which renders standard Russian *po-moemu* as in (19). *Moja dumaj* in this sense is attested in all three dialects of the pidgin (see Neumann 1966:250 for the cognate construction in the Kjaxta dialect). It is not particularly frequent in the Ussuri materials. The second lexical device is *odnako*, a coordinating conjunction 'although' in standard Russian but an adverbial marker of inferentiality in Siberian Russian (and a stereotype of Siberian speech in Russian literature):

(30)   *Sovsem   tixo.   Mnogo   solnca   ne   bylo   vetra.*   *Odnako*,
        absolutely   still   many   sun   NEG.   was   wind

       budet   purga.
       will be storm
       'It's absolutely still. For several days there's been no wind. [I INFER] there's going to be a blizzard.'

Odnako occurs twice in the pidgin corpus. It may be significant that in both occurrences it is used where the main verb is a form of 'be'; *est'* (itself etymologically a form of 'be') is unattested with forms of 'be', and perhaps is ungrammatical with them. This means that *odnako* may have a place in the inflectional marking of evidentiality. A safer assumption, however, is to simply regard it as one of the several lexical Siberianisms in the Ussuri materials.

CROSS-LINGUISTIC COMPARISON

The Ussurian evidential category bears obvious resemblances to the pan-Eurasian evidential perfect, of which it is in fact a representative. The Eurasian evidential is primarily inferential; it may have other meanings, but the inferential use is the salient one, at least in grammatical descriptions. It is a past tense category, usually called a perfect. The Chinese pidgin Russian evidential differs from these in not being a past-tense category. Consequently, it can have predictive future meaning, and it has the tense-based complementary distribution of inferential and immediate meanings described above. Another apparent difference is that the Eurasian evidential can have a reported or hearsay meaning; this is unattested for the pidgin evidential—but then in general there are no hearsay clauses in the pidgin corpus. This means that the lack of tense restriction is the principal, if not the sole, difference between the pidgin evidential and the pan-Eurasian one. (For the Eurasian evidentials see Friedman 1979, Aksu and Slobin, this volume.)

'Evidential' is an appropriate term for the pidgin category since the basic element in its various meanings is evidence rather than propositional content: depending on tense-aspect and person, an evidential predication is either an inference from given evidence or an immediate reaction to it.

The complementary distribution of inferential, immediate, and predictive meanings in the Ussuri pidgin lends itself to a further abstraction. Since (as argued above) predictive is the tense-conditioned converse of inferential, we can reduce the table on p. 247 to the following generalization: The evidential has inferential meaning for punctuals, but immediate meaning for non-punctuals. This generalization disregards the category intersection with person—the extension of immediacy to punctuals in the first person—and claims that the opposition of inferential to immediate is not a true contrast, but that the two are contextual variants. (Recall that the track-reading examples (22–24) showed that even the inferential function of *est'* requires immediacy.)

If we describe evidentials of other languages in sufficiently abstract terms, we find that the same aspect-based conditioning recurs. To facilitate cross-linguistic comparison I will use the term 'perfective' (always in quotes) to group the Chinese pidgin Russian punctual with aspect categories of other languages, and 'imperfective' (in quotes) for the non-punctual and its analogs in other languages. The terms 'perfective' and 'imperfective' label kinds of meanings only, without regard to whether they are lexical classes of verbs (as they are in the pidgin), regular inflectional categories, or contextual variants of one or another tense or aspect category. The use of quotes is intended to make clear that the observation of a recurrent pattern is based on terms used in descriptions of languages. Whether it is a valid universal of languages, rather than a piece of lexicography, is an empirical question. 'Perfective' subsumes meanings like punctual and completive; 'imperfective' subsumes meanings like progressive, durative, iterative, habitual.

Using these terms we can reduce the Chinese pidgin Russian distribution to the following schema:

(31)   Ussurian Chinese pidgin Russian: 'Perfective' conditions inferential;
                        'imperfective' conditions immediate.

The same generalization holds for a number of other languages surveyed in this volume: something the linguist could call 'perfective' is associated with inferential meaning, and something that could be called 'imperfective' is associated with immediate meaning. For instance, in Turkish, the evidential is restricted to accomplished events, except that the readings of surprise and hearsay are not so restricted (Aksu and Slobin, this volume). Leaving aside the hearsay reading (which is unattested in the pidgin), and equating accomplished to 'perfective' and surprise to immediate, we may generalize:

(32)   Turkish: 'Imperfective' is associated with immediate.

In Tibetan (DeLancey, this volume), the evidential markers have inferential meaning only in perfective contexts; in imperfective contexts the meaning is one of surprise or immediate reaction. (*Perfective* is DeLancey's term.) Thus:

(33)   Tibetan: 'Perfective' is associated with inferential;
                        'imperfective' is associated with immediate.

Sherpa '*nok* marks immediate evidence, which is witnessed for the habitual tense, inferential for the past (Woodbury, this volume). Equating habitual with 'imperfective' and past with 'perfective', we get:

(34)   Sherpa: 'Perfective' is associated with inferential; 'imperfective' is not.

To these patterns can be added the general observation that the pan-Eurasian inferential is a 'perfective' category. The very fact that the Eurasian inferential is usually called a perfect, indicates that it is associated with 'perfective' meanings of completedness, punctuality, and the like.

All of these language-specific distributions can be viewed as manifestations of a universal tendency: 'perfective' favors inferential meanings and/or 'imperfective' favors immediate meanings. Schematically:

(35)   Universal covariance.

aspect:	'perfective'	'imperfective'
evidentiality:	inferential	immediate

This distribution is internally motivated. To be immediately perceived and directly reacted to, a situation or event must be ongoing. If it is not ongoing it cannot be immediately perceived, but must be inferred or predicted from the evidence.

(35) suggests the following hypothesis: Languages will tend to group inferential and immediate meanings together into a single evidential form or category, allowing aspect to predict the particular meaning; cross-linguistically, inferential and immediate are contextual variants of a single category.[11]

Of the languages surveyed here, only Sherpa has evidentials other than the inferential-immediate one. The Ussurian pidgin dialect, like the other Eurasian languages, has only a single evidential category. This fact suggests a tentative universal: If a language has only a single grammaticalized evidential, the meaning of that evidential will be inferential-immediate. In other words, a cross-linguistic implicational hierarchy for grammaticalized evidentials is headed by the inferential-immediate type. This universal is quite abstract. It allows considerable language-specific variation in connotations, invariant meaning, and intersection with other categories such as person, tense, and validation. It ranks evidentials only relative to evidentials, not relative to other verbal categories such as tense. It indicates—in answer to the question raised at the beginning of this paper—that the first-ranked evidential category is one and the same, regardless of whether it is embedded in a tense system.

The Balkan languages (Friedman, this volume) allow us to extend this proposed universal even beyond evidentiality. These languages have a non-deictic pragmatic category which is often equated to the pan-Eurasian evidential but which (Friedman shows) is actually more akin to validation than to evidentiality. At least in Balkan Slavic, it is like the Eurasian evidential in being linked to the past tense: morphologically, these are past-tense forms; semantically, even in the analog to immediate meaning the past tense is implicated (Friedman, example 20).[12] The Balkan categories differ from the Eurasian evidentials in that inferential meaning is not only not salient but possibly not at all available (due, no

---

[11] This formulation says nothing about the role of person in determining the semantics of evidentiality. First-person subjects preclude inferential meaning in Chinese pidgin Russian; and a number of papers in this volume show other respects in which first person disfavors various marked evidential meanings. But this is another topic.

[12] This is not true of Chinese pidgin Russian. (24), for example, shows that the immediate meaning is a reaction to a new state of affairs at the instant it comes into existence.

doubt, to their essentially validational, rather than evidential, nature). But—for Slavic as for Albanian—the validational categories do include among their meanings one that can be described as 'immediate' in the sense in which I have used the term (Friedman, examples (20), (21), and notes 15, 17). This suggests an extended universal: The first non-deictic pragmatic category may be either evidential or validational; but whichever it is, it will include immediate meaning among its contextual variant meanings.

The universals proposed here rely crucially on inquiry into basic meaning and contextual variants, a scholarly luxury that has so far been available mostly to languages of the Old World. It remains to be seen what validity they will have outside of Eurasia.

In summary: The Ussurian dialect of Chinese pidgin Russian has an evidential opposition as its sole verbal inflection. The meaning of the evidential is inferential-immediate, with the exact distribution of inferential and immediate readings determined by person and lexical aspect. Both the aspect-based complementary distribution of evidential meanings, and the abstract meaning of the sole evidential, are shared by other languages. The value of the Ussurian dialect materials is not undermined by problems of interpretation and attribution of competence: they still demonstrate that a language can reduce its verbal categories down to evidentiality alone, that evidentiality is basic enough to be viable in a pidgin grammar, and that cross-linguistically the unmarked evidential either is inferential-immediate or at least includes the immediate meaning among its functions.

SOURCES

DU = Arsen'ev 1960b
UK = Arsen'ev 1960a

REFERENCES

Arsen'ev, V. K. 1937. V gorax Sixotè–Alinja. Moscow: Molodaja Gvardija.
_____. 1960a. Po Ussurijskomu kraju. Moscow: Gos. izd–vo geografičeskoj literatury. (Abbreviated as UK when used as source for cited texts.)
_____. 1960b. Dersu Uzala. Moscow: GIGL. (Abbreviated as DU for cited text source.)
_____. 1966. Skvoz' tajgu. Moscow: Mysl'.
Avrorin, V. A. 1959. Grammatika nanajskogo jazyka, I: Fonetičeskoe vvedenije i morfologija imennyx častej reči. Moscow-Leningrad: AN.
Bickerton, Derek. 1975. Dynamics of a creole system. Cambridge: Cambridge University Press.
Čerepanov, S. I. 1853. Kjaxtinskoe kitajskoe narečie russkogo jazyka. Izvestija II otdelenija Imperatorskoj Akademii nauk, II: 10.370–77.
Forsyth, James. 1970. A Grammar of aspect: Usage and meaning in the Russian verb. Cambridge: Cambridge University Press.
Fox, James. MS. Russenorsk: A study in language adaptivity. Revised MA thesis. University of Chicago.
Friedman, Victor. 1979. Toward a typology of status: Georgian and other Non-Slavic languages of

the Soviet Union. The Elements: A Parasession on Linguistic Units and Levels, ed. P. R. Clyne et al., 339–50. Chicago: Chicago Linguistic Society.

Jakobson, Roman. (1944)1971. Franz Boas' approach to language. Selected writings II.477–88. The Hague and Paris: Mouton.

Maksimov, S. 1864. Na vostoke. Poezdka na Amur (1860–61). St. Petersburg.

Neumann, Gunter. 1966. Zur chinesisch–russischen Behelfssprache von Kjachta. Die Sprache 12.237–51.

Nichols, Johanna. 1980. Pidginization and foreigner talk: Chinese pidgin Russian. Papers from the 4th International Conference on Historical Linguistics, ed. by E. C. Traugott, 397–407. (Amsterdam Studies in the Theory and History of Linguistic Science, IV. Current Issues in Linguistic Theory, 14.) Amsterdam: John Benjamins B.V.

Timkovskii, E. F. 1827. Travels of the Russian mission through Mongolia to China, and residence in Pekin, in the years 1820–1821. (Trans. by H. E. Lloyd.) 2 vols. London: Longman, Rees, Orme, Brown, and Green.

Vendler, Zeno. 1967. Verbs and times. In Z. Vendler, Linguistics in Philosophy. Ithaca: Cornell University Press.

PART THREE

*EVIDENTIALITY
IN ENGLISH
AND IN GENERAL*

SIXTEEN

Evidentiality
in English Conversation
and Academic Writing

Wallace Chafe
University of California, Santa Barbara

English has a rich repertoire of evidential devices. It expresses evidentiality with modal auxiliaries, adverbs, and miscellaneous idiomatic phrases, although not, for example, with a coherent set of verb suffixes like those in some California Indian languages. The difference between these Indian languages and English is not a matter of evidentials vs. no evidentials. It is partly a question of how evidentiality is grammatically expressed: is it by suffixes, auxiliaries, adverbs, or what? It is partly a question of what kinds of evidentiality are expressed most readily: are degrees of reliability, or inference, or sensory evidence, or hearsay, for example, especially codable? And partly, too, it is a question of which evidentials are most often used; different languages focus on different kinds of evidentiality more or less of the time. Although English has a large variety of evidential possibilities, it may use them in different proportions than some other languages do.

For English the issue is not just how and when evidentiality is expressed by SPEAKERS. Something else enters the picture when a language has had a long literary tradition and therefore a differentiation into spoken and written styles. Spoken and written language differ from each other in a number of basic ways, and one of these is the expression of evidentiality.

The findings to be discussed here come from a project which was organized to investigate differences between spoken and written English.[1] We have collected several kinds of spoken and written language from each of twenty adults, and have analyzed these data for differential occurrences of a number of features

---

[1] Preliminary reports on this project are available in Chafe 1982 and 1985. The project has been supported by Grant NIE–G–80–0125 from the National Institute of Education. I am grateful for the collaboration of Jane Danielewicz and Pamela Downing.

261

thought to be more prevalent in spoken or written language. Among these features have been some that belong in the category of evidentials, and thus we have a fairly large body of material which sheds some light on the use of evidentials in several styles of English. I will discuss here the expression of evidentiality in dinnertable conversations and academic writing, thereby highlighting the extremes of 'spokenness' and 'writtenness' in our data.

I need to stress that I am using the term 'evidentiality' in its broadest sense, not restricting it to the expression of 'evidence' per se. I will be discussing a range of epistemological considerations that are linguistically coded in spoken and written English. 'Evidence,' taken literally, is one of these considerations, but not the only one. What gives coherence to the set under discussion is that everything dealt with under this broad interpretation of evidentiality involves attitudes toward knowledge. The coherence is reinforced by the observation that various linguistic expressions slide across more than one of the various types within this domain. The refusal of linguistic expressions to restrict themselves to evidence in the narrow sense can be found not only in their synchronic behavior, but also diachronically, where extensions and shifts among these various epistemological considerations are by no means rare (see especially Mithun, this volume).

Our samples of conversational English and academic writing showed approximately the same proportion of evidential markers to the total number of words. In conversation there were 60 occurrences of evidentials per thousand words; in academic writing the proportion was just slightly higher: 64 per thousand words. Differences appeared, then, not so much in the frequency of evidentials overall, as in the frequency of specific kinds of evidentials.

These differences can be attributed to two major differences between speaking and writing. A writer has much more time than a speaker to deliberate on what is being said. Speaking takes place on the fly, but a writer can mull over how best to say what is desired, and has ample time to edit what is produced. As a result, there are certain kinds of epistemological considerations that a writer has time to deal with, and a speaker typically does not. The other major difference between speaking and writing is that a speaker is in direct, face to face interaction with the audience, while a writer sits alone with a pencil or typewriter. Speaking is an involved, social activity; writing is lonely and detached. The result is that speakers pay more attention to direct experience, and to the ways in which their thoughts and expressions match ongoing expectations. We will see below how these two kinds of differences affect the two kinds of language that are produced.

In order to understand what evidentiality in the broad sense involves, it is useful to think in terms of several notions that are illustrated in Figure 1. One notion can be labeled KNOWLEDGE: the basic information whose status is qualified in one way or another by markers of evidentiality. It is shown vertically in the middle of Figure 1. Knowledge may be regarded by a speaker (or writer) as more or less RELIABLE (or valid), as is indicated in Figure 1 with the suggestion of a continuum from the most reliable knowledge, at the top, to the least reliable,

```
source of         mode of                      knowledge
knowledge         knowing                      matched against
                                    reliable
                                       k
                                       n
???          ---> belief      ---> o
evidence     ---> induction   ---> w ---> verbal resources
language     ---> hearsay     ---> l ---> expectations
hypothesis   ---> deduction   ---> e
                                       d
                                       g
                                       e
                                  unreliable
```

Figure 1

at the bottom. Also relevant are various MODES OF KNOWING: various ways in which knowledge is acquired. The modes of knowing shown here are BELIEF, INDUCTION, HEARSAY, and DEDUCTION. Each of them is based on a different SOURCE, which for belief is problematic, for induction is EVIDENCE, for hearsay is LANGUAGE, and for deduction is a HYPOTHESIS. (The placement of these four modes of knowing in Figure 1 does not imply that belief is more reliable, or deduction less reliable than the others. Each mode of knowing can move up and down the scale of reliability.)

On the right side of Figure 1 is an indication that knowledge may be matched against VERBAL RESOURCES (or categories), and also against EXPECTATIONS. Here there is a question of how good the match is. For one thing there is the question of whether the verbal resources which a speaker or writer chooses express more or less well the knowledge to be communicated. There is also the question of the match between a speaker or writer's knowledge and the speaker's, writer's, or others' expectations.

All of these notions receive verbal expression in English under appropriate circumstances. Suppose, for example, I say:

(1)   *I feel something crawling up my leg.*

The idea that something is crawling up my leg is what I will call knowledge. In this case the mode of knowing is induction, based on evidence from feeling. If I went on to say:

(2)   *It's probably a spider.*

the knowledge would be that it's a spider, and I would be showing with the word *probably* something about the degree of reliability of that knowledge. If I had said:

(3) *It might be a spider.*

I would be doing the same, except that I would be indicating a lower degree of reliability. If I said, for example:

(4) *I think it's a spider.*

I would be showing that my knowledge is based on belief. To say:

(5) *It must be a spider.*

would indicate induction alone, without showing the nature of the evidence; and so on.

To the right of Figure 1 is the suggestion that knowledge may be matched against verbal resources, or against expectations. If I said, for example:

(6) *It feels sort of creepy.*

I would be signaling that 'creepy' was an approximate way of characterizing what I was feeling, that the match with this verbal resource (this category or word) was imperfect or fuzzy. On the other hand, if I said:

(7) *Oddly enough it feels good.*

the signal would be that the piece of knowledge expressed by 'it feels good' was contrary to expectation. All of the above examples were concocted in order to clarify the intent of Figure 1. We will meet some real examples presently.

DEGREES OF RELIABILITY

People are aware, though not necessarily consciously aware, that some things they know are surer bets for being true than others, that not all knowledge is equally reliable. Thus, one way in which knowledge may be qualified is with an expression indicating the speaker's assessment of its degree of reliability, the likelihood of its being a fact. Conversational English uses for this purpose adverbs like *maybe, probably,* or *certainly:*[2]

(8s) *We kept thinking maybe they'd be stationed at the Presidio.*

(9s) *But I'm probably not going to do it any more.*

(10s) *He's quite nice, and certainly very cheery.*

---

[2] From this point on, I will distinguish (conversational) spoken examples from (academic) written examples by suffixing 's' or 'w' to the example number.

or modals like *might* or *may:*

(11s)   *The one thing that <u>might</u> shed light on it was something about requests.*

(12s)   *You know I <u>may</u> not really be putting in full time even this quarter.*

Academic writing uses the same expressions, except that it adds a few other adverbs to the set, words like *possibly, undoubtedly,* and *surely:*

(13w)   *The positive and negative decisions in the Johnson-Laird et al. (1978) study may have allowed equal elaboration, but <u>possibly</u> not.*

(14w)   *The answer <u>undoubtedly</u> varies from one situation to another.*

(15w)   *Then this limitation will <u>surely</u> play a part in determining the nature of the 'rules' for reference in any language.*

There is an alternation between *maybe,* used mostly in speaking, and *perhaps,* used mostly in writing. Compare example (8s) above with:

(16w)   *This <u>perhaps</u> served to ward off comments from peers or teacher.*

The incidence of all these expressions of reliability taken together does not differ greatly between conversation and academic writing. Our spoken data showed 4.6 expressions of reliability per thousand words, our written data 6.8.

There is, however, a special kind of reliability which is more important in academic writing than in conversation. Writers, and less often speakers, may be aware that what they are presenting is not categorically true, but rather true in some statistical sense; it may of necessity be true only as an approximation, a tendency, a mean. There is an important difference between a concern with the probability that something is a fact or not a fact and a realization that something may turn out to be true most of the time, but not always. Academic writing, especially, is sprinkled with words like *basically, by definition, essentially, exactly, generally, in some sense, invariably, literally, normally, particularly, primarily, specifically,* and *virtually,* expressions which are less frequent in conversational language. For example:

(17w)   *The need for a personal name is <u>normally</u> felt at the time of a person's birth.*

(18w)   *These are <u>generally</u> taken to be in the area of 'performance'.*

(19w)   *The link between speech formulas and available mental energy is evident in activities like baseball, where players on the field chatter <u>primarily</u> in formulas.*

In other words, writers are prone to worry about HOW true something is. It should be noted that statements like (17w–19w) are necessarily generic statements, since they must allow for an indefinite number of specific instances. The frequency of these expressions of statistical reliability in our samples of academic writing was 10.22 per thousand words, as compared with 4.18 occurrences in conversation.

BELIEF

We can move now from expressions of reliability to expressions that have to do with modes of knowing. In many cases, as we will see, such expressions carry implications as to degree of reliability as well. In other words, mode of knowing implies something about reliability, but not vice versa. We can begin with belief, or opinion (a weaker form of it). Belief is a mode of 'knowing' in which concern for evidence is downgraded. People believe things because other people whose views they respect believe them too, or simply because, for whatever reason, they want to believe them. There may be evidence to support a belief, evidence which a believer may cite if pressed for it by a nonbeliever, but belief is always based on something other than evidence alone. Knowledge arrived at through belief is signaled in conversational English with expressions like *I think, I guess,* or *I suppose:*

(20s)   *I think that a lot of the time I've been misjudging her.*

(21s)   *I guess I was thinking about it in a different way.*

(22s)   *The idea is that Christ followed this pattern, and Moses, I suppose.*

Our conversational written data contained 3.6 occurrences of such expressions per thousand words, as contrasted with only .6 occurrences in our academic written data.

INDUCTION

In contrast to belief, the mode of knowing in which evidence plays a central role is induction or inference. English often signals only that induction has taken place, without any indication of what the nature of the evidence was. The most common marker which serves this function is *must,* which signals an inference with a high degree of reliability:

(23s)   *It must have been a kid.*

Obvious expresses an even more compelling inference:

(24s)   *Well it was just obvious I couldn't work.*

Seem, on the other hand, indicates less certainty about the conclusion:

(25s)   *And she absolutely did not <u>seem to</u> know what was going on.*

Evidently is similar, but less common:

(26s)   *It had <u>evidently</u> been under snow.*

Academic writing marks inductive inference more often than conversation, but the figures are low for both. We found 1.3 markers of induction per thousand words of conversational English and 2.4 in academic writing.

SENSORY EVIDENCE

Languages sometimes go beyond marking simply that knowledge has been acquired through induction to indicate the specific kind of evidence on which the induction was based. Typically such evidence is sensory or perceptual. English may indicate that reliable knowledge has been derived from sensory evidence by using the explicit verbs *see, hear,* and *feel* (the following are constructed examples):

(27)   *I see her coming down the hall.*

(28)   *I hear her taking a shower.*

(29)   *I feel something crawling up my leg.*

That such knowledge is high in reliability is demonstrated by the fact that the following bald assertions are equivalent to (27–29), except for the lack of evidential specification:

(30)   *She's coming down the hall.*

(31)   *She's taking a shower.*

(32)   *Something is crawling up my leg.*

The knowledge derived from sensory evidence may, on the other hand, be treated as less than fully reliable. Lesser reliability is expressed in English with phrases such as *looks like, sounds like,* and *feels like:*

(33)   *She looks like she's asleep.*

(34)   *He sounds like he's mad.*

(35)   *It feels like the door is open.*

In contrast to the confidence shown in (27–29), (33–35) show a degree of doubt. We understand from these sentences that it would be no great surprise to find that she's not asleep, he's not mad, or the door is shut.

The invoking of sensory evidence was a rare phenomenon in our data. We found only 1.1 examples per thousand words of conversation, and virtually none at all in academic writing. The following are conversational examples:

(36s)   *They <u>look like</u> they've been opened at least.*

(37s)   *He <u>sounded like</u> he thought very very slowly.*

(38s)   *Most of the time I <u>feel</u> extremely safe there.*

Though English provides the resources when needed, there may be a real difference between the infrequent invoking of sensory evidence in English and the common marking of it in some other languages.

HEARSAY EVIDENCE

Another mode of knowing is language; that is, we know many things because people have told us about them. Some languages have clearcut devices—particles, affixes, or both—to qualify knowledge as having been acquired through language rather than direct experience. English is less clearcut. There are a variety of phrases which can perform this function: *people say, they say, I've been told,* or more specifically, *Sarah told me, Harry said yesterday.* A real example from our data is:

(39s)   *They were using more verbs than English speaking kids <u>have been said</u> to learn.*

There are several less direct hearsay devices which have been borrowed for this purpose from other functions. One is *it seems,* whose original function was as a marker of induction. In the following example it indicates knowledge obtained through language:

(40s)   *Well Schaeffer <u>it seems</u> had just found the latest article from the Smithsonian.*

Another, which expresses somewhat more doubtful reliability, is *supposed to,* which also has other functions. In the following example it indicates knowledge derived through hearsay:

(41s)   *I think it's <u>supposed to</u> be the most expensive place in Europe to live.*

Apparently is sometimes used in a similar way:

(42s)   *<u>Apparently</u> at the end of a paper she gave, she pulled out a giant hairbrush.*

In academic writing knowledge obtained through language is indicated with the formal device of citing a reference or personal communication:

(43w)   *Craik and Tulving (1975, Experiment 6) suggested that the congruity effect is not due to positive decisions per se, but rather to the likelihood of greater elaboration in those cases.*

These are hearsay evidentials expressed in their most precise and deliberate form.

The number of hearsay devices per thousand words in our sample of conversational English was only .4. In academic writing the bulk of the examples were citations, which of course were very frequent. If we leave citations out of account as not belonging to what are usually considered hearsay evidentials, English does not appear to mark hearsay evidentiality very often. Again, there are other languages which differ conspicuously in this regard.

DEDUCTION

Still another mode of knowing is to invent a model which predicts what will count as evidence. Such reasoning involves an intuitive leap to a hypothesis from which conclusions about evidence can be deduced. Typical markers of deduction are *should* and *presumably:*

(44w)   *He or she <u>should</u> take longer to respond following exposure to inconsistent information than when exposed to no information at all.*

(45w)   *Adults <u>presumably</u> are capable of purely logical thought.*

As with induction, different markers of deduction can imply different degrees of reliability. A lesser degree than in the above examples may be marked with *can* or *could:*

(46w)   *One <u>can</u>—at least in principle—provide the experience that is needed to bring readiness about.*

(47w)   *No normal phonological rules <u>could</u> account for the loss of this h.*

A special kind of hypothetical knowledge is that expressed by *would,* where an outcome is predicted contingent on an unrealized condition. Such hypotheses are common in academic writing, often as a way of avoiding responsibility for evidence:

(48w)   *This claim does not address other retrieval influences that <u>would</u> be consistent with the obtained results.*

In our academic data there were 4.4 occurrences of deduction markers per thousand words. In conversation there were 2.9. A reason for the greater incidence in writing may be that hypothesis formation requires more time for imagination and deliberation, time which is more available to writers than to speakers.

HEDGES

We can now turn from modes of knowing and sources of knowledge to a different epistemological consideration which also receives frequent linguistic coding. Human understanding involves a constant comparing of ongoing knowledge with expectations. Everything we experience has to be checked against what we already know. We interpret particular experiences by attempting to match them with categories and schemas already present in our minds. It is especially with relation to categories (e.g. Rosch and Lloyd 1978) that evidentiality comes into play. Categories make it possible for knowledge to be associated with linguistic labels and thus to be expressed in language. We decide that some creature is appropriately called a *cat,* or some action a *jump.* But the match between a piece of knowledge and a category may be less than perfect. We would say in such a case that the knowledge has less than optimal codability. In conversational English by far the most common markers of low codability are *sort of* and *kind of.* They may be used to qualify nouns, verbs, adjectives, or whole predications:

(49s)   *And they tend to be sort of farmer kinds of people.*

(50s)   *And he started sort of circling.*

(51s)   *And he sort of always has done this.*

The other commonly used hedge in conversational English is *about,* which removes the precision from a categorization that would otherwise be too precise, usually by suggesting something close to but not exactly at a round number:

(52s)   *I have a friend who's about six foot and blond.*

(53s)   *And about two days later my professor called me into her office.*

The hedges *sort of* and *kind of* are entirely absent from academic writing. *About* does occur, but with less than half the frequency of its occurrence in conversation:

(54w)   *. . . a Mohawk community about 30 miles from Montreal.*

Altogether we found 3.6 occurrences of hedging per thousand words of conversation, versus only .4 per thousand words of academic writing.

EXPECTATIONS

Conversational English has a large number of devices which signal expectations of some kind, against which knowledge may be matched. They range from *of course,* which shows that something is in line with expectations:

(55s) . . . *but of course to the audience sounded like sort of a total nonsequitur.*

to *oddly enough,* which indicates a conflict:

(56s) *Well oddly enough it was in Japan.*

In fact and *actually* suggest that a fact goes beyond what one might have expected:

(57s) *In fact this whole week has been awful.*

(58s) *. . . cause German was actually his first language until he started school.*

Or, from academic writing:

(59w) *Furthermore, some speakers appear to apply the rules variably, while others . . . do not in fact use the rules or the underlying forms on which they operate at all.*

Other common expressions which relate in various ways to expectations are *at least, even, only, but, however,* and *nevertheless.*

There were 17 occurrences of such expectation markers per thousand words of conversation, and 13.9 per thousand words of academic writing. Here too academic writing shows less concern than conversational language for aspects of epistemology that involve some kind of on–line matching of knowledge against a prior pattern.

SUMMARY

'Evidentiality' has been used here broadly to cover any linguistic expression of attitudes toward knowledge. So far as we can tell from their language, users of English regard knowledge as factual much of the time, expressing it without any evidential qualification. Some knowledge, however, is judged appropriate to place on a scale of reliability. Positions on this scale may be signaled by adverbs such as *maybe* (*perhaps*), *probably,* and *certainly,* or by the modals *might* and *may.* Writers also use *possibly, undoubtedly,* and *surely.* Both speakers and writers show this kind of concern with the probability of something being a fact or not being a fact. Academic writing, however, also uses a variety of words like *normally* and *primarily* to indicate a statistical tendency rather than a categorical truth.

Speakers, much more often than writers, may indicate that knowledge stems from belief or opinion with phrases like *I think, I guess,* and *I suppose.*

Other expressions show that knowledge has been inductively arrived at: *must, seem* and *evidently* are examples. Such expressions not only mark induction, but provide some indication of degree of reliability as well. They are relatively infrequent, but slightly more common in academic writing than in conversation.

There may also be a marking of the kind of evidence which led to an induction. Conversational English has some straightforward devices for marking sensory evidence as a source of knowledge, *see* and *look like* for example, but these devices are only infrequently used.

There are also ways of indicating hearsay knowledge, like *they say* or *it seems*. These too are infrequent in our material. Academic writing codes hearsay evidence chiefly in the special form of reference citations.

Knowledge arrived at deductively, through hypothesis formation and prediction, may be signaled with words like *should, could,* and *would*. Conversational language shows fewer examples of deductive reasoning than does academic writing.

Another area of epistemology often coded in language has to do with matching knowledge against categories and expectations. A piece of knowledge may match a verbal category more or less well. A less than perfect match is signaled by a hedge like *sort of* or *kind of*. Hedging is largely a property of conversational language, being captured in academic writing only with words like *about*, which hedge precision. Other kinds of expectations are captured with expressions like *in fact, of course,* and *oddly enough*. Academic writing makes less use of such expressions too.

Thus, in general, conversational English and academic writing both show a concern for the reliability of knowledge, as well as for induction. Academic writing shows more concern for deduction, neither makes a big point of marking the kind of evidence per se, and hedging as well as other devices which match knowledge against expectations are more characteristic of conversation than of academic written language. These differences can be seen as stemming from the spontaneity and interactiveness of speaking and the deliberateness and detachment of writing.

REFERENCES

Chafe, Wallace L. 1982. Integration and involvement in speaking, writing, and oral literature. Spoken and written language: exploring orality and literacy, ed. by Deborah Tannen. Norwood, NJ: Ablex Publishing Corp.

———. 1985. Linguistic differences produced by differences between speaking and writing. Literacy, language, and learning: the nature and consequences of reading and writing, ed. by David R. Olson, Nancy Torrance, and Angela Hildyard. Cambridge: Cambridge University Press.

Rosch, Eleanor, and Barbara B. Lloyd (eds.). 1978. Cognition and categorization. Hillsdale, NJ: Lawrence Erlbaum Associates.

SEVENTEEN

Evidentials, Paths of Change, and Mental Maps: Typologically Regular Asymmetries*

Lloyd B. Anderson

Washington, D.C.

INTRODUCTION

Evidentials express the kinds of evidence a person has for making factual claims. They appear in different surface forms, but show patterns of historical development and grammatical function which are similar in language after language. I argue that these regularities result from their basic meanings.

From a typological survey of evidentials we can build a universal framework. We construct a "map" of evidential meanings, showing which meanings are more closely related or more distant from each other. In the process, we are led to a much more precise terminology for distinguishing evidential meanings. With this map we can easily compare languages.

Using the map we can see paths of historical change in a very graphic way: as particular forms change their meanings, they move through the space represented by the map (their category boundaries advance and retreat). Results of this study include new historical hypotheses for evidentials in Tibeto-Burman and California Indian languages, and for moods in Indo-European.

All facets of the reasoning interact in spiral fashion to determine the solution presented here: the map of evidential meanings. The method is explicitly inductive, as it must be in such a new field; results are likely to be more valid this way than if they proceed from a priori logical ideas.

My treatment is divided into three parts: (a) clarifying what evidentials are;

* I am grateful to the organizers of the conference, Johanna Nichols and Wally Chafe, for the opportunity to participate. I have learned far more than I dreamed of in advance.

(b) mental maps of evidential space; (c) evidentials, mood, and modality: typologically regular asymmetries and suppletion.

CLARIFYING WHAT EVIDENTIALS ARE

It is important to distinguish true evidential categories from other forms which SEEM evidential, but are not. The noun form of the term "evidentials" or "an evidential" does not simply include anything one might consider to have an evidential function, that is, to express evidence for something else. Rather, evidentials are a special grammatical phenomenon. Typical evidentials include the following two examples from English. (The words inside brackets, [. . .], are the evidentials; the material not in brackets is the central factual claim of each sentence.)

(1) (circumstantial inference) *John [must have] arrived.* (because I see his coat on the
                                                                        chair)

(2) (hearsay)   *[I hear] Mary won the prize.*   (someone told me)

We can identify archetypal evidentials as in (3). This identification is not an arbitrary definition but results from the empirical findings.[1] Evidentials, so identified, interact strongly with each other as competing choices.

(3a) Evidentials show the kind of justification for a factual claim which is available to
      the person making that claim, whether
            direct evidence plus observation (no inference needed)
            evidence plus inference
            inference (evidence unspecified)
            reasoned expectation from logic and other facts
      and whether the evidence is auditory, or visual, etc.

(3b) Evidentials are not themselves the main predication of the clause, but are rather a
      specification added to a factual claim ABOUT SOMETHING ELSE.

(3c) Evidentials have the indication of evidence as in (a) as their primary meaning, not
      only as a pragmatic inference.

---

[1] In the same way Lyons (1966) was able to frame a universal definition of 'Noun', in which the semantic core is valid for all languages, but the outer limits of what morphologically are treated as nouns will vary from language to language. It was Sally McLendon's remarks at the conference which convinced me of the need for a semantically narrow definition: her own definition was close to (3a). Gordon (this volume) discusses a version of (3b) for Maricopa. Jacobsen (this volume) states that in Makah evidentials are not morphologically a unitary category. But since they are never main predications (3b), they do have some structural properties in common. Some of the forms he discusses only have secondary evidential functions; they are not full evidentials by the criteria used here.

(3d)   Morphologically, evidentials are inflections, clitics, or other free syntactic elements (not compounds or derivational forms).[2]

I will consider each part of the definition. (3c) excludes certain categories which are obviously not evidentials. A marker of experiencer role used on a noun, often a special kind of dative case, may have evidential implications. Yet it is still a case marker, not an evidential. A marker of actual present often allows an inference of direct witnessing or certainty. Yet it is not therefore automatically an evidential.

Circumstantial-inference evidentials often arise by historical change from certain kinds of perfect (those of result state or of current relevance[3]). Consider (4):

(4a)   *The toast is burnt.*

(4b)   *The toast burned. (and the orange juice was sour—a terrible breakfast).*

(4c)   *The toast has burned.*

(4d)   *The toast [must] have burned.*

Here (4a) simply tells the state of the toast observed, and (4b) claims only that the event occurred, that the toast burned, without giving any evidence. But (4c) has its verb in the perfect and may be used to relate a present state (toast now burnt) to a past event (the toast burned). When the present state is used as circumstantial evidence for inferring an unwitnessed past event, English normally adds the epistemic *must* of logical inference: (4d). For this true evidential, the analysis should probably bracket [*must have*] together as in (1), rather than only [*must*] as in (4d).

While the English Perfect (4c) remains primarily a perfect with many non-evidential uses, the "Perfects" of some other languages have historically become evidentials with no need for an additional signal like English *must:* Georgian, Turkish, and Balkan Slavic show this (Aksu and Slobin, this volume; Friedman, this volume), perhaps also Jaqaru-Aymara (see notes 3 and 17).

Part (3b) of the evidential definition distinguishes among the following English sentences, where words which normally carry the strongest stress are capitalized:

---

[2] (3d) is in accord with Jacobsen who notes that the suffixes that are clearly specialized as evidentials are inflections rather than derivational suffixes, what Boas and Swadesh called word-suffixes rather than stem-suffixes. Jacobsen notes that "evidentials may arise from morphemes with . . . concrete meanings . . . mov[ing] to a less central layer of the word" as they change their meaning and cease to be derivational (this volume, 11 and 20).

[3] These and many other varieties of perfect are discussed in Anderson (1982). See also note 17.

(5a)   *[I hear] Mary won the PRIZE.*

(5b)   *[I heard] (that) Mary won the PRIZE.*

(5c)   *I HEARD that Mary won the prize.*

(5d)   *I HEARD she won it, but nobody told me what the prize WAS.*

(5e)   *I already HEARD that, you don't need to tell me AGAIN.*

Of these, only (5a,b) contain evidentials, [bracketed], telling how it is the speaker knows that Mary won the prize. In (5c,d,e) the word *HEARD* is, in fact, the main predication. The proposition that Mary won the prize is here NOT the main predication, so it can be reduced by pronominalization, partially, (5d), or entirely, (5e).

The differences between perception verbs (5c,d,e) and evidentials (5a,b) are at first very subtle. But as a historical change continues, grammatical reanalysis leads to quite distinct structures. The form *[I hear]* in (5a) contains no past tense marker even though the speaker received the information in the past. In this respect it is like (6a,b).

(6a)   *[I understand that] Mary won the PRIZE.*
(6b)   *[I have it on good authority that] Mary won the PRIZE.*

(6c)   *I've got it. = I have it.*

(6d)   *I've gotten it. = I've received it.*

In examples (6a,b), (5a) the evidentials represent states of the speaker, resulting from a prior event as in *[I have heard that] Mary won the PRIZE.* They may represent a lexical reanalysis of 'hear' in the same way that (6d) has changed to (6c), so that *'ve got, 's got* is a new vocabulary item, a stative.

Similar shifts occur in other languages. The Maricopa visual evidential suffix *-'yuu* lacks an aspect suffix *-k* which is present when it is a main verb meaning 'I see': *'-yuu-k* (Gordon, this volume). Like English **understand,** (6a), and **hear,** (5a), which lack a past tense marking, the Makah evidentials *-pi:t, -q̓adi, -caqił* are usually found in the present tense, and never in the past tense (Jacobsen, p. 11). Wintu and Patwin show phonological reductions of an original **mut-** 'hear'.

Perception verbs often give rise to evidentials. Probably this is just because we normally take our own perceptions for granted; perception verbs are then not the main predication of a sentence, and come to be reduced and reanalyzed in various ways.

But when reanalysis has not occurred, there is only the evidential USE of a form which is not itself primarily an evidential. It is important to insist on this aspect of the definition. For most English perception words, there is little or no data to show that they have been reanalyzed. In this they differ from [*hear*], (5a), and [*understand*], (6a). None of the examples in (7) are full evidentials.[4]

(7a)	*It's sour.*	Perception words as main
	It stinks.	predication
(7b)	*It* SMELLS *fresh*	Perception-verb usage
	It LOOKS *fresh.*	
	It FEELS *fresh.*	
(7c)	*That fruit smells like dried fish.*	Perception-verb usage
	(I wonder what chemicals make	
	it have that effect.)	
(7d)	*It smells like dried fish.*	Evidential USAGE
	(='I think it's dried fish.')	
(7e)	*It smells* FRESH.	Evidential USAGE
	It looks FRESH.	
	It feels FRESH.	
(7f)	*[I smell] a pie baking.*	Evidential USAGE

Contrast especially (7c) with (7d), and (7b) with (7e), where the sentences are so reduced that only stress separates them on the surface. Examples (7d,e,f) qualify as evidentials by definitions (3a,b,d) but not by (3c). They are thus borderline.

One purpose of the mental maps I present later is to show clearly these slight shifts in meaning and usage which evidentials gradually undergo in their development.

Several important properties of evidentials are embodied in the definitions given in (3), as we have seen, or are direct logical consequences of them. Since evidentials are used (a) to specify factual claims and (b) to indicate the justification available TO THE PERSON MAKING THE CLAIM, we have the following generalizations:

(8)   Evidentials are normally used in assertions (realis clauses), not in irrealis clauses, nor in presuppositions.

(9a)   When the claimed fact is directly observable by both speaker and hearer, evidentials are rarely used (or have a special emphatic or surprisal sense).[5]

(9b)   When the speaker (first person) was a knowing participant in some event (voluntary agent; conscious experiencer), the knowledge of that event is normally direct and evidentials are then often omitted.

---

[4] For support of this claim, see the discussion of Makah (and see Jacobsen, this volume, p. 23).

[5] For some examples of surprisals, see Gordon on Maricopa, and Aksu and Slobin on Turkish (both, this volume).

(9c)   Often, it is claimed, second person in questions is treated as first person in statements. (But such examples may contain ordinary perception verbs rather than archetypal evidentials, in the sense in which these were distinguished in (7).)

The absurdity of evidentials in irrealis clauses and presuppositions can be seen from (10):

(10a)   *[I hear] Do the dishes!   (imperative)

(10b)   *I asked John to [apparently] come.   (infinitive subjunctive)

(10c)   *If it were the case that John [must have] arrived, . . .

(10d)   *If John had [apparently] arrived, he could help us.   (counterfactuals)

(10e)   *When John [apparently] came, the party got livelier. (presupposition)

In Eastern Pomo (McLendon 1982) the irrealis "cannot occur with evidentials."[6] In Wintu (Schlichter, this volume, following Pitkin's work which she cites) there is a special non-assertive "stem II" of the verb, typically with -u, which is not used with evidentials. (This stem is used for imperatives; interrogatives, negatives; causatives, passives; probability, possibility, potentiality; inevitable/necessary future events; wishes, hopes, and fears.)

Wintu has a "stem I" of the verb, typically with -a, for factual assertions. Evidentials are used with this stem unless the speaker directly observed the subject acting. If the speaker is also the agent of the action, evidentials will only be used to imply an indirect source of the information.[7] I will discuss other languages later which illustrate (9) by having special first-person forms which can be analyzed as having no evidential marking (Tibetan, Kashaya). Detailed discussion of (9c) must be postponed to another occasion.

Distinctions between true evidentials and neighboring non-evidential categories are obviously not easy to make. But it is still possible to construct a reasonable typology of evidential meanings, and to this I now turn.

MENTAL MAPS OF EVIDENTIAL SPACE

Maps of semantic space have been used before. The procedure is fairly straightforward when we have an external "objective" criterion of meaning similarity. The dimensions of color space can be defined in advance in terms such as wavelength/hue and brightness. Thus, Berlin and Kay (1969) were able to use a fixed "map" of color space, locating on it the color terms of each language and establishing their limits of use.

---

6 On Pomo, see Figure 6 and discussion of examples (19).

7 See Schlichter (this volume), examples (8) and (13). This indirect information about the first person might be a source of reanalysis from which a surprisal develops, usable with third-person agents as well.

For more abstract vocabulary, and especially for grammatical categories, this approach is not possible. We do not know the dimensions of our space in advance. But there is another method. We can develop grammar/meaning spaces inductively, finding a "map" which works consistently for many languages.

The fundamental notion presupposed by any semantic space is similarity of meaning. Highly similar meanings should be close together on a map, dissimilar meanings should be far apart (just as on a map of colors).

We can determine similarity of meaning typologically, even without an external "objective" criterion such as that available for color words. If two particular meanings are often expressed by the same surface form (across a random sample of languages), then we can generally infer that the two meanings are similar for the human mind. This inductive inference will usually be valid, although in certain specific situations it will lead to false conclusions and must be corrected (as explained in the next section). This procedure has been carried out for about twenty distinct evidential meanings identifiable in the articles of this volume and elsewhere. Here I only illustrate the procedure.

Consider the three evidential meanings in (11) and their surface forms in two related Pomoan languages.

		Kashaya	Eastern Pomo
(11a)	auditory evidential: ('[I hear] someone coming')	*-V̂nnă*	*-inke*
(11b)	non-auditory non-visual sensory evidential: ('[I smell] a pie baking')	*-qă*	*-inke*
(11c)	inferential evidential: ('John [must]/[seems to] be here now')	*-qă*	*-ine*

Because Kashaya has the same surface grammatical form for meanings (11b) and (11c), namely the suffix *-qă,* it is reasonable to suggest that meanings (11b) and (11c) are similar. By the same reasoning, Eastern Pomo *-inke* shows that meanings (11a) and (11b) are similar.

In the small sample used here, the Kashaya pattern is unique to Kashaya. But the Eastern Pomo pattern is found in many languages: meanings (11a,b) are linked in Maricopa *-(k) 'a-* (Gordon); Wintu *-nther* (Schlichter); possibly Patwin *mut-her* (Whistler); and possibly Sherpa *-i-nok, -ki-nok* (Woodbury) (all authors, this volume).

Because the Eastern Pomo pattern is more common, we can infer that meaning (11b) is more similar to (11a), where it is linked by Eastern Pomo and others, than it is to (11c), where it is linked only by Kashaya. One language, Sherpa, has a single evidential form *-nok* spanning the full range of meanings in (11a,b,c), and others besides (though combined with other elements in different ways for these different meanings). But no language in the sample has a single evidential form used for both meanings (11a) and (11c) while excluding (11b).[8] Thus, it is possible to conclude that the meanings of (11a) and (11c) are not similar in any way other than the characteristics which they share with (11b).

We can now translate such similarity measures into a map of mental space for evidential meanings. The full map of evidential space is complex, so I begin with a simpler extract from it, containing just the points of immediate interest. This is Figure 1.

Just as with an ordinary geographical map, it is useful to have number and letter scales along the top and sides. These are purely to locate particular positions for discussion. Since we are establishing evidential space inductively, the vertical and horizontal dimensions and coordinates do not yet have an interpretation. Such an interpretation will be a RESULT of the analysis, given later.

On the map shown in Figure 1, true evidentials, as defined in (3), are enclosed within a solid rectangle. As argued earlier for the 'I heard' of examples (5c–e), main-predication uses of perception verbs are not true evidentials. Thus perception-verb 'hear' is at point (H5) of Figure 1, outside the rectangle.

Inside the rectangle, at (G6), are the true auditory evidentials, the type of (11a). (English has no true auditory evidentials so the English glosses of (11a,b) are approximations as in (7).) At (F3) are hearsay evidentials, with English examples like (2) and (5a,b). The arrows from (H5) to (G6) and from (H5) to (F3) represent the hypothesis that the perception verb 'hear' often changes historically either into auditory or into hearsay evidentials. Arrows will have this historical meaning throughout. (For some details of arrow use see note 10.)

Point (F6) on the map is for non-auditory, non-visual sensory evidentials, that is, for information gained through smell, taste, etc. English examples include (11b).

Inferential evidentials (types like 11c) are at points (E4, D4, D2). The English examples (1, 11c) and the Eastern Pomo *-ine* of (11c) belong in (D4, D2). Oswalt's description of Kashaya *-qǎ* (this volume) leaves open the possibility that its meaning includes points in the range of (E4–5) as well as (D4, D2) or instead of (D4, D2).

Positions of meanings on this partial map do reflect the similarity measures drawn from the typological survey, as in (11). Meanings (D4) and (G6) are fairly far apart; (F6) is in between, but closer to (G6).

Some Technical Aspects of the Reasoning in Building Mental Maps

The fundamental step in creating mental maps was presented above as an inference from similarity of surface form to similarity of meaning. In one common

---

[8] Interpreted as a synchronic generalization, this last statement may have a marginal exception in Makah (see Figure 4 and the discussion of it earlier). But the relevant form *-pał* is not a true evidential. It is also not an exception to the more sophisticated historical interpretation of this pattern (see example 15). On general problems of the relation between typology or universals of historical change and synchronically observed language types, see Greenberg (1978).

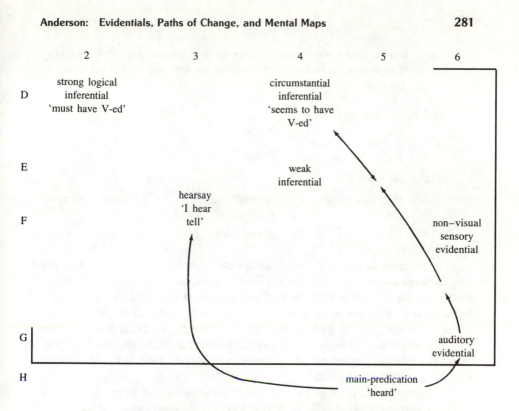

Figure 1.   A partial map of mental space for evidential meanings.

situation this inference is invalid, which we can illustrate with the auditory and hearsay evidential functions, points (F3) and (G6), in Figure 1. In English these both use a form of the word *hear,* derived historically from the perception verb *hear* (H5). Examples are (2, 5a,b) and (11a). We are justified in saying that (F3) is similar to (H5) in meaning, and that (G6) is similar to (H5) in meaning. But we cannot conclude that (F3) and (G6) are similar to each other in meaning. We have no examples in which an auditory evidential (G6) changes into a hearsay evidential (F3), or the reverse. This problem arises whenever a word or grammatical form splits into several descendants, whose similarity to each other has only a historical not a synchronic explanation. Typologically recurring patterns often have such complex relations to their sources.[9]

Ideally we would base our maps only on well-studied examples of gradual meaning change. The fundamental notion would then be not similarity of meaning but derivability of meaning, as in (12):

(12)   A new meaning of a form derives from an old one at first only as a pragmatic inference or extension of use, but later it is reanalyzed to

---

[9] See Greenberg (1978) and other articles in the same volume.

become a new core meaning independent of the old one. (This possibility of extension of use justifies saying that the new and old meanings are "similar".)

A classic example is in (13),

(13a)	*He did not want for food.* (archaic)		* 'lack'	
			↓	
(13b)	*He wants food.*		'desire'	
			↓	
(13c)	*He wants to eat.*	*He wills it thus.* (archaic)	'intend'	* 'intend'
				↓
(13d)		*He will eat.*		future

In practice we do not have enough documentation of such meaning changes to rely on them exclusively. We can combine a small amount of direct historical evidence with a larger amount of evidence of the simpler kind, derived from a typological sample. But we must remain on our guard, knowing where we can go wrong. This compromise procedure is the basis for this study, as it was for the treatment of the perfect in Anderson 1982. Historical derivability, whether documented or plausibly hypothesized, is represented by the arrows in (13), as also in Figures 1 to 10 and 14 to 16.[10]

True mental space has no fixed number of dimensions, yet the paper we write on is two-dimensional. This limits how effectively we can display mental maps. But it is purely a practical limitation.

Building mental maps is very much like doing the kind of multidimensional scaling familiar in modern sociolinguistics. In sociolinguistics, the points are individual speakers, who are more or less similar to each other in terms of various characteristics. For mental maps, the points are particular meanings, more or less closely related to each other. For mental maps, we do not have precise mathematical measurements of degree of similarity. But we have an advantage, in that random statistical variability is a very minor problem. The meanings and uses of particular linguistic forms are usually established across a large number of speakers.[11] When we extract form-meaning patterns by comparative typology, we are in one sense drawing our sample from the largest

---

[10] In example (13) the arrows go only one way, because the historical changes observed go only one way. Arrows with two heads (or, equivalently, connecting lines with NO arrowheads on the maps) indicate an equilibrium balanced between two meanings or uses, so that historical changes can go in either direction.

[11] This does not eliminate all sociolinguistic problems in the validity of the data we use. As all self-conscious analysis of language tends to distort repeatedly in certain ways, our typological samples of language descriptions will be distorted in these same ways.

possible experiment, the result of thousands of years of language use by large parts of humanity.

The meaning spaces built here are based on natural languages. This can be a great advantage, because intuitions, abstract logic, and psycholinguistic experiments all introduce artificial distortions. Even where an external "objective" criterion SEEMS to be available, it may not have the same structure as mental space. In that case, it is not "objective" at all. In a future paper I will argue from natural-language data that color terms are organized in a semantic space somewhat different from the hue-and-brightness dimensions of Berlin and Kay (1969). Just as in the multidimensional scaling used by sociolinguists, the dimensions and coordinates of color space should be defined by the discovered structure of the space. They are results of the analysis, not a precursor to it. Tops and bottoms of maps may even have different coordinate systems!

Even with only twenty evidential meanings we need AT LEAST three dimensions. Most evidentials fit fairly well in one plane. But evidentials of reported speech have complex links which require a third dimension. In Figure 2, which represents major results of this study, we see reportive evidentials as if through a window, the internal square box. The reportives should be conceived as located in an area behind the main plane, but linked to it. In the main plane, the meanings 'conjecture' (G4, English *maybe*) and 'possibility' (G1, English *may*) are adjacent, as they should be, not interrupted by the reportives.

Questions of basic or core meaning (Grundbedeutung), common meaning (Gesamtbedeutung), and primary vs. secondary uses of forms are discussed in Anderson (1982).

We can map evidential systems for individual languages by outlining the range of use of each surface evidential form with an oval. Since we use the same base map each time, we can easily compare languages with each other. In this way we also can test the base map for its claims to universal validity and for any needed modifications: how easily does it fit the evidentials of new languages not in the original typological sample?

I will discuss the topics in the following order:

(14a)   Perception verbs and sensory evidentials

(14b)   Logical expectation and evidentials of reported speech

(14c)   Inferential evidentials and reported speech: Jaqaru and Aymara

(14d)   Typologically regular asymmetries: Tibeto-Burman

(14c)   Evidentially unmarked forms

Throughout the discussion I will illustrate how mental maps can be used both to clarify synchronic description and to develop hypotheses of historical change. In the process, we can also refine terminology.

For each evidential morpheme discussed, examples of its use in sentences will

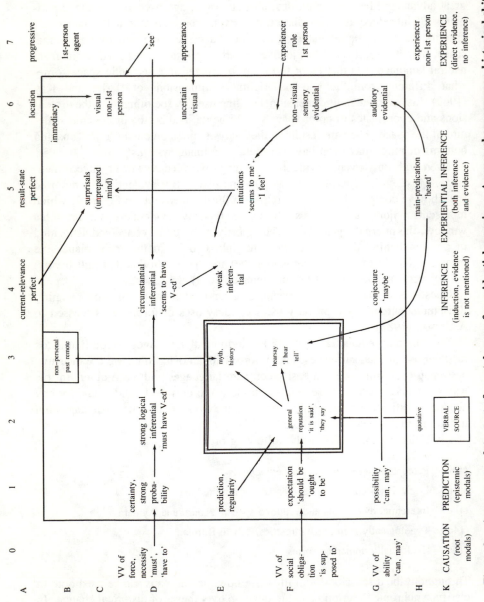

Figure 2. A more complete map of mental space for evidential meanings. Arrows show common historical shifts.

be found in other articles in this volume or in references cited. In some cases, where such examples were not sufficient to determine exact limits of use, I have had help from other authors in this volume.[12]

Perception Verbs and Sensory Evidentials

The difference between perception verbs and evidentials can be very subtle. This can be seen for English in the first part of this paper, especially in example sets (5, 6, and 7). Structural reanalysis is evidenced by very small changes in surface form. The most detailed treatment I know of is Gordon's for Maricopa (this volume). In Maricopa the visual evidential *-'yuu* lacks the aspectual suffix *-k* found on the main verb *-yuu-k* 'see' from which it is derived. The auditory and non-visual sensory evidential *-'a* lacks a passive suffix *-v* found on the main verb *-'a-v* 'hear' from which it is derived. Gordon thus demonstrates that these evidential forms are separate grammatical categories, no longer identical to the main verbs. When we map Maricopa evidentials onto our evidential space (Figure 3), the main verbs appear outside the large rectangle, the evidentials inside it, and the arrows represent the historical changes by which main verbs became evidentials. These two examples just discussed are on the right side of the map.

There is another detailed typological parallel with English worth noting. The Maricopa hearsay evidential VERB-*k-i-sh-'a* has an etymological structure [[[VERB-*k*]-'say']-'hear'] just like English *[I hear [tell [that VERB]]]*.[13]

Makah is another language which clearly shows sensory evidentials originating from perception predicates (Figure 4). Like English evidential **hear,** three of these, **pi:t, -q̇adi,** and **-caqi,** usually occur in the present tense, never in the past tense. The suffix **-ṗaɬ** however "clearly has a primarily descriptive value in describing smells or tastes, but verges on being an evidential which indicates evidence from these sense modalities in certain examples" (Jacobsen, this volume, p. 23). So **-ṗaɬ** is not a true evidential.

Jacobsen cites one type of example which I have not seen elsewhere, and which can help us to refine concepts and terminology. The auditory inferential in 'it sounds like you're getting fat' (if someone says that their clothes are tight) is expressed in Makah by **-q̇adi,** in opposition to hearsay examples (presumably 'I hear that he's getting fat') with **-wa:t.** Accordingly, we should consider **-wa:t** to be a hearsay EVIDENTIAL (reporting the content of what one is told), but not an INFERENTIAL (which, like **-q̇adi,** must infer to something beyond that content).

In English, Maricopa, and Makah, sensory evidentials clearly have a perception-predicate origin. In Kashaya (Figure 5) and Eastern Pomo (Figure 6), the origins of the sensory evidentials are not synchronically obvious.

---

[12] Authors who have been particularly helpful with their comments and corrections of my errors are Gordon, Jacobsen, Oswalt, Schlichter, and Thurgood. They are, of course, not responsible for remaining errors.

[13] It is possible that there is an additional parallel with Makah, see note 14.

Kashaya and Eastern Pomo are the two Pomoan languages I used earlier in example (11) to show how a map of evidential space could be constructed. The difference between them is visually clear on the maps. Kashaya expresses the auditory evidential and the non-visual sensory evidential with two different surface forms, while Eastern Pomo has a single sensory evidential *-inke* for both. In this Eastern Pomo resembles Maricopa and Makah, and also Wintun and Sherpa Tibetan.

The Eastern Pomo *-inke* is also used for the first-person experiencer role, with verbs like 'like', 'afraid', and 'be bitten' (McLendon 1982). Sherpa Tibetan shows the same extension of its sensory evidential *-nok* in its stative/durative (and experiencer) form *-i-nok* with 'feel sick' and in a punctual/habitual (and active/agentive) form *-ki-nok* with 'want to' and 'think' (Woodbury 1982). It is not surprising that the experiencer role should be related to the sensory evidential in more than one language.

In Wintu and Patwin (Figures 7 and 8), a verb *mute-* 'hear' in a "passive" form **mut-her* > *-nther* has become a non-visual sensory evidential (Schlichter's analysis for Wintu, accepted by Whistler as cognate in Patwin, both this volume). The ranges of use are quite similar in the two languages, as seen by the ovals. The "passive" marking is very possibly connected with the fact that the speaker has an experiencer case role in this kind of evidential, as we have seen. Makah may have a passive *-t* on its hearsay suffix *-wa:t* and visual evidential *-pi:t* (Jacobsen, this volume).[14]

To conclude this section, I suggest the following hypotheses:

(15)   Non-visual sensory evidentials often arise by weakening and generalization of an auditory evidential '[I hear] . . .', which (always?) arises from a verb 'to hear'.

(16)   Possible language patterns with overt morphologically distinct sensory evidentials include the following:

auditory	non-visual sensory	visual	unmarked (obvious)	
0	0	0	0	English?
+	0	0	0	English?
+	+	0	0	Pomo, Wintu, Patwin, Jaqaru, Aymara (Sherpa?)
+	+	+	0	Kashaya, Maricopa, (Makah?) (Japanese?) (Lhasa?)

---

[14] Jacobsen's analysis is found on p. 17 and his note 20. There is some possibility that the suffix on *wa:* 'to say' and **pi:* 'to observe' was actually from a verb **'to hear'. The Nootka auditory inferential is *-'in,* which occurs in the "quotative" *-we:?in,* matching Makah *-wa:t* (Jacobsen). The first parts of these last two forms are cognate according to Jacobsen. The second parts might therefore have the same etymological meaning, though not necessarily; this is merely an interesting hypothesis.

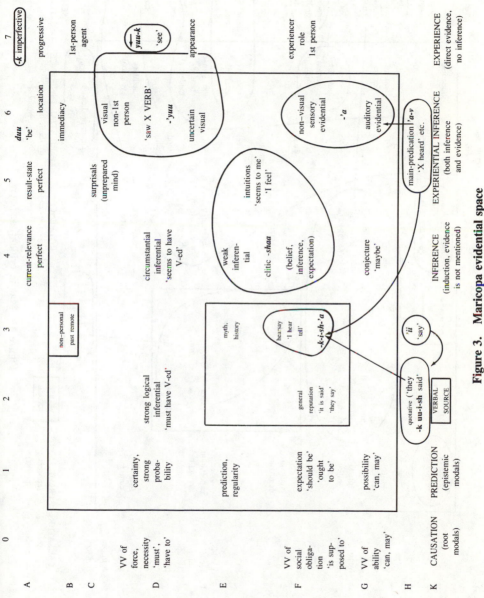

Figure 3. Maricopa evidential space

287

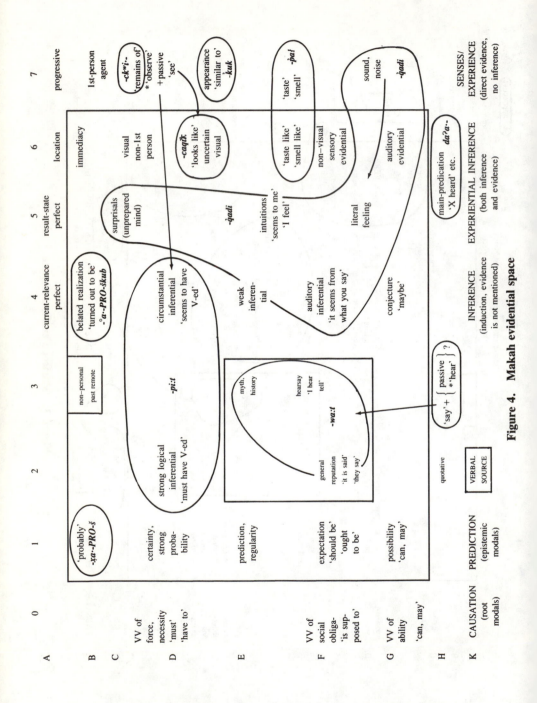

Figure 4. Makah evidential space

288

Logical Expectation and Evidentials of Reported Speech

We must distinguish several different kinds of reported speech, because one or more languages in our sample express these with distinct surface forms. In this area of meanings, however, technical terminology is not well developed. Some authors have used the term "hearsay" for all reportives. But this conflicts with the ordinary-language sense of "hearsay": a more specific unreliability of the information, often from a weak or single source. We need to retain the term in its ordinary-language sense for that specific meaning, as distinct from other kinds of reported speech. To do otherwise causes needless confusion and erects needless barriers between laymen and specialists. We need thus to distinguish AT LEAST four kinds of reportives: (a) hearsay, (b) general reputation, (c) myth and history (these three being evidentials), and (d) "quotative" (marginally an evidential).[15] These are placed toward the left on our maps of evidential space.

We have already seen how a true hearsay evidential can arise from a main verb 'say' (plus 'hear'), in Maricopa, Makah, and English. Reportive evidentials also arise from forms expressing logical expectation or necessity. The range of meanings is clearly shown by the German word *soll:*

Root modal:

(17a) (obligation)   *Er soll es tun.*   'He should do it'

(17b) (past expectation)   *Er sollte könig werden.*   'He was destined to be king.'

(17c) (counterfactual)   *Ich hätte es tun sollen.* 'I should have done it.'

Epistemic modal:

(17d) (general reputation)   *Er soll sehr gelehrt sein.* 'He is reputed to be very learned.'

(17e) (general reputation)   *Er soll es getan haben.*   'He is said to have done it.'

Wintu (Figure 7) shows two morphemes shifting from meanings of logical expectation to reportive evidential senses. Both Schlichter and Pitkin state that this change is historically observable. The form -ʔel originally indicated expectation,[16] based on knowledge of what normally or repeatedly happens in the world:

---

[15] I have tried to use the examples offered in the papers at hand to determine the exact uses of forms; obviously I have not been able to do this completely. There seems as yet to be no good term for the full range of evidentials indicating evidence from verbal communication. I have used "reportive" here, where Jacobsen uses "quotative". Jacobsen points out (p. 8) that "quotative" also has differing uses. l use it in the restrictive ordinary-language sense, only to refer to a form meaning 'This is what X said', what Jacobsen calls "a kind of spoken quotation mark (like Sanskrit *iti*)."

[16] Pitkin's term "experiential" is, as Schlichter notes, subject to confusion with experiencer case. "Experiencer" is needed in its normal use in discussing evidential systems like those of Eastern Pomo and Sherpa. While experience is indeed the SOURCE of knowledge of regularly recurring events, the MEANING of the grammatical form is rather one of expectation (the mental state resulting from the knowledge). For yet a third distinct use of the term "experiential," see note 21. The term "expectation" is more exact than "prediction", as Schlichter has taught me.

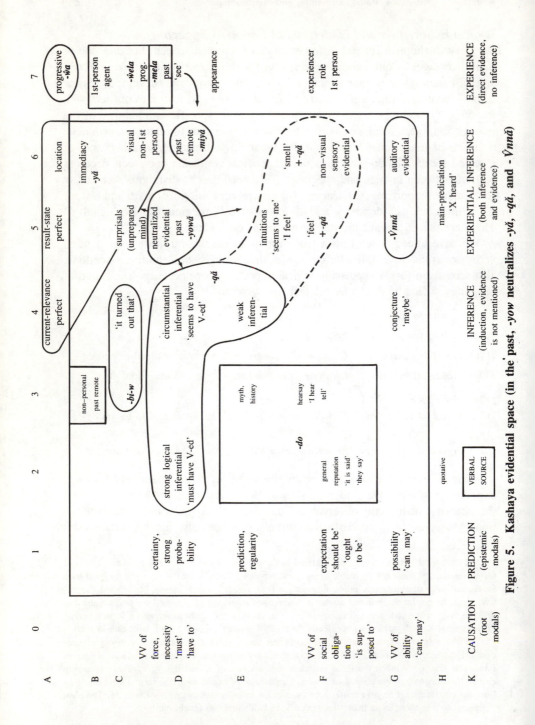

Figure 5. Kashaya evidential space (in the past, *-yow* neutralizes *-yá, -qá,* and *-√nná*)

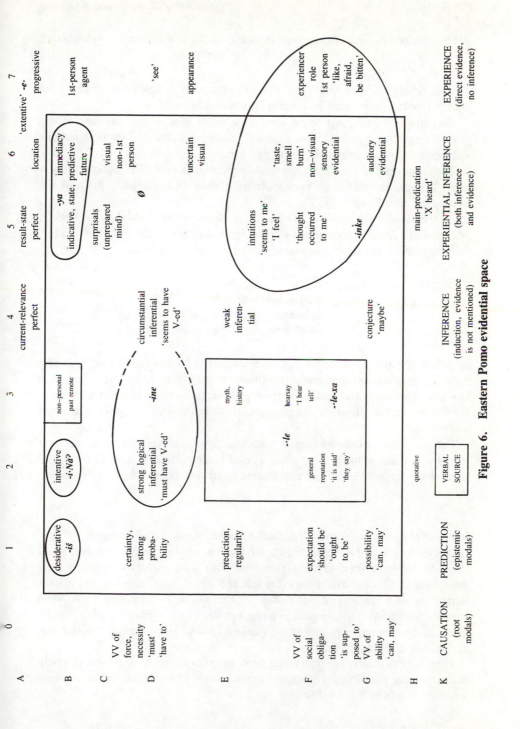

Figure 6. Eastern Pomo evidential space

291

(18)   'The berries [must] be ripe now' (because it's that time of year, not because I've
seen them).

A form *?el* also is used to express generic existence. A link of these two uses
finds a typological parallel in Tibetan (discussed below).

Recently *-?el* has come to be used as a kind of reportive, perhaps of the
general reputation type, as an older evidential *-ke·* was absorbed in combinations
with the conditional *kila* and completive *kir*.

The form *-kEl* has links to potentials and conditionals (Schlichter's discussion). It might derive from a verb meaning * 'should', to judge by the possible
typological parallel of (17).

Eastern Pomo has a suffix *-·le* as a reportive evidential (McLendon 1982),
extended as *-·le-xa* in some uses. Certain irrealis forms contain what may originally have been the same morpheme, in a symmetrical pattern:

(19)   (Eastern Pomo)   Jussive   *-ba?*
                        Subjunctive   *-ba?e·le*
                        Indicative   *-ya*
                        Conditional   *-ya?e·le*

Apparent cognates in some other Pomo languages have a conditional meaning
(Oswalt, personal communication). Although belonging to different language
families, Eastern Pomo and Wintu are geographic neighbors. The strong resemblances in both function and phonological form of *-?el* and *-(?e)·le* demand
study.

Patwin (Figure 8) shows similar historical developments. The verb meaning
'become', which in the present gives a result-state perfect, is used in the future
form *-bo-ti* for prediction and expectation, and this is extended into reportive
evidential functions.

Inferential Evidentials and Reported Speech: Jaqaru and Aymara
Jaqaru (Figure 9) and Aymara (Figure 10) have no obvious sensory evidentials of
the kind we have seen in California. But they have greatly elaborated their
inferential and logical evidentials (the left and upper left portions of the maps).
Jaqaru shows a gradient of fine distinctions as we move from upper left down
towards the right: *+qa, +qilli; +psa, +psilli; +ja, +jilli; +jashi; +ashi*.
These go from strong certainty to the weakest kind of conjecture, and differ also
in the kind of evidence implied.

Here we can clearly see how using these maps to compare languages can help
in discovering plausible etymological connections. (Two of the following were
noted by Hardman, this volume.)

(20)		strong inferential	weak intuitions	'probable'	reportive
Jaqaru		+*psa*	+*ashi*	+*qa*	+*mna*
Aymara		−*pacha*	−*chi*	+*xa*	
				−*chi*+*xa*	−*chi*+*m*

These languages distinguish "non–personal" (unwitnessed) from "personal" (witnessed) pasts. This opposition overlaps partly with the distinction between Perfect and Simple Past in English.[17] The English Perfect in sometimes called an "indefinite past", and is sometimes used when what is reported is inferred, not personally witnessed (*John [must have] arrived.*). The "non-personal" and Perfect are in each language the more marked form: Aymara *-tay-na* vs. *-na*, English *has baked* vs. *baked.*

Aymara divides reportive evidentials, the inner square of the map, into four (!) categories. It links myth/history with non-witnessed remote pasts; it links general reputation with quotative, literal 'said'; and it links true hearsay with weak inferences. Third-hand information is expressed as a combination of non-witnessed remote past with weak inference.

These links and contrasts lock parts of the map into their relative positions. True hearsay must be placed closer to the sensory/inferential evidentials, while general reputation must be placed closer to quotative and, as shown for Wintu and Patwin (Figures 7 and 8), closer to prediction and expectation. The entire map has been arranged using such procedures.

Typologically Regular Asymmetries: Tibeto-Burman

Tibeto-Burman evidentials are embedded in a complex morphological paradigm. Evidentiality interacts with other grammatical categories such as person, participant role, tense and aspect, and does so in an asymmetrical manner. The analyses presented here emphasize these other categories, attributing specifically evidential values to very few forms.

The asymmetries will be treated typologically, by seeking to show that the SAME asymmetries occur in many languages, and suggesting explanations from pragmatic meanings. Mental processes can also produce symmetry within one language. Either symmetry or asymmetry can be regular, typologically recurring.

Lhasa Tibetan and Sherpa are closely related languages. Lhasa patterns are in

---

[17] A detailed comparison would be most interesting. The Jaqaru/Aymara distinction of four past forms, personal vs. non–personal and near vs. remote, would be a good place to refine the map of mental space for the perfect presented in Anderson (1982).

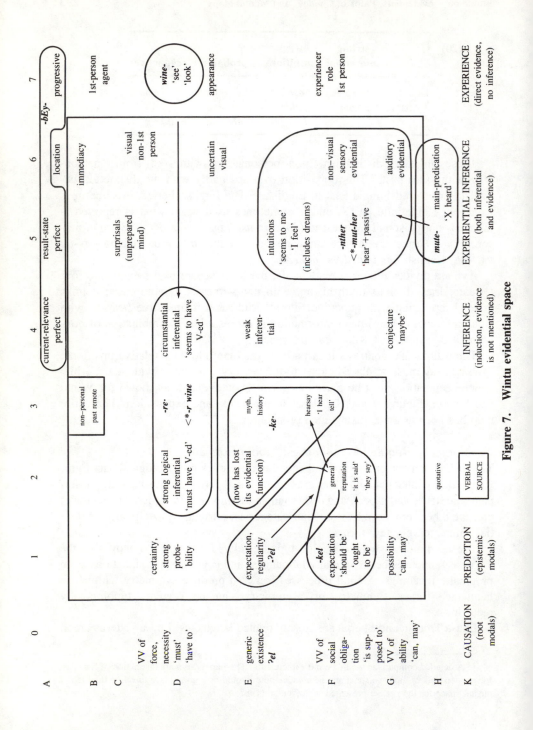

Figure 7. Wintu evidential space

294

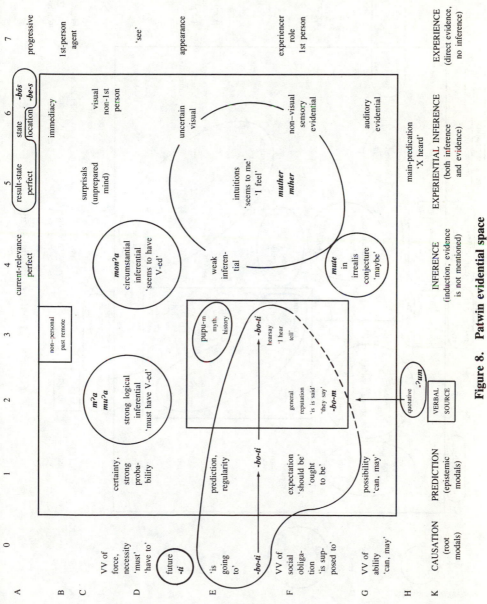

Figure 8. Patwin evidential space

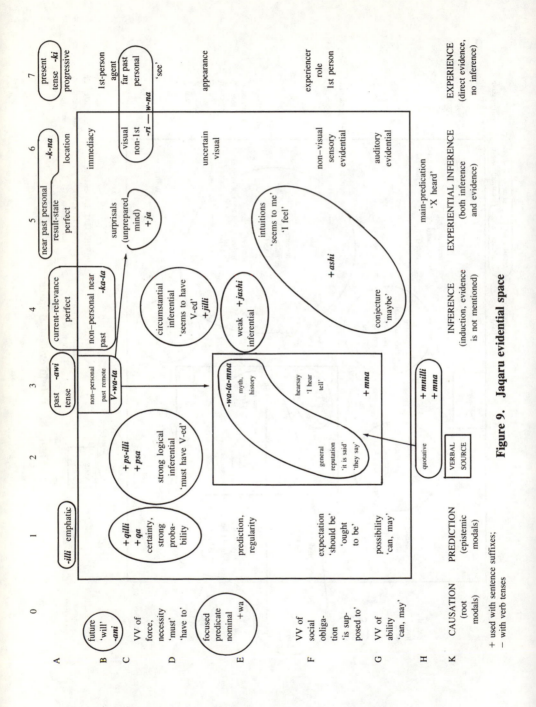

Figure 9. Jaqaru evidential space

296

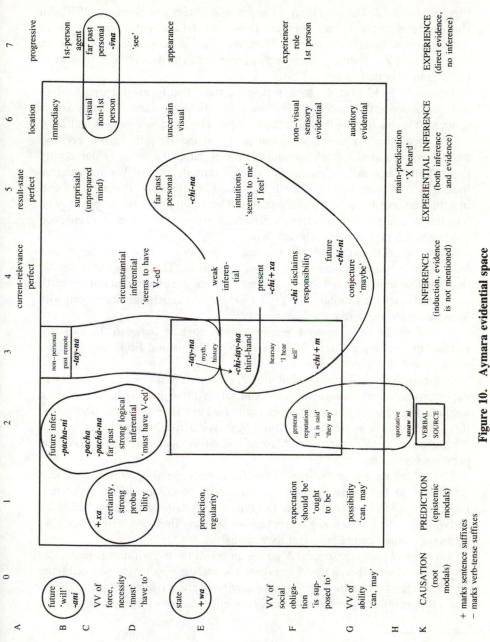

Figure 10. Aymara evidential space

297

Figures 11 and 12. Data in Figure 11 is from Goldstein and Nornang (1970), in phonemic transcription. Data in Figure 12 is from DeLancey (this volume and to appear), in traditional orthography. There are slight dialect differences between these two sources. Sherpa patterns are in Figure 13. The data is from Woodbury (1981) and Schöttelndreyer (1975).

Figures 11 to 13 have the same arrangement, so that forms in corresponding cells are functionally matched. The most specifically evidential forms are in columns (C) and (Ev) at the far left and right sides, and in rows (9) and (10).

The predictive evidentials of columns (C) at the far left, Lhasa -reè and Sherpa -wi, are used to make statements about habitual actions or universally known truths for which no immediate evidence is used, such as 'We make cheese from milk', or example (18) 'The berries must be ripe now' (because it's that time of year, not because I've seen them). These two forms might possibly be historically related: sound correspondences /r ~ w ~ γ/ do exist (Thurgood 1982), though possibly not relevant here.

In columns (Ev) at the right, Lhasa -tuù/-tuq- (rows 3, 4, 6) and Sherpa -nok indicate the existence of some kind of evidence, as in 'The berries are ripe now' (because I've seen or tasted them). These two forms are almost certainly related, as the Jirel language (Strahm 1975) has a pattern very much like Sherpa but with -duk, phonologically like the Lhasa form.[18]

Several of the other morphemes are clearly cognate between the two languages. In the simple past, Lhasa -su/-son- is Sherpa and Jirel -sun.[19] Lhasa rows (4) and (6) -qi- is Sherpa and Jirel -ki-.

In the first-person forms of columns (F, Fcr, Rec) Lhasa has a clear three-way opposition based on aspect and participant role. Although these have evidential implications, they are not primarily evidentials. They are most easily understood if we think of them as yin derived from * 'go', yod derived from * 'be here' (? < * 'have come'), and -yun from * 'come'. Both Tibetan data and typological parallels support this analysis.

Lhasa 'go' is p'yin and 'come' is yon (DeLancey, passim), showing obvious similarities to the verbal inflections. The forms of column (Rec) indicate a participant role as receiver, what DeLancey calls non-agentive including all dative-subject verbs but many others besides such as 'find' and 'remember'. An etymology from 'come' is obviously reasonable.

Typological parallels support * 'go' as an origin for many futures, pasts, and progressives (note Sherpa row 5 in Figure 13, and the upper right part of Figure 17). In the sense 'become', this could easily have given rise to a copula (Sherpa row 1), possibly accounting historically for all instances of Sherpa -in and 'in.

---

[18] Jirel has -kio where Sherpa has -ki-wi. Jirel has -sun, -in, etc.

[19] Compare classical Tibetan ŋa son 'I came/went', which may be an s-causative form of 'oŋ/yoŋ 'come'; DeLancey (to appear) refers to son as a suppletive perfective of the verb 'to go'; an s-perfective of 'come' is also possible.

It is likely that the forms of column (Fcr) which signal current relevance also derive from a form of * 'come', possibly a perfect 'to have come'.

(21a)	DeLancey	Lhasa	*yod*	'current relevance' (orthographic *d* here indicates palatalization)
	Goldstein and Nornang	Lhasa	*yöö*	
	Origin?		**yoŋ-i*	
(21b)		Sherpa	*'woi*	auxiliary of temporary state
	from		*wo-*	past stem of *ḫuŋ-up* 'come' (Woodbury 1981:12)
(21c)		Lhasa	*pə-yöö*	past reportive evidentials
(21d)		Sherpa	*-up-i[nok]*	

It appears that Lhasa *-yöö* either contained an old suffix *-i* (21a,b) or else corresponds to *-i-* (21c,d). Within Sherpa, certain verb stems which Woodbury refers to as "involuntary" (1981 note 6) contain *-i-* where most verbs use *-ki-*, the latter clearly related to the verb 'do', DeLancey's Lhasa *gi-*, Sherpa *ki-*. This last opposition is no longer productive, and a complete list of verbs using *-i-* is needed. (The verb stem *wo-* in (21b) might also be related to a verb 'be, exist, live' frequent in texts, appropriate to the meaning of *'woi*.)

Typological parallels from unrelated or distantly related languages can be helpful. Compare the Chinese *le* perfect-of-current-relevance derived from a verb meaning 'come', *lái* in Mandarin (Li, Thompson and Thompson 1982 note 6, Anderson 1982:234, 239).[20]

Lhasa (Figure 11) shows a very interesting split between column (Ev+) (positive assertion) and column (EvQ) (questioning, negation), which we can explain as follows. Claims about third-person subjects which the speaker has actually observed may be evidentially unmarked as in some other languages (column Ev+). But when questioning or negating such a claim, evidence is more in the forefront of thinking, and the auxiliary *-tuq-* of temporary state (typological analog of Spanish *estar*) is used in an evidential function (column EvQ). The Tibetan uses are obligatory, grammaticalized into paradigms. The same asymmetry exists in English, even though it is not an obligatory category.

---

[20] There are also some intriguing possibilities for cognates. With Mandarin *lái* 'come' compare Sherpa *la* 'raise' plus the *-i-* under discussion. Sherpa *la* is used to express the occurrence (arising) of an emotion or feeling.

The "version" prefixes of the verb in Georgian (a South Caucasian language) are single vowels. One pair *i/u* are most directional and linked to person (1st, 2nd/3rd), which as agents in the Georgian "Perfect" perhaps come closest to Tibetan functions. Sumerian directional forms may also be considered. In both these cases, origins as * 'go' vs. * 'come' are likely.

		C certain, predicted	F first person	Fcr first-person current relevance	Exp experiencer (1st p.)	Ev+ evidenced positive	EvQ evidenced questioned
1 copula, ownership (essential attributes)	+	reè	yĩi				
	Wh	rɛɛ					
	Q	re-pɛɛ					
2 location, existence, having (accidental attributes)	+	yɔɔ̀-reè		yöö yɔɔ yö-pɛɛ̀	tuù	tuù	
	Wh	yɔ̀ɔ-rɛɛ					
	Q						tuq-ɛɛ̀
3 perfect (past still manifest in present)	+	-yɔɔ̀-reè		-yöö	-chu	-šaa	-töö
	Wh	-yɔ̀ɔ-rɛɛ			-chuŋ		-tuq-ɛɛ̀
	Q						
4 present (especially habitual; imperfective)	+	-qi-yɔɔ̀-reè		-qi-yöö̀	(= 04)	-qii	-qi-töö̀
	Wh	-qi-yɔ̀ɔ-rɛɛ					-qi-tuq-ɛɛ̀
	Q						
5 (not distinguished from 4 imperfective)							
6 future	+	-qi-reè	-qi-yĩi	(= F6)	(= F6)	-paa	-pə-tuù
	Wh	-qi-rɛɛ					-pə-tuq-ɛɛ̀
	Q						
7 past (perfective)	+	-pə-reè	-pə-yĩi		-chu	-su	-sôö
	Wh	-pə-rɛɛ			-chuŋ-		-soŋ-ee
	Q						
9 present reportive (hearsay, general knowledge, folklore)	+	-pə-reè					
	Wh						
10 past reportive (3rd-person agent told 1st-person)	+			-pə-yöö̀			

Data from Goldstein and Nornang (1970)

Whenever examples were available, two forms are given: the simple positive in the first row of each cell, and the form for WH-question in the second row. Yes/no-question forms "Q" are illustrated once in columns (C) and (Fcr), but given everywhere in column (EvQ) to show morphophonemic change.

Figure 11. Lhasa Tibetan evidentials

Figure 12. Lhasa Tibetan evidentials

	C certain, predicted	F first person	Fcr first-person current relevance	Rec/Exp receiver/ experiencer toward 1st p.	Ev evidenced
1 copula, ownership, 'be' (essential attributes)	red	yin			
2 location, existence, having, 'be at' (accidental attributes)			yod		'dug
3 perfect				-yuŋ	b=šag (inferential)
4 present (imperfective)	-gi-yod		-gi-yod		-gi-'dug
5 (not distinguished from 4 imperfective)					
6 future	-gi-red	-gi-yin			
7 past (perfective)	-pa-red	-pa-yin		b=yuŋ	s=oŋ
9 present reportive					
10 past reportive	(C9) here?				

Data from DeLancey (this volume and to appear)

There is not enough information to distinguish the meanings of forms in (Ev3) and (C9) or (C10).

Three probable historical morpheme boundaries which are not opaque have been marked with (=).

301

	C certain, predicted	F first person	Fcr first-person current relevance	Exp experiencer (1st-p.)	O temporary state event	Ev evidence
1 copula, ownership (essential attributes)	'in					'nok
2 location, existence, having (accidental attributes)	-wi			-i-nok	'woi	'nok
3 perfect					Pst)'woi (result state)	(PSt) -nok (inferential)
4 present	-i-wi		-i-wi	-i-nok	(non-P.St)'woi (state)	-i-nok
iterative/habitual	-ki-wi			(-ki-nok)		-ki-nok
5 progressive and presaged future	-in ki-wiq				-in 'woi	-ki-nokq
6 future	-ki-wi / -i-wi	-in	-i-wi	(Ev6) here?		-up-nok (only 1st person) (determined to)
7 past (perfective)		(PSt)-in		(PSt)-suŋ	(PSt)-suŋ	(PSt)-nok (inferential includes 3rd-pers. experiencer)
9 present reportive			-up-i-nok	(Fcr 9) here?		
10 past reportive			(PSt)-up-i-nok	(Fcr10) here?		

Data from Woodbury (1981) and Schöttelndreyer (1975).

Verbal inflections are added to the non-past stem unless marked with "PSt" for past stem. The result-state form in cell (O3) is only in Schöttelndreyer; Woodbury has (O4) instead.

Figure 13. Sherpa evidentials

	(C) expected non-1st	(F) expected 1st person	(Fcr) unexpected 1st person	(Rec/Exp) non-visual unexpected (1st?)	(O) unexpected non-1st	(Ev) visual unexpected (non-1st?)
1						
2						
3						
4 non-past	(mɛ̀)	má	é	(ña)	á	ŋá
5 all-the-time, non-surprise? (progressive, imperfective?)	mía					
6 prediction, assumption, non-knowledge	ń			ñá		ŋáa
7 past	mὲ	mà	ὲ	ñà	à	ŋà
8 past all-the-time, non-surprise? (progressive, imperfective?)	mía					ŋàá

Data from Egerod and Hansson (1974:228) and from Thurgood. Parentheses enclose two forms in three-way oppositions where I suspect innovations compared to the Tibetan material, to fit the Akha system of oppositions. With column (F) compare the verb *má* 'be real, true' and the adverb *mámá* 'really, surely' (suggestion from Hansson reported by Thurgood).

Figure 14. Akha sentence particles

303

(22a)   (positive)   He has arrived.   (no evidential)

(22b)   (questioned)   Can you tell if he has arrived?   (evidential function:
                                                          'Is there any evidence present that he has arrived?')

Thus the forms of columns (C) and (EvQ) in Figure 11 are true evidentials, while the other forms are probably evidentially unmarked. Note that in the past tense (row 7, cells Ev+7 and EvQ7) there is no use of evidential *-tuq-*. This is a parallel to Kashaya, where most pasts (not perfects) are neutralized into a single form *-yowǎ* without evidential distinctions. Again an asymmetry. For Sherpa, the most important difference between this analysis and Woodbury's lies in the decision to classify *-suŋ* as evidentially unmarked.[21]

Forms in columns (Ev) are not usually used with first-person subjects. When they are, they have a special sense, as in 'I must be sick', which is a surprise for the speaker. Or they may indicate the non-deliberate nature of the event. The first person was a cause but not a deliberate agent, as in the verbs 'lose, forget, break, spill, cause to fall' or at least not a direct agent, since all derived causatives are in this class (DeLancey, to appear, used the term "non-voluntary"). The etymology of *-suŋ* itself as 'cause to come/go' fits this (see note 19).

Consider now Akha, a Lolo-Burmese language in the Tibeto-Burman family. Its sentence particles are shown in Figure 14. The arrangement here is again different from that of Egerod and Hansson (1974:227–8) or Thurgood, although it is consistent with the uses they report for the forms. They presented a system symmetrical WITHIN Akha; the arrangement here is asymmetrical, but with asymmetries matching almost exactly those of Sherpa, and corresponding column and row labels are added in parentheses. Note that among the "non–sensorial" particles (columns C, F, Fcr and O) those labeled "expected" include the first two, which in Tibetan represented certain knowledge and prediction. Among the "sensorial" particles, which we may take as denoting knowledge linked to temporary conditions rather than pure reasoning (columns Rec/Exp and Ev), the terms "expected/non-expected" were also used by Egerod and Hansson. But here "expected" covers meanings like 'all the time, non-intermittent' and 'non-surprise' and 'luckily' as opposed to their opposites. I have tentatively considered the "visual expected" and non-visual expected to be analogous to Sherpa progressives, and placed them in rows (5) and (8), without examples to verify this in detail.

There are several possible cognates with the Tibetan material. Column (Rec/Exp) *ña* might match Sherpa *-i-nok*.[22] Column (O) *á* might match the *a* of

---

[21] This is a principled analysis, matching a similar decision by Schlichter for Wintu, discussed in the next section.

[22] Akha *ña* might also be compared with classical Tibetan *ñan-* 'hear, obey' and its relatives. Benedict and Matisoff (1972) reconstruct Tibeto-Burman *g-na* 'hear'. Thurgood derives the *ñá* 'will' of immediate intention and purpose from an attested auxiliary verb 'can, able'. But if Figure 14 cell (Exp6) is like Sherpa cell (Ev6), referring to one's own inner feelings or intentions as EVIDENCE for what one will do, a different origin is implied as hypothesis.

Lhasa *-šaa*, *-paa,* or Sherpa *'woi.* Column (Ev) ŋa might match Sherpa *-nok* or else the /ŋ/ in Sherpa *'meŋ-gup-in* 'there are not' where the initial *m-* is the negation (Schöttelndreyer and Schöttelndreyer 1973:77, 80), a verb present also in classical Tibetan *mŋa*ʔ- 'having', I would assume.

Thurgood identifies Akha *é* with Tibetan *yin* < **yin,* a "morpheme found throughout Tibeto-Burman associated with imperfective and/or futurity" (1982:75), though functionally the match seems better to Lhasa *yöö.* In the Bodo-Garo language Nocte there is a form *-min* 'future' which Thurgood decomposes as *m* plus **-yin,* and we might similarly decompose Akha *mέ* into **m-yin.*

Tibetan evidentials are mapped in Figures 15 (Lhasa) and 16 (Sherpa).

Evidentially Unmarked Forms

Not every morpheme which has evidential implications is an evidential. For some languages, the absence of an overt evidential in ongoing present situations has led investigators to label an imperfective aspect marker as an evidential "witnessed present". I do not adopt that approach here (see the definition in (3c)), but rather agree with Schlichter's position on Wintu (this volume, note 12 following Pitkin 1963:173): The suffix *-bEy-* conveys imperfect aspect, not (as Dorothy Lee would have it) a visual evidential. In present-tense contexts, it pragmatically implies visual evidence if not used with another evidential. On the same basis I have considered Kashaya *-ŵǎ* to be an imperfective, not an evidential, and Jaqaru-Aymara *+wa* to be a stative or imperfective auxiliary, not an evidential.[23]

Similarly, certain past markers (mainly punctual) have been taken as past witnessed evidentials. For Aymara, the suffix *-na* is said to mark a personally witnessed or experienced remote past, but "in combinations, the remote is *-V̄na* and is unmarked for data source." It seems more in accord with pragmatic reality to say that *-na* is always unmarked for data source, but in the absence of an evidential to the contrary, it takes the unmarked value, direct personal knowledge.

Exactly this same reasoning led to classifying Sherpa *-suŋ* as a simple past, evidentially unmarked. Kashaya *-yowǎ* also shows neutralization to a single form in the simple past, with loss of evidential distinctions.

Specifically VISUAL evidential morphemes are actually quite rare. Perhaps this is because the most common evidence is visual and thus need not be specifically noted.

The limitations of definition (3c) are necessary in order to avoid including as "evidentials" forms which have little in common with typical evidentials, either in their functions or in their etymological origins.

---

[23] Since "the surface placement of *+wa* is determined by the underlying question" (Hardman, this volume), it appears to be a copular focus marker.

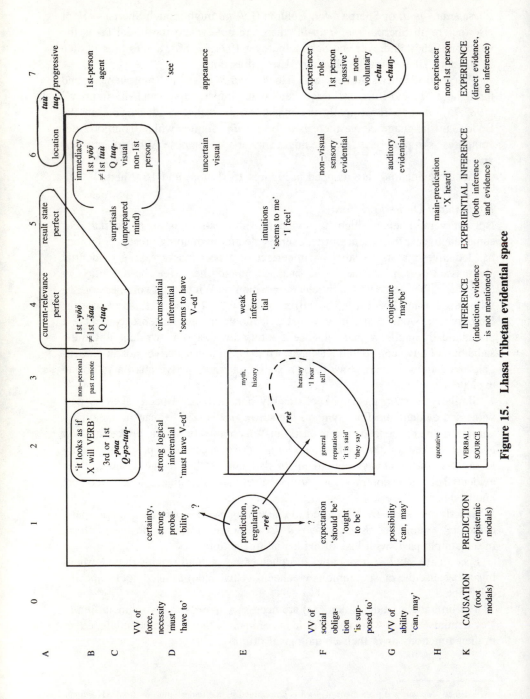

Figure 15. Lhasa Tibetan evidential space

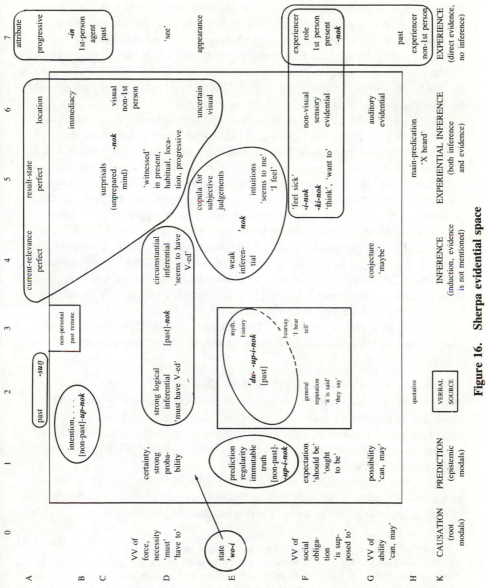

Figure 16. Sherpa evidential space

307

EVIDENTIALS, MOOD, AND MODALITY

Typologically Regular Asymmetries and Suppletion

Some of the asymmetrical links of evidentials with person and tense in Tibetan need to be seen in a wider context. Typological parallels indicate that these can be a matter of mood as well as of evidentiality. The results of a survey of moods,[24] especially in Indo-European, are summarized in the mental map of Figure 17. Toward the top of this map we have at least four different origins for a general future form. The so-called "future" category of particular languages can be a suppletive combination of these different origins.

Thus Latin futures in 3sg. *-et* of some conjugations have 1st sg. forms *-am* with /a/, not /e/. These 1sg. forms are said to be "borrowed" from the subjunctive, which has consistent 3sg. *-at* and 1sg. *-am*. But a 1sg. future has a different kind of "future" meaning from a future of other persons. A speaker can make a statement about his own future action merely by deciding to 'do' it, while for another person's future action the speaker needs to present evidence that the person 'is going to do' it. The asymmetry has a basis in practical conditions.

The Tibetan futures are also suppletive by person. In Figures 11 to 13, cells (C6) and (F6) can perhaps be explained approximately as 'will', predictive for the third person, but deliberate action of the 1st person, thus using different auxiliaries. Cells (O6) and (Ev6) can be rendered as 'is going to' and 'am going to' (current evidence about the future). The difference between third and first-person futures is quite similar to the Latin one.[25]

Many of the asymmetries in the Tibeto-Burman and other evidential systems thus seem to derive historically from systems whose primary use is not evidential.

Evidentials, Modality, and Mood: System Overlap

Many meanings which interact strongly with evidentials have appeared as labels along the boundaries of maps (Figures 2 to 10, 15 and 16). I now offer some interpretation of the overall map coordinates and dimensions, and delimit the semantic nature of evidentials in contrast to other systems. This requires very precise use of terminology.

The lower margin of Figures 2 to 10, 15 and 16 is the primary evidential dimension. Roughly, sources of evidence may be direct experience (at the right), or logical reasoning (at the left), or a combination of the two.

---

[24] Relying on Hahn (1953) and several studies of single languages.

[25] This assumes that the Latin futures in *-e-* are derived from an auxiliary suffix *'be going to', consistent with Hirt's idea that Indo-European optatives go back to such a periphrasis. The Latin "Imperfect Subjunctive" in *-re* is generally recognized as derived from an optative in the form *-se-*, with this same /e/ vowel. Following Hirt we can take this as from *-s-yeH*, the future from *-yeH*, both to be compared with the verb 'go', *-yaH* as it would be written these days. This will be discussed in detail in a forthcoming study of close relations between Latin, Armenian, and Old Irish conjugations.

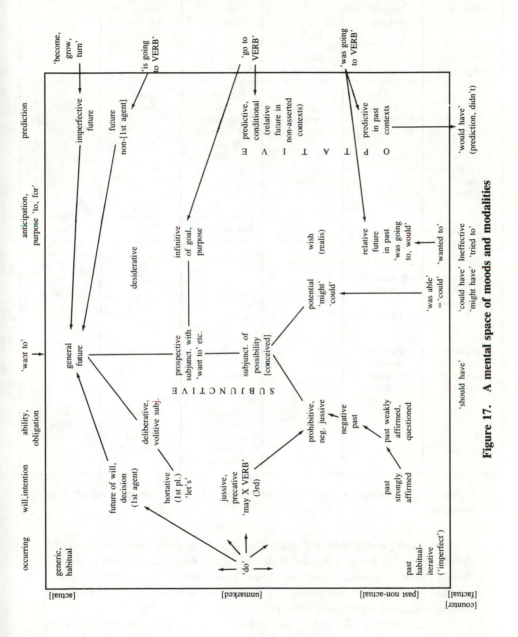

Figure 17. A mental space of moods and modalities

309

actuality (what world)	mood/assertion (asserted, conceived)	aspect	evidentiality (kind of evidence)	modality (strength of evidence or cause)	reason
[recurring] generic tense		habitual, permanent state			
[actual] [present]	[indicative] asserted	[progressive] [temporary state or location]	(unmarked) [direct knowledge] no inference necessary	(unmarked) obvious	facts
[past] directly witnessed		[perfective]			
'am going to'	foreshadowed relative future	[perfect] [inceptive]	[inference from particular kinds or evidence]	probable (obligation, intention)	facts and logic
[non-actual] non-witnessed future or past	[prediction] (future) [optative]				
[counterfactual] or other hypothetical non–actual	[subjunctive] conceived, envisaged, non-asserted		[inference] evidence unspecified	possible 'may, can'	
			[logical deduction] no evidence (epistemic modals)	certain 'must' (causation)	pure logic

Figure 18. Correlated systems: actuality, mood/assertion, aspect, evidentiality, modality

The left margin of the same Figures also appears in a different form along the top of Figure 17, because certain meanings (especially root modals related to causality such as 'should', 'can', and 'must') give rise both to predictive evidentials and to moods and modalities (see the earlier section "logical expectation and evidentials of reported speech").

We can systematically define the core areas of six relevant dimensions in (23), and show some correlations and interactions in Figure 18.

(23a) actuality—what is the claim or proposition about? A present actuality, another real-world past or future, or a hypothetical world?

(23b) mood/assertion—is a claim made at all, or is a proposition merely envisaged as a possibility?

(23c) aspect—what phase of an event is a claim made about?
        i) result (perfect)
          precursor ('is going to')
        ii) entire event (perfective)
          durative, unchanging situation (imperfective)

(23d) evidentiality—what kind of evidence is available for a claim?
        (only relevant to realis claims)

(23e) modality—what is the degree of certainty or kind of CAUSAL source from which one makes a predictive claim

(23f) person (in part)—who is able to make claims of particular kinds?

The scales of Figure 18 suggest how several small mental spaces such as Figures 2 and 17 correlate with each other. Note that Figure 18 shows a close relation between the pair "actuality" and "mood/assertion", and a close relation between the pair "evidentiality" and "modality".[26] Aspect relates to both of these. These correlations do not necessarily imply that meanings in one column can change directly into correlated meanings in another column, though that is sometimes true. Rather, similar content words can be grammaticalized in different ways in different semantic areas. Modalities and evidentials can have common origins.

The semantic spaces and historical meaning shifts studied in this paper suggest one program for the future, as we try to find out how people think and what they think about.

REFERENCES

Anderson, Lloyd. 1982. The 'perfect' as a universal and as a language–particular category. In Hopper, ed., pp. 227–264.

Barnes, Janet. 1984. Evidentials in the Tuyuca verb. International Journal of American Linguistics 50.255–271. [received as this paper was going to press]

Benedict, Paul K. and James A. Matisoff. 1972. Sino–Tibetan: A conspectus. Cambridge University Press.

Berlin, Brent and Paul Kay. 1969. Basic color terms, their universality and evolution. Berkeley: University of California Press.

DeLancey, Scott. (to appear). Categories of non–volitional actor in Lhasa Tibetan.

Egerod, Soren and Inge-lill Hansson. 1974. An Akha conversation on death and funeral. Acta Orientalia 36.225–284.

Givón, Talmy. 1981. Evidentiality and epistemic space. Paper for the Evidentials symposium, University of California at Berkeley.

---

[26] Under the influence of evidential space, I am inclined to put absolute LOGICAL certainty at the opposite pole of the modality scale from the EMPIRICALLY obvious. These are the left and right extreme columns of Figures 11 to 14. From some other points of view (Givon 1982) they would be closely related, since both kinds of assertion claim to be beyond doubting or questioning.

Goldstein, Melvyn C. and Nawang L. Nornang. 1970. Modern spoken Tibetan: Lhasa dialect. Seattle: University of Washington Press.

Greenberg, Joseph H. 1978. Diachrony, synchrony, and language universals. Universals of human language, vol. 1, ed. by Joseph H. Greenberg, pp. 61–91. Stanford, California: Stanford University Press.

Hahn, E. Adelaide. 1953. Subjunctive and optative: their origin as futures. New York: American Philological Association.

Hale, Austin, ed. 1975. Collected papers on Sherpa and Jirel. Nepal Studies in Linguistics II. Kirtipur: Summer Institute of Linguistics. Institute of Nepal and Asian Studies, Tribhuvan University.

Hopper, Paul, ed. 1982. Tense and Aspect: between Semantics and Pragmatics, Amsterdam: John Benjamins B. V.

Li, Charles, Sandra A. Thompson, and R. MacMillan Thompson. 1982. The discourse motivation for the perfect aspect: the Mandarin particle *le*. in Hopper ed. pp. 19–44.

Lyons, John. 1966. Towards a "notional" theory of the parts of speech. Journal of Linguistics 2.209–236.

McLendon, Sally. 1981. Evidentials in Eastern Pomo. Paper for the Evidentials symposium, University of California at Berkeley.

Schöttelndreyer, Burkhard. 1975. Clause patterns in Sherpa. In Hale ed. pp. 1–57.

———— and Heiderose. 1973. Sherpa texts. Clause, sentence and discourse patterns in selected languages of Nepal, Part III. ed. Austin Hale pp. 53–176. Norman, Oklahoma: Summer Institute of Linguistics.

Strahm, Esther. 1975. Clause patterns in Jirel. In Hale ed. pp. 71–146.

Thurgood, Graham. 1982. The Sino–Tibetan copula *wəy. Cahiers de Linguistique Asie Orientale 9:1.65–81.

Woodbury, Anthony C. 1981. Evidentiality in Sherpa verbal categories. MS. prepared for the Evidentials symposium, University of California at Berkeley.

EIGHTEEN

Self-Evidence and Ritual Speech

John W. Du Bois
University of California at Los Angeles

Where got I that truth?
Out of a medium's mouth,
Out of nothing it came,
Out of the forest loam,
Out of dark night where lay
The crowns of Nineveh.
—W. B. Yeats*

What evidence, what authority, can a speaker offer for religious utterance?[1] This question may rarely or never rise to the level of conscious thought for the individual within a traditional society. Nevertheless, the unexpressed demand for authority remains, and is visible in its consequences. It becomes a specifically linguistic issue once it begins to determine the linguistic shape of mythic, prophetic, or ritual utterances. The problem of evidence, or more broadly authority, confronts the utterer of the sacred as well as of the profane; yet the evidential resources which he may draw on in the two spheres are very different. Language reflects this fact. When a speaker turns to provide support for an ordinary utterance, he finds that his language offers, perhaps, a range of linguistic forms

---

*(Reprinted with permission of Macmillan Publishing Company from "Fragments" (*Collected Works*) by W. B. Yeats. Copyright 1933 by Macmillan Publishing Company, renewed 1961 by Bertha Georgie Yeats)

[1] Earlier versions of this paper were presented at the Evidentials Symposium in Berkeley on May 17, 1981 and at the UCLA Linguistics Colloquium on November 13, 1981. I would like to thank the participants of both meetings for their helpful comments, several of which have been incorporated here. I thank Wallace Chafe, Talmy Givón, Dell Hymes, Judith Irvine, Joel Kuipers, Jean-Marie Marandin, Johanna Nichols, and Kenneth Whistler for useful comments and criticism on earlier versions of the paper. I especially thank Elsa Vittaniemi for extensive advice on issues in comparative religion, and for helping in many other ways.

I plan to present a more complete treatment of this topic in a full–length study tentatively titled *Words without speakers: The language of ritual in traditional society* (in progress).

to mark the appropriate source of knowledge: something seen, inferred, heard told. But for a religious utterance, usually something more is needed. And usually, within a traditional society, something more is available: a special form of the language reserved for ritual and similar uses. I will propose below that the characteristic form of these special varieties serves precisely to satisfy the demand for authority: in a certain sense, these speech varieties serve to make the ritual utterance appear as self-evident.

To show how this could be so, I must address three issues. First, the nature of ritual speech. Since I aim here at a general theoretical formulation, I examine ritual speech from as broad a point of view as possible. I survey reports of ritual speech varieties from a genetically and areally diverse sampling of the world's languages, and attempt to determine their characteristic features. Second, the nature of evidence and authority in relation to the general theory of the speech event. Here, I introduce several needed theoretical innovations. Third, the relation between ritual speech form and the social constitution of the speech event. Here, the striking crosslinguistic convergences in ritual varieties discovered in the first section propel to its ultimate solution the theoretical problem of the second. Demonstrating this connection is, of course, the crux of my proposed theory of ritual speech.

RITUAL SPEECH

Ritual speech has not yet received much attention from a theoretical point of view, though it is fairly well attested in a number of individual linguistic ethnographies. Mythic speech has in recent years received considerable serious attention (Hymes 1981; Bright 1982; McLendon 1982), but there are a number of distinct issues which arise for ritual speech that deserve treatment in their own right.

Ritual speech I define as speech distinctively characteristic of ritual. Ritual itself I understand, following Victor Turner, as 'prescribed formal behavior for occasions not given over to technological routine, having reference to beliefs in mystical beings or powers' (1967:19), 'a transformative performance revealing major classifications, categories, and contradictions of cultural processes' (1977:77). (Cf. Geertz (1973b:112) on ritual as, simply, 'consecrated behavior.') The importance of speech in ritual has been stressed especially by Malinowski (1935) and, more recently, by Tambiah (1968, 1979): 'The vast majority of ritual and magical acts combine word and deed. . . . The rite usually consists of a close interweaving of *speech* (in the form of utterances and spells) and *action* (consisting of the manipulation of objects)' (Tambiah 1979:360). Since it is necessary to obtain precise information on both speech (including paralanguage) and ethnographic context, the range of usable sources is limited to a fairly small set of studies—primarily those in the tradition presently embodied in the ethnography of speaking, with early forebears in Malinowski and Sapir. Although there are a few valuable and recent general studies of ritual speech (Basso 1979, Chafe 1981), and several general studies of related matters (of political oratory, Bloch 1975, and Irvine 1979, of performance—much of it in ritual—Bauman 1977), many of the most important and interesting questions have not yet been addressed, or even formulated. Thus, much of what follows covers new theoretical territory.

The survey sample is limited to languages used in technologically simple societies in which traditions of widespread literacy have played no general role. The languages are Quiché (Bunzel 1952; Norman 1980; author's field work), Tzeltal (Stross 1974), Tzotzil (Bricker 1973; Gossen, 1974a, 1974b), and Yucatec (Bricker 1974; Burns 1980), all Mayan languages of Guatemala and Mexico; Cuna (Stout 1948; Sherzer 1974, 1977, 1981, 1982; cf. Lévi-Strauss 1963a), a Chibchan language of Panama and Colombia; Waiwai (Fock 1963), a Cariban language of Guyana and Brazil; Zuñi (Bunzel 1929/30) and Keresan (=Keres) (White 1944), two language isolates of New Mexico; Wintu (Du Bois 1935; Schlichter 1981), a Wintun language of California: Wishram (Spier and Sapir 1930; French 1958; Hymes 1966, 1981), a Chinookan language of Washington and Oregon; Seneca (Chafe 1961, 1981; cf. Foster 1974), an Iroquoian language of New York; Malagasy (Keenan 1974, 1975; Keenan and Ochs 1979), Rotinese (Fox 1974), and Kiriwina (Malinowski 1922, 1935; cf. Tambiah 1968), Austronesian languages of Madagascar, Indonesia, and Trobriand, respectively. Javanese (Becker 1979), an Austronesian language of Java, is also consulted, though on a separate basis, due to the considerable development of literacy in Javanese society. The bias of the sample toward Central and North American languages is partly due to the author's greater familiarity with these languages, but it is, perhaps, just as much a product of the especially active interest in the ethnography of speaking among scholars in this area. I will begin with an extended example of ritual speech from Quiché, followed by a general survey.

The Quiche marriage ritual known as *chupb'al q'aaq'* 'extinguishing the fire' is characteristic of ceremonial speeches delivered by the *k'amal b'eh* 'guide' (literally, 'bringer of the road'), a specialist who, having attained some rank in the traditional religious hierarchy, undergoes several years' apprenticeship to a senior *k'amal b'eh* in order to acquire his ritual knowledge (Norman 1980:389). The following discussion is based primarily on the observations of Will Norman; my own research on Quiché ritual with a *k'amal b'eh* from Olintepeque (carried out in 1975 in conjunction with anthropological field work directed by Janet Shuster Trump) agrees generally with Norman's findings in Nahualá and Santa Catarina Ixtahuacán.

> *Aree k'u   ri   kamiik,   mal k'u tyoox,*
> and-so   the   today   so-thanks
> And so today, so thanks,

karaj ne7   (x)saqirik,
perhaps   it-got-light
perhaps it got light,

karaj ne7   xpakataj   jun   saantalaj   uwach   uleew,
            it-dawned   a   holy   world
perhaps a holy world dawned,

xneek' aama   chu7loq,
I-was-brought   now-here
I was brought now here,

xneeyaaka   chu7loq,
I-was-raised   now-here
I was raised now here,

chwa   ri   nutz' aaq,
before   the   my wall
before my wall,

chwa   ri   nuk' axtuun,
before   the   my-fortress
before my fortress,

chwii   nub' iineem,
above   my-walking
above my walking,

chwii   nuchakaneem.
above   my-crawling
above my crawling.
            (Norman 1980:388; free translation added)

The example differs from colloquial Quiché in several ways. Most strikingly, it is highly parallelistic, with grammatically parallel couplets that are based on a tradition of paired, semantically related lexical items (underlined in the citation above). For example: *k'am, yak* 'bring, raise'; *b'iineem, chakaneem* 'walking, crawling'. The ordering of many pairs is irreversible (**chakaneem b'iineem*). Some words do not appear outside the context of their lexical pair; thus *k'axtuun* 'fortress' only occurs paired with *tz'aaq* 'wall'. The concatenation of meanings in many of the pairs gives rise to a metonymic, metaphoric, or otherwise idiomatic meaning: the pair *tz'aaq, k'axtuun,* literally 'wall, fortress', means 'home'; *k'am, yak,* literally 'bring, raise', means 'hire a *k'amal b'eh*'. Knowledge of the metaphorical significance of most of the pairs is restricted to the specialists. Formation of the couplets themselves is governed by a simple but strict surface syntactic rule. Roughly, the second line is formed by making a copy of the first, starting from any constituent boundary and continuing rightward up to the position of the first paired lexical item, where the second is substituted (for a more precise formulation see Norman 1980:395–97). Quiché ritual speech includes some archaic elements and grammatical processes which, though attested in sixteenth and seventeenth century documents, have been lost in modern colloquial Quiché; for example, the use of *mi* as a recent past tense marker. The ritual text is uttered with a high degree of fluency, without hesitations, in a stylized intonation contour. And, of course, in actual use the speech is embedded in a specific ritual context, with prescribed postures, proxemics, behaviors, attitudes, and trappings.

How much of this is paralleled in other languages? Some of the more significant crosslinguistic convergences in ritual speech characteristics are as follows:

Ritual register. A single meaning is often expressed with two different lexical items, one in colloquial speech, the other reserved for ritual. In Keresan, colloquial *coroyá* 'mountain bluebird' is replaced in ritual contexts by *sto·c; tcá'apɛ* 'eat' is replaced by *posikomɛ́; omʯ́'na* 'you may go now' by *po· tiyak'o'ó* (White 1944:163–64). In Cuna colloquial *iti* 'water' is replaced in magical-curing chants by *wiasali,* and in puberty-rite chants by *nukki kia* (Sherzer 1981:12). In Wintu, the exclamation *ha·haq* 'look upon me' is 'used only by shamans and not related to the word for 'to see, look' ' (Schlichter 1981:107). In Kiriwina, *mulubida* 'bush hen' is *gelu* in ritual speech (Malinowski 1935:219; cf. 1922:432). This ritual register is often built up from elements which are archaic, borrowed, tabooed, or formulaic (see following items).

Archaistic elements. Ritual register often appears to contain archaic elements. In Wintu, 'obsolescent expressions survive longer in shamanistic speech' (Schlichter 1981:109). In Quiché, an old recent past marker, as well as an obsolescent type of adverbial incorporation, is retained in ritual speech (Norman 1980:389). White (1944) rightly cautions against too quick an assumption of archaism for obscure ritual forms; what is certainly significant, however, is the indigenous *belief* in archaism. Thus, Hrdlička was told that 'some of the old men of Laguna know and still use in certain ceremonies an archaic language [called *Hamasija,* said to mean, roughly, 'old, ancient'] which the younger generation can neither speak nor fully understand' (cited in White 1944:166). Such beliefs in the archaism of the ritual speech variety are common, whether or not actual archaism can be demonstrated to the historical linguist's satisfaction.

Borrowed elements. The source of ritual register elements is often a neighboring language (or dialect), even where no superstrate relation exists and the borrowing language does not lack the borrowed term. In Rotinese, the second member of a lexical pair is often borrowed from a neighboring dialect (Fox 1974:80ff), and Tzotzil pairs are often made up of a native and a Spanish term (Bricker 1974:372). In Hopi, in a song from the Powamu ceremony (claimed by one investigator to be 'composed entirely of archaic words') some otherwise obscure terms are probably loans from Keresan, according to White (1944:162).

Euphemism and metaphor. Ritual speech is often highly circumlocutory. In Keresan, colloquial *h'a·wɛ* 'snow' is replaced by ritual *naback'ᵃ po·tca,* lit. 'let a white blanket cover(?)' (White 1944:164). In Cuna *poni* 'evil spirit' is replaced by *urwetule* 'angry person'; *nae* 'walk, go' is replaced by *aypanne,* lit.

'swing back and forth like a hammock' (Sherzer 1981:12–13). The Rotinese formula expressing 'male child' in ritual speech is the pair *popi koa* // *lanu manu* 'a rooster's tailfeathers' // 'a cock's plume' (Fox 1974:75).

Meaning opaqueness.   The effect of the above four points is often obscurity in meaning, even for those members of the culture for whom the ritual is being carried out, such as the patient in a curing ritual—and sometimes even for the ritual practitioner. In Rotinese, 'This ritual code, in its entirety, is probably beyond the comprehension of any of its individual participants' (Fox 1974:83). For Kiriwina, Malinowski speaks of the 'coefficient of weirdness in the language of magic' (1935:218ff). Wintu shamans may call up spirits which speak through them in foreign languages unintelligible to the nonspecialists present (Schlichter 1981:102–03, 105–06; cf. section on mediated speech). The Cuna curer uses a language which is usually not understood by the patient or other persons present, although it is understood by the supernatural *suar mimmi* 'stick babies' to whom it is addressed (Sherzer 1974:272). The mumbled speech of Yucatec shamans is called *xwala' t'aan* 'unintelligible speech' (Burns 1980:309–310).

Semantic-grammatical parallelism.   The basic structural principle governing many ritual languages is semantic and, frequently, grammatical parallelism in which two or more successive lines express synonymous or otherwise closely related meanings. Often such couplets are built on a tradition of lexical pairs. Parallelism is a basic principle of all the Mayan languages I know, and of Cuna, Kiriwina, Rotinese and many other ritual languages (cf. Jakobson 1966, Fox 1974:66, Bauman 1977; see also the Malagasy, Wishram, and Quiché citations below.)

Marked voice quality.   The voice quality which the ritual specialist employs is sometimes marked. In Cuna chanting (*namakke*) the specialist employs a tense voice quality (*wai sae*) accomplished through pharyngeal tightening (Sherzer 1974:273). In Kiriwina, certain types of ritual speech appear to involve a special voice quality (Malinowski 1922:436–437, 1935:224).

Fluidity.   Ritual speech is typically more fluent than colloquial speech. In Seneca, ritual speech is smoother, without false starts, afterthoughts, or other disfluencies (Chafe 1981:134–136). Wintu shamanistic register is characterized by the absence of the 'hesitation-type connective *ʔunaˑ*' (Schlichter 1981:123). If a Zuñi speaker is called on to display impromptu verbal skill in a ritual context, he must handle the ritual vocabulary and rhythms correctly 'and, above all, speak without any hesitation or fumbling and for as long as possible' (Bunzel 1929/30:615).

Intonational restriction.   Ritual speech often has a characteristic stylized intonation contour, eliminating alternatives available in colloquial speech. A Seneca ritual variety is characterized by a set of short prosodic phrases with final rising contour, closed by a phrase with falling contour; 'Almost no intonational variety is possible' (Chafe 1981:140). Cuna ritual speech is described as 'chanted' (Sherzer 1974:273), while Kiriwina is 'singsong' (Malinowski 1935:219).

Gestalt knowledge. The ritual text often appears to be known (and learned) as an indivisible whole. Specialists are often unable to present their chants in line-by-line fragments for the investigator, and they teach the texts (whether to outside scholar or indigenous novice) through many repetitions of the whole. In Kiriwina, 'Magicians as a rule cannot repeat their spells slowly or piecemeal or in an ordinary voice' (Malinowski 1935:224). Mojave memorized texts are traditionally delivered in a rapid staccato, and informants have great difficulty in slowing the sequence down, even though it is composed of short sentences (Devereux 1964:268).

Personal volition disclaimer. The ritual speaker often explicitly disclaims any credit for or influence on what is said. A traditional source is often credited instead. In recreating (in English) the Sunday morning speech of a Chinook 'crier', a Chinook speaker said, 'Me—I'm not telling you this myself. I'm only giving you the revelations which I've learned from somebody else' (Hymes 1981:89). The Iroquois longhouse speaker stresses his inadequacy for the role as he allows himself to be coaxed into it (Foster 1974:364). A Malagasy ritual speechmaker said:

Manao azafady aho,	I excuse myself,
fa tsy tompon'ity . . .	for (I) am not a master of this . . .
tsy tompon-dalana fa mpanohy,	not an originator of paths but a continuer,
tsy tompon-dia fa mpanaraka . . .	not an originator of journeys but a follower . . .
tsy tompon-teny fa mpindrana.	not an originator of words but a BORROWER.

(Keenan and Ochs 1979:144; emphasis in original, line breaks added)

Shifter avoidance. In much of ritual speech, shifters are avoided, especially those which index the speaker as an individual, particularly 'I' (cf. (11) above). In Seneca the words for 'I' and 'you', though frequent in conversation, are present in ritual only in opening and closing remarks (Chafe 1981:142); for the Iroquois it is a harsh criticism of a speaker in the Thanksgiving ritual to say 'He's got too much "I" in there' (Foster 1974:364). The Cuna ritual chant used in grabbing a dangerous snake, 'like all Kuna magical chants, is a third person narrative' (Sherzer 1982:318). The specialist constantly refers to himself (or to his spirit) using a third person nominal or pronominal ('the specialist', 'he'), while he usually refers to the snake by his spirit name (Sherzer 1982:312). (Shifter avoidance does not apply to all genres of ritual speech, however; in some genres, 'I' is quite prevalent.)

Ancestral model. The ritual speech variety is often believed to be the way the ancestors spoke. Very old people, it is believed, may approach this variety; for the Rotinese, ritual speech is 'an ancestral language which they continue'. Some former elders approaching great age are said to have 'ceased to speak ordinary language and uttered only ritual statements' (Fox 1974:83; cf. 455, fn. 4). Tzeltal ritual speech is labeled *poko k'op* 'ancient speech' (the term also subsumes traditional music), and is held to be 'the way and the words that people spoke in ancient times (elegant, stylized, serious, nonmalicious speech . . .)' (Stross 1974:221). Respected elders stereotypically speak a similar variety (1974:224).

Mediated speech. Despite the widespread occurrence of mediation in ritual speech, the unity of this phenomenon has scarcely been recognized; hence, I devote a somewhat fuller discussion to the matter (but see Hymes 1972:60–61). What I mean by mediated speech is the passing of the message through an additional link (or links), so that the simple relation between speaker and hearer is made complex. In its most developed form, the entire speech event may be duplicated, with each role doubly represented. The following shows types of mediated speech used by different groups.

For Wishram, Spier and Sapir (1930; cf. the valuable distillation in Hymes 1966) report on the ceremony for bestowal of a name. In the midst of relatives and friends gathered for this very important occasion, the one who was to be named was flanked by the two individuals who were to carry out the ceremony. The first of these uttered the first sentence of the ritual in a low voice; then the second repeated the same words in a loud voice, and the people answered '*a:xi:*'. This sequence was repeated with the next portion of the ritual text, and so on, to the end. At this point the individual was considered to be, in some sense, a reincarnation of his long-dead namesake, which demonstrates the actual ritual efficacy of the procedure. In this ritual, a duplication of speech roles is quite overt.

Wintu shamans employ an assistant to 'interpret' their utterances for the audience (for example, the person being cured). The shaman enters a sort of trance during his seance, and speaks in a ritual variety characterized by obsolescent words and somewhat opaque metaphor and circumlocution; he may even speak in a foreign language. The interpreter repeats the shaman's message more simply, elaborating any prophecies made. Thus between the shaman's utterance and the patient's comprehension lies an official process of mediation. In fact, the shaman is himself but a further mediator, as shown in the statement of one highly regarded Wintu interpreter: 'Doctors don't know what they say or sing. The spirits tell them their words' (Du Bois 1935:107). The Wishram shaman also had a spokesman 'who repeated aloud what the spirit communicated to the shaman' (Spier and Sapir 1930:213).

The Cuna 'congress chant', encompassing religious, historical, and political content, is chanted by a 'chanting chief' to a 'responding chief', who after each verse responds with the stereotyped feedback *teki* 'it is so', before the assembled villagers. The chant is in *sakla kaya* 'chief's language', a ritual variety distinguished from the colloquial *tule kaya* 'people's language' by distinct paralinguistic features, lexical items, opaque metaphors, and a high degree of semantic-grammatical parallelism. After about two hours of this somewhat opaquely metaphorical chanting, an *arkar* (specialist interpreter) stands up to interpret it to the audience (Sherzer 1974). Notice that the role of the changing chief's addressee is not filled directly by the audience but by the designated responder, another ritual specialist. The audience is further removed from this chanter-responder interaction, as it only receives the message via the interpreter, and then in a different code as well. Thus, the pervasive duplication of speech roles encompasses speaker, addressee, and code. I analyze it as follows:

> chanter : interpreter :: responder : audience :: chief's language : people's language

The message, held to be in some sense constant throughout, binds together the two halves of what, in effect, has become a duplex speech event.[2] The phenomenon of designated responder is also reported in ritual and political functions for Waiwai and other South American languages (Fock 1963), and in myth-telling functions for Yucatec (Burns 1980). The stereotyped feedback characteristic here may be found even where no official responder is designated. In Seneca, some members of the audience interject at the end of each paragraph-like unit the exclamation *nyoh* (like *amen*), beyond which 'It would be unthinkable for a member of the audience to interject a comment' (Chafe 1981:141). (Note also the Wishram response *a:xi:*, above.) The Seneca speaker sometimes closes his eyes as he delivers his ritual monologue (1981:141), underscoring the supression of ordinary speaker-addressee interaction.

In Javanese shadow theater the 'essential audience' ('without whom the play is pointless') are 'spirits, demons and creatures, gods, and ancestors.' The non-essential audience are the people, 'who may or may not be present and who in some sense overhear much of the drama.' Though much of the nonessential audience cannot understand portions of the performance in Old Javanese and Sanskrit, they know that the appropriate members of the essential audience do understand. In all this, the performer is 'above all a man who can be "entered", a "medium"' (Becker 1979:230–232).

In the crosslinguistic convergences above I have presented some of the most salient features which distinguish ritual speech from ordinary speech (cf. also Bloch 1975:13; Bauman 1977:16). These cannot yet be called universals. Only as linguistic ethnographies systematically address each point will it become possible to decide that issue. Taking a somewhat more abstract and fundamental perspective on these features, we can summarize the basic principles of ritual speech under four headings:

---

[2] There is, to be sure, a directionality in this structure; the two manifestations of the duplex speech event are not equal. The utterance of the chief is prior both temporally and conceptually to the derivative utterance of the *arkar*. Such manifest inequality may contribute to preserving the perceived authority of the prime speaker: a failure in oracular prediction is typically laid at the door of its interpreter, not the misread oracle.

1. COMPLEMENTARITY. Some formal features of ritual speech are in social-contextual complementary distribution with those of ordinary speech.
2. CONSTRAINT. A restriction of colloquial speech alternatives narrows the range of expressive variation possible in ritual speech.
3. PARALLELISM. Segments of the message are made to coincide with syntagmatically contiguous segments at the levels of sound, grammar, and meaning.
4. MEDIATION. The immediacy of ordinary speech interaction is modified through mediation and speech role doubling or, simply, by subordination to a generalized nonpersonal role.

EVIDENCE AND AUTHORITY

The problem of evidence is clarified if we first draw a distinction between providing evidence for a statement and providing authority for it. I propose as an initial principle that NO UTTERANCE IS ACCEPTED WITHOUT AUTHORITY. In a large subset of cases, the authority provided will be that of visual evidence, inferential evidence, and so on. But providing evidence is simply a special case of providing authority. This formulation forces us to take seriously two questions. First, what is the domain of applicability of evidentiality? Second, what alternative sources of authority are there besides evidence?

It will be helpful to begin by considering implications of the term 'self-evident'. A statement is sometimes called self-evident if it is considered a basic or foundational tenet of a particular culture—one that is ordinarily presupposed and, indeed, would ordinarily remain unremarked. In such uses as 'We hold these truths to be self-evident, that all men are created equal . . .' the utterers imply that they need not spell out the evidence because any rational person will reach the same conclusion through his own direct examination of the evidence, which is accessible. Again, the term 'self-evident' may be used when a linguist presents several sentences from a language on a handout and says, 'Given examples one through six, the fact that this language is ergative is self-evident'—or even just, 'Given these examples, the conclusion is self-evident.' In all these cases, the speaker effectively distances himself from the proposition he wishes to convey, and simply puts the hearer—or claims to put the hearer—DIRECTLY IN TOUCH WITH THE EVIDENCE, so that the hearer can frame the proposition himself. Indeed, it is the hearer who must actively construct the implicit meaning if he is told nothing more than that 'the conclusion' is self-evident. The 'speaker' may in a sense not be a speaker at all, since he may never actually perform the illocutionary act of asserting the proposition in question. The persuasive potency of such an approach is that the hearer is not asked to take anything on faith; he draws his own conclusions.

I propose a somewhat different, technical definition of 'self-evident': An utterance is self-evident if the evidence (or authority) for it is found in the utterance itself. The utterance does not receive its authority through appeal to external evidence such as seeing or hearing an event, but from characteristics internal to the utterance itself. I include 'authority' in the definition because it is more typically authority, and not evidence strictly conceived, which resides in the utterance. Self-evidence, in this sense, can be established as such only for particular cultures. Members in the grip of a particular culture will accept, perhaps unconsciously, that certain utterances carry their authority within themselves.

But what is the function that evidence ultimately serves? Evidence is used to persuade, and persuasion is a perlocutionary act, involving as it does a change in the state of mind of the hearer. So we are led beyond the utterance itself, and beyond the speaker as well, to consider the role of the hearer. The critical listener sifts through what is said, deciding what he will accept as reliable and what he will not. In this process there are four basic questions, at least, that the hearer may ask in order to gauge the reliability of the utterance. The burden of these questions falls as much on the speaker as on the utterance:

1. How does the speaker know?
2. What are his interests, and how might interests distort assertions?
3. Is he sincere, or is he lying?
4. Is he fallible?

Although there are other matters into which a critical listener might probe, these four—knowledge, interests, sincerity, and fallibility—stand at the core of the problem of reliability. Given that a speaker knows that his utterance will be evaluated in accordance with these questions, he may choose to defer, through quotation, to a second speaker who will withstand the scrutiny better. Thus, the issue of who is being quoted receives its importance, as Aristotle recognized when he distinguished three categories of quoted speakers—in order of increasing value, (a) 'recent' witnesses (i.e. contemporaries) who had an interest in the business at hand, (b) recent disinterested witnesses, and (c) 'ancient' witnesses (e.g. deceased poets and lawmakers) (*Rhetoric*, Bk. 1, Ch. 15). In addition, the linguistic characteristics of the speaker's own speech contribute to persuasion by defining his ethos as trustworthy: 'This trust . . . should be created by the speech itself' (*Rhetoric*, Bk. 1, Ch. 2).

I propose a distinction among participants in the speech event: The PRIME SPEAKER is the individual who is originally responsible for framing the proposition, the original performer of the illocutionary act. The PROXIMATE SPEAKER is the individual who actually utters the sentence, the performer of the utterance act.[3] When a speaker is speaking in his own right he is both prime speaker and

---

[3] This distinction is related but far from equivalent to the distinction made by French scholars (Benveniste, Ducrot, etc.) between the *sujet parlant* and the *sujet de l'énonciation*. On a rather different footing, see Goffman (1974, 1981).

proximate speaker; when he is repeating the words of another he is the proximate speaker only, and the quoted individual is the prime speaker. (In the first case I will speak of an 'ego prime speaker', in the second of an 'alter prime speaker'.)

In addition, I distinguish between arbitrary and indexic (cf. Peirce 1885) signs of speaker reliability. If a speaker marks an utterance with a morpheme indicating certain truth, this is an arbitrary sign of reliability; but if at the same time his voice reveals certain characteristic rhythmic irregularities, he is likely to be perceived as lying, on the basis of what is taken as an index of unreliability. There is a crucial difference between arbitrary and indexic signs of reliability in the extent to which they are subject to speaker control.[4] As Bateson observes, 'Insofar as a message is conscious and voluntary, it could be deceitful. . . . But discourse about relationship is commonly accompanied by a mass of semivoluntary kinesic and autonomic signals which provide a more trustworthy comment on the verbal message' (1972:137). Combining notions from Aristotle and Peirce, I would suggest that the most powerful determinants of ethos are indexic, precisely because they are difficult to manipulate at will.

Anthropologists, sociologists, and linguists have presented some preliminary insights into the problem of authority or validation for religious utterances, especially myth. Regarding myth, Lévi-Strauss states, 'Although experience contradicts theory, social life validates cosmology by its similarity of structure. Hence cosmology is true' (1963b:212). Hymes speaks of a 'circle of validation':

> Why should people say certain things when the first salmon and swallows come? Because in the myth Coyote had said that they should. Why should one believe Coyote said such things? Believe the myth? Because what he, what the myth, said the swallows would do (come with the first salmon) and the people would do when they came, observably is the case. (1981:305–306; cf. 1966:144, 155)

(Hymes also cites validation accrued by the traditional reproduction of received words.) Although such circles of validation are of the highest importance, they operate at the level of semantic content rather than linguistic form: propositions true of the world match propositions true in the myth. This process may not be sufficient where the phenomena of experience are variable or indeterminate. A proposition about the health of a particular individual undergoing a curing ritual may match the world one day and not the next. Thus, in the sphere of indeterminate phenomena authority leans to linguistic form (e.g. in a ritual curing text) because it is within the domain of symbolic form itself that it may still be possible to achieve a validating circle. Geertz has observed that 'the imbuing of a certain specific complex of symbols . . . with a persuasive authority . . . is the essence of religious action' (1973b:112). The question remains of how this is achieved.

---

[4] Though a recent article by Goffman (1978) maintains that individuals manipulate paralinguistic and quasi-linguistic signals to a greater extent than is generally admitted.

In a typology of mood and evidential systems in language, Nichols (1978) defined a class of mood categories in which the speaker takes no active role in framing the situation reported, so that the basis of authority becomes a problem. The category includes nomic, hearsay, mythic, and other moods—to which we might add ritual speech. In the nomic category, that of general truths like 'Glass breaks', the authority is directly available in the experience of each member of the culture. For hearsay/quotation, the appeal for authority is referred to an alter prime speaker. For myth, the speaker may rely at least in part on the semantic circle of validation and the traditional repetition of words heard from an earlier generation. Thus, in Kashaya Pomo myths are told using the 'quotative/hearsay' evidential suffix -do without, however, casting any doubt on the veracity of the myth (Oswalt, this volume).[5] Likewise, Eastern Pomo myths are told in the 'hearsay' evidential mode (McLendon 1982:288).

While for ritual it seems that no ordinary evidence is appropriate, authority must still be found. The possibility of 'self-evidence' was raised earlier, and indeed a precedent satisfying the technical definition as formulated seems to exist in an epistemological category long ago described by Kant. He characterized 'analytic' statements as 'adding nothing through the predicate to the concept of the subject, but merely breaking it up into those constituent concepts that have all along been thought in it, although confusedly' (Kant 1961:48). I would point out that the speaker initially approaches the lexical item which founds the analytic predication (e.g. *bachelor* in *all bachelors are unmarried*) as an object or artifact, and not as part of the process of a speech act. Just as one might examine a geological fault as an artifact in nature or a carved mask as an artifact in culture for the information they might yield, one approaches the word as an artifact in language. Its manifest semantic characteristics are then made the basis of a predication, which is automatically taken as valid without regard to external evidence.[6] In his analysis of the 'continuum of epistemic space' Givón (1982) has made the important observation that the linguistic use of evidence is restricted primarily to the domain of medium certainty, where it is relevant. In the

---

[5] Note that in Kashaya, propositions based on one's dreams, visions, or revelations fall into the category of propositions for which the speaker does take responsibility: they are marked with the 'personal experience' evidential suffix *−yow,* and are taken to be as true as if one had personally experienced them (Oswalt, this volume). Similarly in Wintu, the suffix *-nt^{h}Er* encompasses evidence gained not only through the nonvisual senses of hearing, feeling, taste, smell, and touch, but through 'any kind of intellectual experience or "sixth sense".' It is used in talking about the supernatural and in prophecy (Schlichter, this volume). Though on some level the speaker in such cases is required to do no more than indicate whether his source of knowledge is 'hearsay' or 'personal experience', for ritual speech, at least, I think it is clear that the demand for authority ultimately probes deeper, to the level of indexic rather than arbitrary signs (see below).

[6] Roman Jakobson, in a passing remark on a Russian oral poem, said '. . . the contrariness of 'bald' and 'curly' appears SELF-EVIDENT' (1966:413; emphasis mine). Here the 'self-evident' fact of contrariness (to the extent that it is valid) appears to reside in the words themselves as artifacts in the lexicon (i.e., in *langue*).

domain of highest certainty (which for him includes analytic, as well as a priori synthetic, given-by-revelation, presupposed,[7] and deictically obvious statements) the use of evidentiality is not required. Such statements already have the highest certainty because of the shared contract between speaker and hearer. Nor is evidence found in the domain of lowest certainty, irrealis, where it is impossible. Givón's insight that both analytic statements and religious statements of a certain type achieve the highest certainty without evidence recalls Douglas's important treatment of the implications of analytic truth for symbolic anthropology ('Self-evidence', 1975).[8] We are close here to the problem framed by Geertz as 'the essence of religious action.' I suggest that it is the business of ritual language, as of ritual symbolism, to merge two apparent extremes: to equate the ritual truth with the analytic truth. Such an equation may, of course, depend on a metaphorical sleight of hand, effective just within the framework of a particular culture. The question remains: What in ritual speech provides authority without recourse to evidence?

SPEECH FORM AND THE SOCIAL CONSTRUCTION OF AUTHORITY

While no one would deny that the ritual speaker controls, in some sense at least, the level of the utterance act, it seems to be a function of the particular structure of ritual speech to prevent the ritual speaker from exercising sovereign control at the level of illocutionary formulation. Each of four formal principles contributes to this:

The COMPLEMENTARITY of ritual speech forms, which are distributed in different social contexts from those of colloquial speech, marks the ritual occasion as separate from ordinary experience as encoded in the colloquial variety. The meanings and associations which adhere to a lexical item from the discourses into which it is embedded are kept in two distinct spheres, avoiding contamination between the sacred and the profane.

PARALLELISM has two major structural functions, a negative and a positive. Negatively, it constrains individual variability in syntactic-semantic structure, tending to obstruct personal manipulation of a valued traditional message. Positively, it projects the image of inevitability: a form, first foreshadowed, now indeed occurs. The consequent impression of inalterable completion fails to

---

[7] The position on the nonapplicability of evidentiality to presuppositions has been properly qualified by Mithun (this volume), who notes the occasional use of such phrases as *so-called* before an otherwise presupposed nominal categorization. But this modifier simply acts to reverse the assumption that an unqualified nominal reference will presuppose its appropriateness as a predication of the referent. While the nominal presupposition can be blocked in this way, it remains true that evidence is not in general applicable to presuppositions.

[8] Douglas's work, incidentally, contributed to the title of the present paper.

distinguish inevitability in substance from coincidence in form. Parallelism makes of the message a structured entity, placing it in a class with other symmetrical objects and reiterative or cyclic phenomena. In a sense, the circle of validation has become internalized within the message form. Beyond this, parallelism has an elusive semantic effect, compared by Boodberg to 'binocular vision' (1954–5, cited in Jakobson 1966:402; cf. Jakobson 1966:423).

MEDIATION and the associated doubling of speech event roles act to constrain the ritual speaker's independence and his direct interactive link with the listener. The doubling of roles puts an additional mediated link between the hearer and the ultimate message source, and the expression of individual volition may be precluded (cf. Plato 1953:534). Mediation also interacts with the complementarity principle, leaving its imprint in linguistic form by giving rise to two divergent and complementary varieties, one obscure and symbolically distant, the other clear and accessible.[9]

CONSTRAINTS on ritual speech (beyond those already implicit in the three previous principles) act to subordinate the linguistic indexing of the individual personality to the generalized requirements of the role. In colloquial speech, those traits which are not fully specified by the (categorical) rules of *langue* are available to distinctively index individual personalities. Potential personality indexes, as defined by Sapir (1927) and updated by Friedrich and Redfield (1978), are mostly phonetic—voice, intonation, pitch, rhythm, relative continuity, speed, pronunciation—but variable features in lexicon, grammar, and semantics—word usage, morphology, syntax, rhetorical tropes—may be personally indexic, as may even patterns of discourse interaction (Gumperz and Tannen 1979). Sapir considered the voice 'the lowest or most fundamental speech level' in that it constituted 'a level that starts with the psychophysical organism given at birth' (1927:535). Yet this, and most or all of the other features, may also, with some skill and effort, be modified in order to disguise or even suppress personality. An analysis of this process will give us an important key to ritual speech.

In 'sovereign' speech (ordinary direct speech) the proximate speaker and prime speaker are equivalent; the proximate speaker exerts full control over the utterance. But a shift to an alter prime speaker, whether through mimicry or simple quotation, involves a transfer of control over at least some features of the utterance. This control is not monolithic, but is transferrable by gradations.

---

[9] Parallelism in the message also may be connected with mediation and interpretation. An anonymous nineteenth century writer on parallelism uses the term 'interpretation' (in addition to 'paraphrase' and 'repetition') to describe the function of the second line of a parallel couplet (cited in Jakobson 1966:406). Rotinese couplets often have an alien dialect term effectively 'interpreted' by an indigenous term, and Quiché couplets sometimes pair a term not in general use (i.e., restricted to lexical couplets) with a familiar term. In this way parallel couplets allow the presentation of obscure language along with its clarification, a paradox of interpretability and uninterpretability remarked by Malinowski (1935:213ff).

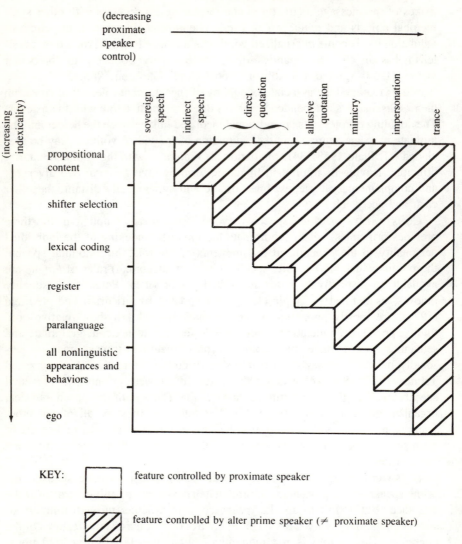

Figure 1.   Hierarchy of Transfer of Control

Figure 1 illustrates the possible gradations and the associated speech categories. Down the left side are ranged the linguistic and behavioral features which are subject to control by either proximate speaker or alter prime speaker, in order of increasing indexicality: propositional content, shifter selection (*I/you*), lexical coding (*apple/fruit*), register (*chalice/cup*), paralanguage (voice, rhythm), and—leaving the domain of strictly linguistic features—nonlinguistic appearances and behaviors, and finally ego itself. Along the top of Figure 1, in the initial category of sovereign speech, the proximate speaker controls all of these features. In the second speech category, indirect speech, control of propositional content alone is turned over to an alter prime speaker. As control of each successive feature is turned over to a second prime speaker, we pass through the rest of the hierarchy of speech categories: quotation, allusive quotation, mimicry, impersonation, and finally, as even ego is released from proximate speaker control, trance.[10]

Once control of and responsibility for an utterance are shifted to another speaker, the character of this new speaker becomes an issue that bears on authority. I propose eight categories of prime speaker, ranged along a continuum of degree of 'personal presence' in the situation at hand (Figure 2). The categories range from the first person (the proximate speaker himself, (a)) through the second person (b) to five categories of third person (c)–(g).[11] Within this set there is a rapid decrease in personal presence: with the myth characters and lesser deities (f) we have already left historical time,[12] and with the nebulous ancestor group we approach a very low level of distinctive personality. The vacant square in the final position (h) represents the possibility, which may prove to be more than theoretical, of an ultimate vanishing point of personal presence.

According to Becker, 'One can roughly specify for any language activity the degree to which the speaker/writer is speaking the past or the present' (1979:213). This implies a continuum comparable in some respects to the present one of personal presence. Distance in the past is associated both with fading of distinctive personality and with increase in authority. Thus, Aristotle distinguishes between recent and ancient witnesses. In Turkish, Slobin and Aksu (this volume) describe a psychological phenomenon whereby recent events, as they recede further into the past (toward 'history'), are likely to shift from the

---

[10] Compare Bauman's partial classification of 'frames' (somewhat different in orientation from the present analysis) into literal communication, performance, insinuation, joking, imitation, translation, and quotation (1977:10).

The difference between mimicry and quotation may be grammatically marked in some languages. Givón notes that in KinyaRwanda, 'direct-quote' complements of 'say' may be marked with either -*ti*, representing 'a more NEUTRAL report', i.e., quotation, or -*tya*, involving 'mimickry of VOICE and GESTURE' (Givón 1982:27; emphasis in original). In English, while the complements of either *say* or *go* may be used to report speech, *go* tends to be used when mimicry is involved, whether of human speech, animal cry, or even ambient noise.

[11] Categories (c)–(e) are, of course, taken over from Aristotle. The existence and ordering of most of the categories, especially (f)–(g), may reflect culture-specific variation. I leave open the locus of a supreme deity.

A very interesting and valuable discussion of 'voice' (in roughly my sense) in music is found in Cone (1974).

[12] See Eliade (1959:68ff) on sacred time in myth and ritual.

a	b	c	d	e	f	g	h
Proximate speaker (= prime speaker)	Addressee	Recent interested witness	Recent dis- interested witness	Ancient witness	Myth characters & lesser deities	Anonymous ancestor group	⌐ ‐ ‐ ‐ ¬ ⌐ ⌐ ‐ ‐ ‐ ⌐

(decreasing
personal ——▶
presence)

Figure 2.   Categories of Prime Speaker: Hierarchy of Personal Presence

suffix of (loosely) indirect experience (*-miş*) to the suffix of direct experience
(*-di*). The origin of ritual speech often recedes beyond even historical time. In the
Trobriand view of ritual speech (as deduced by Malinowski), 'A spell is believed
to be a primeval text which somehow came into being side by side with animals
and plants, with winds and waves, with human disease, human courage and
human frailty' (Malinowski 1935:218).

Though words to be tangible must always be physically uttered by a proximate speaker (or writer), every culture need not have such a requirement of a
final prime speaker. I propose that the first step in establishing authority for ritual
speech is to make it appear to be of apersonal origin, or at least to approach this.
The possibility of apersonal texts is perhaps not entirely alien to linguistics.
Fillmore recognizes a category of 'impersonal' texts (alongside 'monologic' and
'dialogic' texts) in which 'there is no first-person mention of the creator of the
text and no second-person mention of the addressee of the text,' as in the
example, 'Printed in Great Britain by Richard Clay Ltd.' (1974:V–9). Other
investigators have commented on depersonalization through formulaic speech
(Hymes 1972:49, Labov 1972:353), 'anonymization' (not specifically linguistic)
in ritual (Geertz 1973a), and invoking of 'positional identities' in political oratory (Irvine 1979:778ff). The actual obliteration of ultimate personal source for a
spoken text is envisaged in Lévi-Strauss's apt remark that the repeated myth is 'a
message that, properly speaking, is coming from nowhere' (1969:18). Becker,
speaking about Javanese shadow theater performance, defines 'trance speaking'
as 'communication in which one of the variables of the speech act (I am speaking
to you about x at time y in place z with intent a) is denied' (1979:232–33). Here,

> most frequently the variable *I* is paradoxically both speaking and not speaking, or
> speaking involuntarily or nonintentionally. Trance is a kind of incongruence be-
> tween statement and intent (I/not I am speaking to you/not you. . . .) (1979:233)

To deny proximate speaker intentionality in this way is to bleach out a central
aspect of personal presence in the utterance.

While several of the above remarks would seem to allow a quiet place in
linguistic theory for a concept of apersonal speech, the in fact radical conse-

quences of the idea become apparent as soon as we confront established theories of the speech act. Searle maintains that in order for an individual to take a potentially symbolic phenomenon (a noise, a mark on paper) as a message it is necessary that 'he should regard it as having been produced by a being with certain intentions.' How is it possible to reconcile the paradox of apersonal speech with this demand for intention? For Searle the perceiver of the potential symbol

> cannot just regard it as a natural phenomenon, like a stone, a waterfall, or a tree. . . . It is a logical presupposition, for example, of current attempts to decipher the Mayan hierogryphs that we at least hypothesize that the marks we see on the stones were produced by beings more or less like ourselves and produced with certain kinds of intentions. If we were certain the marks were a consequence of, say, water erosion, then the question of deciphering them or even calling them hieroglyphs could not arise. To construe them under the category of linguistic communication necessarily involves construing their production as speech acts. (1972:137)

This insistence on intention presupposes that even if no speaker (or writer) is immediately present, if one goes far enough back one will find him. Intentional man is the sole source of linguistic communication, while nature and accident, lacking intention, are rejected.

But this stance is not universal. The Quiché ritual of divination extracts meaning from 'chance' phenomena which are clearly held to be nonintentional. The diviner who wishes, for example, to determine the name of an enemy who has caused his client's illness, begins by taking a random handful from a large pile of sacred red *pito* seeds and pronouncing a short ritual text (characteristically parallelistic) which invokes the ancestors, among others. In part:

> our first mothers
>   and fathers
> who came before the altars,
> the masters of the pointed stick,
>   the masters of the seeds of the *pito*,
> the masters of divination by corn
>   and by blood,
> come hither! (Bunzel 1952:287; line breaks added)

He then asks, 'Is it _____ (so-and-so)?' and lays out the seeds he is holding in groups of four until the last one has been set down, thus— :: :: :: and so on. The answer depends on the configuration of the final seeds: 'If they come out even [::], the answer is affirmative, if two remain over [:] it is doubtful, if one or three remain [. :.], it is negative' (Bunzel 1952:288). Any intentional control over this message is specifically precluded by the chance number of seeds grasped (though Bunzel makes clear that room to maneuver remains in the process of interpretation, 1952:290f). In place of intention, what validates the significant message is a parallel, symmetrical structure: most effectively, a doubly symmetrical structure (::) but in any case not a nonsymmetrical structure or nonstructure (. :.). As Roland Barthes observes, in popular thought 'to repeat is to signify':

> Repetition always commits us to imagining an unknown cause, so true is it that in the popular consciousness, the aleatory is always distributive, never repetitive: chance is supposed to vary events; if it repeats them, it does so in order to signify something through them; to repeat is to signify, this belief is at the source of all ancient *manteia* '. . . (Barthes 1972:191)

What is structured by repetition is significant, outside language as well as in; yet Searle's intending speaker is nowhere to be found.

Intention is thus revealed to be culture-bound as a criterion of meaning. We are forced to recognize a typological split in cultural canons of symbolism (including language) according to their axiomatic criteria for the imputation of meaning. One type, embodied in most of official Western thought since the Age of Reason, indeed takes intentionality as its primary criterion. A further criterion is structural coherence, to the extent, at least, of following rules of grammar. This cultural type may be called the humanist-rationalist. Here, the meaningful is that which displays structure and is backed by intention (i.e., +intention +structure). Whatever appears structured but is not backed by intention is meaningless. In the second cultural type, however, structure takes precedence over intention in the imputation of meaning. I call this type the manticist. Here, what has structure has meaning, whether the structure is the product of human intention or otherwise (thus, +structure, ±intention).[13] Moreover—and here lies the immediate import of this typological contrast—what the humanist-rationalist tradition discards as coincidence, the manticist may take as not only meaningful but unassailable: it bypasses ordinary criticism because it bypasses the human source of error.

CONCLUSIONS

This inquiry began with the problem of self-evidence. It is found that speaker's ethos is central to perceived utterance reliability. Quotation is exploited as a powerful tool for persuasion, to the extent that it shifts hearer's scrutiny of knowledge, interests, sincerity and fallibility to those who are most able to bear it. In addition to arbitrary linguistic marking, paralinguistic indexic marking contributes crucially to the perception of speaker reliability, as well as of message source. Indexic signs carry special weight because they are not easily subject to volitional control.

---

[13] Of the two other contrasting logical possibilities, -intention -structure represents simply chance phenomena, while +intention -structure is perhaps applicable, in varying degrees, to aphasic and schizophrenic speech.

Analytic truth is accorded the highest reliability; yet no appeal to external evidence is made. The word which founds the analytic predication is approached initially as an artifact of language, rather than as part of the speech act process, in order to extract for assertion the meaning which it presupposes.

The need for marking sensory evidence or quotation arises in the first place from the limitations of the individual speaker, whose asserted knowledge is by itself fallible. He supports it by indicating the source of his external evidence or by quoting someone else who has evidence. But in taking this step he does not yet escape the realm of personal fallibility, for his statement of evidence itself, whether asserted or presupposed, remains the arbitrary utterance of an individual still subject to ignorance, manipulation, insincerity, and fallibility. Quotation and mimicry shift evaluation of these to an alter prime speaker, in the first case arbitrarily, in the second quasi-indexically. But this second person remains subject to the same critical scrutiny. To escape this a source of meaning must be found which stands outside the chain of human fallibility.

Thus ethos reaches its highest importance, and with it the form of the speech itself. In the utterance of the ritual practitioner, the prescribed form of speech tends to obliterate the indexing of individual personality. In place of distinctive voice, intonation, hesitation, rhythm, sentence structure, is a voice made uniform and intonationally inexpressive, a pauseless automatic flow of ritual syllables within given structures, where any imposition of proximate speaker control is checked at every hand. The ethical voice of ritual is not that of a second mimicked individual, with all his idiosyncratic traits, but of an idealized form. It is a voice which can index no personal origin. The groundwork is thus laid for a belief that the ritual practitioner channels words derived from, at best, the nebulous ancestors, or more simply, from nowhere.

Given manticist premises, meaning forms which are found in the artifactual world of language, existing independently of personal intention, can be validated as coherent structures—and hence meaningful—by the symmetry which they manifestly share with their isomorphs in nature. Parallelism promotes a perception of the utterance as an artifact—what we may call a 'speech tool' rather than a 'speech act'—and hence makes possible the manticist equation of ritual speech with analytic truth. The basis of the authority of ritual speech is in the end quite simple. The manticist listener, through the structure of ritual speech and of the ritual event, is put directly in touch with a sourceless message whose authority he can observe in its very form: it is self-evident.

What I have tried to do in this paper is to uncover a function which must underlie the observed correlation of phenomena in the domain of social life with phenomena in the domain of symbolic form. In order to do this it has been necessary to deepen our conception of the constitution of the speech event, taking into account both the positive substance of symbolic form and its efficacy in the larger world, in order to build further toward a theory of language in social life.

REFERENCES

Aristotle. 1932. The rhetoric of Aristotle, trans. by Lane Cooper. New York: Appleton-Century-Crofts.

Barthes, Roland. 1972. Structure of the *fait–divers*. Critical essays. Evanston: Northwestern University Press.

Basso, Keith. 1979. Discussant presentation on ritual language. 78th Annual Meeting, American Anthropological Association, Cincinnati.

Bateson, Gregory. 1972. Style, grace, and information in primitive art. Steps to an ecology of mind, 128–152. New York: Ballantine.

Bauman, Richard. 1977. Verbal art as performance. Rowley, Mass.: Newbury House.

Becker, A. L. 1979. Text–building, epistemology, and aesthetics in Javanese shadow theatre. The imagination of reality: Essays in Southeast Asian coherence systems, ed. by A. L. Becker and Aram A. Yengoyan, 211–243. Norwood, N.J.: Ablex.

Bloch, Maurice. 1975. Introduction. Political language and oratory in traditional society, 1–28. London: Academic Press.

Boodberg, Peter A. 1954–55. Syntactical metaplasia in stereoscopic parallelism. (Cedules from a Berkeley workshop in Asiatic philology, #017-541210.) Berkeley.

Bricker, Victoria R. 1973. Ritual humor in highland Chiapas. Austin: University of Texas Press.

———. 1974. The ethnographic context of some traditional Mayan speech genres. Explorations in the ethnography of speaking, ed. by Richard Bauman and Joel Sherzer, 368–388. London: Cambridge University Press.

Bright, William. 1982. Literature: Written and oral. Georgetown University Round Table on Languages and Linguistics 1981, ed. by Deborah Tannen, 271–283. Washington: Georgetown University Press.

Bunzel, Ruth. 1929/30. Zuñi ritual poetry. Bureau of American Ethnology, Annual Reports, 47.611–835. Washington, D.C.: Government Printing Office.

———. 1952. Chichicastenango: A Guatemalan village. (Publications of the American Ethnological Society, 22.) Locust Valley, N.Y.: Augustin.

Burns, Allan F. 1980. Interactive features in Yucatec Mayan narratives. Language in Society 9.307–319.

Chafe, Wallace L. 1961. Seneca Thanksgiving rituals. (Bureau of American Ethnology, Bulletin 183.) Washington, D.C.: Government Printing Office.

———. 1981. Differences between colloquial and ritual Seneca, or How oral literature is literary. Reports from the Survey of California and Other Indian Languages, no. 1, ed. by Alice Schlichter, Wallace L. Chafe, and Leanne Hinton, 131–145. Berkeley: Department of Linguistics.

Cone, Edward T. 1974. The composer's voice. Berkeley: University of California Press.

Devereux, George. 1964. Mojave voice and speech mannerisms. Language in culture and society, ed. by Dell Hymes, 267–271. New York: Harper and Row.

Douglas, Mary. 1975. Self–evidence. Implicit meanings, 276–318. London: Routledge and Kegan Paul.

Du Bois, Cora. 1935. Wintu ethnography. (University of California Publications in American Archaeology and Ethnology, 36.) Berkeley: University of California Press.

Eliade, Mircea. 1959. The sacred and the profane. New York: Harcourt Brace Jovanovich.

Fillmore, Charles J. 1974. Pragmatics and the description of discourse. Berkeley Studies in Syntax and Semantics, vol. 1, ed. by Charles Fillmore, George Lakoff, and Robin Lakoff. Berkeley: Department of Linguistics and Institute of Human Learning.

Fock, Niels. 1963. Waiwai: Religion and society of an Amazonian tribe. Copenhagen: The National Museum.

Foster, Michael K. 1974. When words become deeds: An analysis of three Iroquois longhouse speech events. Explorations in the ethnography of speaking, ed. by Richard Bauman and Joel Sherzer, 354–367. London: Cambridge University Press.

Fox, James J. 1974. 'Our ancestors spoke in pairs': Rotinese views of language, dialect, and code. Explorations in the ethnography of speaking, ed. by Richard Bauman and Joel Sherzer, 65–85. London: Cambridge University Press.

French, David. 1958. Cultural matrices of Chinookan non–casual language. IJAL 24.258–263.

Friedrich, Paul and James Redfield. 1978. Speech as a personality symbol. Language 54.263–288.

Geertz, Clifford. 1973a. Person, time, and conduct in Bali. The interpretation of cultures, 360–411. New York: Basic Books.

––––––. 1973b. Religion as a cultural system. The interpretation of cultures, 87–125. New York: Basic Books.

Givón, Talmy. 1982. Evidentiality and epistemic space. Studies in Language 6:1.23–49.

Goffman, Erving. 1974. Frame analysis. New York: Harper and Row.

––––––. 1978. Response cries. Language 54.787–815.

––––––. 1981. Footing. Forms of talk, 124–159. Philadelphia: University of Pennsylvania Press.

Gossen, Gary H. 1974a. Chamulas in the world of the sun: Time and space in a Maya oral tradition. Cambridge, Mass.: Harvard University Press.

––––––. 1974b. To speak with a heated heart: Chamula canons of style and good performance. Explorations in the ethnography of speaking, ed. by Richard Bauman and Joel Sherzer, 389–413. London: Cambridge University Press.

Gumperz, John J. and Deborah Tannen. 1979. Individual and social differences in language use. Individual differences in language ability and language behavior, ed. by Charles J. Fillmore, Daniel Kempler, and William S–Y. Wang, 305–325. New York: Academic Press.

Hymes, Dell. 1966. Two types of linguistic relativity (with examples from Amerindian ethnography). Sociolinguistics, ed. by William Bright, 114–167. The Hague: Mouton.

––––––. 1972. Models of the interaction of language and social life. Directions in sociolinguistics, ed. by John Gumperz and Dell Hymes, 35–71. New York: Holt.

––––––. 1981. 'In vain I tried to tell you': Essays in Native American ethnopoetics. Philadelphia: University of Pennsylvania Press.

Irvine, Judith T. 1979. Formality and informality in communicative events. American Anthropologist 81.773–790.

Jakobson, Roman. 1960. Closing statement: Linguistics and poetics. Style in language, ed. by Thomas A. Sebeok, 350–377. Cambridge, Mass.: MIT Press.

––––––. 1966. Grammatical parallelism and its Russian facet. Language 42.399–429.

––––––. 1971. Shifters, verbal categories, and the Russian verb. Selected writings, v. 2, 130–147. The Hague: Mouton.

Kant, Immanuel. 1961. Critique of pure reason, trans. by Norman Kemp Smith. London: Macmillan.

Keenan, Edward Louis and Elinor Ochs. 1979. Becoming a competent speaker of Malagasy. Languages and their speakers, ed. by Timothy Shopen, 113–158. Cambridge, Mass.: Winthrop.

Keenan, Elinor. 1974. Norm–makers, norm–breakers: Uses of speech by men and women in a Malagasy community. Explorations in the ethnography of speaking, ed. by Richard Bauman and Joel Sherzer, 125–143. London: Cambridge University Press.

––––––. 1975. A sliding sense of obligatoriness: The polystructure of Malagasy oratory. Political language and oratory in traditional society, ed. by Maurice Bloch, 93–112. London: Academic Press.

Labov, William. 1972. Rules for ritual insults. Language in the inner city: Studies in the Black English Vernacular. Philadelphia: University of Pennsylvania Press.

Lasch, R. 1907. Ueber Sondersprachen und ihre Entstehung. Mitteilungen, Viennese Anthropological Society.

Lévi-Strauss, Claude. 1963a. The effectiveness of symbols. Structural anthropology, 181–201. Garden City, N.Y.: Anchor.

————. 1963b. The structural study of myth. Structural anthropology, 206–231. Garden City, N.Y.: Anchor.

————. 1969. The raw and the cooked. New York: Harper and Row.

Malinowski, Bronislaw. 1922 [1961]. Argonauts of the Western Pacific. New York: Dutton.

————. 1935. Coral gardens and their magic, vol. 2: The language of magic and gardening. New York: American Book Co.

McLendon, Sally. 1982. Meaning, rhetorical structure, and discourse organization in myth. Georgetown University Round Table on Languages and Linguistics 1981, ed. by Deborah Tannen, 284–305. Washington: Georgetown University Press.

Nichols, Johanna. 1978. Predicate categories checklist. MS, Berkeley.

Norman, William M. 1980. Grammatical parallelism in Quiché ritual language. Proceedings of the Sixth Annual Meeting of the Berkeley Linguistics Society, 387–399. Berkeley: Berkeley Linguistics Society.

Peirce, Charles Sanders. 1885 [1933]. Three kinds of signs. Collected papers of Charles Sanders Peirce, vol. 3, ed. by Charles Hartshorne and Paul Weiss, 210–214. Cambridge, Mass.: Harvard University Press.

Plato. 1953. Ion. The dialogues of Plato, 4th ed., trans. by Benjamin Jowett. Oxford: The Clarendon Press.

Sapir, Edward. 1927 [1949]. Speech as a personality trait. Selected writings of Edward Sapir, ed. by David Mandelbaum, 533–543. Berkeley: University of California Press.

Schlichter, Alice. 1981. Notes on the Wintu shamanistic jargon. Reports from the Survey of California and Other Indian Languages, no. 1, ed. by Alice Schlichter, Wallace L. Chafe, and Leanne Hinton, 95–130. Berkeley: Department of Linguistics.

Searle, John R. 1972. What is a speech act? Language and social context, ed. by Pier Paolo Giglioli, 136–154. Harmondsworth, Middlesex: Penguin.

Sherzer, Joel F. 1974. *Namakke, sunmakke, kormakke:* Three types of Cuna speech event. Explorations in the ethnography of speaking, ed. by Richard Bauman and Joel Sherzer, 263–282. London: Cambridge University Press.

————. 1977. Cuna *ikala:* Literature in San Blas. Verbal art as performance, ed. by Richard Bauman, 133–150. Rowley, Mass.: Newbury House.

————. 1981. The poetic structures of Kuna discourse: A sociolinguistic perspective. MS, University of Texas, Austin.

————. 1982. The interplay of structure and function in Kuna narrative, or: How to grab a snake in the Darien. Georgetown University Round Table on Languages and Linguistics 1981, ed. by Deborah Tannen, 306–322.

Spier, Leslie and Edward Sapir. 1930. Wishram ethnography. University of Washington Publications in Anthropology, vol. 3, no. 3, 151–300.

Stout, D. B. 1947. Ethno–linguistic observations on San Blas Cuna. IJAL 13.9–12.

Stross, Brian. 1974. Speaking of speaking: Tenejapa Tzeltal metalinguistics. Explorations in the ethnography of speaking, ed. by Richard Bauman and Joel Sherzer, 213–239. London: Cambridge University Press.

Tambiah, S. J. 1968. The magical power of words. Man, N.S., 3.175–208.

————. 1979. The form and meaning of magical acts: A point of view. Reader in comparative religion, ed. by William A. Lessa and Evon Z. Vogt, 352–362. New York: Harper and Row.

Turner, Victor W. 1967. Symbols in Ndembu ritual. The forest of symbols, 19–47. Ithaca: Cornell University Press.

————. 1977. Process, system, and symbol: A new anthropological synthesis. Daedalus 106.61–80.

White, Leslie A. 1944. A ceremonial vocabulary among the Pueblos. IJAL 10.161–167.

Whorf, Benjamin L. 1956. Some verbal categories of Hopi. Language, thought, and reality, 112–124. Cambridge, Mass.: MIT Press.

Author Index

A

Adelaar, W.F.H., 138, 142, 145, 149, 149*n*, 150, 153, *154*
Akatsuka, N., 181, *186*
Aksu, A.A., *167*
Aksu-Koç, A.A., 165, *167*
Albino Mendoza, L., 148, *155*
Alcocer, P., *154*
Anderson, L., 275*n*, 282, 283, 293*n*, 299, *311*
Andrade, M.J., 9*n*, 17, 21, 23, *25*
Andrejčin, L., 168, 170*n*, *186*
Aristotle, 323, *334*
Aronson, H.I., 169, 171, 171*n*, 175, 177, 180*n*, 185, *186*
Arsen'ev, V.K., 247, *256*
Avrorin, V.A., 243, *256*
Ayer, A.J., 56, 57, *59*
Azkue, R.M. de, 7*n*, *25*

B

Barbeau, M., 93*n*, *111*
Barnes, J., *311*
Barthes, R., 332, *334*
Baskakov, N.A., 165, *167*
Basso, K., 315, *334*
Bateson, G., 324, *334*
Bauman, R., 315, 318, 321, 329*n*, *334*
Becker, A.L., 315, 321, 329, *334*
Benedict, P.K., 304*n*, *311*
Berlin, B., 278, 283, *311*
Bertonio, L., 113, *136*
Bickerton, D., 243*n*, *256*
Blanca, M., *155*
Bloch, M., 315, 321, *334*
Bloomfield, L., 7, *25*
Boas, F., 3, 4, 5, 5*n*, 9*n*, 11*n*, 13*n*, 17, 24, 24*n*, *25*, 245
Bolinger, D., 7, *25*
Boodberg, P.A., *334*
Bradley, D., 216, *222*
Bricker, V.R., 315, 317, *334*

B (second column)

Briggs, L., 114, *136*
Bright, W., 314, *334*
Bunzel, R., 315, 318, 331, *334*
Burns, A.F., 315, 318, 321, *334*
Burns, D., *154*
Buslaev, F., 177, *186*

C

Campbell, L., *25*
Carlson, B.F., 9*n*, 11*n*, 17*n*, 19*n*, *25*
Cayco Villar, T., 141, 144, 152, *155*
Čerepanov, S.I., *256*
Cerron-Palomino, R., 152*n*, *154*
Chafe, W.L., 6, 7, *25*, 58, *59*, 92*n*, 93*n*, 100*n*, *111*, 161*n*, 272, 315, 318, 319, 321, *334*
Chang, B.S., 207*n*, *213*
Chang, K., 207*n*, *213*
Comrie, B., 164, *167*, 168, *186*
Cone, E.T., 329*n*, *334*
Creider, C., 145, *154*

D

de Dios Yapita Moya, J., 116, 119, *136*
De Rijk, R.P.G., 7n, *25*
Dejanova, M., 175, *186*
DeLancey, S., 203, 207n, 209, 212, *213*, *311*
Demina, E.I., 182n, *186*
Demiraj, S., 180, *186*
Devereux, G., 319, *334*
Dodi, A., 186n, *186*
Douglas, M., 326, *334*
Du Bois, C., 54, *59*, 315, 320, *334*

E

Ebbing, J.E., 113, *136*
Egerod, S., 214, 214*n*, 215, 216, 217, 218, 219, 219*n*, 221, 222, 303*n*, 304, *311*
Eliade, M., 329, *334*
England, N., 116, 119, *136*

337

Subject Index